Schriftenreihe des Forschungsinstituts für Europafragen
der Wirtschaftsuniversität Wien

Band 20

Research Institute for European Affairs
Publication Series

Volume 20

SpringerWienNewYork

Schriftenreihe des Forschungsinstituts für Europafragen
der Wirtschaftsuniversität Wien

Band 20

Research Institute for European Affairs
Publication Series

Volume 20

SpringerWienNewYork

Stefan Griller
Birgit Weidel (eds.)

External Economic Relations and Foreign Policy in the European Union

SpringerWienNewYork

Prof. Dr. Stefan Griller

Mag. Birgit Weidel

Research Institute for European Affairs, Wirtschaftsuniversität Wien, Austria

Financial support was given by the *Bundesministerium für Bildung, Wissenschaft und Kultur,* Wien

Printed in Austria

Typesetting: Camera ready by editors
Printing: Ferdinand Berger & Söhne Gesellschaft m.b.H., A-3580 Horn
Printed on acid-free and chlorine-free bleached paper
CIP data applied for
SPIN: 10849901

ISBN 3-211-83726-4 Springer-Verlag Wien New York

Preface

Expectations for the European Union's role in a more and more globalised and at the same time significantly fragmented international environment are higher than ever before. The Laeken Declaration calls on Europe to "shoulder its responsibilities in the governance of globalisation" and to "develop the Union into a stabilising factor pointing the way ahead for the world". So far the European Union has not proven its ability to meet these ambitious targets. Despite its immense economic importance, it has not been able to assert a corresponding influence on the course of international policy developments.

The main impediments preventing the EU from representing a global political player are home-made. Whereas Member States have bestowed the EU with far-reaching competences ensuring effective action in economic areas, political aspects have been reserved to the intergovernmental domain. The artificial attempt of the Treaty on European Union to uphold clear dividing lines between external economic relations as a subject of the first and foreign policy as a subject of the second pillar undermines a consistent policy-making and significantly weakens the EU's appearance on the international scene. Until today insurmountable sovereignty concerns root in the constitutional dimension of external representation. Given the repercussions of the EU's status under international law, the design of foreign policy constitutes an important prejudice to the question of statehood of the European Union.

Against this background, the contributions in this book illustrate the inextricable link between political and economic aspects in the external relations of the EU and provide an analysis of the complicated consequences for the allocation of competence arising from this artificial separation codified by the TEU.

The studies presented in this volume are the outcome of a research project carried out by the Research Institute of European Affairs at the Vienna University for Economics and Business Administration (*Forschungsinstitut für Europafragen der Wirtschaftsuniversität Wien*) under the responsibility of Professor *Stefan Griller*. The realisation of this project was only possible with the financial support provided by the Anniversary Fund of the

"Oesterreichische Nationalbank" (Austrian National Bank) from January 2000 to September 2001, project No. 8349. Furthermore, we want to thank the Austrian Federal Ministry for Education, Science and Culture for their financial assistance granted for the printing of this volume.

Stefan Griller, Vienna
Birgit Weidel, Vienna

July 2002

Table of Contents

Stefan Griller/Birgit Weidel

External Economic Relations and Foreign Policy in the European Union

I. Preliminary Remarks

In the history of European integration, the distribution of competence between the European Community and its Member States in the area of external relations has always been a matter of controversy. When presence at the international scene is at stake, the individual Member States are concerned to emphasise their autonomy vis-à-vis the outside world. For this reason, it was, for some forty years of European integration, impossible to establish a common foreign policy at European level. With the creation of the Common Foreign and Security Policy (CFSP), the Treaty on the European Union (TEU) has finally created the nucleus for common action in this area. However, the Member States' persisting claim in this domain is manifested in the structure of CFSP. As the intergovernmental character of this policy preserves individual national veto rights, CFSP does not live up to a true common foreign policy but represents merely a coordination of national policies.

Moreover, by introducing the pillar construction, the TEU has codified the division of European foreign policy into two fundamentally different components that had existed since the creation of European Political Cooperation (EPC). In this dual system, mainly economic issues are subject to the supranational EC framework, whereas "political affairs" are reserved to the intergovernmental domain of the second pillar.

This rigid and, to anticipate one of the results of our deliberations, artificial separation of economic and political aspects enshrined in the constitutional set-up of the European Union forms the starting point of this volume. The basic contention is that this delimitation is not respected as it is impracticable in political reality. As this book endeavours to highlight, there is an inextricable link between economic and political concerns, which affects the practical implementation of external EC and EU policy. Particular emphasis is dedicated to the implications of this inseparability on the division of competences between the EU, the EC and the Member States. The analysis of three practical examples illustrates the legal tensions arising from this inadequate distribution of powers. The study is complemented by an examination of the consequences for the representation of the EC in international organisations.

II. The Roots of Sovereignty Concerns

Before entering into the substance of the study, a few remarks should highlight the delicate nature of external polices. Why are Member States so concerned about external relations?

A crucial point is the prominent role of foreign affairs in the debate on statehood. According to practice as well as academe,[1] the division of competences in this field is seen as an indicator for the existence of a state. The degree of centralisation distinguishes, among others, the federal state from an international confederation of states.[2] In a federal state, certain important matters, such as foreign affairs (specifically the conclusion of international treaties), the declaration of war and the conclusion of peace, as well as control of the armed forces, usually fall within the competence of the federation. On this ground, it could – at least in terms of the first decades – be concluded that the Communities should be qualified

1 For a prominent example, see *Kelsen* (1949) 321.

2 *Kelsen* (1949) 316ff.

as confederations, since they lacked the necessary centralisation in foreign and military affairs,[3] despite far-reaching centralisation in economic matters. This view could be reversed by the introduction of a fully fledged external relations policy which would integrate both political and economic aspects in a supranational legal system. Moreover, given the constantly rising importance and number of external *economic* relations involving more or less unexpected *political* repercussions– e.g. in the famous banana dispute – caution might be justified that even reforms of the *commercial* policy might, political implications thus being inevitable, tilt the balance in favour of the emergence of a European state. Although doubts may be expressed against the validity of that scenario,[4] it might still be the "background assumption" of the Member States' concern and their reluctance to introduce substantial reforms in the field. As a result, the goal to maintain their prerogatives often trumps the frequently purported commitment to speak with one voice to the outside world. The consequent reluctance against reforms is not only directed against the integration of intergovernmental into supranational decision taking, but also against any expansion of Community competences within the first pillar, be it by either the widening of exclusive Community competences or the generous use of concurrent competences.

Consequently, external representation and international relations are of eminent constitutional significance, which is reflected in the current debate on the future of the European Union, not the least expecting enlargement.

III. The Two Track System – an Inadequate Mechanism to Cope with the Complexity of International Relations

A. A Shortcut on Foreign Policy in the EU

Intentions to set up a political union existed from the very start of European integration.[5] Governments, aware of the advantages of a collective appearance on the international scene, showed interest in adding weight to their national positions by pursuing them in a coordinated framework at European level.[6] However, various initiatives to integrate this area in the existing structural and

---

[3] *Kelsen/Tucker* (1966) 264, fn. 89.

[4] Compare *Griller et al* (2000) 66ff.

[5] See *Nuttal* (1992) 30ff.

[6] *Regelsberger/Schoutheete/Wessels* (1997) 4.

institutional framework of the EC have failed because of diverging national visions of Europe.[7] Extending the Community method to "foreign policy" was unthinkable to certain member states, let alone to the more sensitive areas of security and defence. The compromise finally achieved in 1970 was the establishment of EPC as an intergovernmental cooperation forum operating outside EC structures. By leaving the final say to national governments, EPC worked through a "pooling of sovereignty rather than a transfer"[8].

A further attempt to install a common foreign policy was launched at the negotiations preceding Maastricht and resulted in the creation of CFSP, the second pillar of the newborn EU. Despite the ambitious goals set out in Title V of the TEU, the new provisions did little more than provide the existing informal mechanism with a legal foundation in a Treaty text. In essence, the intergovernmental features of EPC were retained, preventing CFSP from becoming a common policy rather than a mere coordination of national policies.

Moreover, the introduction of the pillar construction constituted an accreditation of the dualism existing in European foreign policy since the launch of EPC. While CFSP is the forum to deal with "high politics", some components of external relations, perceived as less sensitive "economic politics", are subject to the TEC framework. These external EC competences extend to areas with a mainly economic focus, like commercial policy, development cooperation and financial and economic cooperation with third countries.

B. The Complexity of International Relations

The straight division of economics and politics, as codified in the pillar structure of the TEU, does not, however, reflect political reality. The EU's external activities take place in an international environment which faces a growing level of interaction and cooperation. In the last decades, there has been a remarkable proliferation of international organisations, agreements, working groups and various other initiatives of transnational collaboration. In the wake of continuous globalisation, international relations are increasingly complex. The items of the international agenda are neither confined to economic issues, nor follow the neat separation between economic and political issues. International cooperation

---

7 *Nuttal* (1992) 182.

8 *Nuttal* (1992) 318.

covers areas such as environmental issues, social and labour standards, assistance to developing countries, culture or conflict management. Although these issues are mostly dealt with in a subject-oriented manner, there is general awareness that all these areas cannot be regarded in isolation from each other. Undoubtedly, activities in one field have repercussions on other policy areas. Given this interconnectedness, it is impossible to focus, for instance, solely on economic perspectives, as action might likewise concern a number of other aspects, including foreign policy.

The evolution of the EC serves as an illustrative example for the impossibility to separate economic matters from other policies. In its original version, the EC, formerly called European Economic Community (EEC), was conceived as a purely economic and technocratic organisation – despite its underlying, highly political, rationale to promote peace and security in Europe. Its tasks were limited to the creation of the customs union and the Common Market ensuring the free circulation of economic factors, the establishment of a transport policy and a commercial policy. Nevertheless, it was already apparent even at the time the TEC was drawn up, that economic policy is not independent from other policies. For example, the necessity to reconcile economic interests with other concerns like public health, culture, environment or public security had been recognised by the insertion of Art 30 (former Art 36) TEC, which allowed Member States to pursue their individual national policies in theses areas. However, differences in national non-economic policies turned out to constitute insurmountable obstacles to the realisation of the Common Market. Effective economic integration could only be achieved by harmonisation of "non-economic concerns". Consequently, the competences of the EC have been gradually extended to other policies and the strict economic focus has been abandoned. Today there is widespread consensus that the Community is an organisation pursuing various policy objectives beyond economic integration. While the formulation of common policy-specific objectives and the transfer of respective competence to the EC in fields like environment or social policy did not meet major resistance or dissension, it was impossible to achieve similar progress in the area of "foreign policy".

The complexity of international relations calls for a holistic and integrated approach taking into account existing reciprocities between different policy fields. Although "consistency" has gained a prominent role in EU policy making, the design of the EU external relations has not been adapted to these demands of integrated policy making. The pillar construction does not correspond to the needs of a modern foreign policy.[9] The existing structural and procedural variety constitutes a considerable obstacle to a coherent and comprehensive policy-making.

C. The Political Dimension of EC Competences

Although governments are obviously more prepared to accept restrictions on their competences in the economic field, this does not imply that economic issues lack any political dimension. *Ulrich Immenga's* examination of the attempts to establish a global set of rules for competition policy shows the contrary. Despite a general consensus that the undisrupted functioning of a global economy requires the setting up of uniform multilateral rules, such initiatives are facing opposition. Differences exist in national conceptions and approaches to the various issues, which cannot be reconciled fully in a uniform system. The establishment of global rules is thus always a matter of compromise. Some states might assert their interests at the expense of less powerful states. In any case the outcome will – to differing degrees – entail a loss of political sovereignty, in the sense of independent policy determination for the individual state. For this reason, the establishment of international regimes will always meet difficulties even in areas perceived as politically less sensitive like competition policy.

Another controversial facet are foreign state's trade-restrictions threatening to impair interests of domestic industries. The uneasy relationship between the EU and the US is the best example for the fact that economic questions may quickly turn into top priority issues in the political dialogue. This can be demonstrated by a series of high-profile trade disputes on bananas, hormone-treated beef and, most recently, steel. Frequently political repercussions have outreached the economic interests lying at the heart of the dispute.

One of these cases, which surprisingly produce a preponderant political dimension, is the famous banana dispute, in which the EU was under fire for the preferential treatment granted to bananas of ACP (African, Caribbean and Pacific) origin. *Erich Vranes* not only examines the reasons for the political escalation of this conflict, but

---

9 See also *Regelsberger/Schoutheete/Wessels* (1997) 9.

also reflects on lessons to be learnt from other cases, such as Hormones and the Foreign Sales Corporations. The author reveals the deficiencies of WTO dispute settlement mechanism in finding a satisfactory solution for economic conflicts.

Lukas von Lutterotti draws similar conclusions from his analysis of the affair concerning the Helms-Burton and D'Amato acts and the efforts undertaken on the part of the EC and the EU to avoid negative effects of extraterritorial jurisdiction for European enterprises. The subject of the controversy was the US attempt to impose a restrictive policy vis-à-vis certain countries upon (non US) enterprises by sanctioning investments in those countries. According to the author, the existing regulatory mechanisms, like the WTO dispute settlement system, are inadequate to deal with such measures motivated by foreign policy considerations. In this delicate case, recourse to traditional means of diplomacy, such as bilateral negotiations, proved to be the most effective tool to successfully prevent harmful impacts for European operators.

The transatlantic disputes examined in this volume illustrate that in practice international economic relations bear a considerable potential for conflicts that cannot be comprehensively settled by solely relying on the existing dispute settlement mechanisms. A solution often depends on diplomatic intervention. Thus in order to safeguard its interests and those of its enterprises, even the EC, one of the world's leading economic powers, has to resort to classic diplomacy.

Changes both in the global and the regional environment have driven the EC into the role of a political player. After the end of the Cold War, economic and financial diplomacy have gained more and more importance in international politics.[10] Economic power enables states to exert influence in non-economic areas. Trade measures have become a central means to put political pressure on other states and thus constitute important elements of foreign policy. This development has also influenced the EC's relationship to third countries.

The example of development cooperation demonstrates, even more obviously than that of the recent trade disputes, the political inclination of the EC's acting. In the framework of this policy, the EC is explicitly called upon to pursue "political goals". According to Art 177 TEC, the EC shall contribute to the development and

---

[10] *Cameron* (1997) 100.

consolidation of democracy, the rule of law and respect for human rights and fundamental freedoms. This task certainly belongs to one of the most delicate issues in diplomatic relations. Interventions in this context are frequently perceived as undue interference with internal affairs. The EC's approach is illustrated by *Peter Hilpold's* analysis of the so-called "human rights clauses" in association and development cooperation agreements. These clauses, which link economic and financial benefits to compliance with democratic and fundamental rights standards, constitute the main instrument to promote the political objectives set out in Art 177 TEC. It is evident, that the central element of this mechanism is economic pressure.

Political aspects do not only characterise the EC's relationship to developing countries, but the whole spectrum of cooperation with third countries. In his overview on the various types of agreements and instruments existing in this area, *Bernd Martenczuk* stresses the fact that cooperation policy measures inevitably have political implications. A closer look at these policy activities clearly disqualifies the assertion that foreign policy falls outside the ambit of the TEC. Coherently, *Martenczuk* qualifies cooperation policy as a "component of Community foreign policy".

The conclusion common to these analyses is that a considerable part of "foreign policy" actually belongs to the EC's day to day business. The attempt to uphold clear dividing lines between economic and political issues is thus artificial and indefensible in practice.

D. The Legal Framework of EU External Relations – Discrepancy instead of Consistency

Notwithstanding the inadequacy of this separation, the legal framework for European foreign policy still distinguishes between a supranational "economic" and an intergovernmental "political" component. In the light of the fundamental differences characterising action under these two different systems, the question of delimitation is of utmost importance. The result does not only decide on the actors involved in the decision making process and on the legal quality and effectiveness of the measures adopted, but furthermore bears a fundamental constitutional aspect. The apparent parallelism between EC external policy and CFSP risks an encroachment of intergovernmental features on the supranational EC framework, which could hollow existing EC policies and undermine the achievements of the Community method.

The relationship between the EC and the intergovernmental pillars is determined by two main elements: the integrity of the acquis communautaire and the principle of consistency. Examining the content and legal implications of these principles, *Birgit Weidel* identifies the requirement to safeguard the acquis communautaire as decisive criterion determining the choice between EC or CFSP instruments. However, this shield only covers exclusive competences and areas regulated by secondary EC legislation. Areas coming under concurrent or complementary EC competence are not automatically excluded from the scope of CFSP.

On the one hand, this results in what *Martenczuk* calls the "residual character" of the second pillar: The promulgation of Community law in areas of concurrent or complementary external EC competence will entail a communitarisation of former CFSP issues. Accordingly, CFSP will become increasingly focused on defence and security issues, areas in which there is nearly no scope for TEC action.

On the other hand, there exists a certain danger of "renationalisation", as governments might prefer to take recourse to intergovernmental CFSP instruments in areas of concurrent or complementary EC competence. The endeavours to tackle complex issues, typically involving economic and political aspects, by a combined use of EC and intergovernmental pillar instruments constitute interesting precedents in this respect. They can be regarded as attempts of Member States to recover lost powers in sensitive areas by relocating the relevant decisions to the intergovernmental sphere. In this volume, three examples of cross-pillar mechanisms are examined, which further illustrate and analyse the complicated relationship between the EC and the intergovernmental pillars.

The imposition of economic sanctions, dealt with by *Anita Lukaschek*, has to be considered as an exceptional case, since Art 301 TEC explicitly provides for a two step procedure, according to which a CFSP action constitutes the precondition for a EC measure. Due respect for the acquis communautaire and EC competences requires that the former must be confined to the general political decision to interrupt economic relations, whereas it is an exclusive EC task to determine how this interruption will be carried out in detail.

The control regime for trade in dual-use goods introduced in 1994 also followed a cross-pillar approach by regulating sensitive issues of the control mechanism in a CFSP joint action and leaving technical and procedural aspects to the scope of the EC regulation. As demonstrated by *Birgit Weidel's* second contribution, this approach must be regarded as an infringement of the principle to safeguard the acquis communautaire, since the CFSP measure encroached on the EC's exclusive competence for the Common Commercial Policy (CCP).

A further example is provided by the continuation of *Lukas von Lutterotti's* analysis of the US Helms-Burton and D'Amato affair, which focuses on the legal instruments adopted in order to counteract the sanctions provided for in these US measures. In his critical appraisal of the EU blocking statute, a combination of an EC regulation and a joint action based on the second and third pillars, the author assesses the legality of using a CFSP instrument despite the existence of a potential competence under the TEC. *Lutterotti* especially criticises the choice of a Joint Action, since the act did not provide for any specific action and was apparently adopted as a substitute for an EC instrument because of lacking political consensus on the issue. Instead, it is argued that a common position would be more appropriate to take a general political stand and would not risk affecting the acquis communautaire.

As becomes obvious from these three cases, evasion to the intergovernmental sphere has become an attractive alternative when delicate aspects are at stake. In order to preserve the integrity of the acquis communautaire, it is thus imperative to insist on the distinction between EC and CFSP competences, however difficult this may be. The severe drawback, however, is the detrimental effect on consistency. In comparison to the EC, the intergovernmental pillars are not only characterised by different decision making procedures but also by differences in implementation and effectiveness. This discrepancy can easily lead to incoherent results concerning the substance and the implementation of foreign policy instruments.

However, it should not be overlooked that procedural and institutional diversity also exists inside the EC pillar. Following a sectoral, subject-oriented approach, the TEC's external competences are fragmented in terms of competences and decision-making procedures. The jurisprudence of the European Court of Justice (ECJ) on the EC's external relations has created a "maze" of explicit and implied, exclusive and shared competences. Discussions on the delimitation of those competences are just another manifestation of the struggle for power between the EC and its Member States. Exclusive competence is the most far-reaching encroachment on national political sovereignty, as Member States are in principle completely blocked from taking any autonomous action in these fields. As such restrictions are hard to accept, the Commission frequently faces fierce opposition when it claims exclusive external competence in a specific subject-matter. This explains the endless controversies on the scope of the Community's exclusive competence under the Common Commercial Policy (CCP). Subscribing to a wide notion of CCP, covering the external dimension of the entire Common Market would have entailed the paradox result that the Community's external competence goes beyond its internal competence in this domain. In their examination of CCP and other exclusive external competences, *Anita Lukaschek* and *Birgit Weidel* thus stress the necessity of parallelism between the internal and external sphere.

The practice of concluding international agreements has shown that Member States are anxious to assert their international position whenever possible. The standard recourse to mixed agreements whenever the EC does not dispose of exclusive competence has raised doubts on the very existence and rationale of implied concurrent powers. As contended by *Stefan Griller* and *Katharina Gamharter*, the ECJ has never abandoned this concept in his jurisprudence. In the light of this conclusion, the Nice version of CCP, which establishes concurrent competence for services and intellectual property, seems to be based on a misunderstanding of the previous legal situation.

The complexity of external powers is heightened by "flexible" internal arrangements, such as those of Economic and Monetary Union (EMU), that are also reflected in the external regime. *Barbara Dutzler* analyses the external dimension of EMU and highlights the controversial questions arising from the non participation of three Member States in the third stage of monetary union and the special status of the European Central Bank.

The fragmentation in competence distribution and Member States' reluctance to entrust the Community with tasks in the external area creates particular difficulties for the representation in international organisations. *Barbara Dutzler* examines the EC's status and conduct in international organisations with a view to functionality and efficiency. As already highlighted before, questions of international cooperation are complex and do not respect the boundaries of competence between the EC and its Member States. At the same time, a single spokesperson is an essential precondition for a homogenous and credible representation at the international level. Consequently, the conduct in international organisations cannot strictly conform to the internal distribution of competence in the external field and requires effective implementation of the duty of cooperation. Finally *Dutzler* points out the symbolic and constitutional weight inherent in the issue of external representation. First, it is the stage where restrictions on national political sovereignty become particularly apparent for the outside world. Second, representation in international organisation is, in principle, a privilege of states.

IV. Reflections on Improving Consistency

As the Commission recently put it:

> "The Union's external policy is not easy to define. It goes beyond the traditional diplomatic and military aspects and stretches to areas such as justice and police matters, the environment, trade and customs affairs, development and external representation of the euro zone. Our aim must be to integrate these different areas and make all the resources available work together well."[11]

If this is a valid goal for the future, it has to be concluded that the requirements of Article 3 TEU – to "ensure the consistency of [the Unions] external activities as a whole in the context of its external relations, security, economic and development policies" – have not been fully met in the past.[12]

It might be useful, as a preliminary exercise to proposals on improvements, to reflect on the subject of such an effort. Relying upon *Karl Loewenstein's* conceptual framework, our analysis is premised on the differentiation between policy determination,

---

[11] Communication from the Commission, A Project for the European Union, COM(2002) 247 final, 22. May 2002, at p 12. To the same end, see the discussion paper provided by the Praesidium of the European Convention of 3 July 2002, EU External Action, CONV 161/02.

[12] As *Krenzler/Schneider* (1997) 147, rightly observe, the provision does not constitute an effective instrument to guarantee consistency in the EU's external acting.

policy execution, and policy control .[13] In this system, *policy determination* is incumbent on the government and the parliament of a polity, which are called on to co-operate. The primary instrument for the performance of policy decision is legislation. *Policy execution* is seen as administration, that is the application of the policy decisions as well as of the utilitarian regulations of social relations. *Policy control* is seen as the mechanisms for taming and limiting political power. It is exercised with regard to all power holders, and done by the electorate, the government, parliament and the courts. Even if these categories were developed mainly for states, they are useful for our context.

Looking at the EU, it has already been stressed that external relations is fragmented in several respects. The competence for policy determination differs with respect to "economic" and "political" matters, and even within these matters, the borderlines being more than blurred. Moreover, the division includes at least three "players": the Member States, the European Union, and the European Communities. Procedures and legal instruments are divergent, not only for different actors, but often also for one and the same actor according to the subject matter. Things become even more inscrutable as soon as policy execution and policy control are taken into account.[14] Under these circumstances, it is natural that the delimitation of competences and procedures is not only a predominant exercise in day to day business, but nearly inevitably bound to become extremely controversial and burdensome. Our analysis suggests that a consistent and at the same time workable solution on the grounds of the existing legal framework is not in sight. Given the perspective of EU enlargement, including the eventual doubling of the number of Member States, leaving everything as it stands can only worsen the situation.

Concentrating on *policy determination*, the most obvious, but at the same time radical step to improve consistency would be[15] the

---

13 *Loewenstein* (1965) 42 – 52.

14 We are to a large extent silent on these issues in the following deliberations. However, it should be said that they must not be underestimated; among others, policy control through courts is almost entirely lacking with regard to second pillar activities.

15 By the following we undertake to evaluate political alternatives against the background of our scientific analysis. It goes without saying that every decision for or against amendments of the current system is a *political* decision. We do not claim that science could provide

abandonment of the pillar structure, and the integration of the Common Foreign and Security Policy (CFSP) as well as the Provisions on Police and Judicial Cooperation in Criminal Matters (PJC) into the first pillar. As long as "respecting and building upon the acquis communautaire" (Article 3 TEU) is accepted not only as existing law but also as a guiding principle for future reforms, such reforms should at least point into the direction of integrating CFSP and PJC into the first pillar – as has already been the case in Amsterdam and in Nice. At the same time, the decision making procedures even within the first pillar could be reduced, thereby realising an old desiderate.[16]

Utopian as this suggestion may appear at first glance, it is nonetheless on the political agenda. A recent proposal suggests a three-stage plan similar to the approach taken with regard to European Monetary Union (EMU). The final stage would include the establishment of a "genuine specific political authority", a far-reaching political Union.[17]

The radicalism of such a concept could of course be reduced by upholding differences (within the EC) of organs and procedures involved, admitting at the same time that every such difference may again be the cause for incoherence. The search is for a *better* balance between the need for consistency and the need for differentiation. A candidate for specific, more intergovernmental provisions, at least in the near future, certainly is the military dimension of European security and defence policy.

On the basis of these general observations, some remarks shall be added on the proposal to merge the post of the Commissioner for External Relations and of the High Representative for the foreign and security policy. The proposal is, in essence, a purely organizational reform without explicitly touching on the more fundamental implications mentioned above.

"The EU needs to bridge the gap between the Community side and the inter-governmental side of external policy, headed by the Commissioner for External Relations and Mr CFSP respectively. In

---

sufficient conditions to turn this *political* character into a scientifically proven necessity.

16 See only European Council, Turin 29 March 1996, SN 100/96, no. 2; European Parliament, Resolution from 17 May 1995, PE 190.441, no. 29.

17 Contribution from *Alain Lamassoure* to the European Convention, CONV 46/02 of 14 May 2002.

the long run, these two jobs should merge so that a single 'Foreign Policy supremo' runs EU foreign and security policy."[18] The latter is also what the Commission is suggesting as a remedy.[19] Obviously, the organizational status of such a post – member of the Commission,[20] special organ affiliated with the Council (eventually still within the General Secretariat),[21] or a personal union of a Commissioner and the High Representative – is of crucial relevance.

It should be very clear at the outset that the picture of the Commissioner for External Relations and the High Representative currently "heading" or "running" EC external relations and CFSP is severely misrepresenting the current legal situation. *Policy determination* regarding external relations in the EC is currently differing according to the subject, and is shared between the Council, the Commission, and – to a lesser extent – the European Parliament. Within the second pillar, lacking the monopoly of initiative for the Commission, and the EP restricted to a consultative function, the power is mainly with the European Council and the Council, the Member States remaining the primary actors as long as no consensus can be reached. The High Representative is only "assisting" the Council,[22] which provides for a weaker position than that of the Commission within the first pillar. The Commission is clearly reflecting this situation by proposing not only the merger of the two posts, but also the introduction of "a single source of initiative", i.e. the right of initiative for the Commission, and qualified majority voting.[23]

Consequently, it should be noted that the merger of the roles is only a facet of the more fundamental topic of the division of powers with regard to *policy determination* as addressed above. The merger

---

18 *Everts* (2002) 7, 52.

19 COM(2002) 247 final, at 14.

20 This is what the Commission is saying, when it proposes to secure coherence "by incorporating the High Representative within the Commission": COM(2002) 247 final, at 15 and 16.

21 *Everts* (2002) at 52, proposes to place the new High Representative "inside the Commission – with a special statute – but be answerable to EU foreign ministers. The new Mr Foreign Policy should still be appointed by the European Council, to emphasise the member-states' ownership of the CFSP."

22 Compare Article 26 TEU.

23 COM(2002) 247 final, at 13 and 15.

of the posts without any clarification on decision taking in "economic" and "political" matters would rather increase the confusion, than bring it to an end.[24]

Moreover, it has also to be said that the merger at issue would imply an unprecedented fusion of policy determination and policy execution at EU and EC level.[25] If the new Commissioner/High Representative unifies all powers currently divided between the two posts, this would amount to bringing policy determination and execution partly into one hand.[26] Accountability would be difficult if the concrete person is to be chosen by joint agreement by the President designate of the Commission and by the Council at Heads of State and Government level, but should at the same time perform its tasks under the authority of the President of the Commission.[27] Consequences were even more staggering if the new functionary would "run" EU external policy and be "answerable" to the Council.[28] The role of the foreign ministers would thus be changed from policy determination to policy control, while policy determination would be a matter for the new organ. This would, in effect, create an additional layer in remoteness from and accountability to the electorate.

Our conclusion is that reflections on a better division of competences for policy determination, policy execution and policy control between the EC, the EU, and the Member States should be

---

24 A similar objection is to be raised against the proposal to simple establish a new Foreign Affairs Council – among other also proposed by *Everts* (2002) at 53: "The real need is for the EU to make its huge range of general policies support an overall diplomatic strategy. To achieve that, a new foreign affairs council is needed, to ensure better cross-pillar coherence." As long as the varying competences are not clarified, an organisational reform alone will bring no progress. Suffice it to say that even today it is the same Council which is acting on the grounds of the TEC and of the TEU.

25 Our premise, which cannot be developed in detail, is that the principle of separation of powers – not in an organic, but in a "functional perspective" – is a structural feature underlying the Community legal order; compare e.g. *Lenaerts* (1991) esp at 14.

26 We contend that the High Representative is an *assistant* to the Council (Article 26 TEU) and not a special executive organ with a different status compared to that of the Commission.

27 This is what the Commission is proposing: COM(2002) 247 final, at 14.

28 Compare above fn 21.

the primary task of a reform, and it should be addressed explicitly, and in terms of scope of competences. As mentioned, the direction can only be to (gradually) bring foreign policy further under supranational structure, if the safeguard of the acquis communautaire remains the guiding principle. But it should also be stressed that this cannot, as might be the impression from the most recent debate, be the only task. Equally important would be to improve the division of competences within the EC. A sound and workable solution in the field of external relations cannot be achieved by merging functions or posts, while leaving the underlying concepts untouched.

References:

Fraser Cameron (1997), Where the Commission Comes In: From the Single European Act to Maastricht, in: *Elfriede Regelsberger/Philippe de Schoutheete de Tervarent, Wolfgang Wessels* (eds), Foreign Policy of the European Union. From EPC to CFSP and Beyond, London 1997, 99-108.

Steven Everts (2002), Shaping a credible EU foreign policy, CER study, 2002.

Stefan Griller/Dimitri P. Droutsas/Gerda Falkner/Katrin Forgó/Michael Nentwich (2000), The Treaty of Amsterdam. Facts, Analysis, Prospects, Vienna 2000.

Hans Kelsen (1949), General Theory of Law and State, Cambridge (Massachusetts) 1949.

Hans Kelsen/Robert W. Tucker (1966), Principles of International Law, 2nd edition, New York et al. 1966.

Horst-Günter Krenzler/Henning Schneider (1997), The Question of Consistency, in: *Elfriede Regelsberger/Philippe de Schoutheete de Tervarent, Wolfgang Wessels* (eds), Foreign Policy of the European Union. From EPC to CFSP and Beyond, London 1997, 133-151.

Koen Lenaerts (1991), Some Reflections on the separation of powers in the European Community, CMLRev. 1991, 11-36.

Karl Loewenstein (1965), Political Power and the Governmental Process, 2nd edition, Chicago 1965.

Simon Nuttal (1992), European Political Cooperation, New York 1992.

Elfriede Regelsberger/Philippe de Schoutheete de Tervarent, Wolfgang Wessels (1997), From EPC to CFSP:Does Maastricht Push the EU Toward a Role as a Global Power?, in: *Elfriede Regelsberger/Philippe de Schoutheete de Tervarent, Wolfgang Wessels* (eds), Foreign Policy of the European Union. From EPC to CFSP and Beyond, London 1997, 1-15.

Birgit Weidel

Regulation or Common Position – The Impact of the Pillar Construction on the Union's External Policy

I. Preview

The European Union is characterised by its pillar system. The coexistence of the supranational first pillar, on the one hand, and the intergovernmental second and third pillars, on the other hand, gives rise to a number of legal uncertainties particularly in areas with overlapping competences. The Treaties do not provide for a clear demarcation of competence between the European Community and the European Union. Hence the question arises whether the choice between Community instruments and those of the intergovernmental pillars remains totally free and therefore left to the discretion of the Council. The objective of this article is to identify a system of rules or guidelines determining the choice between Community and intergovernmental instruments. Special considerations will be dedicated to consequences for the European Union's external activities.

II. Introduction

A. The Structural Changes of the Maastricht Treaty

With the entry into force of the Treaty on European Union (TEU) in 1993, the areas of Common Foreign and Security Policy (CFSP) and Justice and Home Affairs (JHA) have officially become part of the European agenda.[1] The inclusion of these policies as the

[1] Both areas have previously been subject of cooperation at European level in a more or less informal context. European Political Cooperation (EPC), known as the predecessor of CFSP, has been formally introduced by the Single European Act without providing for any institutional or procedural framework. On a more casuistic basis, judicial cooperation was also part of this system. The relevant subjects were discussed in various intergovernmental working groups eg the TREVI group combating terrorism. For a comprehensive study on EPC see *Nuttal* (1992).

so-called second and third pillars of the newly created European Union overruled traditional conceptions of European integration as reflected by the history and evolution of the European Community (EC).

Those elements which have paved the way for the EC's transformation from a purely economic organisation into a multifunctional entity, have not been taken over into the new dimensions of European cooperation. By introducing the pillar construction, the drafters of the TEU created a structure which allows for coordinated action outside the rigid mechanisms of the Community method. Instead of extending the supranational features of Community law to the new areas of CFSP and JHA[2], the framers of the treaties opted for a less stringent way of Europeanisation and gave the second and the third pillar a mainly intergovernmental character. As many authors have extensively discussed the differences[3], the most important elements of this distinction shall only be briefly highlighted.

- *Decision making process and institutional balance*: The Council is the predominant institution in the intergovernmental framework. In comparison to the Community system, the position of the Commission is significantly weaker. By sharing the right of initiative with the Member States, this truly supranational body cannot exercise the same influence on policy-shaping as it does in the Community. The Parliament is virtually excluded from the decision-making process in the framework of CFSP and PJC. Whereas decisions are generally taken by qualified majority voting in the Community, unanimity is the rule in the 2nd and 3rd pillar. Every single Member State may veto a common measure.
- *Lack of judicial control and enforcement mechanisms*: Control mechanisms known to the Community system are absent in the intergovernmental pillars. CFSP is totally excluded from the ECJ's jurisdiction. In the area of PJC, the Court may review the legality of certain acts and give interpretative rulings. Due to the lack of infringement proceedings, a Member State's failure to

---

2 With the entry into force of the Amsterdam Treaty the third pillar has been renamed into "police and judicial cooperation in criminal matters"(PJC).

3 See for example *Demaret* (1993) 39ff; *Weiler* (1993) 52ff; *Griller* (1999) 54ff.

implement CFSP or PJC acts is not amenable to judicial review. Furthermore, the important elements of the Community legal order – direct effect and supremacy – do not apply to law generated in the intergovernmental pillar.

For this recourse to intergovernmental mechanisms, the TEU was heavily criticised.[4] It has been regarded as a major threat to achievements of the EC Treaty and to the further progress of European integration. Aspirations for a communitarisation of CFSP and JHA[5] at the early stage of the 1996 IGC soon turned out to be illusionary visions rather than political reality. The Amsterdam Treaty maintained the tripartite architecture of the European Union.[6] Despite its shortcomings[7], the intergovernmental method still dominates the decision-making process in the second and third pillar. European action in the areas of CFSP and police and judicial cooperation continued to be based on a different type of law than Community policies.

B. Overlaps between TEU and TEC

At first sight, the simple coexistence of two distinct categories of law does not appear problematic as long as only "new issues of European cooperation" i.e. areas which have previously not been part of the Community's agenda are concerned. However, some delicate aspects should not be overlooked. A thorough analysis of the Treaty establishing the European Community (TEC) and the

---

4 See for example *Curtin* (1993).

5 See *de Witte* (1997) 54; *Laursen* (1997) 64; *George* (1997) 109; *Pijpers/Vanhoonacker* (1997) 129; *Dinan* (1997) 197.

6 The changes of Amsterdam showed that the initial distrust and objections the TEU encountered were unjustified to a certain extent. A number of minor but nevertheless significant modifications and nuances have been introduced to the second pillar which strengthened the European Union's identity and its capacity to act on the international scene. In the area of JHA even more progress in terms of a deepening of integration could be achieved. The transfer of a major part to the first pillar and the reinforcement of the ECJ's jurisdiction in the field of PJC are the main achievements to be mentioned in this context. For a comprehensive analysis of the Amsterdam Treaty see *Griller* et al. (2000).

7 The deficits have been addressed in the Report of the Reflection Group on the TEU. Even the Council, traditionally a defender of intergovernmental decision-making recognised the need for reforms in this area.

TEU reveals that the distinction between Community policy areas and areas of intergovernmental co-operation is blurred. The tasks the TEU assigned to the second and third pillar cannot always be precisely separated from tasks the Community is entrusted with under the TEC.

The most evident overlap exists in the field of external relations between the Community's express and implied external competences and the second pillar, the CFSP. The whole field of cooperation with third countries beyond purely economic purposes[8] provides a vast field for possible intersections with the second pillar. In addition, the difficulty to establish a clear demarcation also concerns the relationship between the Community and the third pillar. Although the Amsterdam Treaty has mitigated the danger of potential overlaps[9] by transferring various areas ranging originally under the third pillar to Title IV of the TEC, a number of subjects cannot be easily classified: The inclusion of cooperation between customs authorities into Title VI of the TEU might conflict with Art 135 TEC ("customs cooperation"). In the area of data protection measures relating to the collection, storage, processing and exchange of information adopted pursuant to Art 30 para 1(b) TEU might cover elements already regulated by Community instruments concerning data protection based on Art 95 TEC.[10] To continue this list one can further point at Art 280 TEC, which provides for measures to combat fraud affecting the Community's financial interests and its potential overlap with general actions aimed at fighting and preventing fraud in the framework of police and judicial cooperation.

---

8 Until today, the TEC lacks a specific legal basis for this type of relationship with third countries. Agreements of this kind have been based on Art 310 or Art 308 TEC. Upon the entry into force of the Nice Treaty the newly created Art 181a TEC will provide an explicit basis for economic, financial and technical cooperation with third countries. For a more detailed presentation see *Bernd Martenczuk's* contribution to this book.

9 Before the entry into force of the Amsterdam Treaty, the crossing of external borders was one of the problematic issues. See in this context: *O'Keeffe* (1995) 912.

10 E.g. directive 95/46/EC concerning the protection of individuals in relation to the processing of electronic data, OJ L 281, 23. 11. 1995, 31.

C. The Relevance of the Distinction

Due to the fundamental differences between the Community and the intergovernmental system highlighted above, the attribution of an issue to the Community pillar or to one of the intergovernmental pillars has substantial consequences for the legal quality and the effectiveness of a measure adopted. A Community act, directly applicable or capable of having direct affect, setting aside incompatible national law and subject to the jurisdiction of the ECJ, does certainly have more practical importance than a measure stemming from the intergovernmental sphere, the binding force of which is not contested in principle[11], but which lacks the effective enforcement mechanisms of Community law, namely the ECJ's jurisdiction, primacy and direct effect.

Furthermore, the choice of the legal basis decides on the actors participating in the decision-making process. An involvement of the Parliament, the level of the Commission's influence or the consultation of bodies like the ESC or the Court of Auditors depend on that decision. Hence questions of the institutional balance also come into play at that stage. Already within the Community system, disputes concerning the correct legal base take place against the background of the distribution of power amongst Community institutions and thus touch upon fundamental structural and organisational principles. Questions of that type became even more delicate, since the Community is now no longer the only decision making body but supplemented by two intergovernmental fora, in which the powers of institutions like the Commission and the Parliament are manifestly restricted.[12]

With the exception of Art 301 TEC, neither the TEC nor the TEU sets up a clear rule of precedence. Article 301 TEC is the only rule that clarifies the question of precedence in a special case of overlapping areas.[13] In all the cases referred to above, the relevant

---

11 *De Witte* (1998) 53; *Eaton* (1994) 222; *Müller-Graff* (1994) 495.

12 See also *Cremona* (1993) 248.

13 Art 301 TEC, the legal basis introduced by the Maastricht Treaty for the imposition of economic sanctions, constitutes the sole exception to this general rule. This article establishes a two step procedure for the adoption of economic sanctions against a third country. According to this procedure, the Council takes a measure "*where it is provided in a common position or a joint action*". It is clear from the wording that the adoption of a Community measure under Art 301 TEC depends on the existence of a corresponding action under the 2nd pillar. The

provisions do not even make any reference to their counterpart in the other pillar. Likewise the TEU remains silent on the question whether Community instruments can have binding effects on CFSP or JHA acts or the reverse.[14] What are the implications of this absence of specific priority rules? Are the decision-makers absolutely free in their choice of the legal basis as soon as a subject matter cannot clearly be attributed either to the Community or the intergovernmental sphere? The consequences of such a conclusion would be significant:

Before the entry into force of the TEU, concerted actions at European level could only be taken in the framework of the TEC, provided that the latter contained an appropriate legal base. Whenever the Member States decided to proceed on a common basis, they were forced to respect the principles and decision making procedures of Community law. Assuming that the choice between Community instruments, on the one hand, and measures of CFSP or JHA, on the other hand, is free, would allow Member States to escape from the mandatory rules of Community law by having recourse to decisions taken on an intergovernmental decision-making basis when a neat assignment is not possible. In this respect, the concerns that intergovernmental features might encroach upon Community procedures do not appear unjustified. An extensive interpretation of second or third pillar competences in these cases of uncertainty might lead to a gradual displacement of Community measures. It is obvious that such an understanding could seriously undermine the objectives of the European Community and the mechanisms established by the TEC to achieve these aims.[15]

III. Implications Arising from TEU Provisions

Notwithstanding the lack of specific priority rules, the TEU contains general norms with relevance for the relationship between the three pillars and the exercise of powers under the various Treaties. The two central principles will be analysed in the following.

---

contribution of *Anita Lukaschek* to this books deals with the specific questions concerning the imposition of economic sanctions.

14 *Neuwahl* (1994) 236.

15 See *Krenzler/Schneider* (1994) 152, 154f; *Morgan* (1994) 19; *Burghardt/Tebbe* (1995) 8, 12.

A. The Integrity of the Acquis Communautaire

When creating the Union, the Member States committed themselves to safeguard the Community's achievements for the integration process. A number of indications aim at preserving the level of integration guaranteed through the existing acquis communautaire:

- Art 1 (ex-Art A) TEU declares that the Union is *founded* on the European Communities and (only) *supplemented* by the intergovernmental policies, CFSP and JHA. This sentence, albeit probably more programmatic than legally pertinent, acknowledges the central role of the Community which constitutes the fundamental basis for the "process of creating an ever closer union among the peoples of Europe"[16].
- A more precise and compelling formula is contained in Art 2 (ex-Art B) TEU, which sets out the main objectives pursued by the Union. Its fifth indent obliges the Union "*to maintain in full the acquis communautaire and to build on it* with a view to considering to what extent the policies and forms of cooperation introduced by the TEU" – that is to say CFSP and JHA – "may need to be revised with the aim of ensuring the effectiveness of the mechanisms and the institutions of the Community." This stipulation postulates the integrity of the acquis communautaire.[17] It strengthens the Community's position in relationship to the intergovernmental pillars, since it provides for a revision of these policies in order to ensure the effective functioning of the Community.
- The principle of immunity of the acquis communautaire established by Art 2 TEU is repeated in Art 3 (ex-Art C) TEU requiring the Union's institutions to respect and build upon the acquis communautaire.
- Most evidently, the intention to ensure the integrity of the Community system is demonstrated by the insertion of Art 47 (ex-Article M) TEU, which explicitly states that the TEU – apart from provisions amending provisions for the EC, ECSC and the Euratom Treaty and the final provisions of the TEU – does not affect the Treaties establishing the European Communities and subsequent treaties modifying or supplementing them. By explicitly deviating from the general rule of *lex posterior*

---

16 Article 1 TEU first sentence.

17 See in particular *Pache/Hilf* (1995) paras 17-19.

derogat legi priori, Art 47 TEU avoids conclusions that provisions concerning the intergovernmental pillars could be understood as amendments of the TEC.[18]

The inclusion of these provisions clearly reflects the concern of some Member States that the new forms of cooperation might entail a weakening of the Community pillar through an "intergovernmental contamination"[19] of its structures and decision making procedures.[20]

Art 47 TEU clarifies that the introduction of the new policies by the TEU did not change primary Community law. This commitment to safeguard the integrity of the TEC is further reinforced and extended by the requirement of Art 2 fifth indent and Art 3 TEU to maintain and build on the acquis communautaire. Hence, immunity is not solely guaranteed to the legal framework explicitly enshrined in the Treaties but to the entire scope of the Community legal order. As *Everling* pointed out, "... *CFSP and JHA introduced new elements in the* [Union] *legal order but did not affect the present state and unity of the Community legal order.*"[21]

The TEU's concept of the acquis communautaire requires clarification: The traditional notion of the acquis has been elaborated in the context of accessions to the Community and comprises not only the founding Treaties and their political objectives, but also secondary law and other acts of the institutions including the case law of the ECJ and general principles of Community law.[22] In this context, the acquis has aptly been depicted as "a sort of 'snapshot' of the situation" existing at a certain moment.[23]

It has been rightly pointed out that the TEU's reference to the acquis must have a different meaning in comparison to the more static accession concept, which refers to the body of law that

---

18 *Dehousse* (1994) 10, *Pache* (1995b) para 22.

19 This expression is borrowed from *Curtin* (1993) 30.

20 *Gialdino* (1995) 1105; *Timmermans* (1996) 67; *Kapteyn/Verloren van Themaat* (1998) 53.

21 *Everling* (1992) 1072.

22 The term even goes beyond the concept of Community law in stricto senso, since it further includes measures whose legal status inside the system is unclear – for example acts of representatives of the Member States and other measures generally referred to as soft law. *Gialdino* (1995) 1089ff.

23 *Gialdino* (1995) 1092; *Weatherill* (1998) 161.

candidate countries must take over in order to fulfil the accession criteria. Interpreted in that sense the aforementioned provisions would freeze the whole spectrum of Community law at its Maastricht state.[24] Art 2 and 3 TEU certainly do not intend to keep Community law from being adapted or developed further. Accordingly, a different notion of the acquis which does not prevent the natural dynamic evolution of law has to be deployed.

The concrete substance of the acquis referred to in Art 2 and 3 TEU is hardly ascertainable, although the general idea behind this concept seems clear: The purity of the Community framework has to be preserved.[25] CFSP and PJC may not undermine the achievements in the Community or the Community method.[26] The acquis is the platform on which future integration shall stand.[27] It has been suggested to interpret the "acquis" as a kind of "hard core" consisting of the fundamental principles of the Community legal order.[28] These fundamental principles may comprise material issues like the freedoms of the single market or the protection of fundamental rights as well as organisational and procedural elements of Community law. The latter aspect is of particular relevance for the issue of this essay. As highlighted above, the essential differences between the Community and the intergovernmental pillars exist in the decision-making process, the role of the institutions and in the quality and enforceability of measures adopted. Thus protection must logically be directed at the special features of the Community system, by which it differs that significantly from the intergovernmental pillars and other intergovernmental organisations. These fundamental elements may

---

24 *Weatherill* (1998) 161; *Bogdandy/Nettesheim* (1996) 276ff.

25 *Gialdino* (1995) 1105.

26 *Kapteyn/Verloren van Themaat* (1998) 49.

27 *Weatherill* (1998) 158.

28 *Gialdino* (1995) 1089ff. According to *Weatherill*, the notion of the acquis in Art 2 and 3 TEU is neither sufficiently specified to provide an efficient safeguard for the values of the Community, nor does it oblige the Member States to adhere to these values indefinitely. Thus he suggests to substitute this "lip service" by the definition of fundamental values and a commitment to safeguard them in a constitutional document, which should even be immune against alterations by Treaty revisions concocted by Member States in the framework of intergovernmental conferences. *Weatherill* (1998) 153ff.

not be diluted by an enhanced recourse to instruments of the intergovernmental pillars.

These considerations clearly imply that the intergovernmental pillars are not placed over the Communities.[29] The wording of Art 1 TEU "supplemented by the CFSP and JHA" and the passage of Art 2 TEU providing for a revision of these policies in order to ensure the effective functioning of the Community do even indicate to the contrary, namely that the Community supersedes the second and third pillar.[30] Thus, the mechanism embodied in Art 301 TEC has to be considered as an exception rather than a rule and does not establish a general principle.[31] This conclusion applies equally to policy areas with potential overlaps: Community actions are neither degraded to simple implementing acts for second and third pillar decisions, nor is the pre-existence of a CFSP or JHA act a precondition for the Community to adopt a measure.[32]

B. The Principle of Consistency

Apart from the integrity of the acquis communautaire, the TEU establishes another principle concerning the relationship between the Union's pillars:

- According to Art 1 TEU, the Union has to accomplish its task "in a manner demonstrating consistency".
- The first sentence of Art 3 TEU imposes an obligation on the single institutional framework to ensure the consistency and continuity of the Union's activities.
- The second sentence of Art 3 TEU attaches particular importance to the consistency of the Union's external activities.[33] Responsibility for ensuring this consistency is attributed to the Council and the Commission.

The Union is required to carry out its internal and external activities in a consistent and continuous manner. This requirement

---

29 Explicitly in favour of general equality amongst the pillars: *Krenzler/Schneider* (1994) 152.

30 However, it might be more convincing not to overestimate the legal value of these formulas. As *Pechstein* points out correctly, the term „foundation" lacks any legal substance to allow for a dogmatic classification of the European Communities and its legal instruments in the Union system. *Pechstein* (1995) 248.

31 In that sense *Gilsdorf* (1996) 165; *Timmermans* (1996) 68.

32 *Willaert/Marquez-Ruiz* (1995) 40; *Lenaerts/Van Nuffel* (1999) 667.

33 See also Art 13 para 3 TEU.

obviously seeks to avoid that the considerable structural differences resulting from the pillar construction lead to an inconsistent or even contradictory design of Union policies.[34] The single institutional framework is the main instrument to ensure this consistency. It is the institutions' task to further compliance with this principle. The Treaty explicitly charges the Council and the Commission with observing that the implementation of the Union's external policies respects the requirement of consistent action.

The principle of consistency has a twofold meaning. While Art 1 TEU requires the Union to ensure its inner coherence[35], Art 3 para 1 TEU calls for conformity of its actions and measures taken under the different provisions and pillars of the Union.[36] The latter understanding is of particular importance for the relationship between Community and intergovernmental policies, since actions adopted in the different frameworks have to be attuned to each other. In other words, the principle of coherence seeks to avoid contradictory and non-adjusted measures.

In literature it has been questioned whether Art 3 TEU also has legal effects for Community law. As pointed out above, Art 47 TEU stipulates that the TEU – apart from provisions amending provisions for the EC, ECSC and the Euratom Treaty and the TEU's final provisions – does not affect the TEC. This formulation could lead to the conclusion that only amendments contained in Art 46–53 and Titles II-IV of the TEU are relevant for the Community.[37] The few authors, who addressed this issue mainly consider the TEU's Common provisions (Art 1–Art 7) as (implicit) amendments of the TEC.[38] In general, it is assumed that Community actions must be in accordance with the principle of coherence.

---

[34] In that sense *Neuwahl* (1994) 234. In this context, the term "Union policies" is understood in a broad sense comprising Community policies as well as CFSP and PJC.

[35] Consistency and coherence are used synonymously. Elaborating on nuances of these notions: *Cremona* (1999) 169.

[36] *Müller-Graff* (1993) 150; *Hilf/Pache* (1995) paras 9 and 10.

[37] See for example *Eaton* (1994) 221.

[38] *Pechstein/König* (1998) 59ff; *Trüe* (1997) 27ff; *Wichard* (1999) 175.

C. The Relationship between the Acquis Criterion and the Principle of Consistency

According to Art 3 TEU, consistency shall be ensured *while respecting and building upon the acquis communautaire.* Both aspects – safeguarding the acquis communautaire and consistency – have to be taken into account by the legislator. Prima vista, there seems to be contradiction between these two requirements. On the one hand, the provisions on the integrity of the acquis seek to avoid an intrusion of intergovernmental decisions into the Community sphere. On the other hand, consistency even requires a certain level of interaction and might be understood as a certain attenuation of this separation claim. Especially in the area of foreign policy, which is split up between different provisions and different pillars, the danger of inconsistent and contradictory measures is evident. The formulation of a coherent policy requires to take into account all aspects concerning the Union's relationship to a third country or its attitude to a specific thematic issue. It could be argued that the need to adopt such a comprehensive approach necessarily entails that instruments sometimes have to exceed their specific scope and deal with aspects covered by other Treaty provisions. Consequently, foreign policy instruments adopted under the CFSP might also touch upon matters of economic or development cooperation.

However, it should not be overlooked that consistency and the acquis criterion are only partially targeted to the same aspects of policy making. The principle of consistency established by Art 3 TEU primarily aims at ensuring material consistency, that is to say conformity of the substance or content of the Union's actions.[39] Art 3 TEU does not refer to procedural or organisational conformity.[40] Accordingly, the principle of coherence itself is neutral with regard to the choice of instruments. Consistency does not impose an automatic preference of a certain category of law.

The requirement to safeguard the acquis is aimed at the unimpaired functioning and the preservation of the Community method. One important component of the Community method is the specific way of policy-shaping inside the Community system. Contrary to the principle of consistency, the integrity of the acquis therefore extends to procedural aspects. The way decision-making works in the EC is inspired by fundamental considerations

---

39 *Müller-Graff* (1993) 150; *Pechstein* (1995) 254.

40 *Neuwahl* (1994) 236.

concerning the functioning inside the EC, e.g. to ensure the participation of different actors representing particular interests (Commission, Council, Parliament, Economic and Social Committee, Committee of the Regions) or the efficiency of the process and its result. They form the underlying principles of the legislative procedures laid down in the EC Treaty, which in reverse guarantee their due consideration. Respect of these procedural rules is an important premise to preserve the Community method.

The choice of the legal basis determines which procedures are to be followed. This choice has to be governed by the criterion to safeguard the acquis. Thus Art 2 and 3 TEU, read in conjunction with Art 47 TEU, play the central role at a preliminary stage of the decision-making process. Once this choice has been made in accordance with these provisions, consistency comes into play for the specific content of the measure. The relationship between these two principles will be examined again in the context of the Union's external relations.

IV. The Distribution of Competence after Maastricht

When the Council intends to enact legislation in a field that is covered by the TEC as well as by CFSP or PJC, it must respect the acquis communautaire. The "vocation communautiare" establishes a preference in favour of the Community method. How far reaching is this protection? In many areas that can be subject of Community legislation Member States are yet not excluded from acting on an individual basis. Are these areas nevertheless excluded from the scope of the second and the third pillar? In other words, does the integrity of the EC Treaty call for protection that extends to the whole range of Community powers irrespective of their nature or is protection limited to areas falling in the exclusive jurisdiction of the Community?

A. Existence of a General Priority Rule?

The requirement to maintain in full and build on the acquis could be interpreted as to grant unconditional preference to every potential Community competence over alternatives in the 2nd or 3rd pillar. In his analysis on the notion of the acquis, *Weatherill* suggests such a wide interpretation in the context of competence aspects.[41] According to him, respect for the acquis implies "*denial for a free political choice between pillars in deciding the forum for*

[41] *Weatherill* (1998) 158ff.

transnational action". Whenever an adequate basis for action can be found in the TEC, there is no room for action in the intergovernmental framework as "[i]*f something can be done via the EC it must be done via the EC*"[42]. This broad understanding would certainly offer protection for Community competences to the widest possible extent. Obviously *Weatherill* considers "building on the acquis" to be an unconditional commitment to the Community method. However, the acquis which is to be build upon has not totally excluded Member States from acting in spheres of potential Community competence. It is doubtful that "building on the acquis" should be understood in a sense of expanding Community powers in that way. In fact, such a conclusion would render a concurrent competence into an exclusive one with regard to CFSP and PJC. The wording of Art 2 and Art 47 TEU is too vague in that respect as to allow such a far-reaching interpretation.

In this context, it should be mentioned that the ECJ could already have clarified this question. In 1996, the Commission sought an application for annulment under Art 230 (ex-Art 173) TEC against a joint action adopted by Council on the basis of ex-Art K.3 TEU concerning airport transit arrangements.[43] According to the Commission, the measure should have been based on former Art 100c TEC, providing for a Community competence to determine the third countries whose nationals must be in possession of a visa when crossing the external borders of the Member States. The Court dismissed the alleged lack of jurisdiction and considered itself responsible to ensure that acts of the TEU do not encroach upon powers conferred to the Community by the TEC. The Court also affirmed its competence to annul the act in case that it should have been based on Art 100c TEC. After examining the content of the act, the Court however stated that the measures adopted did not fall within the scope of Art 100c and dismissed the action.

The judgment gave rise to various diverging interpretations. It is vital to avoid the confusion of two different aspects. In the beginning of the judgment, the Court announced an annulment of the joint action in case that the act "should have been based on Art 100c TEC". After examining the substance of the measure, the Court did not come to the conclusion that the act did not have to be based on Art 100c but limited itself to the statement that the act

---

42 *Weatherill* (1998) 159.

43 Case C-170/96, *Council v. Commission*, ECR [1998] I-2763.

"does not fall in the ambit of that provision [Art 100c TEC]". One might consider this as mere rhetoric, but strictly speaking, the question whether the act "should have been based on Art 100c TEC" remained open. The conditions for using Community competences or intergovernmental alternatives have (consciously?) not been clarified by the Court. It would have been of particular interest whether the ECJ had made a difference according to the nature of competence or whether the fact that Art 100c TEC provided an adequate legal basis had automatically rendered illegal the joint action. In the latter case the outcome would be tantamount to an unconditional priority of Community competences irrespective of their nature. Exclusive and concurrent Community powers would enjoy automatic primacy vis à vis CFSP and PJC.

B. The Nature of the European Union

The provisions establishing the integrity of the acquis cannot further clarify the question of priority. In order to examine the relationship between the pillars, it is illuminating to explore the very nature and fundamental structure of the Union. During the last years, the debate on the nature of the Union has been carried forward by some profound and thorough studies, which shall constitute the basis for further conclusions on the delimitation between Community and Union activities. In detail, these theories are multifaceted and show considerable variations which will not be considered in this context for reasons of space restraint. The following presentation highlights the two "extreme" positions and gives an overview on the in-between ranging opinions.

1. The Union as a Mere Legal Framework for Coordinated Cooperation

According to *Pechstein* and *König,* the TEU did not create a new autonomous legal entity in form of the Union. The TEU provisions, using expressions like "Member States" and the "establishment of a Union amongst themselves", are conceived as misleading and verbal rhetoric instead of legally pertinent. From these authors' point of view, the Member States consciously retained their sovereignty in the areas of JHA and CFSP, as they did not confer these tasks to the European Community. The "creation" of the Union, as such, is regarded as the evidence that the Member States obviously wanted to prevent the loss of respective powers. By framing CFSP and JHA as intergovernmental policies, they did not intend to transfer any competence to a higher ranging authority.[44] The Union does neither accomplish proper tasks nor does it pursue an own policy.[45] Rather it simply provides the rules for concerted action of the "contracting parties" in the fields of external relations and judicial cooperation and seeks to ensure consistency with related Community policies. Consequently, *Pechstein* and *König* characterise the Union as an institutionalised form of cooperation providing the institutional, legal and procedural prerequisites for the coordination of intergovernmental and Community policies. In essence, the Union is not more than a system of rules (a treaty) rather than an international organisation or a federation of states.[46] Consistently, the Union cannot be regarded as the originator of second or third pillar instruments, since it lacks the capability to act autonomously. Therefore, the instruments provided for the implementation of CFSP and JHA cannot be imputed to the Union or the institutions, but should be attributed to the Member States.[47]

2. From Structural Roof to a Fully Fledged International Organisation

In contrast to this extreme view held by *Pechstein* and *König*, the majority of authors recognises that the nature of the Union goes beyond the concept of a pure legal framework. It is generally understood that the Union is not legally identical with the Member States but a body distinct from Member States[48] and the Community[49]. Generally these theories envisage the Union as an embracing structure for the Communities and the intergovernmental policies. Again the individual positions are quite nuanced. Two main facets of this type can be identified.[50] A more restraint

---

44 *Pechstein/König* (1998) 1. See also *Hilf* (1995) para 28.

45 Of the same opinion *Torrent* (1997) 49ff.

46 *Pechstein/König* (1998) 4 and 47.

47 *Ibid.*

48 *Heukels/de Zwaan* (1994) 200; *Trüe* (1997) 12; *Dörr* (1995) 336, 343ff; *de Witte* (1998) 62; *Tizzano* (1998) 29ff and 34; *Griller* (1999) 45.

49 *Everling* (1992) 1056 and 1063; *Heukels/de Zwaan* (1994) 200; *Dörr* (1995) 344; *Curtin/Dekker* (1999) 94; *Kapteyn/Verloren van Themaat* (1998) 47.

50 This classification has been elaborated by *Bogdandy/Nettesheim* (1996). Being proponents of the unity thesis, they use the term "moderate separation thesis" to characterise the various models distinguishing between Union, Community and Member States.

position views the Union as a horizontal formation of different organisations connected to each other. The Temple model often constitutes the basis for these theories by providing the common roof and foundation as the link between the Community and the intergovernmental pillars. *Heukels* and *de Zwaan* consider the Union to be a "separate entity of integration and cooperation" which "overarches three distinct pillars with own competences and procedures" that, however, lacks competences of its own and legal personality.[51] From a similar point of view, *Hilf* regards the Union as the "roof" for the actors capable of taking legal action, namely the Member States and the European Communities, and denies any transfer of competences to the Union.[52] Nevertheless he recognises the Union's potential to obtain legal personality in course of time.[53] *Everling* seems to go further by contending that the Union is "an organisational framework *within* which the Communities and fields of cooperation are comprehended" that forms a political and juridical unity with the Communities.[54] Although he does not concede legal personality to the Union and thus no legal capacity to act under international law, the Union seems to have certain internal competences.[55] However, the specific powers mentioned are mainly those of the Community forming an integral part of the Union.[56] It remains unclear whether competences have also been directly conferred to the Union by the general provisions, Title V or Title VI of the TEU. In his analysis of CFSP, *Müller-Graff* however concludes that the Union is an independent actor and policy maker in this field.[57]

---

51 *Heukels/de Zwaan* (1994) 200ff. See also *Hilf* (1995) paras 25 and 28; *Lenaerts/Van Nuffel* (1999) 56, 612; *Kapteyn /Verloren van Themaat* (1998) 47.

52 *Hilf* (1995) paras 26 and 35. Similar *Kapteyn/Verloren van Themaat* (1998) 47.

53 For details see *Hilf* (1995) para 39.

54 *Everling* (1992) 1063 emphasis added.

55 *Everling* (1992) 1061 and 1065ff. *De Witte* also submits that the concept of legal personality should be limited to the capacity to act as a subject of international law and should not be regarded as a precondition for the existence of an international organisation. *De Witte* (1998) 62. See also *Dörr* (1995) 338.

56 *Everling* (1992) 1065ff.

57 *Müller-Graff* (1993) 152. See also *Krenzler/Schneider* (1994) 147.

A transfer of genuine Union competences is furthermore explicitly affirmed by *Dörr*, according to whose point of view, the TEU has set up the Union as a legal entity with a proper capacity to act.[58] It constitutes an international organisation and an autonomous actor in the internal relationship to its Member States. In the external sphere, the Union only enjoys limited legal personality.[59] The Communities are inseparable but nevertheless legally independent elements of the Union. Therefore actions taken pursuant to the EC Treaty may not be attributed to the Union.[60] In *Dörr's* view, the Union is a layered international organisation whose Member States have formed other entities, namely the EC, the ECSC and EURATOM, *inside* the Union system.[61]

A more pictorial description of this concept – also referred to as vertical integration model[62] – is offered by *Curtin* and *Dekker*, who compare the Union to a Russian Doll sheltering within its husk another legal person, namely the European Communities.[63] In general, the proponents of that theory concede legal personality to the European Union. In comparison to *Dörr*, they attach great importance to another significant characteristics of the union concept: Albeit being legally distinct entities and notwithstanding the significant procedural and structural differences of the TEC and the TEU, the Union and the Communities are considered to form a unitary legal system.[64] Mainly, the unity of the legal system is based on two arguments, the single institutional framework and the common and final provisions of the TEU. Hence, action in the unitary system is taken pursuant to different procedural rules but

---

58 *Dörr* (1995) 336.

59 *Dörr* (1995) 343f.

60 *Dörr* (1995) 346.

61 *Dörr* (1995) 347. This view has also been supported by *Trüe* (1997) 23f and 59; *Curtin/Dekker* (1999) 101 and *Wichard* (1999) 177.

62 *Bogdandy/Nettesheim* (1996) 274.

63 *Curtin/Dekker* (1999) 101. Similar *de Witte*, according to who the TEU has created a new international organisation , namely the EU, within which the three Communities are encapsulated but nevertheless continue to exist as legally independent suborganisations. *De Witte* (1998) 59.

64 *Trüe* (1997) 27; *Curtin/Dekker* (1999) 97ff; *De Witte* (1998) 58ff; *Wichard* (1999) 178.

nevertheless by identical institutions.[65] Furthermore, the "umbrella provisions" of the TEU apply to the first pillar as well as to the second and the third. Thus, the objectives of the Union are also relevant for the Communities, the principle of coherence also concerns Community action and the respect for fundamental rights has to be guaranteed in the Community order as well. As a result, the TEU has created a unitary legal order but no unitary organisation.[66] Within this unitary legal system, subsystems with significant structural differences continue to exist in form of the TEC and the intergovernmental pillars.[67]

It emerges from these considerations that the term "European Union" can be applied in a twofold sense. The broad notion refers to the overall structural framework comprising the different subsystems encapsulated in the international organisation "European Union". In a more narrow sense, it stands for the entity responsible for the performing of specific functions defined in Title V and Title VI of the TEU. [68]In that context, the Union and the Communities are perceived as distinct legal actors each endowed with specific powers. Albeit tasks are carried out by a single institutional framework, both entities perform proper tasks according to very different procedures.

3. Unity Thesis

Bogdandy and *Nettesheim* have taken one step beyond the thesis of the unitary legal system. The unity thesis suggests that the TEU did not simply entail a fusion of the institutions but also a merger of the entire organisations. The EC and the EU should not be regarded as different and separate entities existing alongside each other, but a unitary system comprising different legal subsystems. The TEC, TECSC and TEA do no longer provide the basis for independent organisations but are merely regarded as partial constitutional documents. Accordingly, the Communities have been fused into the

---

65 Different *Dörr* (1995) 337, who submits that the Union borrows the institutions of the Community.

66 *Trüe* (1997) 27f. This constitutes the most important difference to the unity thesis of *Bogdandy/ Nettesheim*.

67 The structural differences between the subsystems do not form an obstacle to the unity of the Union legal order as such. See *Bogdandy/Nettesheim* (1996) 279ff and *Trüe* (1997) 30f.

68 See *Wichard* (1999) 181ff.

Union.[69] However, *Bogdandy* and *Nettesheim* emphasise that this fusion should not be understood as a dissolution implying the discontinuing of the Communities' activities and the extinction of its legal relationships. Rather the law of the TEU and its structural set-up constitute the further developed stage – a modification or complementation – of the already existing Community legal order.[70]

Based on the assumption that the institutions constitute the central elements of an organisation, the single institutional framework provides the theoretical cornerstone for their theory. Without changing their identity, the Union's institutions exercise powers defined in the various texts – the TEU and the Community Treaties.[71] Coherently, they should be constantly denominated as institutions ("Council..", "Commission...", etc.) "*of the European Union*" whenever appearing as legal actors.[72]

Apart from the single institutional framework, the unity of the organisations is a consequence of the unity of the legal system. The concept of legal unity is defined as systematic linkage between norms being part of a legal system. The Union legal order derives its unitary character from its predecessor – the Community legal order. Since Community law has emerged from a unity of the legislative institutions – a result of the fusion treaties – unity has always and undisputedly been an essential characteristic of the Community's normative system which subsists in the newly created Union legal order. Apart from the responsibility of the actors for achieving unity expressed in Art 2, 3 and 6 TEU, the fact that all provisions are contained in one act (namely the TEU), and that all secondary law emanates from Union institutions, are put forward as arguments in favour of a legal unitary system.[73]

In substance, the Union is one entity with regard to the organisation, its actions and its law.[74] Powers derived from the TEC or the TEU are both attributed to the Union. Thus legal action is always taken by the Union albeit according to the rules of different treaties. Interestingly, *Bogdandy* and *Nettesheim* submit that the unity thesis does not necessarily imply a single legal personality for

69 *Bogdandy/Nettesheim* (1996) 268.
70 *Bogdandy/Nettesheim* (1996) 286.
71 See *Bogdandy/Nettesheim* (1996) 276 and 282.
72 *Bogdandy/Nettesheim* (1996) 281.
73 See *Bogdandy/Nettesheim* (1996) 279f.
74 *Bogdandy/Nettesheim* (1996) 281.

the Union. Albeit favouring such an approach, the existence of a single sovereign organisation without a single legal personality is – although not convincing – at least thinkable.[75]

4. Structural Regrouping

The foregoing illustration has demonstrated the manifold visions of the Union's architecture and the legal concept "union" varying from virtually "nothing" (*Pechstein*) to "everything" (*Bogdandy*). For the specific purpose of this paper, the author suggests a regrouping of the different models into three main categories focussed on the capacity to take legal action:

a) The Dual Relationship

Authors, in particular *Pechstein/König* but also *Hilf* and *Heukels/de Zwaan,* submit that the TEU did not create the Union as an entity with a proper capacity to take legal action. No powers have been transferred to the Union as such. Rather the TEU generated rules for the concerted exercise of *Member States'* competences in the areas of foreign policy and judicial matters. Thus, the Community and the Member States are the sole legal actors implementing the provisions of the TEU. Consequently, interferences created by the provisions of the second and third pillars require a delimitation of competences between these two actors.

b) The Triangular Structure

The second category is formed by those authors who recognise the Union as a legal entity with genuine law making powers distinct from the European Community and the Member States. From this perspective, decision making powers are distributed amongst three distinct legal actors, the Community, the Union and the Member States. In this case, overlaps between the three Union pillars do not raise the question of drawing a line between Member States and Community but between Union and Community.

c) The Unitary Structure

According to the proponents of the unity thesis, the Union has completed and thereby "absorbed" the European Community as a separate legal actor. Competences founded on the TEC are *Union competences* like powers defined in the second or third pillar. The problem of pillar intersections is thus not an issue of demarcating

---

[75] *Bogdandy/Nettesheim* (1996) 284f.

competences between different legal subjects. In any case, the Union is competent to take legal action. Nonetheless, significant procedural and material differences between the law of the first pillar and that founded on the second or the third pillar subsist in the unitary legal system and thus necessitate a clear differentiation within the unitary Union legal order. The question of the correct legal base thus plays an equally important role in this context.

C. Distribution of Competence in the Light of the Different Union Models

1. General Observations

Article 47 TEU clearly implies that the tasks the TEC conferred to the European Community have not been modified by the TEU. In other words, the insertion of CFSP and JHA did not limit or adjust the scope of existing and future Community policies.[76] Consequently, the original ambit as defined by the provisions of the TEC and by the jurisprudence of the Court is also conserved in the areas characterised by potential overlaps with CFSP and JHA policies. Since Community competences existing before Maastricht remained unaltered after the entry into force of the TEU, the Community institutions must enjoy the same powers and margin of manoeuvre.

2. Unitary Structure

According to the unity thesis, the TEC as well as CFSP and PJC are integrated in a single legal system. Community competences have become Union competences. *Within* this unitary system, the different competences have to be "interpreted with respect to the unity of the legal system"[77]. Consequently, there is no free choice between the various legal bases provided by the TEC, CFSP and PJC. The Treaty makers have assigned the different policies to specific provisions providing for particular decision making rules. The scope of former Community provisions has not been modified by the TEU. An issue already attributed to a (Community) provision cannot constitute subject of another provision. Thus, also issues falling in the ambit of a concurrent Community competence can only be regulated according to the rules of Community law and not in the intergovernmental way. The external relations provisions constitute *leges speciales* in comparison to CFSP. Based on the

---

[76] *Müller-Graff* (1994) 505; *Wichard* (1999) 177.

[77] *Bogdandy/Nettesheim* (1996) 283.

assumption that the Union constitutes a unitary system, Community competences, be they exclusive or concurrent, would be fully protected from the intrusion of intergovernmental structures. The result is a general priority rule for action in the Community system.

In the face of the fundamental differences characterising the second and third pillar, the existence of a unitary legal system has been denied.[78] A more pragmatic assessment is reflected by those models which characterise the Union or CFSP and PJC as something distinct from the Community legal order.

3. The Dual and Triangular Structure

In contrast to the unity thesis, the nature of competences plays an important role in the other models of the Union. In fact, the exercise of powers under the various treaty regimes follows the same rules in both, the dual and the triangular models of the Union. In the first concept, action in the Union framework is simply considered as the joint exercise of Member States' individual competences. The borderline between Community tasks and those of the intergovernmental pillars must logically be identical with the boundary between Community and Member States' competences.

In the triangular models, the Union possesses and exercises proper competences of its own, which have been conferred to it by the TEU. Pursuant to Art 47 TEU, the powers of the Community have remained unaffected by the TEU. Thus, the powers the Union acquired flow from competences that remained in the Member States' sphere. No transfer of powers has taken place from the Community to the policies introduced by the TEU. Consequently, the scope of second or third pillar instruments can only comprise areas in which Member States have retained their sovereignty in full or at least to a certain extent.[79] Of course the TEU could only confer powers to the Union to the extent the Member States actually enjoyed. This transfer could only take place within the limits set by Community law. Hence, action in the Union framework is subject to the same restrictions that Community law has imposed on the exercise of remaining national powers.

---

78 *Cremona* (1994) 255.

79 See *Cremona* (1994) 250. A different view has been presented by *Trüe*, who argues that no competences of Member States have been transferred to the Union. Rather new competences have been created and attributed to the 2nd and 3rd pillar. *Trüe* (2000) 159.

In areas attributed to the exclusive competence of the Community, Member States are in principle completely blocked from adopting any regulatory measures. They have irreversibly transferred their powers in that field to the Community which enjoys the exclusive authority to enact legislation. The exclusive nature of Community competences prevents the Member States from taking any action at all, be that individually or jointly in the framework of the second or third pillars.[80] Coherently, the conclusion is also valid for the triangular models. Since Member States have no more sovereignty in the areas of exclusive Community competence, no room for second or third pillar measures could have been created by a transfer of tasks to the Union via the TEU. Hence, areas of exclusive Community competence cannot be subject of CFSP or PJC acts. The Community enjoys an exclusive power to take legal action.[81]

A more complex issue is the question of concurrent or potential[82] competences. In these areas the Community is authorised to take action, but as long as the Community has not acted, Members States fully retain their legislative competences. Given the necessary political consent, the Community can enact rules based on its potential powers thereby preventing the Member States from lawfully adopting incompatible national law. In other words, it depends on the will of the Council, whether it seizes the opportunity to act in the Community framework. Member States have preserved their powers albeit not to an unlimited extent. This preservation of authority is subject to the condition that the Community does not enact legislation in that field. Once the Community has enacted legislation, there is no room for contradictory Member States' action.

In line with the pre-emption doctrine, an extensive legislative activity would advance the Community to the sole legitimate law-making authority. When the Community makes use of its potential competence in an exhaustive way – when it "occupies the field" in a manner that leaves no scope for further Member States' action – the concurrent powers are transformed into exclusive Community powers. As outlined above, exclusivity deprives the Member States of any possibility to enact national legislation. Likewise, the

---

80 In that sense *Pechstein /König* (1998) 67ff.

81 *Pache* (1995a) para 22; *Griller* (1999) 56.

82 About the terminology see *Gilsdorf* (1996) 150.

principle of pre-emption would produce the same results with regard to the scope of CFSP and JHA actions. As soon as the Community has occupied a specific field, the Council would be prevented from adopting and applying legally binding instruments of the second or third pillar in that area.

Once the Community has enacted legislation, Member States are prevented from taking actions, which could affect the Community measure in place. Accordingly, this restriction applies also to action in the Union framework. Community law in force cannot be undermined by acts stemming from the intergovernmental sphere of the Union.[83] The integrity of the acquis does not only preserve Community law in force, but extends its protection to subsequent Community law. First, Art 47 TEU refers to Treaty amendments, which can create "new" Community powers on which the Community may base further actions. Second, the Community has the possibility to expand its existing powers by having recourse to its potential powers. Obviously, such an expansion can be understood as "building upon the acquis". The respect of Community competences thus also implies that a preceding CFSP or PJC act cannot take precedence over subsequent Community law.

In essence, matters falling under concurrent Community powers may be regulated by intergovernmental instruments, as long as they do not affect existing EC law and the Community has not made exhaustive use of its powers. There is no obligation to give precedence to an existing concurrent Community power.[84]

The category of parallel powers does not pose specific problems. In this field, Community action is always perceived as complementary or parallel to the action of Member States. Retaining unlimited control of their legislative powers, they may take parallel action either at national level or jointly under tile V or VI of the TEU.

4. Comparative Summary

The examination of the different types of competence in the light of the three main theories on the nature of the European Union leads to following conclusions: Whereas the complete range of

---

[83] *Everling* (1992) 1063; *Griller* (1999) 56; *Müller-Graff* (1993) 500 and 504; *Weiler* (1993) 54.

[84] With the same conclusion albeit different argumentation *Pechstein/König* (1998) 67f.

Community powers enjoys exclusivity against Union powers in the unitary model, areas in which the Community has not made use of its concurrent powers can be subject of second or third pillar acts in the dual and the triangular models. On the basis of the conclusions concerning the dual and the triangular model, the requirement to preserve Community's competence sets following limitations to the scope of second and third pillar acts:

1) Union law may not contravene or affect Community law.
2) Matters falling into exclusive Community competence cannot be subject of CFSP or JHA measures.
3) Matters falling into concurrent Community competences can be dealt with by Union law, as long as the Community has not enacted specific rules or occupied the field.
4) Where competences are parallel or complementary the decision-makers are free to make use of instruments in the second or third pillar provided that Union law is compatible with Community law.

When the Community has not adopted rules for an area falling within its concurrent competence, the Council is not prevented from regulating this issue by means of the intergovernmental pillars. Member States could be tempted to shift controversial issues, for which no solution has so far been found in the framework of Community mechanism, to the intergovernmental sphere.

V. The Interrelations between the Community's External Policies and the Common Foreign and Security Policy

Due to the splitting of competence between the TEC and the CFSP, the Union's external relations are characterised by a structural dualism. This division into "high" and "low politics"[85] stems from the beginning of the 70s, when the Member States of the European Community started coordinating their foreign policies in the framework of European Political Cooperation. This forum, perceived to complement the economic policies of the EC, was operating outside Community structures on an intergovernmental basis.[86] At an early stage, the delimitation between economic and political matters already proved to be inadequate and infeasible in practice. For the maintenance of this artificial distinction, through

---

[85] *Weiler* (1993) 55.
[86] *Nuttal* (1987) 211ff.

the creation of the second pillar as the forum to govern the Union's foreign policy, the TEU faced heavy criticism.[87]

Given the complexity of international relations and the importance of economic instruments as powerful resources of foreign policy, political and economic aspects cannot be kept separate from each other.[88] Nevertheless, the fundamental structural differences between the pillars require particular vigilance over the preservation of Community competences to safeguard the level of integration achieved. Apart from the difficulty of ensuring consistency of external action under the different Treaty regimes, a clear-cut attribution of competence proves highly problematic. Art 11 TEU provides for a quasi-unlimited scope of the second pillar by stating that CFSP covers "all areas of foreign and security policy". Even if attempted to confine this comprehensive notion by interpreting the CFSP in the light of its objectives specified in the same article, the second pillar's ambit remains extra-ordinarily broad. Consequently, thematic overlaps with the Community's external policies are inevitable: One objective of CFSP is the consolidation of democracy, the rule of law and the respect of fundamental rights. The Community pursues the same goals in the framework of development cooperation.[89] Furthermore, CFSP aims at promoting international cooperation. This component of CFSP is characterised by a vast potential for intersection with virtually all external Community activities, ranging from purely commercial relations to all other kinds of cooperation. In this context, another aspect should not be forgotten: As the ECJ has held in its *ERTA* judgment[90], in addition to the external powers expressly mentioned in the TEC, the Community also disposes of implied external powers in basically all areas of internal competence as far as external action is necessary to achieve the objectives of the Treaty.[91] Hence potential overlaps with the second pillar do not only concern the field of explicit external policies but virtually the entire scope of Community activities.[92] Due to the dynamic

---

87 *Weiler* (1993) 55; *Morgan* (1994) 195f; *Krenzler/Schneider* (1994) 150 and 159f.

88 In this context see *Cremona* (1994) 253.

89 See Art 177 TEC. Even the wording is identical.

90 Case 22/70, *Commission v. Council (ERTA)*, ECR [1971] 263.

91 *Dashwood* (2000) 116ff.

92 The issue of external Community competences is examined in detail in this volume by *Stefan Griller* and *Katharina Gamharter*.

character of Community powers, the demarcation of competences is not a static concept but subject to continuous adaptation.[93]

The impracticability of distinguishing strictly between economic and political aspects in relations to third countries is clearly reflected in the Community's external policy. In the case of development cooperation, the simultaneous consideration of political factors is even enshrined in the TEC by virtue of Art 177 para 2. Association and cooperation agreements regularly contain a chapter on political dialogue.[94] For this reason, most of them have been concluded as mixed agreements. Conditionality, an approach developed in the last decade, makes the continuance of agreements with third countries subject to the respect of democratic values and fundamental rights.[95] By the same token, CFSP measures frequently address economic aspects or refer to Community instruments to implement their objectives.

This legally diffuse situation has lead to attempts to increasingly deal with Community issues in CFSP instruments. Against the background of the central conclusions elaborated in this essay, the transformation of the relevant CFSP articles into comprehensive legal bases for actions in external relations meets serious objections, as it runs counter to the requirement to preserve the integrity of the acquis communautaire.[96] This fundamental principle sets inherent limits to the wide notion of CFSP insofar as it may not encroach on Community competence. Only where the Community has not made use of its concurrent competence, the Council may opt for a concerted action under CFSP. Issues belonging to areas of exclusive Community competence – like the Common Commercial Policy – are *per se* excluded from the scope of CFSP.[97] Furthermore a second pillar instrument cannot regulate aspects that are already subject of Community legislation. Basically, the Council is not allowed to decide on principles or predetermine Community issues

93 *Cremona* (1994) 249ff.

94 The political character of the Community's development and cooperation policy is highlighted by the analysis of *Bernd Martenczuk* in this volume.

95 The contribution of *Peter Hilpold* to this book is dedicated to the issue of conditionality and human rights clauses.

96 Similar *Burghardt/Tebbe* (1995) 8.

97 The imposition of economic sanctions is the sole exception to this rule, because Art 301 TEC is amongst the provisions amending the TEC. Such a modification of the TEC is explicitly endorsed by Art 47 TEU.

which oblige the Commission to present a respective proposal even against its will.[98]

As a result of disputes amongst the institutions and Member States on these questions, an informal *modus vivendi* has been elaborated in 1995 for the adoption of common positions.[99] It recognises the possibility to address subjects of Community action in common positions. However, full respect for the competences of the institutions and the procedures must be ensured. Thus, a common position may only *take note* of Community measures or the intention of the Commission to present a specific proposal without obliging the Commission to set the respective actions. In practice, the requirement to respect the procedures and competences has not been duly observed in several cases. The wording of many provisions would imply an obligation rather than a simple announcement of the Commission's intention to present specific proposals.[100] Given these practical inconsistencies, the *modus vivendi* does not offer a satisfactory solution[101] and should be perceived as an interim regime rather than the way forward.

The issue of thematic overlaps has gained particular relevance with regard to common strategies (CS), introduced by the Treaty of Amsterdam. According to Art 13 TEU, the new instrument's material scope covers areas in which the Member States have important interests in common. A CS defines, *inter alia,* the means to be made available by the Union and the Member States. Paragraph 3 states that a CS is implemented, *in particular,* by joint actions and common positions. The wording already indicates that these instruments are not the only possibilities to give effect to a CS. Current practice reflects that "means to be made available by the Union" also include Community measures and third pillar acts.

So far, the Council has made use of this instrument three times by adopting the CS on Russia, the CS on Ukraine and the CS on the Mediterranean region[102], which constitute interesting precedents. In

---

98 *Burghardt/Tebbe* (1995) 16; Morgan (1994) 197.

99 In this section the author has extensively drawn on an article of *Timmermans* (1996).

100 *Timmermans* (1996) 63.

101 *Burghardt/Tebbe* (1995) 16.

102 Decision 2000/458/CFSP, Common Strategy of the European Council on the Mediterranean region, OJ L 183, 22. 7. 2000, 5; Decision 1999/414/CFSP, Common Strategy of the European Union on Russia,

all three cases, the countries' relations to the Union have already been regulated in comprehensive mixed agreements based on Art 308 or Art 133 combined with Art 310 TEC. With Russia and Ukraine, the Community has signed a partnership and cooperation agreement (PCA) in 1994. The relationship with the Mediterranean region is determined by the Barcelona Process involving a series of association and cooperation agreements. The common strategies' main thrust is to strengthen these pre-existing relations. Calling on the Union to reinforce the activities foreseen in these Community instruments, the CS cover, albeit in very general terms, fields of cooperation already regulated in detail in the agreements themselves. In the chapter "Instruments and Means", common to all three instruments, the Council, the Commission and the Member States are required to review and adjust the existing policies and to make full and appropriate use of existing instruments.[103] The obligations assumed in the measures concerning Russia and Ukraine even go beyond those specified in the PCA: The Union commits itself to make appropriate use of *all relevant instruments and means available to the Union, the Community and the Member States* in order to contribute to the objectives of the CS.[104]

The creation of these new CFSP tools is perceived as a response to the need of more consistent policy-making covering the scope of all Union pillars.[105] Due to its comprehensive material approach, the common strategy has been ascribed a "cross-pillar nature" permitting it to coordinate the full range of Community and Union

---

OJ L 157, 24. 6. 1999, 1; Decision 1999/877/CFSP, European Council Common Strategy on Ukraine, OJ L 331, 23. 12. 1999, 1.

103 See Part I, Chapter "Instruments and Means" Art 2 of the CS on Russia; Art 41 of the CS on Ukraine; and Art 28 of the CS on the Mediterranean region. Note the different wording: Whereas the CS on Russia states that "the European Council *calls on* the Council, the Commission and the Member States..." the CS on Ukraine and on the Mediterranean region use a stricter formula: "The Council, the Commission and the Member States *shall*...".

104 Nevertheless it is also stated that the CS shall be implemented in accordance with the applicable procedures of the Treaties. See Art 38 and 39 of the CS on Ukraine, Part I, Chapter "Instruments and Means" point 1 of the CS on Russia. It is interesting that in the CS on the Mediterranean region only the Member States are required to make appropriate use of all relevant instruments available to them. Art 24 and 27 of the CS on the Mediterranean region.

105 *Spencer* (2001) 36.

external policies and instruments.[106] Recognising the possibility of eventual duplication, *Hillion* suggests granting precedence to CS over other EU measures – thus including Community law. By establishing such a hierarchy, the CS would become a vehicle for consistency.[107]

The concern for consistency in the Union's external relations is very legitimate. Nevertheless, the theory of a CS's unconditional precedence over Community law must be dismissed, since it entails a manifest disregard of the requirement to safeguard the acquis communautaire. The purported cross-pillar nature of CS is nowhere enshrined in the Treaties. The simple fact that the Council has chosen this pillar-overarching orientation for the three common strategies adopted so far cannot itself constitute any evidence on the legality of such an approach.[108] Art 13 TEU is certainly not part of the provisions amending the TEC. There is no indication whatsoever why common strategies should be exempt from the requirement to respect the acquis communautaire. As pointed out above, the principle of consistency does not overrule the integrity of the acquis communautaire. Whilst the latter is primordial for the choice of the legal basis, the former has considerable influence on the substance of the measure. Hence, already at the stage of choosing the legal basis, Community competences must be respected in accordance with the principles developed in this essay.

Respect of the acquis is not only limited to the respect of procedural particularities in the Community decision-making process, but extends to the fundamental principles guaranteed by the EC's legislative procedures. The purpose of these rules would clearly be undermined if the Community were required to simply duplicate the content of the CFSP act. The essence of a Community measure must be the outcome of an autonomous Commission proposal modified by deliberations in the various bodies involved in the Community legislative process and not a package already fixed by the Council in the framework of CFSP. This applies in full extent also to common strategies. Thus, any provision in a CS depriving the Community and its institutions of the possibility to adopt an autonomous decision on the basis and according to the

106 *Hillion* (2000) 295.

107 *Hillion* (2000) 295ff.

108 The ECJ has constantly reiterated this principle, for example in the WTO Opinion. Opinion 1/94, *WTO*, ECR [1994] I-5267, para 52.

specific procedures of the Community framework would affect the acquis communautaire and could be invalidated by the ECJ. Accepting the contrary would inevitably lead to the result that Art 2, 3 and 47 TEU obviously intended to avoid: Member States could defy the constraints of sovereignty linked with supranational decision-making by reverting to intergovernmental mechanisms, where the outcome depends on individual national interests rather than the specific needs of the question at issue. Coherently, a common strategy must neither provide for the adoption of specific measures in the scope of the EC Treaty nor modify the substance of a Community measure. What has been criticised as a lack of concrete action provided for in the CS[109], should more likely be regarded as a consequence of the TEC's integrity.

An all-encompassing instrument defining a comprehensive approach and guaranteeing coordination of action in the external field would certainly be an effective means to ensure a consistent shaping of foreign policy. Given its general nature, the common strategy might appear to be an adequate means to achieve this aim. However, the common strategy itself cannot overcome the problems arising from the different organisational structures of the three Union pillars.[110] Thus, coherence must be achieved in another way. The soft wording the common strategies employ whenever referring to action on part of the Commission in the framework of Community powers suggests that the drafters have been lead by an attempt to ensure coherence whilst respecting the acquis. Formulas like "the Commission will examine ways to deepen the investment dialogue.., the Commission will study the possibility of bringing Community programmes into play for this purpose,.. the Commission will contribute to the above within its powers,.. the Commission is invited to make adequate proposals"[111] do not entail a material predetermination of Community measures. They leave the Commission with a broad margin of manoeuvre allowing it to

[109] *Spencer* notes that the language deployed in the Common Strategy on the Mediterranean region is strong on the need for internal policy coordination but not on how to operationalise it. *Spencer* (2001) 46.

[110] See also *Ojanen* (2000) 374.

[111] These phrases can be found in the CS on Russia (Part III, Chapter "Specific Initiatives", Subchapters "Trade and investment", "Twinning programmes" and "Exchange programmes for students and young scientists") and in the CS on the Ukraine (Art 49, Art 52, Art 62 and Art 66).

make full use of its powers granted under the Community framework. The Community is not obliged to deliver and operationalise a specific act already pre-formed by the CS, but has the possibility to consider in the framework of its own competences how its policies could also contribute to the objectives identified in the CS.

When shaping a measure under the TEC regime, the Community has to observe the principle of consistency. Community institutions are obliged to take CFSP acts into account. Hence, it is evident that CFSP objectives may influence the content of a Community measure to a certain extent. Within these limits, CFSP objectives might have a binding force on EC law. This binding effect cannot oblige the EC to adopt specific acts in order to achieve the goals set out in the CFSP measure.[112] Rather, the Community is required to abstain from measures which would run counter to the objectives of CFSP.[113] In some cases, it will be hard to ascertain whether a CFSP act constitutes a predetermination of the content or just one factor to be taken into account. A mere reference to, or the reproduction of, an already existing Community measure's content does not impair Community competence. However, a CFSP act might contain very precise commitments or a narrowly defined objective, which leaves the Community with no real options how to contribute to the achievement of these goals. In this case, the content would in fact be determined by the Union and not by the Community. As already discussed above, such an encroachment on Community competence is not permissible. Whenever a CFSP measure concerns an area of exclusive competence or an issue already governed by Community law, the act could be invalidated. A CFSP measure may regulate issues touching an area of concurrent competence, in which the Community not enacted legislation yet. Nevertheless, the Commission is not *per se* obliged to present a respective proposal. The Council can request the Commission to do so. The outcome of the process must be consistent but need not necessarily be identical with that of the CFSP measure, given the influence of the Commission and the Parliament in the Community legislative process.

With regard to the inextricable link between economic and political aspects, the question whether a CFSP act actually

[112] *Timmermans* (1996) 67.
[113] *Cremona* (1999) 172.

encroaches on Community powers requires a detailed examination of every single provision in a second pillar instrument. The following considerations, rather than providing watertight rules to draw the borderline, only attempt to identify guidelines:

Some guidance on how to ascertain this boundary might be provided by the Court's considerations in the *Portugal v Council* case[114]. The ECJ was confronted with the question to which extent a development cooperation agreement based on ex-Art 130y (now: 181) and 113 (now: 133) TEC may address issues like energy, intellectual property, tourism, etc without having recourse to other legal bases in the TEC. The Court held that ex-Art 130y TEC constitutes a sufficient legal basis, as long as the clauses referring to other policies do not impose such extensive obligations concerning the specific matters referred to that those obligations in fact constitute objectives distinct from those of development cooperation.[115] In other words, such provisions must not impose duties which do not fall under the subject matter. The application of this principle to the demarcation of CFSP and Community competences might be rejected due to the all-encompassing notion of CFSP defined in Art 11 TEU. However, the obligation to respect the acquis must be interpreted as an inherent limitation to this wide ambit. Community competences must be excluded from the scope of CFSP. As soon as the wording of a CFSP measure would assume commitments in the ambit of a Community policy, the Council is not competent to integrate such a provision in a CFSP act. For example, in the area of Common Commercial Policy, there is no doubt that trade policy is generally embedded in the broad realm of foreign policy. However, this policy follows its own specific rules and principles and might have objectives that do not always coincide with those of CFSP.[116] The definition of these specific objectives and rules is the exclusive competence of the Community. As the Court has stated, the political motivation of a measure does not alter its commercial character.[117] Thus, aspects particular to the nature of trade may not be subject of a CFSP measure.

In essence, the CFSP is the forum to define general political objectives and guidelines, which have to be taken into account by

---

[114] C-268/94, *Portugal v Council*, ECR [1996] I-6177.

[115] See para 39 of the judgement.

[116] Similar: *Cremona* (1999) 172.

[117] Case C-70/94, *Werner*, ECR [1995] I-3189, para 10.

the Community legislator when formulating the external policies of the Community. These powers must not be expanded to decisions on principles and objectives particular to Community policies. In order to safeguard the acquis communautaire the Council must refrain from providing for specific Community actions or commitments the content of which is exclusively subject to the decision-making in the Community method. Accordingly, stipulations in CFSP instruments must not affect the content of existing Community measures or concern exclusive Community competences. Issues falling within an area of concurrent competence, where the Community has not yet generated common rules may be subject of CFSP acts but the Community cannot be obliged to implement these rules. A general reference to respective Community law and competence in CFSP acts, as already provided for in the *modus vivendi,* meets no objections. The principle of consistency requires the Community to assure that its legislation is in line with the objectives of CFSP, but does not entail a predetermination of its content.

VI. Conclusions

For those who call for a coordinated Union foreign policy, the result may be dissatisfactory. Undoubtedly, the strict separation of Union and Community competences in the area of external relations inevitably entails a serious handicap to ensure consistent action in this field. However, given the notably increasing preference to regulate external relations comprehensively in second pillar instruments, it is vital to insist on this strict separation, which is necessary to safeguard the acquis communautaire. It has been demonstrated that consistency cannot be invoked to attenuate the integrity of the EC Treaty. Thus, second pillar instruments, like the common strategy, cannot be construed as a remedy for the fundamental inconsistencies lying at the very heart of the pillar construction. Nevertheless, the protection of Community competence is not watertight. In areas of concurrent competence where no Community legislation is in force, the Council is not prevented from shifting decisions into the intergovernmental sphere. Hence, the danger of "renationalisation" is particularly precarious in this field.

Against the background of these insufficiencies, the merits of maintaining the pillar construction have to be called into question. If Member States are seriously committed to the Union's role as a powerful international actor, they must provide the Union with adequate means to meet the demands related with this task. The current situation does certainly not live up to these needs. The minimum scenario would be an abandonment of the pillar structure without eliminating the structural particularities of the second and third pillar policies. Alongside Community policies, CFSP and PJC could be brought under one Treaty regime albeit maintaining their "intergovernmental" character. The example of Title IV TEC – immigration and asylum – demonstrates the practicability of this idea. Consequently, former Community and Union policies would be considered to form part of a single legal system, what *Bogdandy* and *Nettesheim* have already suggested for the present construction of the Treaties. This step would entail the complete safeguarding of Community competences – thus including areas of concurrent Community competence, where no secondary legislation has been enacted.

Whereas the endeavour to preserve the acquis would be accomplished, the deficiencies regarding coherent policy making cannot be remedied by the simple abolition of the tripartite structure. As long as the influence of the institutions (in particular the Commission and the Parliament) varies that considerably in the field of external relations, the tensions between communitarian and intergovernmental acts will continue to exist. In the long run, there is no other option than adapting CFSP structures to the features of Community law. Everything else would either jeopardy the achievements and the unity of the TEC or entail the failure of promoting the Union into a major political player at global level.

Bibliography

Günther Burghardt/Gerd Tebbe (1995), Die Gemeinsame Außen- und Sicherheitspolitik der Europäischen Union – Rechtliche Struktur und politischer Prozeß, EuR 1995, 1-20.

Armin von Bogdandy/Martin Nettesheim (1996), Ex Pluribus Unum: Fusion of the European Communities into the European Union, ELJ 1996, 267-289.

Marise Cremona (1994), The Common Foreign and Security Policy of the European Union and the External Relations Powers of the

European Community, in *David O'Keeffe/Patrick Twomey* (eds.), Legal Issues of the Maastricht Treaty, London 1994, 247-258.

Marise Cremona (1999), External Relations and External Competence: The Emergence of an Integrated Policy, in *Paul Craig/Grainne de Burca* (eds.), The Evolution of EU Law, New York 1999, 137-175.

Deirdre Curtin (1993), The Constitutional Structure of the Union – A Europe of Bits and Pieces, CMLRev. 1993, 17-69.

Deirdre Curtin/Ige Dekker (1999), The EU as a 'Layered' International Organization: Institutional Unity in Disguise, in *Paul Craig/Grainne de Burca* (eds.), The Evolution of EU Law, New York 1999.

Alan Dashwood (1998), External Relations Provisions of the Amsterdam Treaty, CMLRev. 1998, 1019-1045.

Alan Dashwood (2000), The attribution of external relations competence, in *Alan Dashwood/Christophe Hillion* (eds.), The General Law of E.C. External Relations, London 2000, 115-138.

Renaud Dehousse (1994), From Community to Union, in *Renaud Dehousse* (ed.), Europe After Maastricht – An Ever Closer Union?, München 1994, 5-15.

Paul Demaret (1993), Le Traité de Maastricht ou les voies divers de l'Union, in *Jörg Monar/Werner Ungerer/WolfgangWessels* (eds.), The Maastricht Treaty on European Union, Legal Complexity and Political Dynamic, Brussels 1993, 39-48.

Desmond Dinan (1997), The Commission and the Institutional Reform Process, in *Geoffrey Edwards/Alfred Pijpers* (eds.), The Politics of European Treaty Reform. The 1996 Intergovernmental Conference and Beyond, London 1997, 188-211.

Oliver Dörr (1995), Zur Rechtsnatur der Europäischen Union, EuR 1995, 334-348.

M R Eaton (1994) Common Foreign and Security Policy, in *David O'Keeffe/Patrick Twomey* (eds.), Legal Issues of the Maastricht Treaty, London 1994, 215-225.

Ulrich Everling (1992), Reflections on the Structure of the European Union, CMLRev. 1992, 1053-1077.

Carlo Curti Gialdino (1995), Some Reflections on the Acquis Communautaire, CMLRev. 1995, 1089-1121.

Peter Gilsdorf (1996), Die Außenkompetenz der EG im Wandel – eine kritische Auseinandersetzung mit Praxis und Rechtssprechung, EuR 1996, 145-166.

Stephen George (1997), Britain and the IGC, in *Geoffrey Edwards/Alfred Pijpers* (eds.), The Politics of European Treaty Reform. The 1996 Intergovernmental Conference and Beyond, London 1997, 100-118.

Stefan Griller (1999), "Die Unterscheidung von Unionsrecht und Gemeinschaftsrecht nach Amsterdam", EuR 1999, Beiheft 1, 45-72.

Stefan Griller/Dimitri Droutsas/Gerda Falkner/Kathrin Forgó/Michael Nentwich (eds.) (2000), The Treaty of Amsterdam. Facts, Analysis, Prospects, Vienna 2000.

Meinhard Hilf (1995), Art. A EUV, in *Eberhardt Grabitz/Meinhard Hilf* (eds.), Das Recht der Europäischen Union, 8th instalment, München 1995.

Meinhard Hilf/Eckhard Pache (1995), Art. B EUV, in *Eberhardt Grabitz/Meinhard Hilf* (eds.), Das Recht der Europäischen Union, 8th instalment, München 1995.

Christophe Hillion (2000), Common Strategies and the Interface Between EC External Relations and the CFSP: Lessons of the Partnership Between the E.U. and Russia, in *Alan Dashwood/Christophe Hillion* (eds.), The General Law of E.C. External Relations, London 2000, 287-301.

Ton Heukels/Jaap de Zwaan (1994), The Configuration of the European Union: Community Dimensions of Institutional Interaction, in *Deidre Curtin/Ton Heukels* (eds.), Institutional Dynamics of European Integration. Essays in Honour of Henry G. Schermers, Dordrecht 1994, 195-228.

Finn Laursen (1997), The Lessons of Maastricht, in *Geoffrey Edwards/Alfred Pijpers* (eds.), The Politics of European Treaty

Reform, The 1996 Intergovernmental Conference and Beyond, London 1997, 59-73.

Paul Kapteyn/Pieter Verloren van Themaat (1998), Introduction to the Law of the European Communities. From Maastricht to Amsterdam, Deventer/Boston 1998.

Horst Krenzler/Henning Schneider (1994), Die Gemeinsame Außen- und Sicherheitspolitik der Europäischen Union – Zur Frage der Kohärenz, EuR 1994, 144-160.

Koen Lenaerts/Piet Van Nuffel (1999), Constitutional Law of the European Union, London 1999.

Roger Morgan (1994), How Common Will Foreign and Security Policy be?, in *Renaud Dehousse* (ed.), Europe After Maastricht – an Ever Closer Union?, München 1994, 189-199.

Peter Christian Müller-Graff (1993), Europäische Zusammenarbeit und Gemeinsame Außen– und Sicherheitspolitik: Kohärenzgebot aus rechtlicher Sicht, Integration 1993, 147-156.

Peter Christian Müller-Graff (1994), The Legal Bases of the Third Pillar and its Position in the Framework of the Union Treaty, CMLRev. 1994, 493-510.

Nannette Neuwahl (1994), Foreign and Security Policy and the Implementation of the Requirement of "Consistency" under the Treaty on European Union, in *David O'Keeffe/Patrick M Twomey* (eds.), Legal Issues of the Maastricht Treaty, London et al. 1994, 227-246.

Simon Nuttal (1987), Interaction between the European Political Co-operation and the European Community, YEL 1987, 211-249.

Simon Nuttal (1992), European Political Co-operation, New York 1992.

Hanna Ojanen (2000), The EU and Its "Northern Dimension": An Actor in Search of a Policy, or a Policy in Search of an Actor? EFARev. 2000, 359-376.

David O'Keeffe (1995), Recasting the third pillar, CMLRev. 1995, 893-920.

Eckhard Pache (1995a), Art. L EUV, in *Eberhardt Grabitz/Meinhard Hilf* (eds.), Das Recht der Europäischen Union, 8th instalment, München 1995.

Eckhard Pache (1995b), Art. M EUV, in *Eberhardt Grabitz/Meinhard Hilf* (eds.), Das Recht der Europäischen Union, 8th instalment, München 1995.

Matthias Pechstein (1995), Das Kohärenzgebot als entscheidende Integrationsdimension der Europäischen Union, EuR 1995, 247-258.

Matthias Pechstein/Christian König (1998), Die Europäische Union – die Verträge von Maastricht und Amsterdam, Tübingen 1998.

Alfred Pijpers/ Sophie Vanhoonacker (1997), The Positions of the Benelux Countries, in *Geoffrey Edwards/Alfred Pijpers* (eds.), The Politics of European Treaty Reform. The 1996 Intergovernmental Conference and Beyond, London 1997, 119-141.

Claire Spencer (2001), The EU and Common Strategies: The Revealing Case of the Mediterranean, EFARev. 2001, 31-51.

Christiaan Timmermans (1996), The Uneasy Relationship Between the Communities and the Second Union Pillar: Back To The Plan Fouchet?, Legal Issues of European Integration 1996, 61-70.

Antonio Tizzano (1998), La personnalité internationale de l'Union européenne, RMU 4/1998, 11-40.

Ramon Torrent (1997), Le "quatrième pilier" de l'Union européenne, in *Jaques Bourgeois/Jean-Louis Dewost/Marie-Ange Gaiffe* (eds.), La Communauté européenne et les accords mixtes. Quelles perspectives?, Brussels 1997, 49-63.

Christiane Trüe (1997), Verleihung von Rechtspersönlichkeit an die Europäische Union und Verschmelzung zu einer einzigen Organisation – deklaratorisch oder konstitutiv?, Vorträge, Reden und Berichte aus dem Europa-Institut der Universität des Saarlandes, Nr. 357, 1997.

Christiane Trüe (2000), Rechtspersönlichkeit der Europäischen Union nach den Vertragsänderungen von Amsterdam, ZEuS 2000, 127-176.

Stephen Weatherill (1998), Safeguarding the acquis communautaire, in *Ton Heukels/ Niels Blokker/Marcel Brus* (eds.), The European Union after Amsterdam. A legal Analysis, The Hague 1998, 153-178.

Joseph Weiler (1993), Neither Unity nor Three Pillars – The Trinity Structure of the Treaty on European Union, in *Jörg Monar/Werner Ungerer/Wolfgang Wessels* (eds.), The Maastricht Treaty on European Union. Legal Complexity and Political Dynamic., Brussels 1993, 49-62.

Johannes Wichard (1999), Wer ist Herr im europäischen Haus? Zur Struktur und Rechtsnatur der Europäischen Union nach Amsterdam, EuR 1999, 170-184.

Philippe Willaert/Carmen Marqués-Ruiz (1995), Vers une politique étrangère et de sécurité commune: état des lieux, RMU 3/1995, 35-95.

Bruno de Witte (1998), The Pillar Structure and the Nature of the European Union: Greek Temple or French Gothic Cathedral?, in *Ton Heukels/ Niels Blokker/Marcel Brus* (eds.), The European Union after Amsterdam. A Legal Analysis, The Hague 1998, 51-68.

Stefan Griller/Katharina Gamharter

External Trade: Is There a Path Through the Maze of Competences?

I. Introduction

The division of external relations competences between the EC and its Member States as derived from the scope of Art 133 TEC on Common Commercial Policy (CCP) is among the most disputed issues in the current debate on External Trade and Foreign Policy of the EU.[1] The terms employed in the discussion have mostly been coined by ECJ jurisprudence, the so-called WTO Opinion[2] being the last main occasion for the ECJ to comment on the range of the CCP with reference to the areas newly covered by international trade law, particularly trade in services and intellectual property.

In an attempt to clarify this much discussed topic,[3] the first part of this contribution includes some general remarks on the EC's competence to conclude international agreements Pre- and Post-Nice and the second part is dedicated to formulating an up-to-date system of the various types of competences as established by ECJ case-law. This systematisation is essential for the analysis of the changes foreseen by the Treaty of Nice[4] which are dealt with in the third part.

II. Some Remarks on the EC's Competence to Conclude International Agreements Pre- and Post-Nice

The general framework of the TEC regarding the conclusion of international agreements is, at first sight, confusing. It contains a number of provisions which explicitly foresee the conclusion of

---

1 For a comprehensive presentation of Art 133 TEC as well as other relevant legal bases and for reference to recent literature compare *Vedder* (2001).

2 Opinion 1/94, *WTO*, [1994] ECR I-5267.

3 For a summary of the most recent literary statements on the EC's competence to conclude agreements with third states compare *Griller* (2000a) FN 26.

4 The Treaty of Nice was signed on 26 February 2001 and published in OJ C 80, 10.3.2001, 1. The ratification process is currently under way.

international agreements.[5] Other legal bases provide for cooperation with third countries or international organisations but are silent on the EC´s competence to conclude international agreements.[6]

Concerning the actual conclusion of agreements, the pertinent provisions normally refer to Art 300 TEC, which regulates the applicable *procedure*. According to this provision, international agreements between the EC and third states or international organisations are negotiated by the Commission and concluded by the Council through the adoption of a regulation or decision. The first sentence of Art 300 TEC reads as follows: "Where this Treaty provides for the conclusion of agreements between the Community and one or more States or international organisations ...". This formulation in conjunction with the above-mentioned Arts of the TEC could lead to the assumption that EC competence to conclude international agreements must be explicitly foreseen by Treaty provisions.[7] This would particularly rule out that EC competence to conclude international agreements be implied by internal legislative competence.

But an analysis of the historic development of provisions conferring external relations competence commands a different view.[8] The original EEC Treaty contained only two material provisions explicitly foreseeing the conclusion of international agreements, namely former Art 113 (now: Art 133) TEC on the CCP and former Art 238 (now: 310) TEC on Association Agreements. These two provisions both included passages on the

---

5 Particularly Art 133 TEC (CCP), Art 111 TEC (monetary policy), Art 170 TEC (research and technological development), Art 174 para 4 TEC (environment), Art 181 TEC (development cooperation), Art 181a TEC as inserted by the Treaty of Nice (economic, financial and technical cooperation with third countries) and Art 310 TEC (Association Agreements).

6 E.g. Art 149 para 3 TEC, Art 150 para 3 TEC (education, vocational training and youth), Art 151 para 3 TEC (culture), Art 152 para 3 TEC (public health), Art 155 para 3 TEC (trans-european networks), Art 302 TEC (UN), Art 303 TEC (Council of Europe) and Art 304 TEC (OECD).

7 According to the principle of attribution of powers as laid down in Art 5 TEC. It would remain questionable whether the provisions foreseeing cooperation with third countries encompass the conclusion of international agreements or not.

8 On the following compare *Dashwood* (2000a) 119ff.

procedure of conclusion of such agreements. Moreover, procedural rules were laid down in former Art 228 (now: 300) TEC. Thus, Art 228 TEC would have lacked all range of application if its first sentence - as cited above - would have referred only to explicit attribution of competence through Treaty provisions.

Consequently, it must be concluded that from the start, the TEC has been foreseeing both explicit and implied competences to conclude international agreements. ECJ jurisprudence supports this view and the general admissibility of "implied powers" under EC law nowadays seems largely undisputed.[9]

However, besides the question of scope of the provisions explicitly conferring EC competence, it is disputed on which conditions implied competence comes into existence and if it does, whether it is exclusive or concurrent. In Opinion 2/94 on an EC accession to the European Convention for the Protection of Human Rights and Fundamental Freedoms, the ECJ outlined the basic principles as follows:

"The Community acts ordinarily on the basis of specific powers which ... are not necessarily the express consequence of specific provisions of the Treaty but may also be implied from them. ... [I]n the field of international relations ... it is settled case-law that the competence of the Community to enter into international commitments may not only flow from express provisions of the Treaty but also be implied from those provisions. The Court has held, in particular, that, whenever Community law has created for the institutions of the Community powers within the internal system for the purpose of attaining a specific objective, the Community is empowered to enter into the international commitments necessary for attainment of that objective even in the absence of an express provision to that effect ...".[10]

On the foundation of these principles we will analyse the current situation on EC competence to enter into international agreements as set out by ECJ case-law.

---

9 While we consider that the foundations of implied EC competences lie within the TEC, a number of commentators consider this as a judicial development of the law. Some of them regard it as the permissible substantiation of deficiencies in the Treaty, others view it as an - at least initially - prohibited extension of competences by the ECJ.

10 Opinion 2/94, *ECHR*, [1996] ECR I-1763, paras 25 and 26.

III. The Division of Competences Along the Lines of the Jurisprudence[11]

Our considerations are based on the distinction between exclusive, concurrent and complementary competences as employed in the general discussion on EC competences.[12] We will further differentiate between the respective types of competence as explicitly allowed for by Treaty provisions and between the those implied by Treaty provisions or secondary EC legislation.

The mere existence of exclusive EC competence for a certain matter precludes any Member State activity in the given field. At the same time, exclusive EC competence entails an EC duty to legislate.[13] By concurrent competence we mean that, other than in cases of exclusive competence, as long as the EC has not yet taken legislative measures the Member States are not precluded from passing national legislation. However, as soon as and insofar as EC legislation has been adopted, Member States' legislative competence is limited to the transformation and implementation of this legislation.[14]

In the field of external trade, there seems to be no case for so-called parallel competences, a concept which refers to situations where Member State activity is not precluded by the adoption of secondary EC legislation. However, we doubt the functionality of this separate category even more generally.[15]

---

[11] For an overview of the concepts set out in this chapter compare also *Griller* (2000a) 86ff and *Griller* (2002).

[12] On the - disputed - issue of general division of competences between the EC and its Member States compare *von Bogdandy/Nettesheim* (1994) paras 1ff, on the different types of competence compare paras 11ff. The authors distinguish between exclusive, concurrent and parallel competence. The category of "complementary competence" is drawn from provisions as introduced by subsequent Treaty revisions. For a recent contribution based on the same distinction compare *von Bogdandy/Bast* (2001) 447ff.

[13] Compare e.g. *von Bogdandy/Nettesheim* (1994) para 12. On the dispute concerning the scope of exclusive competence see *von Bogdandy/Nettesheim* (1994) paras 28ff.

[14] Compare e.g. *Jarass* (1996) 188-189.

[15] Competition law tends to serve as the prime example for such "parallel competences". But even in this field, Member States are prohibited to concede activities which are illegal under EC law or, vice versa,

A. Explicit Exclusive EC Competence

Art 133 TEC confers exclusive EC competence in the field of CCP.[16] Measures explicitly envisaged by Art 133 include the adoption of tariff rates, quantitative restrictions, antidumping measures, anti-subsidy measures, measures against unfair trade practices, export policy and the conclusion of tariff and trade agreements. In fields covered by exclusive EC competence only the Community is empowered to act. The ECJ considers unacceptable that "the Member States should exercise a power concurrent to that of the Community, in the *Community sphere and in the international sphere*."[17] As a result, "national measures of commercial policy are ... permissible only if they are specifically authorized by the Community ...".[18] But as the CCP is implemented by organs of the Member States, a denial of any Member State competence would be mistaken.

The initially adopted non-restrictive interpretation of the scope of Art 133 TEC[19] has arguably lost some of its dynamic in the Post-Maastricht era. In Opinion 1/94 however, the ECJ provided clarification with regard to the WTO Agreements:

- The WTO Agreement on Trade in Goods was held to be covered entirely by the CCP.[20]
- Concerning trade in services, the ECJ, in accordance with the General Agreement on Trade in Services (GATS), identified four modes of the supply of services. Only one of them, namely

---

interdict activities unobjectionable under EC law. That is why there seems to be hardly any room to distinguish parallel from concurrent competences. *Jarass* (1996) 189-190 draws the same conclusion. For the opposing view compare *Zuleeg* (1997) paras 5-6 who refers only to exclusive and parallel competences.

16 See Opinion 2/91, *ILO*, [1993] ECR I-1061, para 8. Exclusive competence is not expressly attributed by Art 133 TEC but it has been held by the ECJ that the exclusive competence flows directly from the provision.

17 Opinion 1/75, *Local Cost Standard*, [1975] ECR 1355 (1364) (emphasis added).

18 Case C-70/94, *Werner*, [1995] ECR I-3189, para 12 (with reference to previous judgements).

19 See Opinion 1/78, *International Agreement on Natural Rubber*, [1979] ECR 2871, paras 44, 45.

20 Opinion 1/94, *WTO*, [1994] ECR I-5267, para 34.

cross-frontier supply of services, was considered to fall under Art 133 TEC.[21] Cross-frontier supply of services refers to situations where the service is rendered across borders with no movement of persons involved.[22] More current modes of supply such as active and passive freedom of services, where either the supplier or the customer cross the border, were not considered to be covered by the CCP. Neither was the so-called "commercial presence", i.e. the presence of a subsidiary or branch in a country other than the country of the supplier.[23]

- Intellectual property protection was held to be covered by the CCP insofar as it concerns the prohibition of the release into free circulation of counterfeit goods.[24]
- Lastly, the conclusion of the Agreement on Technical Barriers to Trade and
- The conclusion of the Agreement on Agriculture was held to fall within the ambit of the CCP.[25]

Thus, only limited areas of the WTO Agreement on Trade Related Aspects of Intellectual Property Rights (TRIPs) and the GATS were held to fall within the CCP due to their similarity to trade in goods. This restrictive view on exclusive EC competence in the fields of trade in services and intellectual property protection proved to be among the most disputed issues raised by the ECJ in Opinion 1/94 and set the main challenge for the subsequent Treaty revisions of Amsterdam and Nice. The central point of criticism which led the Commission to seek an extension of the scope of Art 133 during the Amsterdam and Nice IGCs is the extreme fragmentation of external relations competences caused by the allocation of competences for trade in services and intellectual property. Fragmented external relations competences do not only complicate the conclusion of international agreements but also their

---

21 Opinion 1/94, *WTO*, [1994] ECR I-5267, paras 43-47. The sector of transport was entirely excluded from the CCP (Opinion 1/94, *WTO*, [1994] ECR I-5267, para 53).

22 E.g. the conclusion and execution of a credit agreement or insurance contract, or the provision of legal counsel by way of correspondence.

23 In terms of the TEC this would have to be considered part of the "Right of establishment" (Arts 43ff TEC) which causes further problems (compare below at FN 111).

24 Opinion 1/94, *WTO*, [1994] ECR I-5267, para 71.

25 Opinion 1/94, *WTO*, [1994] ECR I-5267, paras 33 and 29.

implementation in EC or national legal orders and the negotiation of eventual subsequent treaty revisions.

The Treaty of Amsterdam, viewed by some as the occasion to review Art 133 in the light of the WTO Opinion,[26] brought no substantial change of the scope of the CCP. New Art 133 para 5 TEC merely empowered the Council to "extend the application of paragraphs 1 to 4 to international negotiations and agreements on services and intellectual property insofar as they are not covered by these paragraphs."[27] The changes envisaged by the Treaty of Nice include further modifications of Art 133 paras 5-7 and will be commented on below.

Apart from the CCP, other Treaty provisions conferring explicit exclusive EC competence include Art 111 TEC (Monetary Policy for EMU Members)[28] and Art 102 of the Act of Accession (conservation of fisheries).

B. Implied Exclusive EC Competence

Besides being expressly attributed, exclusive EC external relations competence may also be *implied* by internal legislative competence, e.g. by competence based on Art 52 TEC (liberalisation of a specific service), Art 71 TEC (transport), Art 95 TEC (general approximation measures) or Art 175 TEC (environment). However, this type of competence becomes exclusive only if qualified common rules have been enacted within the EC. This aspect was firmly established in Opinion 1/94[29] and considered by some commentators as a change of previous ECJ jurisprudence.[30] Member States are prohibited to assume

---

26 Compare *Dashwood* (2000b) 280.

27 For details on the changes made by the Treaty of Amsterdam see *Griller/Droutsas/Falkner/Forgó/Nentwich* (2000) 125ff.

28 Compare e.g. *Torrent* (2000) 223-224.

29 Opinion 1/94, *WTO*, [1994] ECR I-5267, para 77.

30 The ambiguous phrase that external relations competence "may equally flow from other provisions of the Treaty *and* from measures adopted ... by the Community institutions" in para 16 of Case 22/70, *AETR*, [1971] ECR 263 (emphasis added) had left room for the interpretation that exclusive external relations competence might be implied by Treaty provisions without secondary legislation being adopted previously. Compare the clear analysis provided by *Krenzler* (1999) paras 34ff.

"obligations which might affect those rules or alter their scope"[31]. While the AETR judgment suggested that this might be limited to provisions implementing a common policy[32], the ECJ clarified in Opinion 2/91 that this principle is indeed applicable to rules in "all the areas corresponding to the objectives of the Treaty."[33]

According to the WTO Opinion, exclusive competence is implied if the EC has "achieved complete harmonization of the rules governing access to a self-employed activity"[34] or if internal legislative acts contain "provisions relating to the treatment of nationals of non-member countries" or the EC has "expressly conferred on its institutions powers to negotiate with non-member countries" in the "spheres covered by those acts".[35]

Only by way of exception does exclusive external relations competence arise even if internal legislative competence has not yet been exercised. In cases where the objective of an agreement can only be reached in cooperation with third countries "the Community has authority to enter into the international commitments necessary for the attainment of that objective even in the absence of an express provision in that connexion."[36] This was confirmed by the ECJ in the leading case concerning the establishment of a "Laying-Up Fund for Inland Waterway Vessels" which aimed at eliminating over-capacity on certain inland waterways. In addition to a number of EC Member States, Switzerland also had to be involved in the negotiations to successfully reduce the over-capacity on the Rhine river. To constitute exclusive external relations competence without the prior adoption of internal rules, the "participation of the Community" has to be "necessary for the attainment of one of the objectives of the Community".[37]

---

31 Case 22/70, *AETR*, [1971] ECR 263, para 22. Compare Opinion 1/94, *WTO*, [1994] ECR I-5267, para 77.

32 Case 22/70, *AETR*, [1971] ECR 263, paras 15-19.

33 Opinion 2/91, *ILO*, [1993] ECR I-1061, paras 10,11.

34 Opinion 1/94, *WTO*, [1994] ECR I-5267, para 96.

35 Opinion 1/94, *WTO*, [1994] ECR I-5267, para 95.

36 Opinion 1/76, *Draft Agreement establishing a European laying-up fund for inland waterway vessels*, [1977] ECR 741, para 3.

37 Opinion 1/76, *Draft Agreement establishing a European laying-up fund for inland waterway vessels*, [1977] ECR 741, para 4.

Beyond these cases the ECJ rejected the broad notion of "parallelism" between internal and external legislative competence as contended by the Commission.[38] Implied exclusive EC competence was held to arise only if the establishment of common rules is not sufficient to achieve a given objective.[39]

Regarding freedom of establishment and freedom to provide services, the ECJ considered that the attainment of these principles was not "inextricably linked to the treatment to be afforded in the Community to nationals of non-member countries or in non-member countries to nationals of Member States of the Community".[40] Equally, the harmonisation of intellectual property rights did "not necessarily have to be accompanied by agreements with non-member countries in order to be effective".[41] As a consequence, the ECJ dismissed exclusive EC competence to conclude the TRIPs Agreement and the GATS except for the fields covered explicitly by the CCP.[42] Instead, it is well known that the ECJ regarded the EC and its Member States as jointly competent to conclude these agreements.[43] This conclusion however, appears to have resulted mainly from the way in which the Commission chose to formulate the questions answered by Opinion 1/94. It will be submitted in further detail below that the EC would have been vested with the competence - albeit not exclusive - to conclude the entire WTO Agreement.

C. Explicit Concurrent EC Competence

This subchapter outlines *concurrent* or *complementary* EC competences to enter into international agreements as provided for explicitly by the EC Treaty. Legal bases for concurrent or complementary competence are Art 170 TEC (research and technological development), Art 174 para 4 TEC (environment), Art 181 TEC (development cooperation) and Art 181a TEC as inserted by the Treaty of Nice (economic, financial and technical cooperation with third countries).

---

38 See also *Dashwood* (2000a) 128.

39 Opinion 1/94, *WTO*, [1994] ECR I-5267, para 85.

40 Opinion 1/94, *WTO*, [1994] ECR I-5267, para 86.

41 Opinion 1/94, *WTO*, [1994] ECR I-5267, para 100.

42 See chapter III.A.

43 Opinion 1/94, *WTO*, [1994] ECR I-5267, paras 98, 105.

As with most other Community policies, external environmental policy is covered by concurrent competence. Art 174 para 4 TEC authorises both the EC and the Member States "within their respective spheres of competence" to cooperate with third countries and international organisations and to conclude agreements, all this without prejudice to "Member States' competence to negotiate in international bodies and to conclude international agreements".[44]

It appears imperative to interpret this as meaning that the Member States are empowered to act within their sphere of competence *as well as* on behalf of the EC in international fora in cases where the EC is not member of the respective forum. Otherwise the EC would not retain any margin of manoeuvre for the conclusion of international agreements.[45] In the absence of internal approximation measures both the EC and the Member States are competent to conclude international agreements. It is submitted that the EC has the power to enter into international agreements in the absence of secondary legislation and that the Member States are not precluded from doing so either, as long as the EC has not taken any legislative measures.[46] The adoption of EC legislation naturally depends on whether the relevant majorities for the co-decision procedure or the unanimity requirement can be met.[47]

Most other concurrent EC competences differ from Art 174 para 4 TEC insofar as they specify that EC activities in the respective field are *complementary* to Member State activities.[48] This means

---

44 Art 174 para 4 subpara 2 TEC.

45 Recent contributions on this issue include *Heliskoski* (2000) and *Tietje* (2000) with further references.

46 As in all cases of concurrent competence, the Member States must not block the EC´s conclusion of international agreements by taking unilateral measures. If a Member State's obligation arising from a previously concluded agreement is incompatible with an internal or external contractual obligation of the EC and where international law does not provide for a legal solution (which is the case if the other contracting parties are the same) there seems to be a case for analogous application of Art 307 TEC.

47 Art 175 paras 1 and 2 TEC.

48 Art 164 TEC (research and technological development), Art 177 TEC (development cooperation) and Art 181a para 1 TEC as amended by the Treaty of Nice (economic, financial and technical cooperation with third countries).

that overlapping measures taken by the Member States are not precluded by EC legislation. Concerning external competence, the TEC rules that detailed arrangements for cooperation with third countries "may be the subject of agreements between the Community and the third parties concerned" applying the procedure as set out in Art 300 TEC.[49] Such agreements do not prejudice "Member States' competence to negotiate in international bodies and to conclude international agreements".[50] The relationship between Member State and EC legislation in these fields remains unclear.[51] A mutual obligation of consideration has to be assumed.

---

49 Art 170 TEC (research and technological development). Similar wording can be found in Art 177 TEC (development cooperation) and Art 181a para 1 TEC as amended by the Treaty of Nice (economic, financial and technical cooperation with third countries).

50 Art 181 subpara 2 TEC. With equal wording Art 181a TEC. Art 170 TEC does not include the said passage but arguably this does not make a difference.

51 For first cautious assessments compare *Cremona* (1999) 158ff and *Zimmermann/Martenczuk* (2000) paras 5ff.
Concerning development cooperation within the framework of the Fourth ACP-EEC Lomé Convention the ECJ stated in Case C-316/91, *Parliament v Council (Lomé)*, [1994] ECR I-625, para 26: "The Community′s competence in that field is not exclusive. The Member States are accordingly entitled to enter into commitments themselves vis-à-vis non-member States, either collectively or individually, or even jointly with the Community." The Treaty of Maastricht was in force at the time of the judgement but not applicable in Case C-316/91. In para 27 of Case C-316/91 the ECJ mentions an observation of the Spanish Government which stated that Art 130x (now: Art 180) TEC supported the Court's finding. This can be interpreted as the Court's cautious consent. Astonishingly, the more pertinent Art 130y (now: Art 181) TEC is not referred to.
From the above-mentioned the ECJ concludes that the competence to implement the Community's financial assistance is "shared by the Community and its Member States and that it is for them to chose the source and methods of financing" (para 35). This is remarkable with regard to the terminology used by the ECJ. The Court applies the term of "shared" competence to a case in which *either* the EC *or* the Member States must act (in C-316/91 the conclusion is that there is an exclusive obligation of the Member States). We refer to this type of situation as a case of concurrent competence. Shared competence comes to existence only in cases, in which both the EC *and* the

This distinguishes complementary from concurrent competence, in cases of which Community legislation precludes the adoption of Member State measures. Where the EC is vested with complementary competence, its activities must not impair Member State legislation, while Member State measures must equally not interfere with EC legislation. EC competence may also be exercised through the conclusion of international agreements, under the exceptional circumstances outlined above[52] even without prior adoption of secondary legislation.[53]

Member States must act in order to conclude an agreement in its entirety (compare below at III.E).
Compare also Joined Cases C-181/91 and C-248/91, *Parliament v Council (Bangladesh)*, [1993] ECR I-3685, para 16: "... it should be pointed out that the Community does not have exclusive competence in the field of humanitarian aid, and that consequently the Member States are not precluded from exercising their competence in that regard collectively in the Council or outside it."
With regard to the material scope of agreements concluded under Art 181 TEC the ECJ confirmed the principle relevance of the main object of the agreement in Case C-268/94, *Portugal v Council*, [1996] ECR I-6177, para 39. It had been argued that provisions relating to intellectual property, drug abuse control, tourism and culture exceeded the scope of this provision and that additional legal bases were required. However, the ECJ held that "the fact that a development cooperation agreement contains clauses concerning various specific matters cannot alter the characterization of the agreement, which must be determined having regard to its essential object and not in terms of individual clauses, provided that those clauses do not impose such extensive obligations concerning the specific matters referred to that those obligations in fact constitute objectives distinct from those of development cooperation ...". Also in its opinion on the conclusion of the Cartagena Protocol by the EC, the ECJ re-stated this principle (Opinion 2/00, *Cartagena Protocol*, [2001] ECR I-9713).
Besides, it could be deduced from Case C-268/94 para 47 that an agreement on development cooperation may include provisions in fields such as culture where the TEC speaks only of "cooperation" and does not refer to binding agreements, if only the goal of development cooperation remains the essential object of the agreement.

52 Compare chapter III.B.

53 In Declaration No 10 annexed to the final act of Maastricht the Conference considered "that the provisions of Article 111(5), Article 174(4), second subparagraph, and Article 181 do not affect the

D. Implied Concurrent EC Competence

Implied concurrent EC competence can be deduced from internal legislative competence where "the participation of the Community in the international agreement is ... *necessary* for the attainment of one of the objectives of the Community"[54] while transitionally exercised Member State competence does not risk to affect or alter the scope of existing Community rules. This applies mainly in fields where the EC has internal legislative competence and no implied exclusive competence has yet been established. Once the EC has made use of its concurrent competence, however, Member States are blocked insofar as they must not alter these agreements or affect their scope.[55]

As the existence of implied concurrent competence had been challenged in the wake of the WTO Opinion and as it remains of crucial importance in the assessment of the changes made by the Treaty of Nice, we dedicate a more detailed analysis to this type of competence.

1. Implications of Opinion 2/91

Opinion 2/91 deals with the EC's competence to conclude ILO Convention No 170 concerning safety in the use of chemicals at work.[56] At the time of the opinion, the EC's internal legislative competence to adopt minimum requirements in the field of social policy was based on Art 118a TEC.[57] With reference to this internal legislative competence, the ECJ justified the existence of EC

---

principles resulting from the judgement handed down by the Court of Justice in the AETR case." A declaration of the same contents had already been annexed to the final act of the Single European Act (Declaration No 9) at the introduction of Art 130r TEC (now: 174 TEC). As we consider that Art 111 TEC confers exclusive competence, its mention in the declaration appears superfluous.

54 Opinion 1/76, *Draft Agreement establishing a European laying-up fund for inland waterway vessels*, [1977] ECR 741, para 4 (emphasis added).

55 As such agreements would have to be qualified as "Community rules" in the sense of the AETR Principle (Case 22/70, *AETR*, [1971] ECR 263, para 22).

56 Opinion 2/91, *ILO*, [1993] ECR I-1061.

57 Former Art 118a TEC was replaced by Art 137 TEC which is part of the reshaped and significantly extended chapter on social provisions as introduced by the Treaty of Amsterdam.

competence to conclude Convention No 170.[58] As exclusive EC competence was ruled out[59] the ECJ must have referred to concurrent competence.[60]

Transferring this argumentation to a general level, it can be concluded that implied concurrent EC competence to enter into international agreements exists in all fields covered by internal legislative competence as long as this is consistent with the other provisions of the EC Treaty, in particular with the principle of subsidiarity requiring that a Community goal "cannot be sufficiently achieved by the Member States and can therefore ... be better achieved by the Community".[61]

Consequently, it is submitted that the ECJ's statement in Opinion 1/76,[62] as developed by Opinion 2/91, results in *two concepts of necessity* for the establishment of implied EC competences. First, irrespective of the existence of secondary legislation, internal legislative EC competence implies *exclusive* EC competence for the conclusion of international agreements where such a conclusion is "inextricably linked"[63] to the adoption of internal measures for the attainment of a Community goal. Second, *concurrent* EC competence is implied in all cases where the attainment of a Community goal is merely *facilitated* by the

---

58 Opinion 2/91, *ILO*, [1993] ECR I-1061, para 17.

59 Opinion 2/91, *ILO*, [1993] ECR I-1061, paras 18ff.

60 The outcome of Opinion 2/91, that nevertheless the conclusion of ILO Convention No 170 was a matter falling within joint competence of the EC and its Member States (Opinion 2/91, *ILO*, [1993] ECR I-1061, para 39 and tenor), was caused by two factors: firstly, the ECJ held that - differing from the reference in the text - certain passages of the Convention No 170 were indeed covered by exclusive EC competence (paras 22ff, particularly para 25f). Secondly, the ECJ considered cooperation between the EC an the Member States "all the more necessary in view of the fact that the former cannot, as international law stands at present, itself conclude an ILO convention and must do so through the medium of the Member States." (para 37).

61 Art 5 TEC.

62 Opinion 1/76, *Draft Agreement establishing a European laying-up fund for inland waterway vessels*, [1977] ECR 741, para 4 as cited above.

63 Opinion 1/94, *WTO*, [1994] ECR I-5267, para 86.

conclusion of an international agreement, ensuring the optimal use of an internal competence by the EC.[64]

These concepts need to be differentiated from the logic of so-called parallel internal and external EC competences:[65] it is submitted that e.g. EC legislative competence to regulate the right of establishment and the provision of services by its citizens does not automatically imply parallel EC competence in relation with third countries. Nonetheless, competence to conclude international agreements is implied if such agreements facilitate the attainment of the regulative goal of freedom of establishment and freedom to provide services *within the internal market.*

This will regularly be the case because as soon as nationals of non-member countries have established themselves in a Member State or are allowed to provide services according to the respective national laws, internal legislative EC competence also extends to their treatment. The right of "first admittance" remains with the Member States. However, the exercise of the internal EC competence is undoubtedly facilitated by the possibility to conclude agreements on the conditions of mutual "first admittance" because otherwise diverging laws in the Member States could impede EC measures, insofar as these may and have to extend to the treatment of nationals of non-member countries. Consequently, internal legislative competences will normally imply the competence to conclude international agreements insofar as these are "necessary" for the attainment of a Community goal in the sense of Opinion 2/91.[66] Additionally, this view allows for a consistent reading of the ECJ's statement in Opinion 1/94 that *internal* (concurrent) legislative competence implies EC competence for the adoption of

---

64 *Dashwood/Heliskoski* (2000) 14ff and particularly *Dashwood* (2000a) 127ff draw the same conclusion. For critical statements compare below in FN 71.

65 Not to be confounded with the type of parallel EC and Member State competences as referred to above at FN 15.

66 *Dashwood* (2000a) 136-137 has already submitted that in this respect there is hardly any difference to the standard of attribution as laid down in Art 174 para 4 TEC for environmental policy: "Within their respective spheres of competence, the Community and the Member States shall cooperate with third countries and with the competent international organisations."

external commercial measures.[67] The underlying ratio is the same: Where this facilitates the attainment of a Community goal, internal legislative competence also implies external relations competence.

Finally, it has to be added that, though more difficult to distinguish, the foundations for these two concepts of necessity lie in the AETR Judgement. With regard to eventual implied EC competence, the ECJ then stated that it "may equally flow from other provisions of the Treaty *and* from measures adopted, within the framework of those provisions, by the Community institutions."[68] As has been submitted above,[69] the ECJ clarified in Opinion 1/94 that the ambiguous term "and" must be read as alternative. Our argument proves that EC competence might be implied even without prior adoption of secondary legislation, but that normally this competence will be concurrent rather than exclusive. Only if the EC has made use of its concurrent competence the Member States are prevented insofar as they must not alter these agreements or affect their scope.[70]

2. Re-Assessing Opinion 1/94

a) Interpreting Opinion 1/94

The existence of implied concurrent competence, however, has been questioned in the light of the WTO Opinion.[71] Does the ECJ's ruling on shared competence for the conclusion of GATS and TRIPs[72] exclude concurrent competence which would have allowed the EC to enter into these agreements as sole contracting partner? An analysis of Opinion 1/94 casts severe doubt on this assumption: the ECJ manifestly chose to view the Commission's questions as

---

67 Opinion 1/94, *WTO*, [1994] ECR I-5267, paras 90-94.

68 Case 22/70, *AETR*, [1971] ECR 263, para 16 (emphasis added).

69 FN 30.

70 Case 22/70, *AETR*, [1971] ECR 263, para 22.

71 In favour of continued existence see *Dashwood* (2000a) 127ff; *McGoldrick* (1997) 60-61; *Tomuschat* (1997) paras 6,7; *Torrent* (2000) 228ff and apparently *Lenaerts/de Smijter* (1997) 8-9. For a critical view compare *O'Keeffe* (1998) 1456-1457 and *Neuwahl* (2000).

72 Opinion 1/94, *WTO*, [1994] ECR I-5267, paras 98, 105 and Conclusions 2, 3.

regarding *only* exclusive EC competence.[73] It has been submitted that this was even opted for by the Commission in a so-called "all-or-nothing approach".[74] Against this background, the ECJ's statement on shared competence must be regarded as referring solely to the questions on exclusivity. Thus Opinion 1/94 does not rule out implied concurrent EC competence as characterised above. Provided for the respective majorities in both Council and European Parliament (EP), the EC would have been solely competent to conclude GATS and TRIPs based on implied concurrent competence.[75]

Not even the term of "shared competence" employed by the ECJ leads to a different conclusion. The ECJ applies this term both to situations which we refer to as cases of "concurrent" competence - where the EC as well as the Member States are alternatively empowered to act - and to situations where the repartition of competences requires joint action by the EC and the Member States. Case C-316/91 provides an example for the first type of situations,[76] while Opinion 2/91 illustrates the second type.[77] Even if the ECJ considered a joint action of the EC and the Member States indispensable in the case of the WTO Agreements, it has to be re-stated that the answers were given with respect to *exclusive* EC competence.

Though we advocate the aforementioned view, there are certain - though far less convincing - arguments that in Opinion 1/94 the ECJ renounced the concept of implicit, non-exclusive EC

---

73 Though this interpretation of the questions is not the only possible one it is unequivocally the ECJ's understanding. Compare Opinion 1/94, *WTO*, [1994] ECR I-5267, paras 1, 14, 72, 73, 99.

74 *Neuwahl* (2000) 140ff.

75 For the same argumentation compare *Eeckhout* (1997) 17ff (19). The authors cited above in FN 71 draw the same conclusion.

76 Case C-316/91, *Parliament v Council (Lomé),* [1994] ECR I-625, para 35. Compare FN 51.

77 Opinion 2/91, *ILO*, [1993] ECR I-1061, para 12: "Finally, an agreement may be concluded in an area where competence is shared between the Community and the Member States. In such a case, negotiation and implementation of the agreement require joint action by the Community and the Member States (judgement in *Kramer*, cited above, paragraph 60)."

competences.[78] However, the overall thrust of the WTO Opinion, focussing on exclusive competences and silent on Opinion 2/91 does not support this view.[79] That is why our further analysis will be based on the solution presented above. Clarification by the ECJ is eagerly anticipated. The existing uncertainty is a crucial factor in the assessment of the changes made by the Treaty of Nice.[80]

b) The Role of Council Decision 94/800/EC

The Agreement establishing the WTO as well as the Agreements annexed to it were concluded by the EC five weeks after the issue of Opinion 1/94, which had been waited for deliberately. In Council Decision 94/800/EC, the multilateral agreements were approved on behalf of the EC "with regard to that portion of them which falls within the competence of the European Community".[81] The contemporaneity of Opinion 1/94 and the approving Council Decision suggests that this Decision extends solely to those fields of WTO law which are covered by exclusive EC competence.

The preamble of Decision 94/800/EC cites a number of legal bases - regrettably with the customary addendum "in particular" - some of which confer exclusive, others concurrent EC competence according to the above classification. Regarding services and intellectual property within the scope of GATS and TRIPs, approximation competences concerning the right of establishment[82] and the freedom to provide services[83] as well as general

---

78 Compare Opinion 1/94, *WTO*, [1994] ECR I-5267, paras 95, 96, 104, 106 and 109. *Neuwahl* (2000) considers the position on 142ff, invoking these equivocal passages of Opinion 1/94 which upon isolated analysis do support the mentioned argument.

79 Also in its Opinion on the conclusion of the Cartagena Protocol by the EC, the ECJ carefully avoided a statement on this matter (Opinion 2/00, *Cartagena Protocol*, [2001] ECR I-9713).

80 Compare below in chapter IV.

81 Council Decision 94/800/EC (of 22 December 1994) concerning the conclusion on behalf of the European Community, as regards matters within its competence, of the agreements reached in the Uruguay Round multilateral negotiations (1986-1994), OJ L 336, 23.12.1994, 1, Art 1 para 1.

82 Former Art 57, now: Art 47 TEC.

83 Former Art 66, now: Art 55 TEC.

approximation competences[84] are of particular importance along with Art 113 (now: 133) TEC on the CCP.

The eighth consideration of Decision 94/800/EC reads as follows: " [A] portion of the commitments contained in the Agreement establishing the World Trade Organization, including the Annexes thereto, falls within the competence of the Community under Article 113 of the Treaty; ... furthermore, of the remainder of the said commitments some *affect Community rules* adopted on the basis of Articles 43, 54, 57, 66, 75, 84 (2), 99, 100, 100a and 235 and *may therefore be entered into by the Community alone*" (emphasis added) - an express referral to the AETR Principle.[85]

On the other hand, the ECJ's statement, that the Treaty provision authorising the adoption of measures on the movement of capital to and from third countries has not yet been made use of, appears strange at first sight.[86] This must be regarded as a justification for the assumption that former Art 73c (now: 57) TEC *cannot* serve as a legal basis for the conclusion of the Agreements. Apparently regardless of the fact that Art 73c TEC could also confer *concurrent* competence. That is why this passage must be read as referring to the ECJ's view expressed in Opinion 1/94, according to which *exclusive* competence arises only insofar as internal legislative competence has been made use of.[87] This also implies that concurrent competences were not at issue.

The wording of the considerations in Decision 94/800/EC suggests that the WTO Agreements should indeed be concluded by the EC only insofar as they are covered by exclusive EC competence while the Member States should conclude both the parts covered by their exclusive competence and the parts covered by concurrent competences.[88]

---

84 Former Arts 100, 100a and 235, now: Arts 94, 95 and 308 TEC.

85 Compare Case 22/70, *AETR*, [1971] ECR 263, para 22.

86 Consideration 10 of Decision 94/800/EC (FN 81): "[N]o act in Community law has yet been adopted on the basis of Article 73c [now: 57] of the Treaty".

87 For this interpretation compare also *Eeckhout* (1997) 17-18. For a sceptical view see *Neuwahl* (2000) 148-149.

88 Compare also an opinion of the Council's legal service on the question whether the Government Procurement Agreement (GPA) should be concluded by the Member States along with the EC or whether it is covered by the pertinent Arts of Decision 94/800/EC and thus no more

3. Public Procurement as an Example

An additional facet of the competence issue in the field of services arises from Case C-360/93 on public procurement and the legislative developments in the wake of this decision.[89]

In 1993, the EEC and the USA entered into an Agreement on government procurement containing, on the basis of reciprocity, certain obligations to open their procurement markets. Specifically, the EEC was obliged to afford to suppliers, contractors and service-providers of the US and to goods and services originating in the US the award procedures of the pertinent EC directives, namely the Supplies Directive, the Services Directive and the Works Directive. Concerning supplies and works relating to the sector of production, transportation and distribution of electricity, the EEC assumed the obligation to extend the benefits of the Utilities Directive and the Utilities Remedies Directive to US products, suppliers and contractors.[90]

The EP contended the Council's choice of legal basis for the underlying Decisions and argued that they would have had to be based not only on Art 113 TEC but also on Arts 57 para 2, 66 and

---

Member State action is necessary. The legal service clearly states that the EC could have concluded the GPA on the basis of concurrent competences, but chose not to do so: "La question essentielle ... est de savoir si, par ces deux articles, la Communauté a exercé seulement sa compétence exclusive telle qu´elle éxistait à la date de cette conclusion ou si elle a exercé aussi la compétence externe potentielle qui, en vertu de la jurisprudence de la Cour dans l´avis 1/76, découle implicitement des articles du traité qui fondent la compétence interne de la Communauté. De l´avis du Service juridique, la Communauté n´a (d´une facon délibérée) exercé que sa compétence exclusive existante, laissant subsister les compétences des Etats membres pour le reste." (Avis du Service Juridique 5162/95, 24.2.1995, Accord sur les marchés publics conclu dans le cadre du Cycle d´Uruguay. Nécessité de sa conclusion par les Etats membres - unpublished).

89 Case C-360/93, *Parliament v Council (Government Procurement)*, [1996] ECR I-1195. For a detailed analysis compare *Griller* (2000a) 135ff.

90 These obligations were met through the adoption of two Council Decisions based on former Art 113 TEC (now: Art 133 TEC). The decisions resulted in the non-application of Art 29 of the Utilities Directive (now: Art 36 of Directive 93/38/EEC) to US-tenders thus prohibiting the preferential treatment of EC undertakings.

100a TEC.[91] The latter provisions include parliamentary participation foreseeing the so-called co-decision procedure while Art 113 TEC does not provide for any involvement of the EP. The ECJ followed the argument of the EP. First, the Court stated that the Agreement did not only cover services relating to trade in goods but was also concerned, on an independent basis, with the provision of services. Referring to the WTO Opinion, the ECJ held that "in the present state of Community law, only services which are supplied across frontiers fall within the scope of Art 113 of the Treaty (Opinion 1/94 [1994] ECR I-5267, paragraph 53)."[92] The types of service covered by the Agreement could not be "reduced to the sole hypothesis of a trans-frontier supply involving no movement of persons, but relate[d] also to supplies made thanks to a commercial presence or the presence of natural persons on the territory of the other Contracting Party"[93] For these reasons the ECJ annulled the two Council Decisions.[94]

A statement on whether the legal bases invoked by the EP would have given rise to EC competence or whether the Agreement would have had to be concluded under shared competence of the EC and the Member States was carefully avoided by the ECJ.[95]

Another indication that the WTO Opinion might not have changed the competence situation with regard to *implied concurrent competences* in the field of services (and, of course, intellectual property), as advocated by the majority of the Member States, can

---

91 Now: Arts 47 para 2, 55 and 95 TEC.

92 Case C-360/93, *Parliament v Council (Government Procurement)*, [1996] ECR I-1195, para 29.

93 Case C-360/93, *Parliament v Council (Government Procurement)*, [1996] ECR I-1195, para 30.

94 Case C-360/93, *Parliament v Council (Government Procurement)*, [1996] ECR I-1195, para 31. Taking into account the fact that the Agreement in question had already expired before the judgement was rendered, the ECJ, however, conserved the effects of the annulled decisions.

95 Advocate General *Tesauro* did not even consider the second alternative in his Opinion on Case C-360/93, *Parliament v Council (Government Procurement)*, [1996] ECR I-1195, para 11: "...the real issue is whether the two decisions could be validly based on Article 113 alone or whether the Community competence should be based (also) on other provisions of the Treaty."

be found in Council Decision 95/215/EC.[96] The prolongation of the above-mentioned Agreement on government procurement - though including a number of modifications - was based on Arts 57 para 2, 66, 100a and 113 TEC in conjunction with Art 228 para 2 first sentence and para 3 TEC[97] and was concluded *solely* by the EC. The EC and the Member States did *not* conclude an agreement under *shared competence* which would have been the way to go if parts would have been reserved to Member State competence. The adverse argument, that the Agreement was concluded by the EC alone because the system of EC Directives on government procurement establishes *exclusive* EC competence for its conclusion seems almost impossible to uphold.[98] And an unofficial document indicates that the Council acted on the assumption of concurrent EC competence.[99]

---

[96] Council Decision 95/215/EC of 29 May 1995 concerning the conclusion of an Agreement in the form of exchange of letters between the European Community and the United States of America on government procurement, OJ L 134, 10.6.1995, 25.

[97] Now: Arts 47 para 2, 55, 95 and 133 TEC in conjunction with Art 300 TEC.

[98] Compare *Griller* (2000a) 117ff and particularly 122ff for further arguments.

[99] Both the considerations in Council Decision 95/215/EC and the considerations of the Commission in its proposal, COM (95) 18 final, are ambivalent with regard to this matter. However, an opinion of the Council's legal service (Avis du Service Juridique 5163/95, 24.2.1995, Accord sur les marchés publics avec les Etats-Unis d'Amérique. Etendue et fondement de la compétence communautaire - unpublished) which preceded the final version of the preamble of the Council Decision explicitly outlined the two options: either the EC and the Member States could conclude a mixed agreement with the EC acting on the basis of exclusive competences or only the EC could conclude the agreement acting on the bases of exclusive as well as concurrent competence ("conclusion par la seule Communauté, agissant non seulement au titre de sa compétence exclusive existante mais également au titre de sa compétence potentielle"). However clear this statement may be, it does not allow for an unequivocal interpretation of Decision 95/215/EC as it must be classified as a preparatory *internal* act which according to the ECJ is irrelevant for the interpretation if it is not expressed in the legislation. Compare Joined Cases C-283/94, C-291/94 and C-292/94, *Denkavit*, [1996] ECR I-5063, para 29.

E. Shared Competence

In cases where the contents of an international agreement is covered partly by EC competence - be it exclusive or concurrent - and partly by Member State competence, the power to conclude the agreement in its entirety is shared between the EC and the Member States. Such agreements must be concluded jointly by the EC and the Member States with third countries.

Regarding Member State competence this would have to include cases in which - in the sense of Opinion 2/91 - the conclusion of an agreement by the EC is not *necessary* for the attainment of a Community goal as laid down in a Treaty provision conferring internal legislative competence (e.g. for the intra-Community liberalisation of trade in services) because the goal can be sufficiently achieved by Member State activity.[100] Such areas would be reserved for Member State competence, ruling out both exclusive and concurrent EC competence.[101] Shared competence may also come into existence subsidiarily in cases of concurrent EC competence where the EC cannot exercise its concurrent competence, for instance because majority requirements are not met.

As has been shown above, the ECJ's opinion on which of these hypotheses is applicable to parts of the services sector (GATS) and to intellectual property protection (TRIPs) is not clear. We have argued that this is why the said agreements were held to be covered by shared EC and Member State competence and ended up being concluded as mixed agreements. The EC only made use of its exclusive competence - based on Art 133 TEC and the AETR Principle on the impairment of secondary legislation - because the Member States in the Council did not support EC activity based on concurrent competence.

Nevertheless the document clarifies the legal concepts underlying the Council's action in this case.

100 Because of the broad interpretation of the term "necessary" given in Opinion 2/91 such cases will be the exception rather than the rule. Compare chapter III.D.1.

101 A consequence of such a reservation would have to be the prohibition to create EC competence by way of empowerment in an act of secondary legislation. Otherwise areas reserved to Member State competence could be hollowed out by Community legislation.

From a political point of view, this trend towards shared competence appears to be the lowest common denominator between Member State and Community interests. Mixed agreements do however cause a number of both legal and practical difficulties.[102] In Opinion 1/94 the ECJ imposed a duty of cooperation on Member States and Community institutions to ensure the unity in the international representation of the Community.[103] It remains to be seen whether in subsequent judgments the ECJ will have the opportunity to clarify the terms of this obligation and thus render it operational.[104]

F. Association Agreements

Art 310 TEC in conjunction with Art 300 TEC authorises the conclusion of Association Agreements by the Community. According to the ECJ, EC competence exists "in all the fields covered by the Treaty".[105] At least insofar as the contents of an Association Agreement exceeds the contents of a Commercial Agreement, this EC competence will have to be regarded as concurrent rather than exclusive.[106] Shared competence might arise subsidiarily to concurrent competence[107] or if the Association Agreement covers matters outside EC law (e.g. matters falling

---

[102] Compare e.g. *Rosas* (2000) 207ff with further references.

[103] Opinion 1/94, *WTO*, [1994] ECR I-5267, para 108.

[104] See also *Krenzler/da Fonseca-Wollheim* (1998) 240.

[105] Case 12/86, *Demirel*, [1987] ECR 3719, para 9.

[106] However, there is exclusive EC competence insofar as neither a single Member State nor their entirety are empowered to conclude an agreement on the association of third countries *with* the EC. But organisational links may also be established by agreements other than Association Agreements as indicated by Art 300 para 3 subpara 2 TEC ("specific institutional framework"). These agreements establishing a specific institutional framework are not necessarily covered by exclusive EC competence. Consequently, the exclusive competence for the conclusion of Association Agreements is not very helpful in the delimitation of competences as long as no Association Agreement has yet been concluded. On the contrary: The fact that also other international agreements may establish a specific institutional framework makes the demarcation between Association Agreements conferring exclusive competence and other agreements covered by competences according to single Treaty provisions even more difficult. On this issue compare *Lenaerts/de Smijter* (1997) 16ff.

[107] As outlined above.

under the Common Foreign and Security Policy or under Police and Judicial Cooperation).

IV. The Changes introduced by the Treaty of Nice

Significant changes to Art 133 TEC will be brought about by the Treaty of Nice as former paras 3 and 5 (now: para 7) have undergone reformulation and two new paras have been added. We will not comment the negotiation process in detail, suffice it to say that there was an intense debate on various alternative proposals, fuelled by the Commission's initiative and the French presidency. The scrutiny of the new provision will show its intricacy, however, it has to be kept in mind that prior draft versions even exceeded the final version in complexity.[108] Our analysis focuses on the question whether the revision brought the awaited extension of the scope of the CCP and on the implications of the changes made on the system of competences as outlined in the previous chapter.

A. An Extension of the CCP?

1. The Material Scope of New Art 133 TEC

According to the new Art 133 subpara 5 TEC, "agreements in the fields of trade in services and the commercial aspects of intellectual property" are henceforth covered by the CCP, "insofar as those agreements" have not yet been covered by it.

This double emphasis on the domain of trade/commerce forbids the subsumption of services and intellectual property protection under Art 133 TEC in their entirety, including intra-Community aspects. The formulation appears to accommodate fears that Member State legislative competence in the fields of services and intellectual property protection might be eliminated by the introduction of these domains within the scope of the CCP.[109] Moreover, unilateral (autonomous) EC measures do not fall within the range of new Art 133 TEC, another indicator that the emphasis lies on external trade. If the aspect of external trade is missing, there is no competence based on the new Art 133 TEC. The involvement of a third country or an international organisation is

---

[108] Compare CONFER 4790/00 of 3 November 2000, CONFER 4795/00 of 9 November 2000, CONFER 4815/00 of 30 November 2000 und CONFER 4816/00 of 6 December 2000.

[109] Compare *Torrent* (2000) 230-231.

conditional for Community activity. Insofar and as long as this is not the case, external trade competences remain with the Member States - they are empowered both to conclude international agreements and adopt autonomous measures - or remain covered by concurrent internal EC competence. This may serve as the first example for the interplay between the Pre- and Post-Nice situation: As there is no evidence that existing powers of the EC were meant to be curtailed, the absence of EC competence for autonomous measures based on new Art 133 TEC must not lead to the conclusion that such competence can not be based on a different Treaty provisions.

According to the ECJ, cross-frontier supply of services and the prohibition of the release into free circulation of counterfeit goods had already fallen within the scope of the CCP Pre-Nice.[110] Consequently, the questions arise, which other aspects of these sectors will be covered by the Post-Nice provision and whether or not controversies as the one surrounding the conclusion of the WTO Agreements will soon be a thing of the past.

That the latter hope is in vain, at least, for the sector of services, must be concluded from two shortcomings in new Art 133 TEC, namely the *scope of "services"* that this Art is referring to and its silence on the questions of *foreign direct investment*.

While trans-frontier supply of services was subsumed under Art 133 TEC in the WTO Opinion, the other modes of supply as covered by Art I GATS such as active and passive freedom of services and the so-called "commercial presence" were not held to fall within the scope of the CCP. New Art 133 TEC para 5 now extends the CCP to the services sector. This means that active and passive freedom of services will henceforth be included in the CCP, but this does not hold true for the establishment of a commercial presence. For the notion of "services" as employed by the TEC diverges greatly from the notion of "services" as defined by the GATS. The TEC differentiates between the provision of services and the right of establishment, including the set up and the management of undertakings.[111] Systemic interpretation of the Treaty of Nice however commands that terms employed in newly

---

110 Compare above at FN 21 and 24.

111 Compare on the one hand, Art 49ff TEC and on the other hand, Art 43ff TEC.

introduced Treaty provisions be interpreted in the sense in which they have been used in pre-existing Treaty provisions. This is why the notion of services of new Art 133 TEC must be viewed as covering the same scope as the notion of services of Arts 49ff TEC. As these Arts do not include the establishment of a commercial presence, such presence can neither be covered by new Art 133 TEC. This is one reason why new Art 133 TEC will not provide a valid legal basis for consistent EC activity within the WTO framework.[112]

That new Art 133 TEC is silent on *foreign direct investment* is another indicator that the "commercial presence" will not be covered by is its scope. Considering the long lasting debate on the extension of EC competences in the field of the CCP[113] and the negotiating history of the Nice IGC, it appears impossible that this omission happened accidentally. Consequently, it cannot be compensated by extensive interpretation of the new provision.

The issue of foreign direct investment had already been part of the negotiations during the 1996/97 IGC leading to the Treaty of Amsterdam. In the so-called Dublin II Paper of the Irish presidency,[114] there was a proposal to introduce a new Art 113a TEC which would complement former Art 113 (now: 133) TEC. This proposed Art explicitly authorised the conclusion of agreements in "the areas of services, intellectual property *and direct foreign investment* not covered by Art 113(1)".[115] But the outcome of the negotiations was Art 133 para 5 TEC in the version of the Treaty of Amsterdam, no longer including the area of foreign direct investment. The negotiations on the Treaty of Nice took a similar turn: draft versions of new Art 133 included the areas of services, intellectual property *and foreign direct investment* but were

---

[112] For an apparently different view compare *Vedder* (2001) para 60. In how far the "commercial presence" in the sense of the GATS might moreover fall under the TEC provisions establishing the movement of capital (Art 56-57 TEC) could be an equally controversial question but will not be elaborated here.

[113] For a brief account compare e.g. *Krenzler/da Fonseca-Wollheim* (1998) 234ff.

[114] CONF 2500/96 of 5 December 1996, chapter 11.

[115] Emphasis added.

dropped in the very last moment, leaving it impossible to assume that the matter was overlooked.[116]

It could be argued that the regulatory focus of direct investment lies on questions concerning the capital market and not on questions on freedom of establishment. But the establishment of a commercial presence inevitably includes an investment decision. That is why the deliberate omission of foreign direct investment in the new version of Art 133 TEC and the inclusion of the term of "services" without modification to the notion employed in the TEC seems to eliminate the possibility that an establishment in the sense of "commercial presence" as referred to by the GATS be included in the scope of new Art 133 TEC.[117]

While according to ECJ case-law freedom to provide services includes investment insofar as it concerns the set-up of infrastructure such as an office, chambers or consulting rooms, the "temporary nature of the activities in question" must not be lost.[118] The GATS, on the other hand, does also cover regular, continuous and periodical activity, i.e. activity falling under the freedom of *establishment* as defined by the TEC.

It remains to be seen whether this differentiation will mean that consistent activity of the EC concerning the "commercial presence" will be facilitated or exacerbated as compared to its activity in the fields of services and intellectual property. If, as we have argued, implied concurrent competence for these areas has been existing all along, the EC's margin of manoeuvre for the regulation of the commercial presence will be broader than for the area of services and intellectual property, as Art 44 and Art 47 TEC provide legal

---

116 Summary CONFER 4790/00 of 3 November 2000 aimed at the extension of para 1 (Option 1 for Art 133 TEC), Revised Summary CONFER 4810/00 of 23 November 2000 provided for concurrent competence (Option 1 for Art 133 TEC) and finally in Revised Summary CONFER 4815/00 of 30 November 2000 direct investment did no longer appear.

117 Against this background the Commission's view as expressed on its web-site (http://europa.eu.int/comm/trade/faqs/rev133_en.htm, last visited in July 2002) does not seem to be much more than wishful thinking: "It is however unfortunate that Investment is not now also included in Article 133 (except for services, via 'mode 3'of the GATS)."

118 Compare Case C-55/94, *Gebhard*, [1995] ECR I-4165, para 27.

bases for concurrent competence, making co-decision procedure and thus qualified majority voting in Council applicable.

2. Explicit Concurrent EC Competence

Art 133 para 5 subpara 4 clearly states that EC competence in the fields newly covered by the CCP is - only - concurrent. The persisting competence of the Member States to enter into agreements with third countries and international organisations is limited solely by the requirement of compliance "with Community law and other relevant international agreements."

Autonomous measures of the Member States are not referred to, apparently because the entire paragraph only deals with the conclusion of agreements. Consequently, it can be assumed that the situation with regard to autonomous measures remains unmodified and that there is no indication for *e contrario* reasoning, meaning that the Member States continue to be competent to adopt autonomous measures as long as these comply with EC law.

However, the terminology employed in new Art 133 para 5 subpara 4 is rather perplexing. International agreements concluded by the EC also constitute EC law which Member States must respect.[119] What other international agreements the differentiation of new Art 133 para 5 subpara 4 refers to cannot be seen very clearly. Rather, it appears that this formulation is superfluous.

The principle of supremacy of EC law commands that Member States comply with existing EC law both in the conclusion of agreements and in the adoption of autonomous measures. Inversely, this can only mean that the EC competence newly introduced by Art 133 para 5 TEC is a *concurrent* one. The EC is empowered to conclude agreements on trade in services and commercial aspects of intellectual property if the required majority can be met in Council. Insofar as this is the case, the EC acquires competence. As long as the EC does not acquire competence, the Member States are alternatively empowered to act both by way of the conclusion of agreements and the adoption of autonomous measures.[120]

---

[119] Compare below at FN 121.

[120] Compare also *Herrmann* (2001) 272. Conversely, *Vedder* (2001) seems to conclude that the revised provision establishes exclusive EC competence (para 60).

The Member States are bound by agreements concluded by the EC because their provisions form an integral part of EC law.[121] But this does not mean that also the implementation of such agreements automatically falls under EC competence. As long as no secondary EC legislation has been enacted, new Art 133 TEC does not appear to abolish Member State competence to implement agreements concluded by the EC. The pertinent passage of the ILO Opinion remains applicable: "even if the competent authority ... is an authority of one of the Member States, the Community may nevertheless assume the ... obligation for external purposes."[122] Indications that external competence does not necessarily comprise competence to implement can also be found in the *Kupferberg*-Case[123] and the case on development cooperation.[124] And new Art 133 TEC explicitly excludes the adoption of internal measures, as covered by Art 133 para 1 TEC. This is why there is room to argue that the Member States remain competent for the implementation of agreements concluded by the EC on the basis of the new provision, as long as no secondary legislation has yet been enacted.[125]

However, in cases where secondary EC legislation exists which needs to be modified or precludes Member State activity, the EC itself is bound to take legislative steps for the implementation of international agreements. But this implementing acts must not be based on new Art 133 TEC, which only authorises the conclusion of agreements. Appropriate legal bases are Art 49, Art 52, Art 55 in conjunction with Art 47 and Art 95 TEC. Generally, international agreements invalidate secondary EC legislation to the extent that

---

121 Compare only Case 181/73, *Haegeman*, [1974] ECR 449, first tenor; Case 104/81, *Kupferberg*, [1982] ECR 3641, paras 13ff and Case C-61/94, *Commission v Germany*, [1996] ECR I-3989. For the disputed case of WTO law compare below at FN 127.

122 Opinion 2/91, *ILO*, [1993] ECR I-1061, para 34.

123 Case 104/81, *Kupferberg*, [1982] ECR 3641, para 12: "The measures needed to implement the provisions of an agreement concluded by the Community are to be adopted, according to the state of Community law for the time being in the areas affected by the provisions of the agreement, either by the Community institutions or by the Member States."

124 Case C-268/94, *Portugal v Council*, [1996] ECR I-6177, para 47.

125 Before the adoption of the Treaty of Nice compare *Torrent* (2000) 228ff, the proposal reported on p 232 resembles the solution adopted in the Treaty of Nice. Similarly, compare *Cremona* (2000) 9ff.

they are directly applicable.[126] Only with regard to WTO law the ECJ has categorically ruled out direct effect.[127] Consequently, the political and legal margin of manoeuvre for the implementation of WTO law is broader than for other international agreements. However the Banana-Case showed that this does not preclude responsibility at the international level.

3. Implied Exclusive EC Competence?

Considering the broad formulation of new Art 133 para 5 TEC ("...insofar as those agreements are not covered by the said paragraphs..."), it might be argued that henceforth this provision will also be the only legal basis *implying* the conclusion of agreements on trade in services and trade related aspects of intellectual property.[128] Only the fields that were held to be covered by the CCP in the WTO Opinion would not face any changes as they would not fall under new Art 133 para 5 TEC. The major difference for the category of implied exclusive competence would be the new procedural requirements and limitations which will be briefly commented on below.[129]

But we assume that better arguments support the inverse view: new Art 133 para 5 TEC will not henceforth serve as the sole basis for implied exclusive competence. We argue that the situation as regards implied exclusive competence is not changed by new Art 133 para 5 TEC. Art 49, 52 and 95 TEC will remain the legal bases for agreements based on implied exclusive EC competence.

Another aspect which contradicts the above mentioned position according to which implicit exclusive competences will be covered solely by new Art 133 para 5 TEC is the absence of any indication of the intention to facilitate the establishment of this type of competence. Our interpretation, on the other hand, allows for a

---

[126] Because these agreements are also binding on the institutions of the Community: compare Joined Cases 21 to 24/72, *International Fruit Company*, [1972] ECR 1219, paras 5/6 and 7/9 and Case 104/81, *Kupferberg*, [1982] ECR 3641, para 11.

[127] The most recent ruling on this issue is Case C-307/99, *OGT Fruchthandelsgesellschaft mbH*, [2001] ECR I-3159. For a critical analysis of the ECJ's position compare *Griller* (2000b).

[128] On this type of competence compare chapter III.B.

[129] This argumentation would be compatible with new Art 133 para 5 subpara 4 TEC. By definition agreements of the Member States would not come into consideration.

consistent understanding of new Art 133 para 5 subpara 4 TEC. Its formulation refers to the standard case in which the Member States are competent to act as there is no conflicting EC legislation. It does not concern cases of implicit exclusive EC competence as these do not fall under new Art 133 para 5 TEC at all.

The third possible argument, that the Treaty of Nice abolishes implicit exclusive competences altogether, is neither supported by the text nor by the negotiating history.

What confuses at first sight, however, is the term "or" in new Art 133 para 5 subpara 2 TEC. If a unanimous Council decision is required for the negotiation and conclusion of an agreement both if no secondary legislation has yet been enacted and in cases where unanimity is required for the adoption of internal rules, this necessarily implies that the provision is equally applicable where internal rules have already been enacted. Otherwise, the first part of the provision would be redundant. But according to the AETR Principle, these cases typically lead to the establishment of exclusive EC competence insofar as secondary EC legislation could be altered or its scope affected. Additionally, under exceptional circumstances exclusive competence might be implied even in the absence of secondary legislation.

However, also assuming that new Art 133 para 5 TEC does not refer to implied exclusive competences, there is a reading of the new provision consistent with the requirements of the AETR Principle: we argue that new Art 133 para 5 TEC only refers to minimal standards as dealt with in the ILO Opinion which do *not* establish exclusive EC competence. And only under very specific circumstances is exclusive EC competence implied even in the absence of secondary legislation.

Consequently, it is submitted that the strict requirements set out in the WTO Opinion for the establishment of implied exclusive EC competence remain valid in the fields of trade in services and intellectual property. New Art 133 para 5 TEC is not applicable in cases of implied exclusive EC competence.

4. Restrictions and Exceptions to the Exception

According to new Art 133 para 6 subpara 1 TEC, the provision does not apply to cases where an agreement contains provisions which would go "beyond the Community's internal powers, in particular by leading to harmonisation of the laws or regulations of the Member States in an area for which this Treaty rules out such harmonisation."

This manifestly links external relations competence to internal EC legislative competence and can thus be seen as a reference to the "logic of parallelism" between internal and external EC competences as advocated before the adoption of the WTO Opinion. The second part of the phrase and new Art 133 para 6 subpara 2 TEC provide further clarification: the provision extends restrictions on the EC's internal powers, i.e. the exclusion of certain subject matters as well as certain modes of the adoption of internal legislation, to the conclusion of international agreements.

On the other hand, the formulation suggests, that the characteristic requirement for the establishment of internal legislative EC competence, namely the attainment of a *intra-Community* goal such as the facilitation of trade in services or the establishment of a common set of rules protecting intellectual property, is not conditional for creation of external relations competence. Consequently, an international agreement on trade in services or intellectual property could be concluded even without added value within the EC. This type of competence also comes into existence if an agreement only promotes international trade. In this respect, the new provision is broader than the previous requirements for the establishment of concurrent competence as outlined above.

Examples for areas in which the Treaty rules out harmonisation are education and vocational training,[130] culture,[131] public health[132] and social policy.[133] Such prohibitions of harmonisation may not be circumvented by the conclusion of international agreements. On the other hand, the disputed question whether the power to cooperate with third countries as provided for in Arts 149, 150 and 151 TEC includes the conclusion of agreements is answered in the affirmative.

However, the question remains whether the new provision is applicable *only* to constellations for which the EC was *not* previously empowered to conclude agreements on its own. Maybe

---

130 Paras 149 and 150 TEC.

131 Art 151 TEC.

132 Art 152 TEC.

133 Art 137 para 1 lit j and k in conjunction wich para 2 TEC (as revised by the Treaty of Nice).

the drafters of the new provision had in mind that there are no implied concurrent EC competences. But this interpretation of new Art 133 para 6 TEC is not imperative. It could equally be argued that independently, the new provision provides for concurrent competence in the fields of trade in services and intellectual property insofar as exclusive EC competence is not established by other Treaty provisions. Still, internal limitations of the legislative competence (prohibitions of harmonisation) have to be taken into account, with the exception of the condition of the attainment of an intra-Community goal.

This interpretation also casts light on the scope of new Art 133 para 6 subpara 2: the special provision on "agreements relating to trade in cultural and audiovisual services, educational services, and social and human health services" is applicable "in this regard". This must be viewed as referring to - putative or actual - prohibitions of harmonisation as dealt with in new Art 133 para 6 subpara 1. In other words, as long as agreements in the cited fields do not include provisions on internal harmonisation of laws, obliging the Member States to adapt their national legislation, they may be concluded under new Art 133 para 5. For example, if an agreement deals with complementary cooperation measures concerning cultural or educational policy, it could be concluded exclusively by the EC based on new Art 133 para 5. On the other hand, provisions dealing with the approximation of laws "fall within the shared competence of the Community and its Member States" and thus need to be adopted according to Art 300 TEC including the common accord and ratification of all Member States.

However, the reference in new Art 133 para 6 subpara 2 to internal limitations of the legislative competence ("[i]n this regard")[134] results in even further differentiation. The cited fields (cultural and audiovisual services, educational services, and social and human health services) are not entirely excluded from internal

---

[134] Compare also http://europa.eu.int/comm/trade/faqs/rev133_en.htm, last visited in July 2002, where the Commission states that: "The parallelism is also reflected in paragraph 6: to the extent that the Treaty itself (Articles 149 to 152) excludes internal harmonisation in the policy areas of education, human health and culture, and therefore expressly maintains the internal sharing of competences, it would not have been logical that trade negotiations could result in such an harmonisation via the back door. The text confirms this. "

competence for the approximation of laws. There is existing secondary legislation particularly in the fields of audiovisual services and social policy and its permissibility is generally undisputed.[135] Also in the field of health policy there is internal competence for the harmonisation of laws.[136] Insofar as new Art 133 para 6 subpara 2 specifies subpara 1, the scope of existing internal approximation competences becomes crucial for the scope of new Art 133 para 4 TEC. Agreements only fall within shared competence of the EC and its Member States where such internal approximation competence does not yet exist.

This is another aspect of the changes introduced by the Treaty of Nice which will impede consistent future EC activity within the WTO framework, particularly with regard to EC competences covering parts of the fields falling under "shared competence". Based on our argument that the EC could have made use of its implied concurrent competence for these areas even before the reformulation of Art 133 TEC by the Treaty of Nice, we consider this amendment a major step backwards.

---

[135] Compare only Council Directive 89/552/EEC of 3 October 1989 on the coordination of certain provisions laid down by Law, Regulation or Administrative Action in Member States concerning the pursuit of television broadcasting activities, OJ L 298, 17.10.1989, 23 as amended by Directive 97/36/EC of the European Parliament and the Council, OJ L 202, 30.7.1997, 60, and Council Directive 93/83/EEC on the coordination of certain rules concerning copyright and rights related to copyright applicable to satellite broadcasting and cable retransmission, OJ L 248, 6.10.1993, 15, as well as *Rebhahn's* (2000) outline of EC social policy. Also Art 137 TEC as reformulated by the Treaty of Nice allows for approximation measures, even though under more restrictive conditions. Only new Art 137 *para 2* TEC rules out harmonisation for certain issues.
These internal legislative competences are bound to have implications for other cited fields which in turn would have repercussions on external relations competences: e.g. the mentioned directives on television and satellite broadcasting can be assumed to include aspects of cultural policy in the sense of Art 151 TEC (supposing, of course, that television does not entirely lack a cultural dimension). Insofar, agreements on such issues would also be covered by new Art 133 para 5 TEC.

[136] Art 152 para 4 lit a and b TEC.

Apparently, the new provision was introduced mainly in reaction to pressure applied by France trying to protect its cultural policy - prominently including the film industry - from an alleged WTO threat. Thus, difficulties concerning the special treatment of audiovisual products, which had already emerged during the Uruguay Round,[137] have now been extended to additional areas of economic activity.

It could be questioned whether what has been left of the AETR Principle after the WTO Opinion will still be applicable in the light of the new provisions, i.e. whether regardless of the limitations established by new Art 133 para 6 subpara 2 there is still room for exclusive EC competence in these fields. As we have argued that implied *exclusive* competences are not covered by the new provisions we conclude that on the basis of implication exclusive EC competences may still be established. However, such implication is only possible where there is internal competence for approximation measures which e.g. is not the case for cultural policy in general.

The situation as regards international agreements in the field of transport remains unchanged. According to new Art 133 para 6 subpara 3 they "shall continue to be governed by the provisions of Title V and Art 300." This must be read as referring to the pertinent passages of the WTO Opinion.[138] The ECJ stressed that even in the field of transport and against the background of the AETR Judgement there is no broad exclusive EC competence but that the Member States are competent to adopt secondary legislation.

---

[137] The current state of WTO law does not provide for a "cultural exception" as has been advocated by some during the Uruguay Round negotiations. Even though the emission and subsidisation of audiovisual products is part of the annexed lists of exemptions to the Most-Favoured-Nation Treatment as laid down in Art II of the GATS there are no additional obligations of the Member States in this field. However, it has to be kept in mind that this exemption does not apply to audiovisual products falling under the provisions of free movement of goods, such as products recorded on a sound- or visual-storage-medium. The exemption only applies to services covered by the GATS, particularly the emission of television programmes. On the disputed legal situation compare *Hahn* (1996) with further references.

[138] Opinion 1/94, *WTO*, [1994] ECR I-5267, paras 76ff.

5. Procedural Rules

As this contribution focuses on a systematisation of external trade competences and their material scope, procedural requirements and the changes made in this field by the Treaty of Nice are commented on only briefly. The general rules for the conclusion of agreements covered by the CCP were not substantially amended by the Treaty of Nice.[139] Agreements are concluded according to a multistage procedure:[140] The Commission makes recommendations to the Council which authorises the Commission to open the necessary negotiations. The Commission carries out these negotiations in consultation with the so-called Art 133-Committee, composed of representatives of the Member States.[141] The Council may issue directives for the conduct of negotiations.

The pertinent provisions of Art 300 TEC, main legal basis for the conclusion of agreements by the EC, remain applicable. However, they foresee a variation of the general procedural rules of Art 300 in the conclusion of agreements covered by the CCP insofar as the EP's involvement is not mandatory. Nonetheless, in practice the EP is also informed on CCP agreements on the basis of a non-binding declaration of the Council.[142] As with all agreements, those which establish a specific institutional framework, have important budgetary implications or "entail" the amendment of an act adopted under the co-decision procedure require the *assent* of the EP.[143]

The Council decides the conclusion of an agreement by qualified majority.[144]

The Treaty of Nice ties in with these provisions but foresees variations for specific cases. Firstly, new Art 133 para 5 subpara 2 TEC requires the unanimous adoption of provisions "for which

---

[139] Compare, however, the irritating provision of new Art 133 para 3 TEC, commented on below in chapter IV.A.7.

[140] Art 133 paras 3 and 4 and Art 300 TEC. For a detailed account compare *Vedder* (2001) paras 79ff with further references.

[141] The Treaty of Nice additionally provides that the "Commission shall report regularly to the special committee on the progress of negotiations."

[142] So-called *Luns-Westerterp*-Procedure.

[143] Art 300 para 3 subpara 2 TEC.

[144] Art 133 para 4 in conjunction with Art 300 paras 1 and 2 TEC.

unanimity is required for the adoption of internal rules or where [an agreement] relates to a field in which the Community has not yet exercised the powers conferred upon it by this Treaty by adopting internal rules."

The second part of the phrase is understandable only upon the assumption that Art 300 para 2 TEC, which contains identical wording, is not applicable to commercial agreements. This may be concluded from the fact that Art 300 para 2 TEC explicitly mentions Art 310 TEC (Association Agreements) but is silent on Art 133 TEC. Thus, provisions requiring unanimity for the adoption of internal rules could be hollowed out by competence to conclude commercial agreements. New Art 133 para 5 subpara 2 TEC tries to prevent this in the fields of services and intellectual property.

However, as the pertinent legal bases for services and intellectual property already foresee qualified majority voting,[145] the applicability of the new provision could be questioned.

Differing from this principle, the TEC foresees unanimity e.g. in cases where the implementation of a directive involves in at least one Member State amendment of the existing legal principles governing the professions with respect to training and conditions of access for natural persons.[146] Based on new Art 133 para 5 subpara 2 TEC, the conclusion of an international agreement in such a field henceforth also requires unanimity. The new provision overrides the argumentation that such international agreements primarily have to be classified as commercial agreements which - though governed by special rules - are concluded by qualified majority voting.

Compared to Art 300 TEC, the second part of new Art 133 para 5 subpara 2 TEC tightens the voting requirements for the adoption of international agreements in cases where the EC has not yet made use of its internal legislative competence. Unanimity is required for the conclusion of any international agreement in these fields.

Secondly, new Art 133 para 5 subpara 3 requires unanimity for the negotiation and conclusion of "horizontal agreement[s] insofar as [they] also concern the preceding subparagraph or the second subparagraph of paragraph 6." The term "horizontal agreement", introduced into the TEC for the first time, appears to target agreements which cover a multitude of topics, e.g. both financial

---

[145] Art 53 and 95 TEC.

[146] Art 47 para 2 TEC in conjunction with Art 55 TEC.

and insurance services *and* social or audio-visual services. An example for such a horizontal agreement would be the WTO Agreement which, however, is not covered by the new provisions in its entirety.[147]

Thirdly, new Art 133 para 6 subpara 2 TEC requires both a "Community decision taken in accordance with the relevant provisions of Art 300" and a "common accord of the Member States" for the negotiation of "agreements relating to trade in cultural and audiovisual services, educational services, and social and human health services". It has been submitted above that this restriction exempts the said fields from concurrent EC competence as established by new Art 133 para 5 TEC, authorising the conclusion of agreements by the EC alone.[148] On the other hand, new Art 133 para 6 subpara 2 foresees "shared competence" and the application of Art 300 TEC. This reflects the quest to establish EC competence regardless of internal limitations of the legislative competence (prohibitions of harmonisation), even though this EC competence needs to be exercised jointly with the Member States. Insofar as the new provision also excludes exclusive *Member State* competence it may be regarded as an extension of EC competence as compared with the situation Pre-Nice. Because without such shared competence, no EC competence whatsoever (exclusive or concurrent) could be established in fields where there is no internal EC legislative competence.

Unanimity in the Council is required both for the negotiation and the conclusion of agreements according to new Art 133 para 5 subpara 3. However, this applies only to "horizontal agreement[s]", i.e. agreements which also include provisions on topics not falling under new Art 133 para 6 subpara 2. There is no provision regulating the conclusion of agreements which exclusively contain issues covered by para 6 subpara 2. It has to be assumed that for these cases the same requirements will have to be met as if the EC held approximation competences or exclusive competence to conclude international agreements in the respective field. For example in the field of cultural policy this would mean unanimity, for parts of the social policy this would result in a requirement of qualified majority. But as agreements are concluded jointly with the

[147] As outlined above.
[148] Compare chapter IV.A.4.

Member States and thus require their assent, this question might be of minor relevance.

6. Explicit Exclusive EC Competence for Intellectual Property Based on a Council Decision

New Art 133 para 7 TEC allows for the extension of the "application of paragraphs 1 to 4 to international negotiations and agreements on intellectual property insofar as they are not covered by paragraph 5" by unanimous Council decision. Agreements on intellectual property are not covered by paragraph 5 if they do not only include *commercial aspects* of intellectual property. However, as the TRIPs Agreement covers "trade-related aspects" of intellectual property rights, the restriction imposed by this limitation does not appear to be very burdensome. The stimulating effect on trade brought about by the enhancement of legal certainty through the adoption of rules on the term of protection in all participating States is obvious also in the domain of intellectual property. This was confirmed by the ECJ in the WTO Opinion, even though not considered sufficient for the establishment of an exclusive EC competence based on Art 133 TEC.[149] Thus, other than in the domain of services (GATS),[150] it can be assumed that new Art 133 para 5 TEC fully covers the TRIPs Agreement as regards its material scope.

Against this background, the second possible limitation deserves closer scrutiny. However, this limitation is understandable only on the basis of Art 133 para 5 TEC as introduced by the Treaty of Amsterdam. This provision empowered the Council to "extend the application of paragraphs 1 to 4 to international negotiations and agreements on services and intellectual property insofar as they are not covered by these paragraphs." Even though the Council did not adopt any measures based on Art 133 para 5 TEC its application would have established *exclusive* EC competence for services and intellectual property.

---

[149] Opinion 1/94, *WTO*, [1994] ECR I-5267, paras 57-58. *Herrmann* (2001) draws the same conclusion based on a different interpretation of the WTO Opinion: according to the ECJ, the TRIPs Agreement was not aimed at the regulation of international trade but at an international harmonisation of copyright protection (271-272).

[150] Compare above after FN 110.

The introduction of this version of Art 133 para 5 TEC by the Treaty of Amsterdam was clearly a response to the WTO Opinion in which the ECJ had argued that these domains generally were not covered by the CCP. New Art 133 para 5 TEC as re-formulated by the Treaty of Nice now explicitly encompasses services and intellectual property. Nevertheless the last part of new Art 133 para 7 TEC does not refer to Art 133 paras 1-4 but to *new Art 133 para 5 TEC*. Consequently, it remains largely incomprehensible which agreements in the field of intellectual property could fall under the new category "not covered by paragraph 5".[151]

As new Art 133 para 6 subpara 2 TEC constitutes a derogation from Art 133 para 5 subpara 1, fields mentioned in this provision are not covered by para 5. But should this lead to the assumption that by unanimous Council decision exclusive EC competence could be established in fields where there had not even been consensus for the introduction of concurrent competence?[152] Both the contextual interpretation of new Art 133 para 7 TEC and its evolution based on current Art 133 para 5 TEC make this assumption seem unsustainable. Does this mean that all agreements on intellectual property can henceforth be concluded on the basis of new Art 133 para 5 TEC (either by the EC, by the Member States or jointly by the EC and its Member States)? It is submitted that new Art 133 para 7 TEC targets the same goal as the current Art 133 para 5 TEC - to provide a legal basis for *exclusive* EC competence regarding the conclusion of agreements in the field of intellectual property. *In this respect*, agreements are also not covered by new Art 133 para 5 TEC. Additionally, this reading of new Art 133 para 7 TEC clarifies the introductory passage of para 7 ("Without prejudice to the first subparagraph of paragraph 6..."): it aims to exclude applicability of the restriction laid down in para 6 subpara 2. If ever there will be a consensus on the establishment of exclusive EC competence, this competence could encompass *all* aspects of international agreements in the field of intellectual property.

---

[151] Of course agreements dealing with the prohibition of the release into free circulation of counterfeit goods - which were held to be covered by the CCP already in the WTO Opinion - are not covered by new Art 133 para 5 TEC. But from the outset new para 7 could not refer to this category.

[152] *Herrmann* (2001) 273 seems to foster this opinion.

The relevance of new Art 133 para 7 TEC lies in its function as a basis for exclusive EC competence. But its scope is restricted compared to the Amsterdam version - it solely refers to intellectual property and no longer applies to trade in services.

7. A New Obligation of Consistency?

According to the last sentence of new Art 133 para 3 subpara 1 TEC "[t]he Council and the Commission shall be responsible for ensuring that the agreements negotiated are compatible with internal Community policies and rules." Taken seriously, this new provision requires that international agreements henceforth be negotiated and concluded only if they do not require any changes in pre-existing EC law including secondary legislation.[153] For example, obligations in the field of agricultural policy as entered into in the context of the WTO Agreements could no longer be assumed as their implementation would require the change of secondary EC legislation.[154] Previous to the adoption of an international agreement, envisaged changes would have to be negotiated within the EC. Needless to say that this would virtually paralyse the EC as an international actor.[155]

But the negotiating history of the Treaty of Nice does not indicate that such a drastic change was ever seriously raised as an issue. That is why Art 300 para 3 subpara 2 TEC must remain applicable, stating that international agreements may "entail" the amendment of secondary EC legislation. The meaning of the newly introduced sentence in Art 133 para 3 subpara 1 TEC consequently has to be reduced to the commonplace statement that Commission and Council have to take possible future amendments of EC legislation into account during negotiations. And it obliges the institutions to act according to the procedural requirements as laid

---

[153] The provision must not be regarded as referring solely to an obligation of transformation both because of its systematic position and because such an obligation is already included in Art 300 para 7 TEC.

[154] As an illustration compare the package adopted in order to implement the agreements concluded during the Uruguay Round in the agricultural sector. It comprises eight Council Regulations and one Council Decision all published in OJ L 349, 31.12.1994.

[155] *Herrmann* (2001) 274 sees the dilemma but does not draw any alternative conclusion. Rather, he assumes that the "obligation of consistency" would have to be qualified as a mere appeal without legal consequences.

down in new Art 133 paras 5 and 6 which *differ depending on the state of internal legislation.*

B. The New Art 133 TEC - a Misunderstanding?

It has been submitted above that even without the changes brought about by the Treaty of Nice, TEC provisions *imply* far-reaching *concurrent EC competence* for the conclusion of international agreements in the fields of services and intellectual property.[156] If this view is shared, the Treaty of Nice does not bring about the awaited further extension of EC competence. Rather, it reduces the EC's margin of manoeuvre, particularly by extending the unanimity requirement and introducing the obligation to conclude mixed agreements in the fields referred to in new Art 133 para 6 subpara 2 TEC.

For domains covered neither by the "classic" CCP nor by the new provisions - e.g. freedom of movement of persons and capital, environmental protection, transport - the legal situation remains unchanged. Concurrent competences based on these "other" legal bases partly exceed those deriving from new Art 133 TEC. That is why the said unanimity requirement and obligation to conclude mixed agreements are not applicable. Equally, implied *exclusive* EC competences for services and intellectual property are not affected.

A statement of the Commission to be found on its web-site seems to mirror a different view: "The guiding principle of the new Art 133 is to align the decision-making mechanism for trade negotiations on internal decision-making rules: in the area of services, for example, it is illogical that decisions are taken by qualified majority on Internal Market directives, but trade negotiations on the very same subject fall under a rule of consensus (effectively requiring unanimity)."[157] This assumption seems to be based on the unsubstantiated concept that services have not yet been covered by implied concurrent EC competence. Only upon this premise - contrary to the view expressed in this paper - does the Treaty of Nice extend the EC's competence to enter into international commercial agreements.

It is deplorable, however, that this essential question does not seem to have arisen during negotiations. Depending on the

---

156 Compare above in chapter III.D.

157 http://europa.eu.int/comm/trade/faqs/rev133_en.htm, last visited in July 2002. Compare also FN 117 and 134.

respective premise, the negotiators involved must have had totally different implications of the new provisions in mind.

V. Conclusion

By systematizing the different types of competence along the line of ECJ jurisprudence we have tried to indicate a path through the maze of external trade competences as based on the central provision of Art 133 TEC. Expectations ran high that the Treaty of Nice would eventually facilitate this attempt. But regrettably, closer scrutiny of the newly introduced provisions does not invalidate the impression of the reader upon first sight: new Art 133 TEC is a complicated set of restrictions and exceptions to the exception and contributes very little to the consolidation of the CCP. The changes made lack the potential to strengthen the EC's capacity as an actor on the international scene, particularly within the WTO System. The fragmentation of competences will continue to paralyse any consistent EC action vis-à-vis its trading partners and its implementation will necessitate overwhelming administrative effort.

The introduction of *explicit concurrent* EC competence for trade in services and intellectual property does not fit into the system of the CCP. The Member States remain competent for the conclusion of international agreements if majority requirements are not met within the Council and thus keep a firm grip on any EC activity.

If analysed favourably, the changes introduced with regard to the disputed type of *implied concurrent competence* could be viewed as a clarification: at least its mere existence can no longer be questioned. But upon a less benevolent view they appear nothing more than a blatant misinterpretation of the Pre-Nice situation. We have argued that more global bases for implied concurrent competence have been existing all along, governing this type of competence in a way far less complicated than the one chosen by the Treaty of Nice. On the basis of these assumptions we conclude that the continuation of the current system would be preferable to *this* reformulation, both from the point of view of transparency and of feasibility.

But what are the reasons for the persistence of this maze-like situation with regard to external trade competences and who are its authors? It would be misleading to put the blame on a lack of ability of IGC negotiators. Even the textual shortcomings are usually caused by the unbalanced exertion of political pressure. Rather, the difficulties seem to be rooted in the simmering conflict over sovereignty fought out between the EC and its Member States. States represented by the Commission in the negotiation of international agreements and replaced by the Council in their conclusion might appear condemned to silence in international fora. This could raise suspicion on the remainder of their sovereignty. But this opens a whole new dimension to the topic: Art 133 TEC is no longer about Commercial Policy but stands in the centre of the debate on the future shape - and constitution - of the Union.

Bibliography

von Bogdandy, A./Bast, J. (2001), Die vertikale Kompetenzordnung der Europäischen Union, EuGRZ 2001, 441-458.

von Bogdandy, A./Nettesheim, M. (1994), Art 3b EGV, in *Grabitz, E./Hilf, M.* (eds.), Das Recht der Europäischen Union (formerly: Kommentar zur Europäischen Union), 7th instalment, München 1994.

Cremona, M. (1999), External Relations and External Competence: The Emergence of an Integrated Policy, in *Craig, P./de Búrca, G.* (eds.), The Evolution of EU Law, New York 1999, 137-175.

Cremona, M. (2000), EC External Commercial Policy after Amsterdam: Authority and Interpretation within Interconnected Legal Orders, in *Weiler, J.H.H.* (ed.), The EU, the WTO and the NAFTA: towards a Common Law of International Trade? Oxford 2000, 5-34.

Dashwood, A. (2000a), The Attribution of External Relations Competence, in *Dashwood, A./Hillion, C.* (eds.), The General Law of E.C. External Relations, London 2000, 115-138.

Dashwood, A. (2000b), E.C. External Relations Provisions Post-Amsterdam, in *Dashwood, A./Hillion, C.* (eds.), The General Law of E.C. External Relations, London 2000, 279-286.

Dashwood, A./Heliskoski, J. (2000), The Classic Authorities Revisited, in *Dashwood, A./Hillion, C.* (eds.) The General Law of E.C. External Relations, London 2000, 3-19.

Eeckhout, P. (1997), The Domestic Legal Status of the WTO Agreement: Interconnecting Legal Systems, CMLRev. 1997, 11-58.

Griller, S. (2000a), Das Government Procurement Agreement als Bestandteil des Europarechts und des nationalen Rechts, in *Rill, H.P./Griller, S.* (eds.), Grundfragen der öffentlichen Auftragsvergabe, Wien 2000, 79-206.

Griller, S. (2000b), Enforceability of WTO Law in the European Union. Annotation to Case C-149/96, *Portugal* v. *Council*, JIEL 2000, 441-472.

Griller, S. (2002), Die gemeinsame Handelspolitik nach Nizza - Ansätze eines neuen Außenwirtschaftsrechts? in *Griller, S./Hummer, W.* (eds.), Die EU nach Nizza. Ergebnisse und Perspektiven, Wien 2002.

Griller, S./Droutsas, D.P./Falkner, G./Forgó, K./Nentwich, M. (2000), The Treaty of Amsterdam. Facts, Analysis, Prospects, Wien 2000.

Hahn, M.J. (1996), Eine kulturelle Bereichsausnahme im Recht der WTO? ZaöRV 1996, 315-352.

Heliskoski, J. (2000), Internal Struggle for International Presence: The Exercise of Voting Rights Within the FAO, in *Dashwood, A./Hillion, C.* (eds.), The General Law of E.C. External Relations, London 2000, 79-99.

Herrmann, C. (2001), Vom misslungenen Versuch der Neufassung der gemeinsamen Handelspolitik durch den Vertrag von Nizza, EuZW 2001, 269-274.

Jarass, H.D. (1996), Die Kompetenzverteilung zwischen der Europäischen Gemeinschaft und den Mitgliedstaaten, AöR 1996, 173-199.

Krenzler, H.G. (1999), Außenwirtschaftsrecht, in *Grabitz, E./Hilf, M.* (eds.), Das Recht der Europäischen Union, 13th instalment, München 1999.

Krenzler, H.G./da Fonseca-Wollheim, H. (1998), Die Reichweite der gemeinsamen Handelspolitik nach dem Vertrag von Amsterdam - eine Debatte ohne Ende? EuR 1998, 223-241.

Lenaerts, K./De Smijter, E. (1997), The European Community's Treaty-Making Competence, in YEL 1996 (1997), 1-57.

McGoldrick, D. (1997), International Relations Law of the European Union, London 1997.

Neuwahl, N. (2000), The WTO Opinion and Implied External Powers of the Community - A Hidden Agenda? in *Dashwood, A./Hillion, C.* (eds.), The General Law of E.C. External Relations, London 2000, 139-151.

O'Keeffe, D. (1998), Book review of *McGoldrick, D.*, International Relations Law of the European Union, CMLRev. 1998, 1455-1457.

Rebhahn, R. (2000), Art 136 EGV, in *Schwarze, J.* (ed.), EU-Kommentar, Baden-Baden 2000.

Rosas, A. (2000), The European Union and Mixed Agreements, in *Dashwood, A./Hillion, C.* (eds.), The General Law of E.C. External Relations, London 2000, 200-220.

Tietje, C. (2000), vor Art. 302-304 EGV, in *Grabitz, E./Hilf, M.* (eds.), Das Recht der Europäischen Union, 15th instalment, München 2000.

Tomuschat, Ch. (1997), Art 228 EGV, in *von der Groeben, H./Thiesing, J./Ehlermann, C.-D.* (eds.), Kommentar zum EU-/EG-Vertrag, volume V, 5th edition, Baden-Baden 1997.

Torrent, C. (2000), The "Fourth Pillar" of the European Union After The Amsterdam Treaty, in *Dashwood, A./Hillion, C.* (eds.), The General Law of E.C. External Relations, London 2000, 221-235.

Vedder, C. (2001), Art 133 EGV, in *Grabitz, E./Hilf, M.* (eds.), Das Recht der Europäischen Union, 17th instalment, München 2001.

Zimmermann, A./Martenczuk, B. (2000), Art 181 EGV, in *Schwarze, J.* (ed.), EU-Kommentar, Baden-Baden 2000.

Zuleeg, M. (1997), Art 3b EGV, in *von der Groeben, H./Thiesing, J./Ehlermann, C.-D.* (eds.), Kommentar zum EU-/EG-Vertrag, volume V, 5th edition, Baden-Baden 1997.

Anita Lukaschek/Birgit Weidel

Exclusive External Competence of the European Community

I. Preface

As a matter of principle, the European Community disposes of competence to act only in areas where powers have been conferred upon it by the Treaty establishing the European Community (TEC) in pursuance of the objectives assigned to it therein[1]. The numerous TEC provisions bestowing the Community with such competences do not indicate which type of competence has been established. Legal doctrine has developed three main categories of competence – exclusive, concurrent and complementary.[2]

Whereas concurrent or potential[3] competence prevents Member States from taking unilateral action provided that the Community has already enacted legislation, exclusivity requires a general avoidance of Member States action in a particular field of action even in the absence of Community law. This far-reaching limitation of national sovereignty explains the considerable resistance which attempts to conclude international agreements on the basis of exclusive Community competence have encountered.

External exclusivity can flow directly from the TEC or result from the Community's exhaustive law making activity in areas of internal concurrent competence. There are few examples of the former type of external exclusivity. The present article endeavours to discuss these rare cases of an exclusive Community competence directly derived from express TEC provisions. Due to its practical importance, particular attention is dedicated to the Community's Common Commercial Policy (CCP). In addition, the article

1 Article 5 para 1 TEC.

2 Compare *Griller/Gamharter* at 69 with further references and explanations on the inconsistency in the terminology and meaning of the third category of competence – herein referred to as "complementary".

3 *Gilsdorf* (1996) 150.

examines the Common Fisheries Policy (CFP), the fixing of exchange rates and the conclusion of Association Agreements.

II. The Common Commercial Policy – Reflections on the Current State of Play and Future Perspectives

A. Introductory Remarks

Due to the vagueness that characterises the TEC provisions governing the CCP, it was principally left to the European Court of Justice (ECJ) to shed light on the notion of this policy. The ECJ has often had the opportunity to pronounce on this issue as, given its political importance, CCP has been frequently the subject of inter-institutional conflicts or disputes between the Community and its Member States. Trade policy measures have become pivotal instruments of foreign policy, an area which lies at the very heart of national sovereignty. Apart from political aspects, the ECJ's varying jurisprudence attracted extra-ordinary attention in academic writing. The aim of this contribution is to provide a concise presentation of the status quo of the debate on the scope and nature of CCP.

B. The ECJ's Concept of Article 133 TEC

The reasons for the intense academic debate on this jurisprudence is that in its early judgments on CCP, the ECJ combined exclusivity with an extensive interpretation of the scope of CCP. Two decades later, showing a much more pragmatic attitude, it revised its expansive jurisprudence in its famous opinion on the WTO[4]. Whilst abiding to the exclusive nature of former Art 113 (now Art 133 TEC)[5], the ECJ set clear limitations to the ambit of CCP. This section will briefly outline the development and the central arguments of the ECJ jurisprudence.

1. The Exclusive Character of CCP

The CCP was the first Community policy to which the ECJ ascribed an exclusive character flowing directly from the Treaty. In its *Opinion on the Understanding on a Local Cost Standard*, the ECJ affirmed the Community's competence to conclude an agreement concerning credits for the financing of local costs. Examining the concept of CCP, the ECJ pointed at the intrinsic link

---

4 Opinion 1/94, *WTO*, [1994] ECR I-5267.

5 For reasons of simplicity, we will subsequently only refer to the new numbering introduced by the Treaty of Amsterdam.

between the operation of the Common Market and the necessity to adapt particular interests of Member States to each other in order to defend the common interests of the Community. These considerations lead the ECJ to the conclusion that the concept of CCP excludes unilateral action on part of the Member States. Granting a concurrent competence, which allows Member States to pursue their interests separately, would inevitably entail the risk of compromising the effective defence of the common interests of the Community. Allowing Member States to adopt positions differing from the viewpoint of the Community would "distort the institutional framework, call into question the mutual trust within the Community and prevent the latter from fulfilling its task in the defence of the common interest"[6]. In the *Donckerwolcke* case the ECJ reaffirmed the full transfer of responsibility to the Community in the area of CCP and purported that national commercial policy measures may only be adopted on the basis of a specific Community authorisation[7].

The position that the ECJ adopted on the nature of the Community's competence in commercial matters in these early days remains the status quo. Subsequent case law concerning CCP has maintained the principle of exclusivity.

2. The Expansive Character of CCP

The second element that characterised the early jurisprudence on CCP was the broad interpretation the ECJ gave to this policy. The cornerstone of this approach was laid in its opinion on a commodity agreement negotiated under the auspices of UNCTAD concerning Natural Rubber[8]. Despite the fact that the rubber agreement – due to the prominence of development policy aspects – differed significantly from traditional commercial agreements, it was deemed to fall within the ambit of Art 133 TEC. The ECJ explicitly dismissed any interpretation which would "restrict the common commercial policy to the use of instruments intended to have an effect only on the traditional aspects of external trade to the exclusion of more highly developed mechanisms...".[9] Art 133 TEC must be understood "from a wide point of view and not only having

6 Opinion 1/75, *Local Cost Standard,* [1975] ECR 1355 at 1364.

7 Case 41/76, *Donckerwolcke,* [1976] ECR 1921, para 32.

8 Opinion 1/78 *International Agreement on Natural Rubber*, [1979] ECR 2871.

9 Ibid, para 44.

regard to administration of precise systems such as customs and quantitative restrictions"[10]. The enumeration contained in Art 133 TEC is conceived as non-exhaustive and does not exclude the application of this provision to "any other process intended to regulate external trade".[11] If the Community were not in the position to avail itself of more elaborate means, it would not be possible to carry on any worthwhile common commercial policy.[12] Again the ECJ drew a link to the operation of the common market and warned of potential distortions of internal trade that a restrictive interpretation would entail.[13] In the GSP case[14], the ECJ complemented these arguments by stating that the TEC provisions governing CCP took possible changes into account. According to the ECJ, the reference in Art 131 TEC to the harmonious development of world trade presupposes an adaptation of CCP to changes in international relations.[15]

3. The Shift in Opinion 1/94

Obviously this open concept allowed for an expansive application of Art 133 TEC. Combined with the doctrine of exclusivity, the ECJ's findings resulted in an extremely wide competence for the Community in the field of external relations. In such a politically sensitive area, this approach was rather unpopular with national governments anxious to preserve their sovereign authority in the external sphere.[16] However, this jurisprudence was also criticised in academic writing, for example, *Gilsdorf* observed that the concept of exclusivity was not imperative for non-traditional areas of commercial policy. Interestingly he predicted already in 1989 that insistence on the exclusive nature of CCP would risk restrictions on the scope of that policy.[17]

The turning point came in 1994 with the Opinion on the WTO[18], when, by excluding certain types of services and almost the entire area of intellectual property from the scope of Art 133 TEC, the

---

[10] Para 45.
[11] Para 45.
[12] Para 44.
[13] Para 45.
[14] Case 45/86, *Commission v Council,* [1987] ECR 1493.
[15] Case 45/86, *Commission v Council,* [1987] ECR 1493, para 19.
[16] See also *López Escudero* (1999) 1162 and 1171.
[17] *Gilsdorf* (1989) 197 and 198.
[18] Opinion 1/94, *WTO*, [1994] ECR I-5267.

ECJ set clear boundaries to the scope of CCP. Albeit reaffirming "the open nature of the common commercial policy"[19] as a basic premise of its observations, the ECJ's findings constitute a de facto abandonment of its non-restrictive interpretation. Whereas considerations on effectiveness and the functioning of the Common Market have once prompted the ECJ to an unrestricted interpretation, the "overall scheme of the Treaty"[20] served as the main argument to confine the scope of CCP in the WTO-Opinion.

4. CCP – the External Dimension of the Common Market?

As becomes apparent from the early jurisprudence concerning CCP, the operation of Common Market has played a central role for the definition of the scope and nature of Art 133 TEC. The unimpaired functioning of intra-Community trade influenced the ECJ's findings on the *scope* of CCP.[21] Apart from that, it served as the main argument to support the *exclusive nature* of CCP.[22]

Undeniably there exists an intrinsic link between an internal market without frontiers that also covers the free movement of goods imported from third countries with a uniform external commercial regime. The realisation and effective functioning of this Common Market does not only require harmonisation and the abolition of trade barriers at internal level but also depends on a uniform regime concerning economic relations with third countries. In *Donckerwolcke*, the ECJ highlighted this conditionality by stating that "the assimilation of products imported from third countries may only take full effect, if these goods are subject to the same conditions of import ... irrespective of the States in which they were put in free circulation"[23]. In the absence of such a common external regime differences in national commercial policies can lead to deflections of trade or cause economic difficulties in certain Member States.[24]

---

19 See para 41.

20 Para 42.

21 Cf. Opinion 1/78, *International Agreement on Natural Rubber*, [1979] ECR 2871, para 45.

22 Compare Opinion 1/75, *Local Cost Standard*, [1975] ECR 1355, at 1363-1364.

23 Case 41/76, *Donckerwolcke*, [1976] ECR 1921, para 25.

24 Cf para 27 of the judgment.

With the completion of the Single Market, discussions started whether the scope of CCP went beyond the external complement of the customs union.[25] This debate arose against the background of important developments at international level in this area. In the course of the Uruguay Round the concept of trade underwent a significant expansion. Matters dealt with were no longer limited to quotas and customs tariffs but concerned trade in services, the protection of intellectual property and all kind of non-tariff barriers – aspects likewise essential for the completion of the Single Market. In the light of the intimate interconnection it was argued that CCP does not only cover trade in goods but should be conceived as the external dimension of the entire Common Market. The question how far aspects of the Common Market should be reflected in the scope of CCP has been subject to intense legal studies.[26] Ultimately the answer has been given by the ECJ with its Opinion on the WTO in which it implicitly rejected the idea of congruence between the ample scope of the Common Market and that of CCP. In contrast to prior judgments, the ECJ did not consider the operability of the Common Market when it examined the application of Art 133 TEC to services. Rather it analysed the scope of CCP from a wider angle by taking into account the limits set to this policy by the general structure of the TEC.[27] In this way, the ECJ has not dismissed or denied the existence of a link between CCP and the Common Market. It just highlighted that the Common Market itself is not enshrined as a uniform concept in the TEC but consists of various TEC provisions governed by very different procedures. Given this non-uniformity at the internal level, it does not appear consistent to maintain such uniformity for the external sphere. Coherently CCP cannot be defined as the legal basis for regulating all external relations of the Common Market.

One aspect should be added in this context: In any event, it would be mistaken to limit the rationale of CCP to an external harmonisation competence, as that does not perfectly mirror its actual field of application. Commercial policy also includes measures which do not have a counterpart in the internal regime like protective measures. Notwithstanding the obvious links

---

25 *Jacobs* (1996) 3f.

26 See, for example *Eeckhout* (1993).

27 Cf Opinion 1/94, *WTO*, [1994] ECR I-5267, para 42.

between internal and external aspects of the Common Market, Art 133 TEC inheres a certain autonomy.

The *exclusive nature* of CCP also emanates from the need to preserve the functionality of the Common Market.[28] The logic behind the ECJ's reasoning is clear: If Member States were allowed to follow their own (unharmonised) commercial policies with regard to third countries by e.g. imposing national import restrictions, this would certainly lead to deflections of trade, distort competition on the internal plane and thereby impair the functioning and unity of the common market. Exclusivity at the external sphere thus serves as an essential complement for the efficiency of internal harmonisation. Under these aspects, the recognition of an exclusive Community competence by the ECJ is well justified. However, in a number of areas, internal harmonisation has not been completed or proceeded until today. If the undistorted functioning of a Common Market is not even ensured at the internal plane, there is no need for exclusivity to protect it against potential harms caused by unilateral and inconsistent national trade policy measures. An imperative need to ensure the functionality of the Common Market by an exclusive external regime thus only arises in the event of the existence of an internal common regime which could be distorted by inharmonious national action.

C. The Scope of Article 133 Revisited

Kept in rather general terms, the effective TEC provisions governing the CCP do not provide much guidance to define the ambit of that area. According to Art 131 (ex-Art 110) TEC, the harmonious development of world trade, the abolition of trade restrictions and the reduction of customs barriers constitute the objectives of CCP. Apart from providing a non-exhaustive list of measures, Art 133 TEC, the core provision of that policy, only adds that CCP "shall be based on uniform principles". The enumeration in Art 133 TEC refers to concrete instruments like tariff changes, but also contains very general formulas like "measures of liberalisation". Despite this editorial inconsistency, it can be inferred that CCP covers tariff measures, quantitative restrictions, export policy, anti-dumping, anti-subsidy and other protective measures as well as the conclusion of tariff and trade agreements.

---

28 Compare Opinion 1/75, *Local Cost Standard*, [1975] ECR 1355, at 1363-1364.

This provision also indicates that commercial policy is formed by the combination and interaction of two main components, namely unilateral internal or "autonomous" measures and external or conventional measures i.e. agreements. The ECJ has confirmed this classification and underlined that none of these components enjoys priority over the other.[29] The TEC provisions do not offer further indicators for the specification of the content of CCP.

It thus has to be ascertained along the guidelines established by the case-law of the ECJ, whether a measure is covered by the scope of Art 133 TEC. The qualification as a CCP measure depends on various complementary, mutually conditional or even concurrent elements. The following chapters endeavour to structure these elements developed by the ECJ's jurisprudence on CCP, which is, in view of the complexity of the issue, a difficult venture. An additional difficulty arises from the fact that many cases examined by the ECJ with regard to the scope of Art 133 TEC concerned conventional instruments comprising a set of measures which were eventually not deemed to fall within the scope of CCP because of their material complexity. Drawing general assumptions from judgments concerning such comprehensive instruments is problematic and not always instructive.

The definition of CCP's scope deployed here is divided in three main steps.

First, the notion of trade policy has to be defined with respect to its subjects (subject-orientated approach). Does trade only concern the exchange of goods or does it also include other economic factors like services or human capital? In this context, it also has to be examined whether the specific nature of a subject can exclude it from the scope of CCP, be it that by virtue of specific rules (e.g. for agricultural products) or by virtue of the subject's characteristics (e.g. arms or weapons).

The second step consists of identifying the general character of a trade policy measure and the different instruments available to regulate trade.

Third, it has to be clarified whether the specific aim of a trade policy measure can constitute a decisive aspect for the applicability of Article 133 TEC. This goal-orientated approach seeks to delimit the ambit of CCP by focusing on the intention and the overall objective of a commercial policy measure.

---

[29] Opinion 1/75, *Local Cost Standard*, [1975] ECR 1355, at 1363.

It must be noted that these approaches bear mutually conditional elements: The subject orientated scope delimitation also draws on purposive elements in order to identify the various subjects coming within the scope of CCP whereas the goal-focused determination of the extent and scope of a CCP already presupposes the trade instruments to be identified. Consequently, the considerations in the next chapters cannot always follow a clear-cut distinction.

1. The Scope of Article 133 under a Subject-Orientated View

In a first step, it has to be identified, what can be the subject of international trade. In view of the undeniable link between CCP and the Common Market, it is tempting to look at the systematics established in the latter context. According to the TEC, the internal market consists of four main components: goods, persons pursuing a professional activity (workers and self-employed persons), services and capital. It must be clear from the outset that the attempt to draw parallels between the Common Market and the international conception of trade bears important limitations with regard to the specific objectives of Community. Undoubtedly, the grade of economic integration that the Community endeavours to achieve inter alia by realising a single market, goes far beyond the interconnection of economic relationships existing on a global level. However, the reference to the Common Market appears nevertheless quite helpful as it serves as a starting point for the investigation how far these four elements – if reflected in the concept of world trade – also come within the notion of the CCP. The WTO Opinion is certainly the most elusive judgment the ECJ gave in this respect.

a) Trade in Goods

As far as *goods* are concerned, there is certainly no need to discuss the general question of applicability of Art 133 TEC. From its very beginning, international trade has been related to the product sector. Doubts only existed whether the special character of a product can exclude it from the scope of CCP. The WTO opinion brought final clarification to most of these uncertainties.

Opinion 1/75 already dealt with the issue of Art 71 ECSC Treaty, according to which Member States' competence in commercial matters remains unaffected by the ECSC Treaty. The ECJ held that this provision cannot render inoperative the TEC provisions vesting the Community with the power to conclude international agreements in the realm of CCP.[30] The question whether ECSC products also come within the ambit of Art 133 TEC was not specifically addressed in this ruling. In the WTO Opinion, the ECJ held that coal and steel products are not per se excluded from the scope of CCP. According to the ECJ, an external agreement of a general nature which encompasses all types of goods can only be concluded by the Community. The Member States' competence laid down in Art 71 ECSC Treaty only refers to agreements specifically concerning steel and coal products.[31] Nuclear products are generally encompassed by the CCP. Since the Euratom Treaty does not contain specific rules relating to external trade, the TEC's commercial regime is applicable.[32]

Another issue of disagreement was the treatment of agricultural products. According to the ECJ, this product sector, albeit obtaining a special position in the TEC itself, does not automatically fall outside the ambit of Art 133 TEC. The ECJ based its reasoning on the fact that the purpose of the Agreement on Agriculture was the establishment of a fair and market-orientated trading system on a world-wide basis – an objective which does not belong to the goals of Common Agricultural Policy (CAP) set out in former Art 39 (now: Art 33) TEC. The fact that implementing measures might have to be based on Art 37 (ex-Art 43) does not prevent the adoption of international obligations on the basis of Art 133 TEC.[33]

Obviously the nature or specific features of a product are irrelevant for application of Art 133 TEC. This conclusion is supported by statements in other ECJ's rulings related to the specific character of products. In Opinion 1/78, the ECJ rejected the idea that the political importance of a product can be a reason for

---

[30] Opinion 1/75, *Local Cost Standard*, [1975] ECR 1355, at 1365.

[31] Opinion 1/94, *WTO*, [1994] ECR I-5267, para 27.

[32] Opinion 1/94, *WTO*, [1994] ECR I-5267, para 24.

[33] Opinion 1/94, *WTO*, [1994] ECR I-5267, para 29. The ECJ was obviously led by goal-orientated considerations when answering the question whether a product which is subject of a specific Community policy could nonetheless be covered by a CCP measure. In our systematic, we propose to leave goal-orientated reflections aside in the first step of identifying the subjects of CCP. Whether the specific objective of a measure excludes the applicability of Art 133 TEC should only be considered in the third stage.

excluding it from the domain of CCP.[34] Similarly in the *Leifer*-case concerning dual-use products, the ECJ affirmed that the foreign policy nature of these products cannot take them outside the scope of CCP.[35] Consequently the whole range of products is covered by CCP.[36] The only restriction in the goods sector might result from the exemption established in Art 296 TEC concerning trade in arms. However, this exception is to be understood as a general authorisation to derogate from TEC rules and does not as such preclude a priori the adoption of Community measures.[37] Hence, also arms are in principle not excluded from the scope of CCP.

b) Trade in Services

The status of *services* was one of the main issues raised in the WTO-Opinion. As the Commission pointed out, the export of services plays a dominant role in trade relationships of developed countries. In the light of the emerging importance of the service sector in international transactions and the open-ended nature that the ECJ has ascribed to the concept of CCP, the question was whether it would subscribe to an interpretation of CCP including trade in services. It is well known that the ECJ endorsed this view advocated by the Commission only to a very limited extent. Referring to the classification of services undertaken in the GATS (General Agreement on Trade in Services), the ECJ held that – due to their similarity with trade in goods – only cross frontier supplies, which do not involve the transboundary movement of persons, fall within the ambit of CCP.[38] In contrast consumption abroad, commercial presence and presence of natural persons necessarily entail the crossing of external frontiers by third country nationals. The existence of a specific TEC chapter concerning the free movement of persons and the distinction in Art 3 TEC between CCP and "measures concerning the entry and movement of persons" excludes these types of services from the concept of CCP.[39] Relying on the same argument – the existence of a specific TEC title on transport – the ECJ rejected the application of Art 133

---

34 Opinion 1/78 *International Agreement on Natural Rubber*, [1979] ECR 2871, para 49.

35 Case C-83/94, *Leifer*, [1995] ECR I-3231, para 11.

36 *López Escudero* (1999) 1167.

37 *Grabitz/von Bogdandy/Nettesheim* (1994) 26.

38 Opinion 1/94, *WTO*, [1994] ECR I-5267, para 44.

39 Opinion 1/94, *WTO*, [1994] ECR I-5267, paras 45-47.

TEC to transport services. It recalled its *ERTA* judgment[40], which concerned the transport sector, and the doctrine of implied external competence established therein. The logic that the ECJ applied in that case – the idea that external competence does not only arise from an express conferment in the Treaty, but can be derived from other TEC provisions like those on transport – is based on the assumption that transport matters are not covered by the scope of CCP.[41] In contrast to goods, the ECJ has hence adopted a more restrictive approach on services. Furthermore, it should be noted that the TEC does not qualify "commercial presence", which is defined as permanent establishment in another country, as a mode to supply services but regulates this aspect in its chapter on free movement of persons.

c) Trade and the Movement of Persons

The integration of *persons* into the concept of the Common Market is a specific feature of the Community, which aims to create an area without internal frontiers that also comprises the free movement of persons. The mobility of human capital encouraged by the design of the TEC is certainly not reflected in international trade relationships. Questions concerning the transboundary movement of persons are only subject of the international trade regime to the extent to which they are linked to the supply of services. With the exception of cross frontier supplies, the modes of supplying services defined in GATS necessarily imply the crossing of borders either by the supplier or the consumer of a service. However, the focus lies on removing obstacles to the supply of services and not on the movement of persons as such. GATS is not applicable to measures affecting persons seeking access to the employment market and measures regarding citizenship, residence or employment on a permanent basis. The parties are not prevented from regulating the entry of persons or their temporary stay, as long as they do not nullify or impair the benefits under a specific commitment.[42] In this respect GATS obligations exercise an

---

40 Case 22/70, *ERTA*, [1971] ECR 263.

41 Paras 48-53. On the apparent inconsistencies with the ECJ's findings concerning agricultural products see for example *Tridimas/Eeckhout* (1994) 162-163; *Bourgeois* (1995) 776; *Dutheil de la Rochère* (1995) 465.

42 See GATS, paras 2 and 4 of the Annex on Movement of Natural Persons Supplying Services under the Agreement.

influence on the rules concerning the transboundary movement of persons.

Summing up, the movement of persons or human capital to the extent to which it is enshrined in the TEC is generally excluded from the notion of international trade. However insofar as the crossing of borders by persons is a precondition for the supply of services, certain aspects are necessarily covered by the international regime. As already outlined in the section on services, the interpretation the ECJ has adopted in this respect does not correspond to the international concept of trade. Services entailing the movement of persons are precluded from the ambit of CCP.

d) The Flow of Capital

The WTO-Opinion has not addressed the question whether the scope of CCP also includes the movement of *capital*. In the *Centro-Com* case[43], the ECJ had the opportunity to clarify some aspects of this question: Financial transfers constituting the payment for the supply of goods or services (if covered by Art. 133 TEC) are considered as necessary adjuncts to the export or import of services or goods and thus come within the ambit of Art 133 TEC.[44] The relationship between CCP and free movement of capital has not yet been subject to the ECJ's jurisprudence.

Whereas financial services are considered as a special type of services[45] in the global context, the Common Market regime draws a distinction between free movement of services and free movement of capital. In the light of the importance the ECJ attached to the existence of a specific TEC chapter in its WTO-Opinion, it is generally assumed in literature that the movement of capital (as defined by the TEC) escapes entirely from the scope of CCP.[46] This argument is supported by the fact that the relevant TEC provisions

43 Case C-124/95, *Centro-Com*, [1997] ECR I-81, para 41.

44 *Gilsdorf* (1989) 205; *Vedder* (2001) 20. On the theory of necessary adjunct see also *Lukaschek* in this volume at 335.

45 Financial services comprised and defined in the GATS include insurance and insurance related services as well as banking and other financial services (for example: credits, money transmission services, trading with options, foreign exchange, cheques or transferable securities, asset management etc.) See GATS, para 5 of the Annex on financial services.

46 *Vedder* (2001) 20 with further references.

specifically refer to the transfer of capital to third countries.[47] In contrast to services, the entire field of capital movement – including cross-frontier transfers – is excluded from Art 133 TEC. This leads to a rather complicated situation concerning the banking and insurance sector: Financial services provided by these institutions frequently involve the movement of capital, which is covered by the rules of the TEC chapter on capital and payments.[48] An additional complication results from the lack of an exhaustive definition of capital movement. According to the non-exhaustive enumeration in Directive 88/361[49], certain direct investments, investments in real estate, transactions in securities, credits, loans, guarantees, transfers in performance of certain insurance contracts, the physical transfer of financial and real capital and other operations have to be regarded as movement of capital. An important feature is the investment character of such transfers.[50] Direct investments related to the provision of services or the establishment in the territory of another Member State fall outside the scope of Chapter 4 TEC.[51]

The consequence of the exclusion of capital movements from the scope of CCP is a further restriction of the service sector covered by CCP. Financial services, even if they do not involve the movement of persons, fall outside the scope of CCP, as soon as they are linked with the transfer of capital.

The result of this survey on the potential subject matters of CCP measures can be summarised as follows: Whereas goods are generally covered by Art 133 TEC, services do only come within its ambit, if they are not related to transport and do neither involve the movement of persons nor the transfer of capital for investment purposes. On this basis, it has to be established which instruments are at disposal to regulate trade relations concerning these matters.

---

47 *Grabitz/von Bogdandy/Nettesheim* (1994) 31.

48 *Knobl* (1992) 29; *Servais* (1995) 33; *Usher* (2000) 11f.

49 See Annex I of Directive 88/361/EEC of the Council for the implementation of Article 67 of the Treaty, OJ L 178, 8.7.1988, 5.

50 *Bröhmer* (1999) 740 and 742; *Usher* (2000) 11f. See also Cases 286/82 and 26/83, *Luisi and Carbone*, [1984] ECR 377.

51 Being linked with modes of service supply, which entail the crossing of borders by third country nationals, also these types of foreign direct investment are excluded from the scope Art 133 TEC.

2. The Identification of Trade Instruments

The distinguishing aspect of a CCP measure, as opposed to other rules governing economic relations, is its transboundary character: A measure will only constitute a trade policy measure, if it provides instruments and procedures which regulate Community trade *with third countries*. Measures which regulate the exchange of products or economic relations in a general way – without making distinctions between intra-Community trade and external trade – cannot be qualified as trade policy measures, as they lack the transfrontier element. In line with this reasoning, the ECJ has denied the applicability of Art 133 TEC to the TRIPS Agreement in its opinion on the WTO. Albeit recognising the inter-linkage between intellectual property aspects and trade in goods, the ECJ pointed out that intellectual property is not a special phenomenon of international trade but equally concerns internal trade.[52] The argumentation employed shows goal-orientated aspects: The ECJ stated that the rationale of TRIPs is not to regulate the external trade and to protect the market from distortions but predominantly aims at a general strengthening and harmonisation of intellectual property rights. Save a small number of border measures, the agreement principally deals with measures which similarly concern internal and external trade. For this reason the agreement could not be classified as a trade policy measure.

Subsequently, trade specific instruments will be identified. The description starts with those instruments, the commercial character of which is undisputed. According to Art 133 TEC, CCP comprises changes in tariff rates and the conclusion of tariff agreements. However, the TEC contains another provision dealing with customs matters, namely Art 26 (ex Art 28) TEC, which provides for the fixing of Common Customs Tariff duties. Since decision-making under both provisions follows the same rules, the question of the legal base is politically uncontroversial. Law-making practice shows a finalist approach: Whereas Art 26 TEC provides the legal basis for autonomous tariff changes pursuing internal Community policy objectives, (additional) recourse to Art 133 TEC is made, when these changes are (also) motivated by commercial considerations.[53] The question of demarcation extends to the entire area of customs legislation. Since 1992 Community customs law is

---

[52] Opinion 1/94, WTO, [1994] ECR 5267 para 57.

[53] *Vedder* (2001) para 50.

consolidated in the Community Customs Code[54], which has been adopted on the bases of Arts 28, 133 and 95 (ex-Art 100a) TEC.

Commercial defence instruments aim to protect Community producers from economic detriments caused by unfair trade practices or trade barriers implemented in third countries. This category includes antidumping and anti-subsidies measures and the new commercial policy instrument.[55]

Measures promoting exports to third countries also come within the domain of CCP. Due to the far-reaching restrictions imposed by GATT and the absence of a harmonised Community system for export aids, this sector lacks practical importance.[56]

Measures limiting or prohibiting the export or import of goods are typical trade policy instruments. Due to the liberalisation achieved by the GATT, quantitative restrictions have largely been abolished in the Community system.[57] However, measures of liberalisation, which figure on the non-exhaustive list of Art 133 TEC are not limited to these trade barriers. A number of obstacles to trade do not arise from quantitative restrictions but other measures having an equivalent effect. In many cases, the overall rationale pursued might be detached from purely commercial considerations. Frequently, trade measures simply constitute instruments for the exercise of other policies. Whether and under which circumstances these measures fall within the ambit of Art 133 TEC is the subject of the next chapter.

---

[54] Council Regulation 2913/92 establishing the Community Customs Code OJ L 302, 19.10.1992, 1.

[55] For more details see *Vedder* (2001) paras 118ff.

[56] *Vedder* (2001) para 148. The agricultural sector constitutes certainly an exception to that statement. Export refunds paid to the exporters of agricultural products are integral parts of the Common Market Organisations adopted in the framework of the Common Agricultural Policy and do not fall within the scope of Art 133 TEC.

[57] Certain restrictions still exist for the import of textiles. See *Vedder* (2001) para 105. In the export sector, restrictions concern, for example, dual use goods and certain products of strategic importance (i.e. crude oil). *Vedder* (2001) paras 99ff. Furthermore the Community is empowered to adopt safeguard measures in economically critical situations. See Art 16 of Council Regulation (EC) No 3285/94 on the common rules for imports OJ L 349, 31.12.1994, 53 and Arts 6 and 7 Council Regulation 2603/69 establishing common rules for exports, OJ L 324, 27.12.1969, 25.

3. A Goal-Orientated Scope Delimitation

As noted at the outset, the identification of the subjects and instruments falling within the ambit of CCP is only one step in delimiting the scope of Art 133 TEC. Even if a subject or measure is in principle embraced by the "instrumental" or "subjective" scope of Article 133 TEC, the provision's applicability is not always beyond controversy. This is in particular the case, when objectives not pertaining to trade policy such as e.g. environmental policy, development policy or foreign policy objectives are followed by a classical trade policy instrument. The goal-orientated approach thus focuses on the question whether the use of those instruments under Article 133 is permissible only in pursuit of trade policy goals, or whether it is rather their objective aptitude to alter trade flows which suffices for their qualification as commercial policy instruments.

The question whether such "non-genuine" trade measures are nonetheless covered by Article 133 TEC has provoked a long-lasting discussion between the Community institutions focusing on two different approaches:

The subjective or purposive approach, supported by the Council, emphasises the aim of a trade policy measure, namely the one of altering or influencing the flow of trade. Any other (albeit only additional) aim pursued by a measure prevents it from falling within the scope of CCP. According to the Commission's opposing view, the fact that a measure objectively influences the flow of trade suffices to found an exclusive Community competence on the basis of Art133 TEC. (the so-called objective or instrumental approach). The fact that the autonomous measure or the trade agreement at issue actually serves ends of other policies does not alter its CCP nature.

The ECJ was first confronted with these contravening views when it had been requested to give its opinion on the Community's power to negotiate and conclude the Natural Rubber agreement, the purpose of which was closely linked with development policy considerations.[58] In this opinion, the ECJ fundamentally stated that it is not possible to adopt an interpretation of Art 133 TEC the effect of which would be to restrict the CCP to the use of instruments intended to have an effect only on the traditional

[58] Opinion 1/78, *International Agreement on Natural Rubber*, [1979] ECR 2871.

aspects of external trade to the exclusion of more highly developed mechanisms such as those in the agreement at issue. A "commercial policy" understood in that sense would be destined to become nugatory in the course of time. Albeit liberalisation of trade might have been the dominant idea at the time the TEC was drafted, it does not prevent the Community from developing a commercial policy aiming at a regulation of the world market for certain products rather than a mere liberalisation of trade.[59] Furthermore, a restrictive interpretation of CCP would risk causing disturbances in intra-Community trade by reason of the disparities which would then exist in certain sectors of economic relations with non-member countries.[60]

The ECJ thus acknowledged that non-commercial-policy objectives (in the case at issue, development policy aims) underlying a Community trade measure do not constitute a reason for precluding the use of Art 133 TEC as the legal base. This fundamental assumption can also be inferred from the decision in another case equally concerning a trade measure pursuing development-policy objectives.[61] The ECJ stressed the progressively stronger link between trade and development in modern international relations reflecting a new concept of international trade relations in which development aims play an increasingly role. It held that in defining the characteristics and the instruments of the common commercial policy, the Treaty took already into account possible changes as to the concept of common commercial policy and reiterated its reasoning in Opinion 1/78.[62]

The ECJ came to a similar conclusion when it had to qualify the status of trade policy measure pursuing foreign policy objectives. Stating that "Member States cannot treat national measures as falling outside the scope of CCP on the ground that they have foreign and security objectives"[63], the ECJ clearly opted for a instrumental approach. The decisive element accounting for the trade character of the measures at issue was the fact that the measures objectively prevented or restricted the export of certain

---

[59] Para 44.

[60] Para 45.

[61] Case 45/86, *GSP*, [1987] ECR 1483.

[62] Paras 17f.

[63] Case C-70/94, *Werner*, [1995] ECR I-3189, para 10.

products.[64] Again, the ECJ drew upon the arguments already established in Opinion 1/78, namely that the implementation of a common commercial policy required a non-restrictive interpretation of that concept in order to avoid disturbances in intra-Community trade caused by disparities existing in certain sectors of economic relations with non-member countries[65].

The pursuit of environment policy objectives by means of commercial policy measures was evaluated by the ECJ in the Chernobyl case[66]: The Greek government challenged the use of Art 133 TEC as the legal base for a regulation subjecting the release into free circulation of certain agricultural products originating in non-member countries to compliance with maximum permitted levels of radioactive contamination. According to the ECJ, the TEC provisions empowering the Community to take specific action on environmental matters leave intact the powers held by the Community under other provisions of the TEC, even if the measures to be taken under the latter provisions pursue at the same time any of the objectives of environmental policy. Stressing the horizontal character of environmental policy concerns and the requirements of environmental protection, the ECJ concluded that a Community measure cannot be part of Community action on environmental matters merely because it takes account of those requirements[67].

By contrast, a comprehensive environmental policy measure that bears inevitable side effects on trade which are only of secondary nature, shall not be concluded under Art 133 TEC. This conclusion has been confirmed by a recent opinion of the ECJ[68] on the question whether Art 133 TEC could serve as legal base for the conclusion of the Cartagena Protocol on Biosafety, which specifically focuses on the transboundary movement of living modified organisms (LMOs) resulting from modern biotechnology that may have

---

64 Case C-70/94, *Werner*, [1995] ECR I-3189 and Case C-83/94, *Leifer*, [1995] ECR I-3231. Compare also Case C-124/95, *Centro-Com*, [1997] ECR I-81 and Case T-184/95, *Dorsch Consult*, [1998] ECR II-667, para 74, concerning the embargo competence of the Community under ex-Art 113 TEC. See in this context *Lukaschek* at 329ff.

65 *Werner* and *Leifer*, both at para 9, referring to Opinion 1/78 of the Court [1979] ECR 2871, para 45.

66 Case C-62/88, *Hellenic Republic v Council*, [1990] ECR I-1527.

67 Paras 19 and 20.

68 Opinion 2/00, *Cartagena Protocol*, [2001] ECR I-9713.

adverse effect on the conservation and sustainable use of biological diversity. A central element of this Protocol is the establishment of the advance informed agreement procedure for transboundary movements of LMOs.

The ECJ rejected the use of Art 133 TEC as legal base on the grounds mentioned above and considered that, if accepted, it would effectively render nugatory the specific TEC provisions on environmental policy, for, as soon as it was established that EC action was liable to have repercussions on trade, the envisaged agreement would have to be placed in the category of agreements which fall within commercial policy[69]. The question considered in this context shows parallels to that considered in Opinion 1/94 in context with TRIPS. In both cases, the agreements have not been regarded as trade policy instrument for their rationale and predominant component does not relate to trade.

The main aspect dealt within the present section is slightly different: It concerns the case where a measure of a purely commercial nature (e.g. an import or export restriction) is adopted with an overall objective not related to trade. In such a constellation, the measure only provides a trade policy instrument to achieve the specific policy goal. With respect to this question it is sustained here that – in clear prevalence of an objective view – the fact that a measure is (even exclusively) destined to pursue non-commercial-policy goals, does not prevent it from coming within the scope of Article 133 TEC, if it has an objective influence on trade flows which exceeds the extent of inevitable repercussions. These objective effects thus prevail over potential Member States' prerogatives in other fields concerned by the measures' objectives if not safeguarded by Community law itself (e.g. by way of safeguard or derogation clauses).

In a number of cases, however, trade instruments are just an integral part of a comprehensive set of measures destined to achieve a specific non-commercial objective. Such integrated measures will not fall within the ambit of Art 133 TEC, even if the trade instruments play an essential role.[70] Frequently, such acts will also

---

69 See para 40 of the Opinion.

70 Cf the Cartagena Protocol: Undoubtedly the Advanced Informed Agreement mechanism for imports of LMOs constitutes the core element of this agreement with the highest practical importance. Nevertheless it is not the only element contributing to a safe handling

not pass the second stage of the test applied here, as they do not exclusively cover trans-frontier circumstances.

D. A Look into the Future - Art 133 TEC after the Nice Treaty

With the entry into force of the Nice Treaty, the scope of Art 133 TEC will appear in a different light. The main novelties have been brought about by new para 5 and the insertion of paras 6 and 7, which are reproduced subsequently:

Paragraphs 1 to 4 shall also apply to the negotiation and conclusion of agreements in the fields of trade in services and the commercial aspects of intellectual property, insofar as those agreements are not covered by the said paragraphs and without prejudice to paragraph 6.

By way of derogation from paragraph 4, the Council shall act unanimously when negotiating and concluding an agreement in one of the fields referred to in the first subparagraph, where that agreement includes provisions for which unanimity is required for the adoption of internal rules or where it relates to a field in which the Community has not yet exercised the powers conferred upon it by this Treaty by adopting internal rules.

The Council shall act unanimously with respect to the negotiation and conclusion of a horizontal agreement insofar as it also concerns the preceding subparagraph or the second subparagraph of paragraph 6.

This paragraph shall not affect the right of the Member States to maintain and conclude agreements with third countries or international organisations insofar as such agreements comply with Community law and other relevant international agreements.

6. An agreement may not be concluded by the Council if it includes provisions which would go beyond the Community's internal powers, in particular by leading to harmonisation of the laws or regulations of the Member States in an area for which this Treaty rules out such harmonisation.

In this regard, by way of derogation from the first subparagraph of paragraph 5, agreements relating to trade in cultural and audiovisual services, educational services, and social and human health services, shall fall within the shared competence of the Community and its Member States. Consequently, in addition to a Community decision taken in accordance with the relevant provisions of Article 300, the negotiation of such agreements shall require the common accord of the Member States.

---

of LMOs. Consequently it cannot be characterised as a trade policy instrument.

Agreements thus negotiated shall be concluded jointly by the Community and the Member States.

The negotiation and conclusion of international agreements in the field of transport shall continue to be governed by the provisions of Title V and Article 300.

7. Without prejudice to the first subparagraph of paragraph 6, the Council, acting unanimously on a proposal from the Commission and after consulting the European Parliament, may extend the application of paragraphs 1 to 4 to international negotiations and agreements on intellectual property insofar as they are not covered by paragraph 5.

For reasons of completeness it should be mentioned that para 3 has been amended by an obligation on the Council and the Commission to ensure that agreements are "compatible with internal Community policies and rules".[71] Furthermore, the Commission is now explicitly required to deliver a report on the progress of negotiations to the special committee.

1. Subject Matter Related Aspects

From a subject-orientated point of view, the scope of CCP appears to have undergone a significant reorientation. According to para 5, Art 133 TEC will henceforth extend to the negotiation and conclusion of agreements concerning trade in services and commercial aspects of intellectual property, as far as these agreements have not already been covered by CCP. The wording undoubtedly implies that this expansion does not include autonomous commercial policy measures.[72] Only *agreements* dealing with trade in services and intellectual property aspects can be concluded pursuant to Art 133 TEC. Secondary autonomous trade policy measures or measures implementing obligations arising from such agreements have to be based on those TEC provisions,

---

[71] A strict reading of this requirement would imply that agreements may not contravene existing Community law. Compare *Griller/Gamharter* 107 and *Herrmann* (2001) 274. According to *Krenzler/Pitschas*, this "conformity requirement" deals with substantial legal compatibility of trade agreements with internal law. In order to avoid a paralysis of foreign trade policy, the authors favour an interpretation which qualifies this provision as a special occurrence of the principle of conferred powers. Contradicting rules in existing Community legislation would have to be amended before the entry into force of the agreement. *Krenzler/Pitschas* (2001) 298f.

[72] *Herrmann* (2001) 271, *Griller/Gamharter* in this volume at 90.

which constitute the legal bases for internal action in the field of services and intellectual property.

The wording of para 5 subpara 1 suggests that the Treaty of Nice will put an end to the different treatment of *services* according to the distinction the ECJ has drawn in the WTO-Opinion. With the exception of the transport sector[73], the new version of Art 133 TEC seems to incorporate all types of services into the scope of CCP.[74] However, para 5 does neither contain a reference to the GATS nor a corresponding definition of the term "services". The fact that the TEC deploys a different notion of "services" than GATS raises serious doubts on whether the Nice version of Art 133 TEC actually covers the whole range of services as defined by GATS. Good reasons exist for the assumption that commercial presence, which is conceived as establishment in the TEC regime, remains outside the ambit of CCP.[75] Ultimately, the answer depends on whether the scope of CCP is to be defined in the light of the global context (hence WTO-orientated) or in conformity with the internal system set up by the TEC. It should be recalled in this context that the ECJ has taken both aspects into account. In the WTO-Opinion, systematic internal constraints have obviously trumped over an interpretation of CCP adapted to the global concept of trade. Given the ECJ's varying approach, the outcome is hard to predict. For reasons of consistency, an all-encompassing interpretation seems more favourable than the maintenance of the distinction between cross border supplies and other types of services. In any case, as will be discussed later, the concern for consistency cannot be met by the modifications of the Nice Treaty, since the distinction in the service sector still bears importance in another context.

In the area of intellectual property, only "commercial aspects" can constitute the subject of an agreement based on Art 133 TEC. Relying on the resemblance of this phrase with the "Agreement on Trade-related Aspects of Intellectual Property Rights (TRIPS)", some authors submit that this definition actually comprises the entire scope of TRIPs.[76] However, in the WTO-Opinion, the ECJ stressed the fact that TRIPs is aimed at *harmonising* the protection

---

73 See para 6, subpara 3.

74 Cf. *Vedder* (2001) 27 (para 60); *Krenzler/Pitschas* (2001) 302.

75 See *Griller/Gamharter* in this volume, 91ff.

76 *Krenzler/Pitschas* (2001) 302; *Vedder* (2001) para 60.

of intellectual property rights.[77] Its main argument for excluding the applicability of Art 133 TEC was the different procedure to be followed for a harmonisation at internal level, which provides for the participation of the European Parliament. As the new version of Art 133 TEC has not abolished this difference, considerable doubts remain on the complete integration of TRIPs into the scope of CCP.

Para 6 contains another restriction to the expansion of CCP. According to subpara 1, an agreement cannot be concluded "by the Council" pursuant to Art 133 TEC when the Community lacks the internal powers to regulate that area. This applies "in particular" to agreements entailing a harmonisation of areas, in which an internal Community competence to harmonise that field is excluded by virtue of the TEC.[78] The provision reflects the principle of parallelism of internal and external powers, the ECJ has adhered to in its WTO-Opinion. The rationale behind this idea is clear: The competence granted to the Community under CCP shall not be used in a manner to circumvent internal restrictions imposed on Community competence in other fields. Interestingly these additional limits[79] to the scope of CCP arising from internal constraints do obviously only apply to the "new areas" that para 5 has brought under the scope of Art 133. The wording of para 5

---

77 *Herrmann* (2001) 271.

78 The TEC rules out harmonisation in the areas of employment (Art 129 TEC), education (Art 149 and 150 TEC), culture (Art 151 TEC) and public health (Art 152). Furthermore the Art 137 (2) in the version of the Nice Treaty precludes harmonisation of certain aspects in the field of social policy.

79 In contrast to *Krenzler/Pitschas*, it is submitted that para 6 constitutes a genuine additional restriction of para 5. The authors consider para 6 as an ultra-vires prohibition, which corresponds more or less to the principle of conferred powers. In their eyes, the inclusion of this provision is superfluous and of merely declaratory character. See *Krenzler/Pitschas* (2001) 308f. However new para 5 has actually conferred powers on the Community to conclude trade agreements in services and intellectual property pursuant to Art 133. It constitutes a new separate legal basis for the conclusion of agreements in these areas. In the absence of para 6, the restrictions contained in the other parts of the TEC concerning the internal powers of the Community would not automatically apply to this provision. Consequently para 6 does not only have a declaratory character but imposes substantial limits to the interpretation of para 5.

indicates that para 6 is exclusively conceived as an exemption to para 5 and not to the entire scope of CCP.[80]

Subpara 2 qualifies the exception of para 6 with regard to services. Pursuant to this provision, agreements concerning trade in cultural, audiovisual, educational, social and human health services shall "in this regard" come under the shared competence of the Community and the Member States. The reference to subpara 1 ("in this regard"), which is obviously directed at the issue of harmonisation, implies that subpara 2 is construed as a specification or clarification of subpara 1. Hence agreements containing harmonisation measures related to services in the sectors mentioned are not totally excluded from the scope of CCP, but have to be concluded by both – the Community and the Member States.[81] In contrast, agreements harmonising commercial aspects of intellectual property in areas, the internal harmonisation of which is precluded by the TEC, cannot be concluded on the basis of Art 133 TEC.[82]

2. The Rebuff of Exclusivity

As outlined in the beginning, measures adopted on the basis of CCP fall within the exclusive competence of the Community. After the entry into force of the Treaty of Nice, this feature of Art 133 TEC will be a thing of the past. Pursuant to subpara 4 of para 5, the extension of CCP to services other than cross border supplies and to trade-related aspects of intellectual property does not affect the Member States' competence to conclude agreements as long as they comply with Community law. In essence, this represents an abandonment of the absolute exclusivity of the CCP. In areas falling within the scope of CCP by virtue of para 5, the Community's competence is no longer exclusive but concurrent.[83] In this respect, the different legal treatment in the service sector caused by the distinction between cross-border supplies, on the one hand, and consumption abroad, commercial presence and presence of natural persons, on the other, continues to exist. It will depend on the will of the Council whether the Community concludes solely a trade agreement concerning services. Furthermore, it has to be

---

80 See also *Hermann* (2001) 272.

81 Compare *Herrmann* (2001) 272; *Griller/Gamharter* in this volume, 99.

82 Due to the lack of implied competences in these areas, the Community is totally precluded from concluding such agreements.

83 In that sense *Herrmann* (2001) 272.

borne in mind that subpara 2 of para 6 has explicitly laid down a shared competence in case an agreement entails the harmonisation of trade in cultural, audiovisual, educational, social and human health services. Consequently, global agreements encompassing various types of services will have to be concluded as mixed agreements.

By virtue of para 7, the Council is empowered to extend the application of paras 1-4 by unanimous vote to "international negotiations and agreements on intellectual property insofar as they are not covered by para 5". In this case, the entire range of intellectual property – and not only commercial aspects – could be subject of an agreement concluded on the basis of Art 133 TEC. This stipulation resembles the current version of para 5, which provides for the possibility to bring agreements on services and intellectual property under the scope of CCP. However, the Council has never made use of this authorisation. Supposedly para 7 will suffer the same fate. In the absence of any reference to the limitations laid down in para 5, the provision appears to envisage the expansion of *exclusive* competence to agreements on intellectual property not embraced by para 5. Given the Member States' reticence to grant further powers to the Community in this area, it is most unlikely that such a decision will ever be adopted in the Council.

3. Further Issues and Evaluation

Apart from altering the scope and nature of Art 133 TEC, the Treaty of Nice has also introduced significant procedural changes applicable to the new areas of CCP, which shall be outlined here in short.[84] Instead of qualified majority voting, unanimity is required when corresponding internal rules have to be adopted by unanimity or the Community has not yet made use of its internal powers.[85] Likewise horizontal agreements concerning the aforementioned areas of cultural, audiovisual, educational, social and human health services have to be concluded and negotiated by unanimous vote.[86] Like the exception laid down in para 6, these requirements

---

[84] A detailed discussion on the new procedural rules can be found in this volume in *Griller/Gamharter* 102ff.

[85] See the second subpara of Art 133 (5) TEC in the version of the Nice Treaty.

[86] Subpara 3 of para 5.

demonstrate the intention of the drafters to establish a parallelism between the internal and external regime.

In a general evaluation of the revised Art 133 TEC, criticism has to be directed to the complex drafting, which stands in blatant contrast to the purported acknowledgement to the simplification and transparency of legislative texts. Vague formulations like "commercial aspects of intellectual property" give rise to additional uncertainties, which require further clarification. Apart from these editorial shortcomings, the innovative feature of this provision has to be put into question. Whilst new Art 133 TEC will amplify the scope of CCP, it will not expand the external powers of the Community. By establishing concurrent competences in the field of services and intellectual property, the revised version has done nothing else than creating additional powers parallel to those existing before pursuant to the doctrine of implied powers.[87]

The system established by paras 5 and 6 leads to two general observations. First, it must be regarded as a clear rejection of exclusive external Community competence. Thus the trend continues towards 'mixity' involving the joint participation of Member States and the Community in international agreements. Second, the link-up to intra-Community rules reflects an attempt to obtain a parallelism between internal and external powers and constraints. From the viewpoint of the Member States – but also from an interinstitutional point of view – this endeavour appears understandable, since all actors have a legitimate interest to safeguard their influence and competences concerning decision making on the internal plane. As the Community is bound to implement the commitments engaged in international treaties in the internal sphere, the decision-makers might be faced with the duty to adopt rules they would not have agreed on in the internal decision making process. Clearly their powers would be undermined by the duty to implement international obligations. The harmonisation procedures for the internal and external sphere prevents these kinds of problems. The disadvantage of this solution results from the complexity of internal competence distribution. This complicated system is hardly ascertainable for the outside world and might entail uncertainty and confusion for third countries about the identity and authority of their negotiation partner.

---

[87] See in detail *Griller/Gamharter*.

III. Common Fisheries Policy (CFP)

A. The Exclusive Character of CFP

Another policy field, where exclusive competence directly flows from primary Community law, is the CFP. The development of CFP and, in particular, its external aspects, dates back to the ECJ's findings in the *Kramer* case. As the relevant Treaty provisions concerning CFP do not make any reference to the external powers in this area, the ECJ had recourse to its doctrine of implied powers. According to this ruling, it follows from the powers and duties established on the internal level that the Community has competence to enter into international commitments for the conservation of the resources of the sea.[88]

In a later judgment, the ECJ fundamentally stated that from the date of the expiration of the transitional period laid down by Article 102 of the Act of Accession on 1 January 1979, the "power to adopt, as part of the common fisheries policy, measures relating to the conservation of the resources of the sea (...) belonged fully and definitely to the Community. Member States are therefore no longer entitled to exercise any power of their own in the matter of conservation measures in the waters under their jurisdiction. (…) (T)he transfer to the Community of powers in this matter (is) total and definite"[89].

Like in the case of CCP, the need for exclusivity emanated from the internal system governing the policy area. The scope of CFP vis-à-vis CCP gets defined by the diverging objectives the two Community policies follow. In principle, fish is a product which can – like all agricultural products – be subject of a CCP measure[90]. In the *Kramer* case, the ECJ stated that the nature and the circumstances of 'production' of the product in question as well as their aims should be taken into consideration[91]. Agreements can, however, also be concluded on a double legal basis if they relate not only to fisheries policy but also CCP issues.[92]

---

88 Joined cases 3, 4 and 6/76, *Kramer* , ECR [1976] 1279.

89 Case 804/79, *Commission v United Kingdom*, ECR [1981] 1045, paras 17, 18 and 20.

90 *MacLeod/Hendry/Hyett* (1996) 243.

91 *Kramer*, paras 56-59.

92 E.g. Council Regulation (EEC) 3954/92 on the conclusion of the Agreement on relations in the sea fisheries sector between the European Economic Community and the Kingdom of Morocco and

As CFP forms part of CAP, fishery policy consequently underlies to a certain extent the same rules and conditions as other areas of agriculture. Again the specific nature of the product in question demanded the development of an own legal regime, which takes account of these particularities and the specific needs[93].

B. The Member States as Trustees of the Community

Well understood, the exclusive nature of CFP completely excludes the existence of a parallel or concurrent national power. Nevertheless the ECJ took the stance that action taken by the Member States is compatible with the concept of exclusivity under certain circumstances. In a number of cases, it acknowledged the Member States' authority to act wherever the Community failed to adopt the measures in question. Such measures must be necessary and can be taken only on an interim basis in close cooperation with the Commission[94]. This authorisation to act in very exceptional cases does however – as the ECJ was anxious to stress – "not in any case restore to the Member States the power and freedom to act unilaterally in this field"[95]. Indeed the construction does not entail an authorisation to take national action but basically enables the Member States to unilaterally take 'Community action' wherever a failure to act occurs on the part of the Council. The Member states are thus acting as trustees of the Community[96]. This trusteeship model developed in the context of CFP is, in principle, also applicable to other exclusive Community policy fields such as e.g. CCP.[97]

IV. Exchange Rate Policy

The TEC provisions on monetary policy contain detailed arrangements for the external dimension of this issue. Art 111 para

---

laying down provisions for its implementation, OJ L 407, 31.12.1992, 1.

93 See *Thiele* (1999) paras 48ff.

94 Case 804/79, *Commission v United Kingdom*, ECR [1981] 1045, paras 30 and 31.

95 Case 804/79, *Commission v United Kingdom*, ECR [1981] 1045, para 20.

96 *Streinz* (2001) 55, dogmatically characterises the construct as extraordinary law making power conferred upon the Member States by the Commission on the occasion of a legislative state of emergency.

97 *Vedder* (2001) para 11.

1 TEC confers express external competence upon the Community institutions to determine the exchange rates for the Community currency in relation to "non-Community currencies". The Council is empowered to conclude formal agreements on an exchange-rate system in accordance with the procedure laid down in para 3 of the same article. As Member States participating in the third stage of the Economic and Monetary Union (EMU) have unreservedly transferred their monetary competences to the Community[98], the latter's authority to enter into agreements is of exclusive nature.

Whereas the exclusive nature of monetary policy, which has deprived the Member States of the Euro group from the capacity to act autonomously in that area is uncontroversial, the exercise of these powers inside the Community system has given rise to fierce debates in academic writing.[99] In essence, the dispute roots in the non-participation of three EC members in the third stage of EMU combined with the autonomous status of the European Central Bank (ECB). Relying on these facts, it has been argued that the conclusion of exchange rate agreements is an exclusive ECB competence rather than a Community competence.[100] The issue is subject of a detailed discussion in another part of this book and shall therefore not be further elaborated in the context of this article.[101]

V. Association Agreements

The first TEC provision that – apart from CCP – expressly conferred an external competence upon the Community was Art 310 (ex Art 238) TEC. The first paragraph of Art 301 provides: "The Community may conclude (...) agreements establishing an association involving reciprocal rights and obligations, common action and special procedures". The extent and nature of this power, however, was (and still is) not plain. Even an evaluation of the numerous agreements, which have been concluded on the basis of that provision, does not provide a definite and conclusive answer to the following questions: What is an association? What are its

---

98 *Zilioli/Selmayr* (1999) 276, *Torrent* (1999) 1231. See also *Dutzler* in the present volume at 451.

99 See in particular *Zilioli/Selmayr* (1999) and for the opposing view: e.g. *Torrent* (1999).

100 *Zilioli/Selmayr* (1999) 292.

101 See *Barbara Dutzler's* contribution on the external dimension of EMU.

essential or characteristic elements and which are the necessary or potential subject-matters of regulation?

The provision's wording neither offers a precise definition or characterisation of this form of cooperation with a third country, nor indicates the limits of the Community's powers. Furthermore, the nature of the Community's powers under this article raises a multitude of open questions. Undertaking a vague attempt of a definition, "association" is broadly understood as a more intense form of cooperation, characterised by reciprocal rights and common action[102]. The requirement of reciprocity which can be inferred from the wording of Art 310 TEC, however, does not prove to be an essential element according to Community practice so far.[103] The ECJ speaks of "special privileged links with a non-member country" in the context of associations.[104] Association agreements regularly provide for the establishment of own association organs (e.g. Association Council) which are responsible of common action management in the framework of the association under participation of representatives of both parties, the Community and the "associated" State. The fact that the term "association" indicates a very special and particularly intense form of cooperation also led to its avoidance in some agreements' "labelling" for obvious political reasons even though Art 310 TEC apparently served as the legal basis.[105] Conversely, not every form of cooperation which is called an association actually establishes an association with the Community.

In practice, association agreements are adopted on the Art 310 (ex Art 238) in connection with Article 300 (ex Art 228) TEC. Frequently they are also concluded as so-called mixed agreements, in which the EC Member States are parties to the agreement alongside the Community. This practice does not facilitate the delimitation of powers the Community disposes of with respect to associations. Associations may be concluded in pursuance of a variety of purposes, such as development policy objectives[106], as pre-accession instruments aimed at preparing third States for their

---

[102] *Fried* (1995) 123ff.

[103] *Peers* (2000) 160ff.

[104] Case 12/86, *Demirel*, [1987] ECR 3719, para 9.

[105] Cooperation agreements with the Mashreq and Maghreb countries; see *Fried* (1995) 123 with further references.

[106] E.g. Cotonou Agreement of 23 June 2000 (OJ 2000 L 317, 3 -353).

potential future membership (such as in particular the so-called Europe agreements[107]), or aimed at the strengthening of economic links by way of reciprocal abolition of customs and measures having equivalent effect or even the creation of a Customs Union with a common tariff (free trade agreements[108]).

Accordingly, also the subject-matters regulated by the association vary from trade preferences to free movement of goods, services or workers, from technical and financial cooperation to liberalisation in agriculture, from regulation of future political dialogue to regulation of competition matters. The range of subject-matters which may be regulated under an association appears unlimited – can the same be held true for the Community's powers? In *Demirel,* the ECJ confirmed that associations might cover "all fields covered by the Treaty"[109]. Accordingly, the prevailing view maintains that the associations can cover the entire scope of the TEC[110].

Another question is whether the Community's powers originate from that very provision or rather from another provision being the substantive legal basis. In other words: Does Article 310 TEC confer genuine substantial powers on the Community or does it rather provide for a mere procedural attribution of powers? As regards the substance of the agreement the distribution of powers derives from other TEC provisions.[111] If the latter is held to be true, does the nature of the Community's depend on the underlying substantive power?

All these questions are subject to lively disputes. It is held here that Article 310 TEC constitutes a very specific power conferring provision for the field of associations. Comparable to Article 301

---

[107] Signed with Poland and Hungary on December 16, 1991 (OJ 1993 L 348, 1 and L 347, 1), with Slovakia and the Czech Republic on October 4, 1993 (OJ 1994 L 359, 1 and L 360, 1), with Bulgaria and Romania on March 8, 1993 and February 1, 1993 (OJ 1993 L 358, 1 and L 357, 1), with Estonia, Latvia, Lithuania on June 12, 1995 (OJ 1998 L 68, 1, L 26, 1 and L 51, 1) and with Slovenia on June 10, 1996 (OJ 1999 L 51, 3).

[108] See in particular EEA Agreement (OJ 1994 L 1, 3-36), FTAs with Malta and Cyprus (OJ 1971 L 61, 1 and OJ 1973 L 133, 1).

[109] Case 12/86, *Demirel,* [1987] ECR 3719, para 9.

[110] See *Herrnfeld* (2000) para 5.

[111] On the distinction between substantial and procedural division of powers see *Dashwood* (2000) 121.

TEC concerning sanctions against third States[112], it expressly confers upon the Community a broad external competence to act in the framework of an association, covering the whole subject-matter of the Treaty which is independent of the enactment of internal legislation in the relevant field. Likewise the nature of this express horizontal competence of the Community to "associate" with third countries must be judged from this angle. The competence to enter into the specific type of cooperation called association must be exclusively reserved to the Community. Nevertheless Article 310 TEC does not touch upon the repartition of powers between the Community and the Member States with regard to the subject-matters regulated in an association agreement.

Insofar the Community's competence to conclude association agreements does not constitute a genuine substantial provision for it respects the attribution of powers determined by TEC provisions regulating the respective subject. It is substantial only insofar as it establishes an express horizontal competence covering the entire subject-matter of the Treaty.

VI. Conclusions

A few conclusions may be drawn on the concept of exclusivity derived directly from the TEC. As already stated at the starting point of our observations, exclusivity in external relations has in principle not been a very popular concept. In fact the only provisions explicitly establishing an (exclusive) *external* competence are Art 133 TEC (CCP) and Art 111 TEC (exchange rate policy). Such scarcity highlights that this type of exclusivity is an exception. In most cases, external exclusive Community competence is a consequence of the promulgation of internal rules. The need for an exclusive external regime is based on the existence of counterpart at the internal level. In contrast, a "genuine" exclusive external competence does not need a counterpart on the internal level.

On a close examination, however, the accuracy of this statement must be called into question. It should be observed that the so-

---

[112] Insofar as it also confers a horizontal, broad-ranging external competence upon the Community with regard to a special type of relationship with third countries. Of course Article 310 TEC lacks the specific "cross pillar" function Article 301 TEC stands for, see *Lukaschek* in this volume at 343ff.

called genuine exclusive Community competences are also intimately related to internal regimes. The Community's exclusive power to regulate foreign exchange rates is a necessary complement to the common monetary policy and the uniform currency. Likewise the ECJ has justified the exclusivity of CCP with the necessity to protect the operation of the Common Market. The central argument invoked by the ECJ in order to preclude any concurrent competence on part of the Member States was the effective defence of the *common interests* of the Community.[113] This reasoning nevertheless presumes that the common interests are already defined at Community level. In many areas that could have been potentially covered by CCP such common interests have not been formulated and Member States still enjoy a certain margin of discretion to pursue their own interests and policies. Denying this discretion in the external sphere by granting an exclusive competence to the Community in these areas is not only doomed to failure because of political reasons, but likewise seems paradoxical from a legal point of view. Against this background, the call for parallelism between internal and external powers is well justified as soon as the regulation of international relations has implications for the internal regime.[114] Opinion 1/94 can be regarded as the first step in this direction, while the Nice version of Art 133 TEC has also obviously subscribed to the concept of parallelism. In the light of these developments, there seems to be no future for an autonomous exclusive external competence which is not reflected in the internal regime.

Bibliography

Jacques H.J. Bourgeois (1995), The EC in the WTO and Advisory Opinion 1/94: An Echternach Procession, CMLRev. 1995, 763-787.

Jürgen Bröhmer (1999), Kapitel 4. Der Kapital- und Zahlungsverkehr, in *Christian Callies/Matthias Ruffert* (eds.),

[113] Cf Opinion 1/75, *Local Cost Standard*, [1975] ECR 1355, 1363-1364.
[114] See also *Chalmers* (1996) 56; *Cremona* (1999) 239.

Kommentar zum EU-Vertrag und EG-Vertrag, Neuwied/Kriftel 1999, 738-762.

Damian Chalmers (1996), Legal Base and the External Relations of the European Community, in *Nicolaus Emiliou/David O'Keeffe* (eds), The European Union and World Trade Law, After the GATT Uruguay Round, Chichester 1996, 46-61.

Marise Cremona (1999), External Economic Relations and the Amsterdam Treaty, in *David O'Keeffe/Patrick Twomey*, Legal Issues of the Amsterdam Treaty, Oxford 1999, 225-247.

Alan Dashwood (2000), The Attribution of External Relations Competence, in *Alan Dashwood/ Christophe Hillion* (eds.), The General Law of E.C. External Relations, London 2000.

Jacqueline Dutheil de la Rochère (1995), L'ère des compétences partagées. A propos de l'étendue des compétences extérieures de la Communauté européenne, RMC 1995, 461-471.

Piet Eeckhout (1993), The External Dimension of the Internal Market and the Scope and Content of a Modern Commercial Policy, in *Marc Maresceau* (ed.), The European Community's Commercial Policy after 1992: The Legal Dimension, Dordrecht et al. 1993, 79-101.

Rachel Fried (1999), The Relations between the EC and International Organisations, The Hague 1999, 123-126.

Peter Gilsdorf (1989), Portée et délimitation des compétences communautaires en matière de politique commerciale, RMC 1989, 195-207.

Peter Gilsdorf (1996), Die Außenkompetenzen der EG im Wandel – Eine kritische Auseinandersetzung mit Praxis und Rechtsprechung, EuR 1996, 145-166.

Eberhard Grabitz/ Armin von Bogdandy/ Martin Nettesheim (1994), Europäisches Außenwirtschaftsrecht, München 1994.

Stefan Griller (1995), The Common Commercial Policy Instruments after the Uruguay Round – with some Implications for Austria, in *Fritz Breuss* (ed.), The World Economy after the Uruguay Round, Vienna 1995, 269-338.

Christoph Herrmann (2001), Vom misslungenen Versuch der Neufassung der gemeinsamen Handelspolitik durch den Vertrag von Nizza, EuZW 2001, 269-274.

Hans-Holger Herrnfeld (2000), Artikel 310 EGV, in *Jürgen Schwarze* (ed.), EU-Kommentar, Baden-Baden 2000, 2411-2424.

Francis Jacobs (1996), The Completion of the Internal Market v the Incomplete Common Commercial Policy, in *Konstadinidis Stratos* (ed), The Legal Regulation of the European Community's External Relations after the Completion of the Internal Market, Aldershot 1996, 3-18.

Peter Knobl (1992), Europabankrecht, in *Stefan Griller* (ed.), Banken im Binnenmarkt, Wien 1992, 25-476.

Horst Günter Krenzler/Christian Pitschas (2001), Progress or Stagnation?: The Common Commercial Policy After Nice, EFA Rev. 2001, 291-313.

Manuel López Escudero (1999), Quelques remarques critiques à propos de la jurisprudence de la Cour de Justice sur la politique commerciale commune, in Mélanges en hommage à Michel Waelbroeck, Volume II, Bruxelles 1999.

MacLeod, I./Hendry, I./Hyett S. (1996), The External Relations of the European Communities, New York 1996, 241-344.

Steve Peers (2000), EC Frameworks of International Relations: Co-operation, Partnership and Association, *in Alan Dashwood/Christophe Hillion* (eds.), The General Law of E.C. External Relations, London 2000.

Dominique Servais (1995), Ein Europäischer Finanzraum, Luxemburg 1995.

Rudolf Streinz (2001), Europarecht, Heidelberg 2001.

Gereon Thiele Artikel 34 EGV, in *Christian Calliess/Matthias Ruffert* (eds.), Kommentar zu EU-Vertrag und EG-Vertrag, Neuwied, Kriftel 1999.

Ramon Torrent (1999), Whom is the European Central Bank the Central Bank of?: Reaction to Zilioli and Selmayr, CMLRev. 1999, 1229-1241.

Takis Tridimas/Piet Eeckhout (1994), The External Competence of the Community and the Case-Law of the Court of Justice: Principle versus Pragmatism, YEL 1994, 143-177.

John Usher (2000), The Law of Money and Financial Services in the European Community, New York^{2} 2000.

Christoph Vedder (2001), Artikel 133 EGV, in *Eberhard Grabitz/Meinhard Hilf* (eds.), Das Recht der Europäischen Union, 17th instalment, 2001, München.

Chiara Zilioli/Martin Selmayr (1999), The External Relations of the Euro Area: Legal Aspects, CMLRev. 1999, 273-349.

Barbara Dutzler

The Representation of the EU and the Member States in International Organisations – General Aspects

I. Introduction

The issue of an adequate Community and Member States representation in an international organisation (IO) has always been a controversial one. This area of confrontation derives from the deep-rooted competence conflict between the Member States and the Community which has been transferred to the international level already very early.[1] After all, participation by the Community presupposes own Community competences in the IO's area of intervention, competences which have been transferred to the Community by its Member States, which in these areas are no longer competent.[2] At the core of the discussion therefore lies the interplay between the powers of the Community and those of the Member States, seen through the veil of membership arrangements.

As if this was not enough, the discussion gains an extra weight by the promotion of arguably rather procedural questions to matters of principle, due to the symbolic weight contained in the loss of membership status by a Member State for the sake of Community presence.[3] There is certainly some truth in the observation that the fact of being present has become a thing in itself, in the sense that participation serves the precious purpose of manifesting and consolidating the very membership.[4] In addition, the limitation of national sovereignty of the Member States by the Community is openly visible for Third Parties participating in the various IOs, fact which must not be underestimated.[5]

It is obvious that it is not an easy task to reconcile these practical limitations with the principle of co-ordination and Community unity vis-à-vis the rest of the world, which according to the European Court of Justice (ECJ) should guide Community presence at

---

1 See Vedder's account of the work of Grabitz, *Vedder* (1995) 796.
2 *Dormoy* (1997) 40.
3 So *Hilf* (1997) 294, speaking of an "Existenzfrage".
4 See *Heliskoski* (2000) 94.
5 Cf. *Ehlermann* (1983) 6.

the international level. In the present contribution, besides an overview of the legal basis and of the ECJ's case law on the development and more recent incidents of Community representation, particular attention is therefore paid to the establishment of codes of conduct or so-called "gentlemen's agreements". In a final chapter, the main findings are summarised and a rather pessimistic conclusion on the probability of a noticeable improvement in the near future is drawn.

As a last introductory remark, if hereinafter the term *representation* is used, this relates to the question which institution or person is entitled to speak, whereas under *participation* in the strict sense, the status of the Community within the framework of an IO is dealt with.[6]

II. Foundations of Community Representation

The following chapter starts with an overview of the most important principles governing external *Community* representation in terms of internal division of powers. The question as to which principles should guide external representation when both Community and Member States are competent is dealt with in chapter II.B.

A. Authorisation and Limitations Contained in Arts 302-304

1. Legal Basis

From the fact that there is no express Treaty provision for the Community to join IOs, one could well assume that such a membership was not contemplated at the outset.[7] Arts 302-304 EC Treaty are only concerned with the maintenance of relations and cooperation with various IOs, in particular the UN (Art 302 Para 1 EC), Council of Europe (Art 303 EC) and the OECD (Art 304 EC), which is far from establishing membership relations.[8] The purpose of these Articles is twofold: first, there is an outward dimension, confirming the intention of the Community to participate in the international institutional co-operation. The second dimension is the internal constitutional one, which relates to the requirement of ensuring unity in the international representation of the Community,

6 *Cf. Brückner* (1990) 175, *Louis* (1999) 10.

7 *Sack* (1995) 1228.

8 *Schröder* (1997) para 4.

as laid down in Art 2 TEU (assertion of identity on the international scene) and developed in the case law of the ECJ.[9]

Art 302 Para 1 EC instructs the Commission to establish relations with the organs of the UN,[10] while Arts 303 and 304 address the Community to establish forms of co-operation with the Council of Europe[11] and the OECD, respectively. Although the reference in Arts 303-304 to the Community may be interpreted as pointing to the possibility of co-operation between these bodies and the other Community institutions,[12] Art 302 Para 2 EC, which authorises the *Commission* to maintain all appropriate relations with all IOs, can be identified as the general norm to which the other Articles are *leges speciales*.[13] Apart from the organisations specifically mentioned (UN, Council of Europe, and OECD), it is therefore in the discretion of the Commission to determine if, and if so, how, i.e. which kind of liaisons, it should maintain with which organisation. Although the Commission is far from using this wide margin of discretion, and co-operations have always been subject to consultation between the Council and the Commission,[14] it is submitted that

---

9 *Tietje* (2000) para 1, preliminary remarks to Art 302-304.

10 Also in the framework of the CFSP, there is an Article which deals with Member States co-ordination in the UN Security Council (Art 19 Para 2 2nd Sentence TEU). It is clear that in this area, in which the Member States may conclude internationally binding agreements in the implementation of the objectives of the CFSP, conflicts could arise as to the intertwining of areas within Community competence and those falling under the CFSP, so *Tietje* (2000) para 3, preliminary remarks to Art 302-304. A remedy might be Art 3 TEU, aiming to ensure consistency between the three pillars of the TEU, and the principal division of matters dealt with under the EC Treaty and the CFSP (legal commitments as opposed to political commitments), cf. *Frid* (1995) 146.

11 As the growing distance between the EU and the Council of Europe shows, this explicit reference could not prevent that many agreements on different levels of co-operation were inefficient. The differences in competences and functions would constrain concrete results of co-operation to singular questions, cf *Zieger* (1974) 121-122. A recent "singular question" is the Council of Europe Convention on Information Society.

12 So *MacLeod/Hendry/Hyett* (1996) 168.

13 *Frid* (1995) 127.

14 As can be inferred from Section 5 of the Luxemburg Accords 1966, "the Council and the Commission will consult together on the advisability of, the procedure for, and the nature of any links which the

this provision gives the Commission at least a fall-back position in the whole range of external relations of the Community.[15] This assumption requires a closer look on the type of authorisation entailed in those Articles.

2. Typology of Relations and Internal Division of Power

In an attempt to set up a typology of relations between IOs, *Grabitz* differs between (i) the status within the organs of an IO (membership, associated member, observer), (ii) technical co-operation (not within the organs, but in the various fora), and (iii) organised relations (not the position *within*, but *to*, an IO, including the setting up of common fora and joint committees).[16] Besides full members and associated members, a further class of membership is partial membership, which comprises the admission of non-members to full membership of certain organs.[17] Although it must be stressed that the EC will not necessarily be a member identical to the other members,[18] and in spite of interim solutions due to the developing practice of the Community's participation in IOs,[19] the most important distinction is between membership and non-membership. If set in relation with the authorisation contained in Arts 302-304 EC, it is usually assumed that all but full membership (the "tip of the iceberg") is covered by Arts 302-304 EC. Hence, although these Arts do not contain any procedural requirements, and the relations could be organised by the Commission in a wide variety of forms – informal technical contacts, working arrangements by exchange of letters,[20] mutual information agreements, common meetings, or administrative relations in the form of grant-

Commission might establish with international organizations pursuant to Article 229 of the Treaty", reprinted in EuR Heft 1 1966/73-74. See *Frid* (1995) 126-127.

15 *Tietje* (2000) Art 302 para 1.

16 Cf. *Grabitz* (1974) 57.

17 This is mainly the case in the UN, see *Frid* (1995) 168-169.

18 Therefore, *Dormoy* differs between exclusive and cumulative participation, see *Dormoy* (1997) 45.

19 *Frid* speaks of "enhanced membership", see *Frid* (1995) 175.

20 E.g. with UNEP. It is the most common form for liaisons with IOs, so *Frid* (1995) 127.

ing of an observer status, with or without right of speaking – it would not be possible to *join* an IO.[21]

There are two main arguments supporting this view: First of all, it should not be forgotten that the reference to GATT, which had been included in the then Art 229 Para 1 of the Maastricht Treaty, had been removed by the Amsterdam Treaty, obliging the Commission under the present version of (now) Art 301 Para 1 only to uphold relations with the UN and its specialised agencies. This is certainly an indication for an interpretation against a continuance of the legal significance of Arts 302-304 EC in case of a formal membership of the Community in an IO.

This view is challenged on the grounds that it was formalistic and would not take into account the enormous variety of forms of co-operations *below* the level of membership, for which the Commission had a monopoly in representing the Community.[22] Since formalised membership as the tip of the iceberg was different just in degree, it would not be understandable to negate Commission powers relating to formal membership. The counter argument to this rejects the thesis of the sole competence of the Commission in all forms of co-operation below membership,[23] for the reason that an observer status serves as the substitute for a not yet achieved member status. From an internal point of view, an observer status would therefore have a higher rank, so that it was not automatically included in Art 302. This is supported by the observation that in fact, although the EC as an observer may not vote, it is sometimes awarded special rights going beyond the rights of a plain observer, for instance the right to speak and introduce amendments as in the Commission for Social Development.[24] In addition, the number of cases in which the Community does not dispose of more than the status of an observer is large – for instance in virtually all institutions of the UN family[25] – whereas there are only few cases in which the Community is a member of an IO.[26]

---

21 *Sack* (1995) 1229.

22 Cf. *Tietje* (2000) Art 302 para 5.

23 Cf. *Schröder* (1997) paras 11 and 13.

24 The CSD is a subsidiary organ to the Economic and Social Council, see *Dormoy* (1997) 53.

25 SEC(93) 361 on the participation of the Community in the UN.

26 The FAO, the WTO, the NAFO, the EBRD, the ISBA, the KEDO, and as party to international treaties, such as the various Agreements on Commodities, see *Sack* (2001) 280-281.

The second argument which supports the view that a formal membership agreement could not be concluded by the Commission draws on the usual process of becoming a member, which involves the ratification of the constitutive treaty of an IO.[27] As this treaty-making power is contained in Art 300 EC,[28] now expressly including "agreements establishing a specific institutional framework by organising co-operation procedures" (Para 3), it is clear that from a systematic point of view, Arts 302-304 EC cannot contain such a competence.[29] Moreover, it has been argued quite convincingly that any wider interpretation of the authorisation contained in Arts 302-304 EC to include the power to join a particular IO as a member does not correspond with the wording, in particular of Art 302 Para 1 (relations with *organs*, not IOs).[30] Art 300, on the other hand, does not present itself as the correct legal base for the conclusion of a membership agreement either, because the establishment of an IO, as mentioned in Para 3, is rather exceptional, as most IOs have been in existence for quite some time. Nevertheless, in the absence of a more specific provision, concrete accession projects should follow as closely as possible the procedure of Art 300 EC.[31]

However, this does not resolve the question which of the Community bodies, Commission or Council, is to be given a central role within a certain IO, once accession has taken place. In other words, must the main thrust of representational activities – taking part in conferences and working parties, holding of speeches, voting – be carried out by the Commission, due to the responsibility for the maintenance of appropriate relationships awarded to it by Art 302 Para 2 EC? Further attention to this will be paid in chapter III.B., for the moment it suffices to say that in the Maastricht negotiations, in spite of the opportunity to discuss the subject, the external role of the Commission did not receive further attention.[32]

---

27 *Dormoy* (1997) 38.

28 As recognised very early by the ECJ, this power entails the right to participate in the establishment of an IO and, subsequently, in its organs. Opinion 1/76 *Inland Waterway Vessels* [1977] ECR 741, para 5.

29 *Tietje* (2000) para 4, preliminary remarks to Art 302-304.

30 So *Grabitz* (1974) 74, *Schröder* (1997) 5/530 para 4.

31 So convincingly *Sack* (1995) 1230.

32 Cf. *Frid* (1995) 160, with reference to *Cloos* et al. (1993) 360 n. 54.

3. Conclusion of Agreements by the Commission

Another important question is the exact scope of the Commission's powers in relation to the competence reserved for the Council concerning the conclusion of international agreements pursuant to Art 302. In particular, attention should be drawn on the exemption clause contained in Art 300 Para 2 EC, under which the Council's powers to sign and conclude such agreements are "subject to the powers vested in the Commission in this field". It is obvious that there will be borderline cases in which it will be hard to decide whether the envisaged form of co-operation could be pursued by the Commission alone, by virtue of Art 302 EC, or whether it was to be concluded by the Council under Art 300 EC.

For our purposes, the ECJ judgement *French Republic v. Commission* seems authoritative, when the Court had to decide on exactly the question whether an international agreement had been rightly concluded by the Commission, or whether it should be declared void, following the application of France, which considered the Council under Art 300 Para 1 EC as the competent authority for the conclusion of the agreement.[33] In the view of France, the agreement in question was not *administrative,* as, for instance, "the establishment of relations with the organs of the United Nations and the other international organizations referred to in Article 229 [now 302] of the EEC Treaty" would be.

This interpretation was taken up by Advocate General *Tesauro* who characterised arrangements establishing forms of co-operation between authorities acting in the exercise of their discretion, amounting to concerted actions, as a not-binding agreement.[34] As the ECJ found that the Agreement produced legal effects and was binding on the Community, it concluded that the "autonomous general provision" of Article 300 should have been used.[35]

It is noted, though, that it is not only the legal nature – binding or not – which matters, but also the nature of the agreement. Otherwise, would the Commission in fact lack any powers to conclude internationally binding agreements, the exemption clause in Art 300 Para 2 (the Council concludes agreements "subject to the powers vested in the Commission) would be senseless. It is only useful if one assumes that international agreements concluded by

---

33 Case C-327/91 *France v Commission* [1994] ECR I-3641.

34 Opinion of AG *Tesauro* in *France v. Commission* para 22.

35 *France v. Commission*, paras 23-28.

the Commission may bind the Community,[36] but would be limited in their *substance* to "certain expressly specified cases", *inter alia* Arts 302-304.[37] Hence, any agreement concluded by the Commission has to be examined regarding "the identity of its addressees and the will of the contracting parties, its contents and any provision for penalties in the event of non-compliance"[38] in order to establish its nature: if it was legally binding on the Community and designed in its substance to establish more than just concerted practices, it would have to be concluded under Art 300 by the Council.

The differentiation between co-operation between administrations, on the one hand, and co-operation between organisations, on the other, therefore seems useful, as the latter includes participation in the activities of the IOs themselves, involving contractual obligations or decision-making, requiring conclusion under Art 300. Only co-operation between administrations may be governed by Art 302 EC, as it does not concern the substantive activity undertaken within the framework of each of the organisations.[39] One should be aware that this reduces the role of the Commission to a purely technical one in the overall framework of an external "policy-making-power"[40] of the Community, a finding which is not unequivocally accepted in the academic discussion.

B. Division of Competences between Community and Member States and Modalities of Representation

1. Admissibility of Participation

Having established the limits of the authorisation contained in Arts 302-304 EC, it does not come as a surprise that this does not cover, from a normative perspective, the question whether the Community should participate at all. This is, as the ECJ's judgement in *Kramer* implies, not problematic, as Community power to enter into international commitments "arises not only from an express conferment by the Treaty, but may equally flow implicitly from other provisions."[41] The only test which has to be met is based

36 So *Tietje* (2000) preliminary remarks para 9.

37 Cf. Opinion of AG *Tesauro* in *France v. Commission* para 24.

38 Opinion of AG *Tesauro* in *France v. Commission* para 18.

39 *Frid* (1995) 129. See also *Schröder* (1997) para 3, and *MacLeod/Hendry/Hyett* (1996) 167.

40 After a well-known *dictum* by *Grabitz* (1974) 77.

41 Joined Cases 3,4 and 6/76, *Kramer* [1976] ECR 1279, paras 19-20.

upon the concept of *effet utile*, and bears the question whether external action is *necessary* in order to effectively ensure the attainment of the goal set.[42] It follows that necessary action will not remain limited to fields of exclusive Community competence, but include fields in which Member States have concurrent competence. Participation in an IO only by the Member States, on the other hand, is restrained by the principle that any envisaged participation must not concern activities which are to be conducted within the context of the Community by "common action" or change the "internal constitution of the Community by the alteration of essential elements of the Community structure as regards both the prerogatives of the institutions and the position of the Member States vis-à-vis one another."[43]

2. Exclusive Community Competences

Along these lines, the Community's participation is determined by the scope of its competences.[44] By way of illustration, in the case of exclusive Community competence, in *Kramer* the ECJ insisted that "those institutions and the Member States will be under a duty to use *all the political and legal means* at their disposal in order to ensure the participation of the Community in the Convention and in other similar agreements."[45] This obligation on the part of the Member States to work towards the awarding of full membership status of the Community if its competence was fully or partially identical with the area of responsibility of the respective IO could also be inferred from Art 307 in combination with Art 10 EC.[46]

From this, one could conclude that mixed participation in cases of exclusive Community competence was contrary to EC law. This reasoning seems to be used by *Grabitz* who calls the application of the so-called "UNCTAD-Formula" in some cases unlawful.[47] A characteristic feature of this formula, which had been used for instance at ECOSOC, ENCTAD or IAEO, is that the Community is

---

42 See *Dolmans* (1985) 19.

43 Opinion 1/76 [1977] *Inland Waterway Vessels* ECR 741 para 10-11. This is called *loyauté structurelle,* in difference to the principle of *loyauté fonctionelle* as expressed in *ERTA*, see *Blanquet* (1994) 277.

44 *Frid* (1995) 156.

45 Joined Cases 3,4 and 6/76 *Kramer* [1976] ECR 1279, paras 44-45, emphasis added.

46 So *Pernice* (1991) 277.

47 *Grabitz* (1974) 79.

represented by a bicephalous delegation consisting of Commission and Presidency of the Council. This contrasts to the "Rome-Formula", where the Community and Member States form one single delegation, the speaker being a member of the Commission. The difference lies mainly in the assumption of the role of the speaker: whereas the Commission under the Rome-Formula is "in principle" the speaker, under the UNCTAD-Formula either the Presidency of the Council or the Commission make a statement.[48]

However, if "exclusive" competence means that Member States are prevented from legislating independently or assuming obligations which would conflict with rules set by the Community or impair their utility or force, then participation of Member States in agreements in areas of exclusive Community competence could be accepted.[49] As an example for a case in which the ECJ considered continued Member State participation in an IO was justified was the *ERTA* judgment, when the Court took notice of the fact that the negotiations on ERTA had been carried out *before* the powers in question had been conferred on the Community. A change of the procedures "at that stage of the negotiations [...] might well have jeopardized the successful outcome of the negotiations". In such a situation, it would have been on the Council and the Commission to reach agreement "on the appropriate methods of cooperation with a view to ensuring most effectively the defence of the interests of the Community". As this had not happened, the ECJ accepted the joint action by the Member States in the Council "in the interest and on behalf of the Community" also for the future.[50]

To summarise, there are both external and internal constraints to the substitution of the Member States by the Community in IOs. The external obstacle could consist in the risk for the fait of the negotiation (ERTA) or non-acceptance by other parties to the IO in question,[51] whereas the internal obstacle could be a blocking of the decision-making process in the Council.[52] But nonetheless, the powers of the Member States to act in fields of Community competence are only *pouvoirs de crise*, flowing from the principle of

---

48 *Schloh* (1974) 94.

49 Cf. *Dolmans* (1985) 95.

50 Case 22/70 *ERTA* [1971] ECR 263, paras 86-90.

51 This happened e.g. 1971 at the Wheat Conference by the Soviet Union, see *Schloh* (1974) 97.

52 So *Blanquet* (1994) 114.

necessity, and are limited to what is strictly necessary and are accompanied by control effectuated by the Commission or possibly the ECJ.[53]

3. Shared Competences

In line with these considerations on the lawfulness of continued Member State participation in IOs, Member States may not only participate on behalf of the Community in fields of its exclusive competence, in spite of the responsibility of the Commission to maintain the relations and co-operations. In addition, whenever the subject-matters with which the IO deals is broader than the exclusive powers of the Community, which is the rule,[54] forms of representation have to be found which ensure that both the Community and the Member States are adequately represented in their respective fields of competences.[55] In such cases, the fewer discretionary powers to decide on the contents of engagements the Member States have, the greater the need for co-operation and co-ordination.[56]

In spite of the advantages, which arguably, a wider interpretation of exclusive Community competences would bring in terms of internal and external strength,[57] Member States and Council are openly in favour of mixed (as opposed to exclusive) participation. Whereas acceptance of mixed participation therefore reduces inter-institutional tensions, it leads to a number of difficulties. In particular, as responsibilities are split between the Community and Member States, neither party can individually exert full powers of membership.[58]

---

53 *Blanquet* (1994) 118.

54 So *Timmermans* (2000) 239.

55 Most writers question both the meaningfulness and compatibility with EC law of mixed agreements, because they are open to abuse by Member States who can seek to include provisions in an agreement for the purpose of making it a mixed one, see the references in *McGoldrick* (1997) 79-80. Despite this danger, mixed agreements are also seen as beneficial to the Community insofar as they tie together Community and Member States in a growing network, which strengthens the overall framework of European integration, so *Weiler* (1983) 39.

56 *Dolmans* (1985) 45-46.

57 *Ehlermann* (1983) 7.

58 *Schermers* (1983) 836.

Beside the legal status of the Community in the IO, which involves the question whether the Community should gain an independent position when its Member States are also members of the same IO, the main aspects of participation will have to be determined. One of the issues to be resolved in this respect is the exercise of voting rights: should the Community have a vote of its own, possibly in addition to those held by the Member States,[59] should there be an alternative exercise of voting rights in accordance with the respective competences, should the Community express the collective votes of the Member States as in the International Cocoa Agreement, or is it enough if the Member States exert their voting rights collectively whenever the Community is competent as in the International Tin Agreement?[60] Other matters to be addressed include the number of votes attributed to the Community,[61] its right to speak and participate in all working parties, and the co-ordination and presentation of the views of the Community and the Member States. How these issues are resolved differs from forum to forum and "owe as much to habit and history as to law and logic."[62]

4. A Question of Perspective?

Important in this respect is the perspective under which these issues are analysed: From the perspective of Community law, what matters is the internal division of competences which determines the level (observer, member) and the nature (sole or joint) of the participation of the Community and the Member States in other IOs. This focus on the internal division of competence is challenged on the grounds that it leads to exaggerated results, due to its disregard for political realities, when a full membership status for the Community, in case of exclusive competence, and double membership of both Community and Member States competences, in case

---

[59] The EBRD is one of the very rare cases, *MacLeod/Hendry/ Hyett* (1996) 175.

[60] In *Schermers'* opinion, the latter provision does not adequately reflect the Community's position and should be avoided, *Schermers* (1983) 834.

[61] As the "one member, one vote" concept leads to a dramatic loss of voting rights, a mixed agreement, it may also be in the interest of the EC to preserve its voting powers, so *McGoldrick* (1997) 84.

[62] *MacLeod/Hendry/Hyett* (1996) 172. For an extensive survey *Feenstra* (1983) 207ff.

of mixed competence, was not achievable.[63] As *Frid* points out, it is unrealistic to assert that once the division of powers is sorted out, "the institutional problem of whether or not the Community can effectively exercise its powers within the framework of another IO is also resolved."[64] Not every IO is as pragmatic as the GATT,[65] an attitude which was indeed very helpful in the establishment of an adequate status of the Community.[66]

The ECJ's stance in this matter has clearly been an internal one. In *International Atomic Energy Agency*, the ECJ denied any necessity to set out and determine the division of powers between the Community and the Member States, "it being understood that the exact nature of the division is a domestic question in which third parties have no need to intervene."[67] This strategy is, of course, only possible where IOs do not request an exact delimitation of Community powers in relation to Member States powers as a condition of Community participation, which, however, is increasingly the case.[68] It might be for this development that the ECJ changed its view and declared that the extent of the respective powers of the Community and the Member States would determine the extent of their respective responsibilities in relation to performance of their obligations. The requests that the Community should declare the extent of its competence in its instruments of approval showed that this consideration was taken into account at international level.[69]

---

63 See for instance *Schröder* (1997) para 6-7.

64 *Frid* (1995) 160.

65 See *Schloh* (1974) 90.

66 Before the 1994 GATT reform and WTO establishment, although formally, only the Member States were members of the GATT, the Community acted as a quasi-full or *de-facto* member, as it did not only participate in the organs of the GATT, in working parties and in committees, but starting from 1961 also signed the protocols, in addition to the Member States. On the other hand, it did not participate in the financing, and it did not have a right to vote on its own, *Grabitz* (1974) 64. As the appearance of the Community as a party to the Agreement had been accepted by all other parties by tacit consent, the ECJ assumed that the Community had taken over the competences in the area governed by the GATT, Joined Cases C-21-24/72 *International Fruit Company* [1972] 1219.

67 Ruling 1/78 *IAEA* [1978] ECR 2151 para 35.

68 See *Macleod/Hendry/Hyett* (1996) 161 n.81 for a list of cases in which declarations of competence were demanded.

69 So in Opinion 2/00 *Cartagena Protocol*, [2001] ECR I-9731

The result of this attitude is the sanctioning of shared competences and the passing of the buck back to the political actors. The soundness of this approach will be considered *infra.* The important point here, however, is the underlying assumption that the main difficulties have internal, rather than external, reasons. This is certainly correct, as the requirement of effective co-operation between the Community and Member States in order to achieve meaningful participation in the work of an IO in cases of joint participation has to meet three substantial requirements: First, procedural arrangements have to be found which do not jeopardise the homogeneity of the Community as an external actor. Second, at the same time they have to ensure adequate Member States participation, and meet, third, the demands of active members, by allowing the conclusion of agreements or the adoption of positions without being too complicated and time-consuming. The complexity of these requirements deserves a closer analysis of the duty of co-operation, including examples for procedural arrangements and possible legal benchmarks.

III. Duty of Co-operation

A. Article 10 and its Interpretation by the ECJ

1. Kramer and IAEA

The duty of co-operation owes its existence and its status as the guiding norm of the actions of the Community and the Member States in the field of external relations essentially to the ECJ. It is therefore necessary to take a closer look at its development before continuing with its practical relevance in the framing of the so-called gentlemen's agreement. Article 10 EC reads as follows:

> "Member States shall take all appropriate measures, whether general or particular, to ensure fulfilment of the obligations arising out of this Treaty or resulting from action taken by the institutions of the Community. They shall facilitate the achievement of Community tasks.
> They shall abstain from any measure which could jeopardize the attainment of the objectives of the Treaty."

From an early stage, Article 10 received the attention of the ECJ in the fields of external competences. In the *Kramer* cases, the ECJ referred to the duty of the Member States to use all their political and legal means at their disposal to ensure the participation of the

Community in IOs only after having underscored the duty imposed on the Member States by Art 10 EC Treaty. The ECJ continued:

> "Member States participating in the Convention and in other similar agreements are now not only under a duty not to enter into any commitment within the framework of those conventions which would hinder the Community in carrying out the tasks entrusted to it [...], but also under a duty to *proceed by common action* within the Fisheries Commission."[70]

Starting with this statement of principle, two different subjects are to be considered. First, the judgment was made against the background of exclusive Community competence. Nonetheless, the obligation of the Member States to proceed by common action and to ensure Community participation, applied in a situation when the Member States remained still competent to assume commitments within the framework of the North-East Atlantic Fisheries Convention. Their competences were only of a transitional nature, as the Community had by then not fully exercised its powers. In fact, it is evident that reference to the principle of solidarity contained *inter alia* in Article 10 EC is needed exactly in cases in which not only the Community, but also the Member States are competent to act, be it transitorily or permanently.[71] Member States are therefore under the obligation to enable the Community to exercise its powers, and under the prohibition to agree to the terms of a draft convention or rules of procedure for negotiations unless they contain provisions enabling the Community to become a party on conditions compatible with Community law.[72]

---

70 Joined Cases 3,4 and 6/76 *Kramer* [1976] ECR 1279, paras. 44-45, emphasis added. Other examples when the Court recognised on the basis of Article 10 that the Member States are under an obligation not to enter into any commitment within the framework of an international agreement which could hinder the Community are C-61/77 *Commission v Ireland* [1978] ECR 417, para 65; C-141/78 *France v United Kingdom* [1979] ECR 2923, para 8; C-32/79 *Commission v U.K.* [1980] ECR 2403, para 10; C-804/79 *Commission v U.K.* [1981] ECR 1045, para 28.

71 The Member States are therefore *gestionnaires de l'intérêt commune* in areas which are "ni compétence communautaire, ni compétence etatique propre", but by an act of co-operation, the Member States serve the Community interest, see *Blanquet* (1994) 103-104.

72 *Lang* (1990) 670.

In other words, and this is the second implication, the issue at stake is interference, or conflicts arising from particular measures adopted by the Member States which interfere with Community law. Although the ECJ seemed to deduce from Art 10 EC, contrary to its language directed at the Member States only, a *reciprocal* duty of co-operation binding also the Community institutions,[73] it is doubted that Art 10 EC was the legal basis imposing this obligation on the Community institutions. On the contrary, Art 10 is regarded as *lex generalis*,[74] as a source of inspiration,[75] since the obligation to co-operate is more specific than the general principle of loyalty under Art 10.[76] Fact remains, though, that regardless of the question whether the mutual duty of sincere co-operation is applied by virtue of Art 10 EC or by a more general rule of which Art 10 is just an example, it is a duty which creates concrete legal obligations.[77]

It was only two years later that the ECJ had the possibility of further defining the impact of the duty of co-operation in the external sphere. When referring to the draft convention on nuclear materials, which concerned in part the jurisdiction of the Member States and in part that of the Community, it ruled that it could be implemented only "by means of a close association between the institutions of the Community and the Member States *both* in the *process of negotiation and conclusion* and in the *fulfilment* of the obligations entered into."[78] Although the ECJ had applied this duty of co-operation in the context of the EAEC Treaty, some years later, in Opinion 2/91 on *ILO*, all doubts were removed regarding the applicability of this principle also in the context of the EC Treaty, "since it results from the requirement of unity in the international representation of the Community."[79] Though, this is only one significant aspect of this judgement.

---

73 See e.g Case 2/88, *Zwartveld* [1990] ECR I-3365 para 17, C-234/89 *Delimitis* [1991] ECR I-935 para 53. Further references in *Lang* (1990) 677 n. 77.

74 *Blanquet* (1994) 281.

75 See *Heliskoski* (2000) 96, and *Zuleeg* (1997) 124.

76 *Timmermans* (2000) 241.

77 *Tridimas* (2000) 59.

78 Ruling 1/78 *IAEA* [1978] ECR 2151, para 34.

79 Opinion 2/91 *ILO* [1991] ECR I-1061 para 36.

2. ILO and WTO

The case was opened by the Commission which sought a ruling by the ECJ on the question whether the Community was competent to conclude Convention No. 170. This convention, covering safety in the use of chemicals at work, had been drawn up in the framework of the International Labour Organisation (ILO). The ECJ found itself competent to address, in line with the Commission's request, the respective competences of the Community and the Member States within the area covered by Convention No. 170. In particular,

> "It is not for the Court to assess any obstacles which the Community may encounter in the exercise of its competence because of constitutional rules of the IO."[80]

In spite of this apparent self-restriction, the Court could not avoid touching upon the general problem of the participation of the Community in the ILO standard setting.[81] Evidence of this is para 38, where the ECJ repeated, in different terms, the general principle applicable in all cases where the conclusion of an agreement falls within the joint competence of the Member States and the Community. Both "must take all necessary measures so as to best ensure such co-operation both in the *procedure of submission* to the competent authority and *ratification* of the Convention and in the *implementation* of commitments resulting from that Convention".

A further reiteration of this principle can be found in Opinion 1/94 *WTO*, which is remarkable for our purposes as it clearly shows the relevance of the concern that combined membership might have a negative effect on the ability of the Community to defend its interest. It is noticeable that although the Council contested any necessity for the ECJ to touch upon institutional provisions, which aimed solely at the "management" of the substantive provisions,[82] the ECJ did not remain silent on this subject. Having said that, it must be added that the ECJ did not share the concerns of the Commission, which feared that even if the Member States – out of political reasons – were to retain certain powers instead of being subject to Community procedures with a Commission spokesman as they would if the Community concluded the Agreement alone, they

---

80 Ibid, para 4.

81 *Frid* (1995) 151.

82 So in VII, essence of the dispute, Opinion 1/94 I-5285.

could be legally unable to exercise, for example, the right to take cross-retaliation measures.[83]

The ECJ addressed these fears when mentioning the concern that the Community's unity vis-à-vis the rest of the world could be undermined and its negotiating power be weakened, because of "interminable discussions whether a given matter falls within the competence of the Community, so that the Community mechanisms will apply, or whether it is within the competence of the Member State, in which case the consensus rule will operate".[84] But although the ECJ called this concern "quite legitimate" it stressed that

> "any problems which may arise in implementation of the WTO Agreement and its annexes as regards the co-ordination necessary to ensure unity of action where the Community and the Member States participate jointly cannot modify the answer to the question of competence, that being a prior issue. As the Council has pointed out, resolution of the issue of the allocation of competence cannot depend on problems which may possibly arise in administration of the agreements."

It then continued by reiterating the principle of the duty of coordination set out in *IAEA* and *ILO* and stressed that this duty to cooperate was all the more imperative in the case of agreements such as those annexed to the WTO Agreement, which were inextricably interlinked, and in view of the cross-retaliation measures.

If it is argued that the duty of co-operation had the effect of making Member States and the Community each other's prisoner,[85] it therefore seems to be overlooked that it is not the duty of co-operation which has this effect, but the factual circumstances such as the close inter-connection of subject-matters at international level meeting uneasily with the division of competences between Community institutions and Member States. The duty of co-operation is but the remedy, the instrument necessitated to achieve the objective of unity in the international representation of the Community.

Two concluding remarks should be added. First, it seems as if in substance, the arguments invoked by the United Kingdom convinced the ECJ. In particular, the UK had stated that the multilateral negotiations for the GATS annexes on financial services manifested

---

[83] Opinion 1/94 *WTO* [1996] ECR I-5267, chapter XIV 5346.

[84] *WTO* para 106ff.

[85] So Editorial (1995) 388.

the very balanced bargaining power which the Commission had claimed to be unobtainable in the absence of exclusive Community competence.[86]

Second, it is often regretted that the ECJ apparently neither wanted nor was able to pin the Community and the Member States down to an actual substance of the duty to co-operate,[87] although it underscored the goal of carrying out the interests of the Community and the Member States as a whole only with one voice.[88] It is, in *Hilf's* view, therefore, regrettable that the ECJ restricted itself to explicitly formulating a wish, which should have been much more stringent and demanding, in particular in the light of the experiences with the simultaneous membership of the Community and the Member States under the FAO Agreement, as the Commission at that time had already filed its application.[89] In fact, the ECJ has not yet answered the fundamental question of the limits of the duty of co-operation. This can be seen subsequently, when it is tried to pin down the implications of the ECJ's demand that the duty of co-operation must be observed in three stages, in the negotiation, the conclusion, and the execution.,

3. The Legal Duties

As to the first obligation[90] flowing from the duty of co-operation, co-operation in the negotiation, this is the most controversial field, as it relates to the achievement of a common position and the question of the consequences of a failure. In particular, the question arises whether in the latter case the Member States are free to act. On the one hand, it is argued that this would be incompatible with the unity in the international representation of the Community,[91] and hence, if co-ordination failed, there should be no action, i.e. no

---

86 See *WTO* I-5373 and *infra*, at III.B.3.(code of conduct).

87 *Hilf* (1997) 299. See also Editorial (1995) 387, where it is criticised that the Court side-stepped such questions as to how that co-operation should be organised, according to what procedures and on what legal basis.

88 This happened again in Opinion 2/00 *Cartagena Protocol* para 17, when the ECJ only reiterated the duty of co-operation, by pointing out that the procedure of Art 300(6) EC was "not intended to solve difficulties associated with implementation of an envisaged agreement which falls within shared Community and Member State competence."

89 *Hilf* (1997) 299.

90 See also *Timmermans* (2000) 242.

91 So *Krenzler/da Fonseca-Wollheim* (1998) 23.

participation in the negotiation at all. Otherwise, Community powers would be usurped by the Member States.[92] On the other hand, it is held that this could only apply in such cases in which the matter fell within the exclusive competence of the Community. In respect of matters in which competence was shared, the duty of close co-operation amounted only to an obligation to use best endeavours to reach a common position.[93]

As an attempt to assess these arguments, first of all, where parts of a subject fall within purely national competence, attention must be drawn to the deletion of Art 116 EEC, which had established a quite effective procedure of co-ordinating Member State action in IOs of an economic character for matters of "particular interest to the common market" remaining within national competence. The deletion of this Article has been called an "unconsidered and anachronistic act",[94] but was probably due to the fact that it was disliked by the Member States as it allowed Community decisions on the exercise of purely national competence by qualified majority.[95] Although the facts presented to the ECJ in the course of the *WTO* Opinion would have allowed a consideration of this question, a similar obligation on the Member States to proceed only by common accord was not established. But at the same time, Member States acting outside the Community framework in questions where they could not agree upon a common action must, at a minimum requirement, take into account, if not the common interest, the interests of the other Member States. As can be inferred from case law, if they were "adversely affected" by a Member State which did not show the need for this action and where no consultation took place, Art 10 EC would be applicable.[96]

A different reasoning could be applied in cases where the matter in question was only of ancillary national competence so that an uncoordinated action by the Member States outside the Community framework could not be justified.[97] The assumption is that the exercise of such "virtual competences" would oust national competence,[98] so that by failure to agree on a common position, the situa-

92 *Timmermans* (2000) 242.
93 *MacLeod/Hendry/Hyett* (1996) 149. Similar *McGoldrick* (1997) 83.
94 *Sack* (1995) 1228.
95 Editorial (1995) 387.
96 Case 32/79 *Commission v. U.K.* [1980] ECR 2403 para 58.
97 Opinion 1/78 *Rubber* [1979] ECR 2871 para 56.
98 *Timmermans* (2000) 241.

tion would be reversed (Community competence ousted by national competence). The same principles could be used for the ratification procedure, which, due to constitutional difficulties and sensitivities, do not follow a uniform procedure.[99] After all, the Member States have effectively the power to delay Community ratification by delaying their own ratification.[100]

B. Codes of Conduct

1. Introductory Remarks

It could be argued that given the need for the closest possible collaboration between the Community and the Member States, such collaboration should take the form of the adoption of a code of conduct.[101] Obviously, the variety of subject matters and of the constitutional provisions of the IOs in question brings with it a considerable variety of Community internal procedures concerning the implementation of the duty of co-operation. Before in the following, some examples for such agreements will be examined, attention must be drawn to the fact that, as a rule, gentlemen's agreements in spite of their "considerable political significance"[102] do not possess legally binding effect. According to the ECJ, though, Art 10 EC may have the effect of imposing legally binding force on a specific measure which would not otherwise be legally binding. The key question is hence whether non-binding acts such as resolutions in the particular field to which they apply make specific the duties of co-operation which the Member States assume under Art 10.[103]

In other words, whenever procedures for organising co-operation or the modalities of *how* to carry out the duties resulting from Art 10 are set out by non-binding legal acts, this may not prevent their binding force.[104] This principle, which has been applied also in the *FAO* judgement, was perceived as reducing markedly the political room for manoeuvre and, as a consequence, any interest of the

---

99 *MacLeod/Hendry/Hyett* (1996) 155.

100 *McGormick* (1997) 87.

101 So the Netherlands Government in Opinion 1/94, I-5387.

102 See opinion of AG Tesauro, C-327/91 *France v. Commission* [1994] I-3641 para 22, in which he considered such agreements to be an example for "the unusual category of non-binding agreements" in international law.

103 Case 141/78 *France v. U.K.* [1979] ECR 2923 para 8.

104 *Lang* (1990) 668-669.

Member States to agree on such informal procedural arrangements.[105]

2. Proba 20

Proba 20 was adopted in 1981 as an internal, unpublished document[106] in order to translate into practice the findings of the ECJ in Opinion 1/78.[107] This arrangement concerns the negotiation of Commodity Agreements and is a "political deal [...] setting aside any legal/institutional consideration which refers to the respective competence of the Community and the Member States". There is, in principle, a joint delegation expressing the joint position with a single voice. The joint position is established beforehand in the Council bodies and expressed normally by the Commission.[108] Also the Member State holding the Presidency or other Member States may present the joint point of view, "depending on tactical or technical advisability". In addition, in order to support and develop the joint position, Member States may make additional statements, in agreement with the normal spokesman and the Presidency. There might also be subjects (technical points or items of interest to some Member States only) which do not require a joint position. But independently of this, additional statements by Member States could be warranted also by their "stature and experience."

In the light of these provisions, the conclusion that this arrangement, which has been a role model for a range of subsequent arrangements in the field of raw materials, was a "victory" for the Member States[109] cannot be dismissed outright. Nevertheless, the "deal" was successful insofar as it allowed co-operation without too much friction between the Community and the Member States.[110] This implies that the declaration annexed to PROBA 20, in which four Member States claimed the right to make national statements if national fundamental concerns were not taken into account and persistent attempts to reach a joint position proved fruitless, has not been used in practice. The Commission thus traded off a strong

---

105 *Tietje* (2000) preliminary remarks to Art 302-304, para 12.

106 5887/81 PROBA 20.

107 *Sack* (1995) 1253.

108 Though, if formal votes are taken, voting rights (in accordance with the joint position) are exercised by the Member States on an individual basis.

109 *Sack* (1995) 1253.

110 *Timmermans* (2000) 243.

position on exclusive competence for an agreed strong position as negotiator.[111]

3. WTO Code of Conduct

Submitting that the question of the feasibility of joint competence was a concern to the ECJ in Opinion 1/94, the code of conduct applied thereinafter deserves further attention. The code of conduct which the Council presented to the Court during a hearing and which had been agreed in May 1994 between the Council, the Member States and the Commission on the post-Uruguay-Round negotiations on services may serve as a starting point.[112] It authorised the Commission

a) to negotiate on behalf of the Community and the Member States in the negotiations and discussions on trade in services conducted either under the authority of the Preparatory Committee or of the Council for Trade in Services of the WTO,[113]
b) to inform the Member States "as far in advance as possible" of the time and place of all negotiations to be held
c) to express positions reached on all issues according to the relevant decision-making procedures
d) to ensure that representatives of all Member States are in a position to attend all substantive meetings and negotiations, "noting that the Member States may ask the Presidency to attend on their behalf"
e) to circulate promptly to the Member States any notes, formal or informal, produced by the GATT Secretariat and other participants, including the Commission itself, which have not been sent to the Member States directly.

As to point c, the expression of positions reached "according to the relevant decision-making", a declaration by the Council was entered in the minutes of the Council, which specified that this clause meant, in the case of national competence, consensus. The

---

[111] *McCormick* (1997) 111.

[112] As provided for in the Ministerial Decision made at Marrakech on 15 April 1994, see the Council's answer to Question 4 of the ECJ in Opinion 1/94 *WTO* [1994] ECR I-5257, I-5365.

[113] The progress made in the negotiations should be reviewed regularly by the Council on the basis of reports by the Commission. The Council reserved "its rights to give the Commission appropriate directives in due time".

Commission added a declaration which stressed that "in implementing the relevant decision-making procedures, every effort should be made to reach consensus."[114]

From this arrangement, some interesting principles can be deduced. First of all, there is a single common spokesman also for matters which do not fall wholly or at all within the exclusive competence of the Community. This role is assumed by the Commission. In spite of the suggestion that this was not required as a matter of law, as the ECJ had not spoken of a unity of representation of the Community and the Member States where competence was shared but of a duty of co-operation,[115] it is clear that that duty "flows from the requirement of unity in the international representation".[116] Whereas sole representation by the Commission satisfies this requirement, this would have to be proven for any other procedural arrangement.

Second, for matters falling within the competence of the Member States, there is a clear obligation to *make an effort* to reach a consensus, which does not amount to an *obligation* to reach consensus. The Member States can therefore express their views on questions within national competence if, and only if, it proved impossible to adopt a common position. As to the danger that such a clause may be an incentive *not* to make the best effort to reach agreement,[117] prohibiting unilateral action in such a case would be an excessive reaction if set in relation to the aim of putting more pressure on the Member States to come to an agreement. It is submitted that such a prohibition could be justified only where evidence showed that Community participation was brought to a total standstill.

Third, any decisions on this are taken within the Council, even in non-Community matters, "in order that it may fully perform the role assigned to it by the TEU".[118] This refers to the requirement of coherence in the external actions of the EU laid down in Art 3 TEU, and indicates an interesting self-perception of the Council as representing the Member States, also in the Community framework,

---

[114] Ibid.
[115] *Hyett* (2000) 250.
[116] Opinion 1/94 *WTO* [1994] ECR I-5257, para 108.
[117] *Sack* (1995) 1255.
[118] See the Council's response to Question 11 of the Court in 1/94, I-5384.

whereas it would be for the Commission to represent the Community.[119]

A more general code of conduct in relation to the WTO as a whole, though, as proposed by the Commission after the Opinion, had not been concluded by the Council in spite of intense discussions from 1995 to mid-1996.[120] The reason for this was the non-acceptance of the - sensible - procedures sketched out above by some Member States, in particular the principle of single representation by the Commission.[121]

4. FAO-Arrangement

The third example, the FAO code of conduct, deserves further analysis for two reasons. First, within the UN system, the FAO is still the only organisation where the constitutive act was modified in order to allow for a participation of the Community.[122] Nevertheless, the statutory position of the EC is less favourable than in the WTO, as its membership rights are accessory to that of the Member States and can only be exercised alternatively.[123] Secondly, the restrictions placed on the membership of the EC and the alleged unwillingness of the Member States "to yield even an inch of diplomatic territory to the EC"[124] resulted in a case before the ECJ, in the course of which the code of conduct played an important role.

To cut the facts of the case[125] to its barest essentials, there were interminable discussions over the question whether the Commission or the Member States were competent to conclude an Agreement drawn up within the FAO which fell within joint competence. Triggered by the principle of alternative exercise of membership, which governed the Community's position within FAO,[126] the Council and the Commission had agreed on an "Arrangement" setting up a co-

[119] This would conflict with a division of roles between the Council for political and the Commission for technical matters, see *Groux* (1983) 95.

[120] *Timmermans* (2000) 244.

[121] So *Krentzler/da Fonseca-Wollheim* (1998) 230.

[122] Part of the difficulties stemmed therefore from the fear of setting a precedent, as the UN family is governed by similar rules, *Frid* (1993) 242.

[123] See *Heliskoski* (2000) 79ff for a detailed analysis.

[124] *Sack* (1995) 1244.

[125] C-25/94 *FAO-Fishery Agreement* [1996] ECR I-1469.

[126] Art II:8 FAO Constitution.

ordination procedure. It provides that in matters of exclusive competence, the Commission is entitled to speak and vote, whereas in matters of national competence, the Member States speak and vote. In matters of shared competence, the aim is to achieve a common position by consensus. *If* a common position can be achieved, the joint position will be presented by the Presidency, if the "thrust of the issue" lies in an area outside the exclusive competence of the Community, whereas the Commission expresses the joint position when the thrust of the issue lies in an area within the exclusive competence of the Commission.[127]

The agreement in question covered, on the one hand, matters within the Community's exclusive competence (conservation of the resources of the sea), and, on the other, matters within national competence (registration of vessels and the right to fly the flag of a Member State). The Commission had agreed with the indication of shared competence, and a common position was reached and was acted upon by the Member States, so that the conflict arose only as regards the question of voting. Therefore, according to AG *Jacobs,* the terms of the Arrangement, which were obviously intended to provide a structure for co-operation were observed, so that there was no breach of the obligation of co-operation.[128]

The ECJ, though, did not reject the application as inadmissible due to the lack of a genuine dispute of substance between the parties,[129] as advised by the AG. By contrast, whereas *Jacobs* seemed to regard only a dispute over the extent of competence of the Community as being able to elevate the case to the attention of the Court, the ECJ rightly devoted its attention also to the "merely procedural" issue who should be entitled to vote. The decisive point rested on whether the agreement concerned an issue "whose main thrust lies in an area within the exclusive competence of the Community".[130] It did not prove difficult for the ECJ to establish that this was the case for the Agreement, but the concept behind its argumentation is remarkable.

The ECJ broke the ground by recalling that the duty of close cooperation, flowing from requirement of unity in the international representation of the Community, was essential when the subject-

---

[127] *FAO* para 6-7.

[128] Opinion of AG *Jacobs* in *FAO*, para 68, 71-72.

[129] Critically *Helikoski* (2000) 87-89.

[130] *FAO* para 40.

matter of an agreement fell partly within the competence of the Community and partly within that of the Member States. It then continued: "[...] section 2.3. of the Arrangement [...] *represents fulfilment* of that duty of co-operation."[131] This step not only brought the Arrangement within the realm of Community law,[132] but, even more important, its substance was at the same time sanctioned by the Court. In spite of the problems inherent in any effort to define competence in terms of the "thrust of the issue",[133] this provision as set out in section 2.3. was not contested by the ECJ. This should be contrasted with the view of the Advocate General that even when the subject-matter of the vote came only partially within the Community's exclusive competence, the right to vote should be attributed to the Community. He doubted that in such cases of partial exclusivity the Council had the discretion to attribute the right to vote either to the Community or to the Member States.[134] However, this assumption was implicitly rejected.

What are the implications of this finding? As has been observed, the success of clauses similar to section 2.3. of the FAO Arrangement depends on good faith, a requirement which is apparently inconsistent with the temptation of the Member States in cases of joint competence to try to keep the main responsibility[135] and with a very sensitive Commission. Although in the *FAO* case, the ECJ had no difficulty to prevent abuse of the ambiguous criteria used in the Arrangement, the judgment showed the "unworkable situation" which existed apparently behind the scenes at the FAO.[136] Interestingly, though, there was no conflict in substance, as a common position had been reached. Far from being merely procedural,[137] the issue of voting proved to be at the heart of the dispute. The *leitmotiv* of the concern of the Member States seemed to be the pure sym-

---

[131] *FAO* para 49, emphasis added.

[132] *Heliskoski* (2000) 94.

[133] *Sack* (1995) 1256.

[134] Opinion of AG Jacobs in *FAO* [1996] ECR I-1472, para 74.

[135] *Sack* (1995) 1256. According to *Frid,* referring to the reciprocity of the duty of co-operation, the Member States could take advantage of it and advance the need of joint participation in matters in which the Commission claimed sole Community participation, *Frid* (1995) 152.

[136] *Hilf* (1997) 297.

[137] But so AG *Jacobs* in *FAO* para 74.

bolism contained in the fact that the Community would take the vote.[138]

5. Further Implications

To conclude, the admission of the Community as a Member of the FAO led to a reinforcement of the idea that an elaboration of a specific and precise declaration of competence is a necessary prerequisite for admission of the Community to IOs in general.[139] Still, in cases where such codes of conducts are missing, the principle of the duty of co-operation is in itself not concrete enough to allow that unambiguous guidelines concerning the extent of co-operation required are deduced from it – and it could be argued that this is not for the Court to do. By declaring inter-institutional agreements admissible for legal review, it is again for the Member States and the Commission to agree on both practicable and sensible code of conducts. If this exercise is successful, the ECJ is clearly determined to devote some attention to their content, which indirectly leads to the definition of some standards for the exercise of joint competence.

It has also become clear that such codes of conduct, if they are to be practicable, cannot strictly adhere to the legal division between respective competences of the Community and the Member States. First, and important, condition for a successful negotiation in terms of credibility and continuity is a single spokesperson.[140] In addition, a divergence of views can be resolved at internal level, by adoption of a common position, in order to reduce any temptation (for third parties) to test, or (for the Member States) to leave, the agreed position. Such a procedure is therefore appropriate to reinforce the principle of Community solidarity, which entails both a positive obligation (co-ordination and collaboration) as well as a negative obligation (prohibition of certain ways of behaviour of the Member States).[141]

Solidarity is essentially at stake if the Commission pursues a policy informed by the wider interests of the Community as a whole which does not necessarily reflect any particular interest of the Member States. Though, the interest of the Community is also a collective interest, and if there is a difference between the collective

---

[138] *Heliskoski* (2000) 99. See *McGoldrick* (1997) 99ff on the different strategic aspects of approaching questions of competence.

[139] So *Dormoy* (1998) 328.

[140] See *Groux* (1983) 94.

[141] *Blanquet* (1994) 228-231.

interest and the interest of some Member State, this is "une problematique *d'intérêt général* qu'il faut adopter."[142] The usual remedy is protection of the interest of the Member States by Community procedures designed to secure consensus, by the adoption of a common position. Hence, in return for the concession by the Member States to respect the necessity of external unity, there is the safeguard of a possible veto which is necessary as the fields of shared competences will arguably be the ones in which sensitive policy fields are touched.

IV. Recent Developments

As most recent developments show, prospects regarding a united appearance at external level are not conclusive.

A. International Coffee Agreement

Very recently, one of the commodities agreements covered by Art 133 EC which had been concluded by the Community jointly with the Member States under the PROBA 20 Agreement, the International Coffee Agreement, had to be renegotiated, due to the expiration of the 1994 agreement in September 2001.[143] There is certainly some truth in the observation that the decision to give a mixed character to a negotiation and to the conclusion of an agreement created a precedent which could be overturned only with difficulty. The commodity agreements would be the best example, as the Commission had proposed on several occasions sole Community participation, which the Council rejected.[144] Since the last fruitless endeavour, however, the ECJ has revised its stance of *Natural Rubber*, in which it had agreed to the notion of shared competence because of the Member States' financing of the buffer stock.[145] In its *WTO* opinion, it dismissed the argument that contribution to the expenses of the WTO was enough to justify the participation of the Member States in the conclusion of the agreement.[146] Consequently, the Commission in its recent proposal endorsed the view that the contributions by the Member States to the

---

142 *Blanquet* (1994) 113.

143 94/570/EC Council Decision concerning the conclusion of the International Coffee Agreement 1994, OJ L 222, 26/08/1994 1, extended by 1999/803/EC, OJ L 313 , 07/12/1999.

144 *Groux* (1983) 90.

145 Opinion 1/78 *Natural Rubber* [1979] ECR 2871, 52-60.

146 Opinion 1/94 *WTO* [1994] ECR I-5267 19-21.

operating budget of the Coffee Agreement, where no financial instrument existed, were not enough to justify their participation in the conclusion of the Agreement. The new Agreement should be negotiated by the Commission.[147]

On September 20, Coreper formulated a decision in which it accepted exclusive Community competence, nevertheless authorising the Member States to conclude the Agreement at the same time as the Community and "to participate on a temporary basis in the new Agreement [...] in order to avoid certain temporary operational difficulties."[148] At the same time, the Member States are obliged to ensure that the Community's participation in the Agreement is governed by the applicable Treaty provisions, i.e. to ensure that, within a year from its entry into force, the provisions of the International Coffee Agreement which create operational difficulties for the sole Community membership, are amended.[149]

In particular, Article 4 of the Agreement would have to be changed, as the EC has not full membership rights. For instance, it does not itself have any votes but in the case of a vote on matters within its competence it casts collectively the votes of its Member States, and is not eligible for election to the Executive Board but may only participate in the discussions of the Executive Board on matters within its competence.[150] One key problem will certainly be the question whether the Community as the single participant will then dispose of a voting right of its own – and consequently the number of votes will be reduced dramatically from 15 times 5 to 1 times 5 – or whether it will continue to express the voting rights of its Member States, although they are no longer members.

The Council decision was taken as it was on September 24,[151] without the votes of three delegations. In particular the German abstention was caused by the future exclusion of the Member States from the work of the Coffee-Agreement, by the question how the Member States should fulfil the obligation resulting from Article 3, and by doubts whether the depositor of the UN would accept such a

[147] COM (2001) 513 final of 13/09/2001, explanatory memorandum.

[148] Council Decision on the signing and conclusion on behalf of the EC of the International Coffee Agreement 2001, 11953/01.

[149] Article 3, 11953/01.

[150] Article 4 International Coffee Agreement 1994, OJ L 222, 26/08/1994.

[151] 2001/877/EC, Council Decision on the signing and conclusion on behalf of the EC of the International Coffee Agreement, OJL 326 11/12/01.

conditional ratification. Other declarations as well stressed the importance of continued Member State participation in the Coffee-Agreement, even as spokesman or similar in order to allow the Community to benefit from the experience acquired by the national experts. The actual code of conduct which will rule Community participation in this forum should thus receive some attention. Future will have to tell whether it was a wise decision by the Commission to overturn the old deal of mixed commodity agreements. It will be telling whether this agreement is going to serve as a precedent for the other commodities agreements, for which PROBA 20 remains relevant.[152]

B. Kyoto Protocol

Another interesting development is the status of the Community in the much debated Kyoto Protocol to the UN Framework Convention on Climate Change,[153] for the conclusion of which and the joint fulfilment of commitments thereunder the Commission recently presented a proposal.[154] As under Art 24 a "regional economic integration organisation" may participate even if none of its Member States are Parties, the Community would be accepted as a Party to the Protocol in its own right. In case of organisations one or more Member States of which is a Party to the Protocol (as for the EC), the organisation and its Member States must not exercise rights under the Protocol concurrently, but must decide on their respective responsibilities and inform the Parties thereof (also of

---

[152] So far, the unchanged International Cocoa Agreement 1993 has been extended for two further years, see COM (2001) 514 and 11950/01.

[153] Decision 1/CP.3. The text of the Kyoto Protocol, which had been adopted already in 1997, is annexed to COM (2001) 579.

[154] COM (2001) 579. The Commission suggests, as the legal basis for conclusion, Art 174 Para 4 in conjunction with Art 300 Para 2 first sentence (i.e., qualified majority) and Para 3 EC. This decision is not uncontested, as it follows from Art 300 Para 2 2nd sentence that if the agreement relates to a matter for which unanimity is required, the Council is to act unanimously, so that it is necessary to consider whether internal Community rules corresponding to the provisions of the Protocol would be adopted on the basis of Art 175 Para 1 (qualified majority), or on the basis of Art 175 Para 2 (unanimity). Cf. the clear stance of the ECJ in Opinion 2/00 *Cartagena* [2001] ECR I-9731, para 43-44.

any substantial modification).[155] This implies that the participation of the Community will mirror its internal division of power, which partly fall within the Community competence and partly within that of the Member States. The result of this provision is yet another field of joint participation which necessitates respect of the legal duties flowing from the duty of co-operation – for instance in the field of ratification, where the Commission presses for simultaneous ratification, and joint implementation.

The latter aspect, joint implementation, is most interesting for our purposes, as Art 4 to the Kyoto Protocol provides that joint fulfilment of the commitments is possible, under the condition that the combined aggregate reduction commitment does not exceed the assigned amounts inscribed in Annex B. The EC therefore was able to achieve consensus on the point that it could redistribute its targets among the Member States as long as the outcome still amounted to an overall reduction for the European Community of 8%.[156] As these redistributed targets have to be officially notified to the Secretariat of the Convention (Art 4 Para 2), the proposed Council decision now carries an annex to the Kyoto Protocol defining the responsibilities of the EC as a whole and of the individual Member States (the 'Community bubble' concept.)[157]

In particular, Para 6 of Art 4 is remarkable, as it establishes that if the EC fails to achieve its commitments, each Member State is responsible for its level of emissions as notified. In other words, although Annex B foresees an individual commitment of each Member State to reduce its emissions by 8%, each Member State is only responsible for the limit agreed upon according to Community law.[158] It goes without saying that this is not only an important achievement – although easier in the framework of international agreements than within already established organisations[159] – but

---

[155] See the EC declaration in Annex C, which reproduces, essentially, Art 174 Para 4 and the objectives set out in Para 1 EC. Hence, the declaration is framed "in the most general terms possible", which is but one strategy to resist declarations of competence, *McGoldrick* (1997) 112.

[156] Political agreement on Community internal redistribution was reached on June 16, 1998, see the Council conclusions on the "Burden sharing" agreement, Press release No 9132/97, http://ue.eu.int/newsroom.

[157] See Bulletin EU 10-1997, 1.2.183.

[158] The "burden sharing" will be binding on the Member States, see Article 2 of the proposed Council decision, COM (2001) 579.

[159] *Sack* (1995) 1238.

may serve as an example where the legal standards set by the ECJ seem to have flown in the negotiation of an international agreement.

V. Conclusion

As regards the question of bringing in line the Community's formal status in IOs with its competences, the outlook has to be rather pessimistic. At the external front, recent developments have been called a confirmation of the traditional principles of the intergovernmental character of IOs, that is to say, participation is still the monopoly of States and entities other than States have no choice but to accept their "anterior" status.[160] If in the case of exclusive competences, the Community alone took part, the elevation of the Community to the status of a state would be complete, as the Community then would have the same status as the other members of the organisation.[161] This point is justified insofar as it emphasises the political nature of the question of external Community representation, where exactly because of this view, any progress seems to be regarded as the opening of Pandora's box. Though, it should be clear that from the transfer of exclusive competences and the Community's sole participation in a certain IO alone, there would not be a change to its status as IO, which is a member of another IO: this would not turn the Community in a state.

Political considerations are sometimes suspected to guide also the ECJ in cases relating to the division of competences, by shying back from decisions which would not be acceptable to the Member States.[162] The opinion on the Cartagena Protocol could be easily reconciled with this view. Nevertheless, the critique appears unjustified insofar as the ECJ has set clear lines along which efforts should be made. It is on the Member States and Community institutions to translate into actual practice a principle which the ECJ spelled out more than 20 years ago: that performance of the duties of co-operation is, in particular, necessary in fields in which worthwhile results can be only attained by co-operation of all the Member States.[163] External relations, as a whole, is such a field, as

---

[160] *Dormoy* (1998) 331. See also the discussion of the EC's participation in the IMF in *Dutzler's* contribution of the Community representation in EMU, at 448ff (in particular 470ff).

[161] So *Dormoy* (1998) 329.

[162] So *Hilf* (1997) 294-295.

[163] C-141/78 *France v. U.K.* [1979] ECR 2923, para 8.

here, "the only requirement is to take sensible steps in presenting a united front to international partners".[164]

The root of the problem seems to be the *implicit* assumption that sole EC authorisation to become a party to an international agreement was an acceptance of its exclusive competence over the subject of the agreement, and that this would also apply internally, even without express Treaty provisions or express rules.[165] *Cartagena*, where the Member States and the Council suspected that the Commission wanted to extend exclusive Community competence in order to avoid the practical difficulties resulting from the conclusion of mixed agreements and continuance of Member States' presence proves this very point.[166] Arguably, the situation could be remedied if it was accepted that external representation and external competences do not necessarily need to be treated as an entity. There are good reasons to disentangle both and to accept that not only exclusive Community competence does not have to result in exclusive Community representation (Member States used as trustees) but that this cuts both ways, that internally shared competence does not necessarily have to result in external joint participation. The legitimacy of the venture to give predominance to political considerations on legal institutional problems depends on its success, so *Groux* for PROBA 20, which arguably, has met the test.[167]

It has been argued from the side of the Member States that they were the last to have intention of undermining the enormous bargaining power which they exercised collectively, but their overriding interest was to deploy that bargaining power in the most effective way possible.[168] If this was true, then that principle demanded self-restraint by the Community when ranking the aim of formal acceptance of its dignity as international actor higher than the aim of effective negotiation.[169] But at the same time, also the Member States are called upon to thoroughly review their position to support formal membership of the Community at their place if this was warranted by the competences mainly concerned and would add to

---

164 *Dashwood/Heliskoski* (2000) 19.

165 See the discussion in *McGoldrick* (1997) 106.

166 Opinion 2/00, *Cartagena,* [2001] ECR I-9731.

167 *Groux* (1983) 96.

168 Compare also the arguments given in *Brückner* (1990) for the UN.

169 See *Schermers* (1983) 837, cf. also *Sack's* account of the FAO (1995) 1246.

a more efficient participation of the Community in IOs, which is in the collective interest of all parties involved. After all, the persuasiveness of a bargaining power which amounts merely to a repetition by different actors of the same common position appears small in comparison to the power of a unified voice.

Bibliography

Blanquet M. (1994), L'Article 5 Du Traité C.E.E., Recherche sur les Obligations de Fidélité des États Membres de la Communauté, Paris 1994.

Brinkhorst L. J. (1994), The European Community at UNCED: Lessons to be Drawn for the Future, in: *Curtin D./Heukels T.* (eds.), Institutional Dynamics of European Integration, Essays in Honour of Henry G. Schermers, Vol. II, Dordrecht et. al. 1994, 609-617.

Brückner P. (1990), The European Community and the United Nations, EJIL 1990 174-192.

Cloos J., Reinesch G., Vignes D., Weyland J. (1993), Le Traité de Maastricht: genèse, analyse, commentaires, Bruxelles 1993.

Dashwood A., Heliskoski J. (2000), The Classic Authorities Revisited, in: *Dashwood A., Hillion C.* (eds.), The General Law of E.C. External Relations, London 2000, 3-19.

Dolmans M. J. F. M. (1985), Problems of Mixed Agreements, Division of Powers within the EEC and the Rights of Third States, The Hague 1985.

Dormoy, D. (1998), Recent Developments Regarding the Law on Participation in International Organisations, in: *Wellens K.* (ed.), International law: Theory and Practice, The Hague 1998, 323-332.

Dormoy, D. (1997), Le Statut de L'Union Européenne dans les Organisations Internationales, in: *Vitoria R.* (ed.), L'Union Européenne et les organisations internationales, Bruxelles 1997, 36-55.

Editorial (1995), The Aftermath of Opinion 1/94 or how to Ensure Unity of Representation for Joint Competences, CMLRev. 1995, 385-390.

Ehlermann C. (1983), Mixed Agreements A List of Problems, in: *O'Keeffe/Schermers* (eds.), Mixed Agreements, Dordrecht 1983, 3-21.

Feenstra J. J. (1983), A Survey of Mixed Agreements and their Participation Clauses, in: *O'Keeffe/Schermers* (eds.), Mixed Agreements, Dordrecht 1983, 207-248.

Frid R. (1993), The European Economic Community: A Member of a Specialized Agency of the United Nations, EJIL 1993, 239-255.

Frid R. (1995), The Relations between the EC and International Organisations, Legal Theory and Practice, The Hague 1995.

Grabitz E. (1974), Die Stellung der Gemeinschaft und ihrer Organe in internationalen Organisationen, in: *Carstens/Börner* (eds.), Die Aussenbeziehungen der Europäischen Gemeinschaft, KSE 25, Köln et.al. 1974, 47-81.

Groux J. (1983), Mixed Negotiations, in: *O'Keeffe/Schermers* (eds.), Mixed Agreements, Dordrecht 1983, 87-96.

Heliskoski J. (2000), Internal Struggle for International Presence: The Exercise of Voting Rights within the FAO, in: *Dashwood A./Hillion C.* (eds), The General Law of E.C. External Relations, London 2000, 79-99.

Hilf (1997), Ungeschriebene EG-Außenkompetenzen im Außenwirtschaftsrecht, ZfV 3/1997, 293-301.

Hyett S. (2000), The Duty of Co-operation: A Flexible Concept, in: *Dashwood A./Hillion C.* (eds), The General Law of E.C. External Relations, London 2000, 248-253.

Hummer W. (1995), Enge und Weite der „treaty making power" der Kommission der EG nach dem EWG-Vertrag, in: *Randelzhofer* et.al. (eds), Gedächtnisschrift für Eberhard Grabitz, München 1995, 195-226.

Krenzler H. G., da Fonseca H. (1998), Die Reichweite der gemeinsamen Handelspolitik nach dem Vertrag von Amsterdam – eine Debatte ohne Ende?, Europarecht 3/1998, 223-241.

Lang J. T. (1990), Community Constitutional Law: Article 5 EEC Treaty, CMLRev. 1990, 645-681.

Louis J. V. (1999), Les Relations Internationales de L'Union Economique et Monétaire, EUI Working Paper LAW No 99/10.

MacLeod I., Hendry I. D., Hyett S. (1996), The External Relations of the European Communities, Oxford 1996.

McGoldrick D. (1997), International Relations Law of the European Union, London New York 1997.

Osteneck K. (2000), Artikel 302-304 EGV, in: *Schwarze J.* (ed.), EU-Kommentar, Baden-Baden 2000.

Pernice I. (1991), Die EG als Mitglied der Organisationen im System der Vereinten Nationen: Konsequenzen für die Politik von Mitgliedstaaten und Drittstaaten, EuR 3/1991, 273-281.

Sack J. (1995), The European Community's Membership of International Organizations, CMLRev. 1995, 1227-1256.

Sack J. (2001), Die Europäische Union in den Internationalen Organisationen, Bedeutung der Beteiligung sowie Aktion und Einfluss von Gemeinschaft und Mitgliedstaaten in diesen Gremien, ZEuS 2/2001, 268-284.

Sander G. G. (2000), Gesundheitsschutz in der WTO – eine neue Bedingung des Codex Alimentarius im Lebensmittelrecht? ZEuS 3/2000, 335-375.

Schermers H. G. (1983), International Organizations as Members of Other International Organizations, in: *Bernhardt R.* et al. (eds.), Völkerrrecht als Rechtsordnung Internationale Gerichtsbarkeit Menschenrechte, FS für Hermann Mosler, Berlin et al. 1983.

Schloh B. (1974), Die Stellung der Europäischen Gemeinschaft und ihrer Organe in internationalen Organisationen, in: *Carstens/Börner* (eds.), Die Aussenbeziehungen der Europäischen Gemeinschaft, KSE 25, Köln et.al. 1974, 83-102.

Schröder M. (1997), Vorbemerkung zu den Artikeln 229-231, in: *Groeben/Thiesing/Ehlermann* (eds.), Kommentar zum EU-/EG-Vertrag, Baden-Baden 1997, 5/529-5/545.

Tietje C. (2000), Artikel 302-304 EGV, in: *Grabitz E./Hilf M.* (eds.), Das Recht der Europäischen Union, München 2000.

Timmermans C. (2000), Organising Joint Participation of EC and Member States, in: *Dashwood A./Hillion C.* (eds), The General Law of E.C. External Relations, London 2000, 239-247.

Tridimas T. (2000), The WTO and OECD Opinions, in: *Dashwood A., Hillion C.* (2000), The General Law of E.C. External Relations, London 2000, 48-60.

Vedder C. (1995), Die Integrationskompetenz der EG in der Rechtssprechung des EuGH, in: *Randelzhofer* et.al. (eds), Gedächtnisschrift für Eberhard Grabitz, München 1995, 795-817.

Vitoria R. (1997), L'Union Européenne et les organisations internationales, Bruxelles 1997.

Weiler J. H. (1983), The External Relations on Non-Unitary Actors: Mixity and the Federal Principle, in: *O'Keeffe/Schermers* (eds.), Mixed Agreements, Dordrecht 1983, 35-83.

Zieger G. (1974), Die Stellung der Europäischen Gemeinschaft und ihrer Organe in internationalen Organisationen, in: *Carstens/Börner* (eds.), Die Aussenbeziehungen der Europäischen Gemeinschaft, KSE 25, Köln et.al. 1974, 103-150.

Zuleeg M. (1997), Kommentar Artikel 5, in: *von der Groeben/Thiesing/Ehlermann*, Handbuch des Europäischen Rechts, Baden-Baden 1997, 39-47.

Ulrich Immenga*

The Need for Multilateral Rules as a Consequence of Globalization and Liberalization

I. Elements of the Present Discussion

Around the world there is a raising appreciation and acknowledgement of the virtues of competition. The principal points are the decline of socialist countries, the raise of market economies and the implementation of competition laws by about 80 states at present.

Politically most important was the initiative of the European Union in 1995. Based on a report of a group of experts, the EU officially proposed the development of international rules.[1] The EU should be considered the most appropriate proponent of an

---

* Professor of Law, doctor honoris causa, Department of International and Foreign Economic Law, University of Göttingen.

[1] *European Commission* (1995).

internationalization of competition laws. There are less own political interests. The Commission's competition policy is strong and increasingly supported by the Member States. And most important, the Community has gained abundant experience in the creation and application of supranational rules.

The first WTO ministerial conference, held in Singapore in December 1996, directly addressed the issue and established a Working Group on the Interaction between Trade and Competition Policy. About 60 states participated in this group which presented a comprehensive report on its deliberations in November 1998.

There was a strong feeling to continue these efforts in 1999 at the ministerial conference in Seattle. The European Union and other governments (e.g. Austria and Germany) expressed their political interest to include the issue of international competition rules again on the agenda. Unfortunately, the conference failed.

There is a widespread academic consensus at least to develop conceptions of a set of international rules. Several academic circles have been set up to present papers with concrete proposals and even the draft of a code of international rules.[2]

These elements might put into question the subject of my report. Why is it still necessary to elaborate on questions of the need of international competition rules? First, these elements are not unilaterally welcomed. In particular the official policy of the United States holds against developments in this sense. They are considered to be premature. Second, it has to be realized that there are many complex issues of law and politics on the table to broaden a consensus and cautiously to develop the present status of international competition law.

II. The Need for International Rules: Six Reasons

First, from a trade policy perspective, the interrelation of private and public trade barriers has to be recognized clearly. The Uruguay Round successfully liberalized tariffs and non-tariff trade barriers to permit a freer flow of goods and services. These achievements might be seriously diminished if private firms could replace previously existing public barriers of trade by restraints of competition. The competition rules of the EC-Treaty demonstrate the necessity to accomplish an internal market. Otherwise, market

---

[2] E.g. *Zäch* (1999); *Fikentscher/Immenga* (1995); *Ullrich* (1998).

sharing agreements and other restrictive behaviours might replace state barriers.

Second, given the globalization of the economy, there are more and more competition problems which transcend national boundaries. International cartels or mergers on a world scale are most prominent examples. Competition authorities therefore have a prime interest in cooperating to solve these problems together in order to enhance the effective enforcement of competition rules.

Third, as a result of a lack of rules on the international level, firms which are present in several countries are sometimes subject to different national competition rules. Procedures vary considerably, mergers or concerted practices might be authorized in one country and prohibited in another.

Fourth, actions against anticompetitive practices might be less rigorous in some countries than in others. Distortions of competition may be a result.

Fifth, most countries apply in international cases the so called effects-doctrine. Competition rules apply independently of their origin from foreign countries if domestic markets are affected. This approach can lead to conflicts between competition authorities. In absence of international rules, there are legal and practical obstacles to seeking on foreign territories the information necessary.

Sixth, developing countries in particular should have an interest in ensuring effective controls on anticompetitive behaviour. The worldwide lowering of governmental market access barriers may leave them more exposed to the risk of anticompetitive practices. In a system of multilateral rules they may be protected best.

All these problems are liable to undermine the positive results of the former Uruguay Round agreements. Nevertheless, as already mentioned, there are strong US objections based on arguments which are generally political in their character.

III. US-Objections

It has been stated that the US Chamber of Commerce, the US Council for International Business and the Antitrust Division of the Department of Justice all oppose actual WTO negotiations on competition policy at this time.[3] The arguments are as follows:

There is a fast increasing number of competition laws around the world. The former Soviet Bloc countries are generally dedicated to

[3] These arguments are taken from *Davidow* (1999) 29-43.

demonopolisation measures because they know well that they really need this kind of legislation. Developing countries have largely joined the bandwagon. Others, like Indonesia, are now succumbing to pressure from World Bank and International and Monetary Fund experts who now deem competition law to be a necessary part of a free market society operating under the rule of law. In the framework of these developments the time of multilateral rules has not yet come.

The United States might have thought of the WTO dispute settlement as a way to delegitimise any effort by the EU to fine Boeing for acquiring McDonnell-Douglas. But the United States has sufficient diplomatic strength left to preserve its interests in such matters directly. This is the most political point, though sometimes hidden, which seems to have important weight in the discussions.

The EU proposal aims toward making the WTO not merely a dispute settler, but also an investigator and enforcer. These are roles the WTO does not play in any other field.

It is thought that a WTO system would likely follow an EU, not US type approach, since the EU has had a far greater success than the US in selling its competition law approach to other nations. Twenty-three countries now conform their competition laws to EU norms, and most developing countries find the EU's commission-based, administrative law, abuse control model more compatible with their existing laws and capacities than would be a US type system.

The developing countries largely see international competition rules as a way to investigate or punish powerful multinational enterprises, many of which are American.

It has been observed, however, that the momentum for quicker WTO action on competition may be irresistible. The EU becomes a stronger force each year. The US may have to become involved rather than forfeit all influence on the contents of the project.

IV. The Lack of Present Rules to Provide Adequate Relief

A. The Effects-Doctrine

The application of national competition law to international restraints of competition is mostly based on the effects-doctrine. This doctrine was first introduced into US antitrust law in 1945 when the famous ALCOA-decision declared invalid contracts concluded abroad but showing effects on national imports.[4] § 130 II 1 of the German Law Against Restraints of Competition explicitly states that the law also applies to restrictive practices outside its territorial reach as far as they cause effects within it. The European Commission has referred to the effects-doctrine on several occasions whereas the European Court of Justice hesitates to rely on the effects-doctrine and rather refers to the territorial principle or the single economic unit theory.[5] In general, the effects-doctrine is acknowledged by the majority of the international community although its validity and ambit remain controversial.

The effects-doctrine originates from the national claim to intervene by law in conduct abroad. Hence, being directly extended to foreign countries, jurisdiction becomes extraterritorial and does not seldomly evoke international conflicts as the legal conceptions of competition and industrial policy tend to differ significantly. Especially the severe extraterritorial application of the US antitrust laws has caused numerous foreign governmental reactions (e.g. blocking statutes).[6]

It may not be concluded, however, that implementing the effects-doctrine into national law is absolutely inappropriate a method. The prerequisites for an approach to a competition order based on the effects-doctrine would be, first, that national antitrust laws consist of almost equal substantive law, and second, that in practice the law is effectively applied. Consequently, national authorities would prosecute the national and international effects of restrictive practices quite similarly. Even with regard to trade between countries favoring comparable conceptions of competition policy, these prerequisites, which demand widely harmonized national laws, are not given, however.

Therefore, the effects-doctrine is mostly recognized as an instrument to unilaterally effectuate national competition policy. The more the governmental conceptions diverge, the greater is the likelihood of conflicts arising. In order to promote international understanding and at least to rudimentarily deal with issues of competition on an international level the effects doctrine has been specified and modified.

---

4 *United States v. Aluminum Co. of America*, 148 F. 2 nd 416, 444 (2nd cir. 1945).

5 *Rehbinder* (1998) 71.

6 See in detail *Griffin* (1998) 64ff.

B. Balancing of Interests

The evolution of a balancing of interests-test proved to be considerably important. Accordingly, the exercise of jurisdiction is not unilaterally limited but rather evaluated by respecting foreign interests colliding with the extraterritorial jurisdiction in a particular case. This respect refers to the international principle of courtoisie or comity although it is not an approved general principle of international law and its application remains uncertain. The reduction of governmental interests in exercising jurisdiction is called negative comity whereas the recently introduced positive comity requires efficient enforcement of the law (see below C).

Especially the US courts presented several approaches to a precise balancing. In the landmark decision *Timberlane Lumber Company v. Bank of America*[7] the idea of balancing was expressed as follows:

An effect on United States commerce, although necessary to the exercise of jurisdiction under the antitrust laws, is alone not a sufficient basis on which to determine whether American authority should be asserted in a given case as a matter of international comity and fairness.

Still, definite principles of balancing interests necessarily imply a consensus on which aspects shall be included and how they shall be evaluated. In the Timberlane case the following seven elements were considered relevant:

- the degree of conflict with foreign law or policy
- the nationality or allegiance of the parties and the locations or principal places of business of corporations
- the extent to which enforcement by either state can be expected to achieve compliance
- the relative significance of effects on the United States as compared with those elsewhere
- the extent to which there is explicit intention to harm or affect American commerce
- the foreseeability of such effects
- the relative importance of effects within the United States as compared with those abroad.

The difficulties in evaluating these factors are evident, and the attempts to likewise establish principles of an international antitrust law have not produced the desired results. Due to the fact that the

7 549 F. 2d 597, 613 (9th Cir. 1976).

conflicts in question arise from interfering policies of sovereign nations, legal solutions appear to be almost unworkable, anyway. Not surprisingly, rather serious conflicts are regularly solved in the course of diplomatic negotiations.

C. Bilateral Agreements

Bilateral agreements referring to the cooperation of antitrust authorities shall ensure competition in international trade by reducing the conflicts of extraterritorial jurisdiction.[8] Accordingly, bilateralism implies the unilateralism of the effects-doctrine. Up to a certain extent, bilateral agreements based on international law can reduce the difficulties existing in current international antitrust law. These agreements obligate the contracting parties to mutually notify restrictive practices, to exchange information, to harmonize enforcement and to develop provisions concerning confidentiality. Such agreements were concluded in particular between the United States and Canada, Germany, Australia, and the European Community. Another agreement was signed by Australia and New Zealand. The participation of the United States in most cases can be interpreted politically: Since bilateral agreements and their application are subject to the consent of both participants, the United States can continually safeguard their interests. On the other hand, multilateral agreements often contain compromises and tend to diminish national sovereignty, especially when adopting the principle of majority rule.

In the course of the evolution of bilateral agreements, new elements have been included which define potential conflicts at an early stage and thus make their outcome more predictable. In this context, the agreement between the European Community and the United States (1991) should be mentioned.[9] In analogy to the above mentioned US court decisions, Article IV contains a catalogue of competing interests to be evaluated when exercising jurisdiction.

Even more considerable and of fundamental significance is the principle of positive comity, without precedent introduced in Art. V of the agreement. Whereas negative comity reduces the exercise of jurisdiction with regard to foreign interests, positive comity is based on the participants' general understanding to effectively apply national laws to conduct causing restrictive effect within the other country's territory.

---

8 See in detail *Immenga* (1996) 155-165.

9 *Campbell/Grundmann* (1997) 1973ff.

Without a dispute settlement system, however, conflicts arising from diverging conceptions of a particular bilateral agreement are unlikely to be solved. Without a positive comity-clause, bilateral agreements cannot be applied to business behaviour affecting imports. Furthermore, the existence of such a clause remains ineffective as long as the national law fails to prohibit restrictive practices, e.g. export-cartels. In addition, even the most progressive agreement between the European Community and the United States cannot solve politically sensitive cases on both sides of the Atlantic as the Boeing/McDonnell Douglas case has proved.[10]

In essence, the present system of unilateral jurisdiction, mitigated by bilateral agreements, is not capable of preventing restrictive business practices which undermine the liberalization of international trade. Therefore, the need for an international competition order still exists. Nevertheless, bilateral cooperation plays a vital role in this process and should be continued both qualitatively and quantitatively. Due to the exchange of information, valuable experience in exploring and legally evaluating restrictive practices across national borders is gained.

V. Basic Considerations to Develop Multilateral Rules

The WTO system should, to preserve a consistency of rules and institutions and to promote political acceptance, be extended along the lines of the present system in order to develop international competition rules as a plurilateral agreement.

There is a rising consensus on the interrelation of competition and trade issues. The respective rules have to be developed in consistency. It should be considered to what extent trade rules, for example those against dumping, could be substituted by competition rules.

Already at the present stage of developments in competition policy, it seems to be possible to achieve a general consensus on lower levels: a ban on clearly anti-competitive behaviour. To achieve a more stable framework for international trade the political impact should be diminished. Competition Policy has to be changed from discretionary policies to law. Provisions governing the conditions of market access should be strictly law-oriented and governed by a rule of law and due process. This is a condition to

---

10 *Banks* (1998) 309-311.

restrict politics in trade issues and to ensure efficiency in a liberalized economic system.

VI. Five Principles of a Draft International Antitrust Code (Outlook)

A large consensus that the WTO is the right institutional framework for implementing a set of international competition rules exists. The *Draft International Antitrust Code* (DIAC)[11] proposed by a group of academic experts and practitioners has to be seen in this context. The DIAC is an ambitious academic model designed as a *plurilateral trade agreement* in the sense of Annex 4 to the WTO Agreement in order to integrate competition rules into the broad WTO legal framework by an initially limited number of like-minded countries to be progressively extended. The basic principles of the DIAC are as follows:

First, implementation into the WTO System: The WTO offers the opportunity of plurilateral agreements under Annex 4 to the Agreement establishing the WTO. To implement international competition rules in this way means that the contracting parties are bound by international public law. The agreement does not, however, bind all parties to the WTO as multilateral agreements do, but only those who signed the plurilateral agreement. This procedure offers an evident advantage. The rules will, initially, apply only to those countries that are particularly interested and experienced in matters of international competition.

Second, transformation into national law: The still ruling concept of national sovereignty requires that the rules of the plurilateral agreement are implemented as national law. By way of this transformation, the rules have to be qualified legally as national law and, as part of a internationally binding agreement, as connected to public international law. This twofold legal qualification has to be taken into account to solve enforcement issues.

Third, national treatment: A further principle, well known on the international level and part of the GATT, is the requirement of national treatment. In the present context it means that national and international competition has to be treated without differentiation.

Fourth, minimum standards: An international code requires equal standards which are internationally applicable. These

---

[11] See note 2.

standards should be minimum standards to ensure that there will be at least a minimum of internationally equivalent provisions. It follows that those countries that are disposing of an anti-competitive legislation might have a two-tiered system, a bottom line of internationally standardized laws, and beyond them diverging national laws. This approach allows countries to develop their own rules for national competition issues.

Fifth, transborder cases: As an international code, its rules should deal with international cases only. Exclusively national cases are the preserve of national authorities and courts. The code has to apply to transborder situations. These provisions of the DIAC are applicable to restraints of competition that are affecting at least two parties to the agreement. A party is considered to be affected whenever there are economic effects within its territory or otherwise on its commerce.[12]

VII. Institutional and Enforcement Issues

These five principles are basically underlying both the DIAC and the EC expert report mentioned above.[13] There are some differences, however, with regard to enforcement issues and corresponding institutional requirements.

The EC expert report considers it necessary that an international body shall be entrusted with three functions:

First, to serve as a forum for drafting and permanently reviewing, adapting, and, insofar as possible, extending the common principles for incorporation in the various national laws and for their enforcement;

Second, to establish a register of anti-competitive practices which would initially concern only practices satisfying specific criteria. It follows that some notification requirements have to be established;

Third, to provide a structure for settling disputes between participating countries. According to the report, the WTO settlement mechanism seems to correspond fairly closely to the structure which might be established to arbitrate on disputes concerning action by competition authorities. In the following, the report refers in detail to the functions of such a panel. Violations would trigger international 'secondary obligations' recognized in

---

12 See in detail Art 3 Sec. 1(b) DIAC.

13 See note 1.

GATT/WTO law, for example cessation of the illegal act and possibility of authorization of countermeasures pending the withdrawal of the illegal act.

The efficiency of international competition rules depends on their enforcement. While the EC expert report's recommendations are cautiously framed with regard to the limited competences of the WTO, the DIAC develops new institutional means of enforcement which, however, largely respect national authorities.

To deal with enforcement issues, two kinds of problems have to be distinguished:

- violations with regard to the implementation of the Agreement;
- violations with regard to the application of the Agreement's rules.

The first type of disputes between the parties to the Agreement might be resolved according to the existing dispute settlement mechanism of the WTO. If the Agreement has not been implemented into national law, or has been implemented in an inadequate form, any party might call upon the panel of the WTO. There is a breach of international public law in the event of any violation of the Agreement. The remedies provided by the dispute settlement system will be applied. The DIAC comes close to this conception.[14]

The second type of disputes concerns a violation of national law implementing the rules of the Agreement. Two kinds of violations may occur. The national authorities might not enforce their laws. This might happen in international conflicts. A country may refuse to act against domestic restraints of competition which protect markets against the entry of foreign companies. Or, national authorities might apply the rules of the Agreement in a way considered wrong. Since the rules of the Agreement are not self-executing, it is necessary to provide an international control of these kinds of violations. The more cautious approach of the EC expert report refers to a specific dispute settlement panel, which has to be set up. The sanctions, however, are limited.

The DIAC presents a really new conception, which is not as strong as a self-executing character of the Agreement, but ensures international enforcement of the transformed national law. The conception is a step beyond the present WTO system, since it requires an International Antitrust Authority IAA as a new

---

[14] Art 19 Sec. 2(e); Art 20 Sec. 2.

institution. However, it has to be emphasized that the issuing of administrative orders by the IAA directed against private persons as initiators of a restraint of competition is not possible. Its powers are restricted to bring actions before national courts. This is the so-called international procedural initiative; the new idea which respects national sovereignty while ensuring the application of the rules of the international Agreement in a domestic court system.

The DIAC provides for the right of the IAA to bring actions against national antitrust authorities in individual cases before national law courts, whenever a national antitrust authority refuses to take appropriate measures against individual restraints of competition; the right to sue private persons and undertakings as alleged parties or initiators of a restraint of competition before national law courts seeking for injunctions against the execution of the restraint; and, finally, the right to national appeal, even when the IAA is not a party to the case, under the same conditions as parties to the case.

This conception offers an appropriate opportunity in the form of a compromise between national and international interests to enforce transborder competition rules. This system might be completed by additional civil law sanctions for instance that anti-competitive practices are not enforceable at law.[15] In this way domestic courts will play the decisive role in applying the international rules.

VIII. Conclusions

Obviously, there still will be a long period of time to bring issues of international competition into an adequate legal form. Within the next future it will be generally accepted, however, that the globalization of the economy inevitably requires rules which respond to the changing conditions of business. It will be crucial to overcome the potential impact on national sovereignty. This is predominantly an institutional issue. Having solved this problem it should be possible to gradually develop a generally accepted set of rules of substantive law.

---

[15] See *European Commission* (1995) 25.

Bibliography

J. D. Banks (1998), The Development of the Concept of Extraterritoriality under European Merger Law and its Effectiveness under the Merger Regulation following the Boeing/Mc Donnell Douglas Decision 1997, E.C.L.R. 1998, 306-311.

James S. Campbell/Silvia Grundmann (1997), Wettbewerbsrecht und seine internationale Durchsetzung: Kartellbehörden in Drittstaaten und ihre Beziehungen zur EG-Kommission am Beispiel des EG-US-Kartellrechtsabkommens in: *Immenga/Mestmäcker* (eds.), EG-Wettbewerbsrecht, Kommentar, Vol. II. 1997, 1963 - 1991.

Joel Davidow (1999), US Antitrust at the Fin de Siècle, World Competition, Vol. 22 No. 3, 1999, 29 - 43.

European Commission (1995), Policy in the New Trade Order: Strengthening International Cooperation and Rules, COM (95) 359 endg.

Wolfgang Fikentscher/Ulrich Immenga (1995) (eds.), Draft International Antitrust Code, Baden-Baden 1995.

Joseph P. Griffin (1998), Foreign Governmental Reactions to U.S. Assertions of Extraterritorial Jurisdiction, E.C.L.R. 1998, 64-73.

Ulrich Immenga (1996), Wirkungsgrenzen bilateraler Verträge für eine internationale Wettbewerbsordnung, in: *Jörn Kruse/O. G. Mayer* (eds.), Aktuelle Probleme der Wettbewerbs- und Wirtschaftspolitik, Baden-Baden 1996, 155 - 165.

Eckard Rehbinder (1997), Einleitung: Geltungs- und Anwendungsbereich, in *Immenga/Mestmäcker* (eds.), EG-Wettbewerbsrecht, Vol. I, 1997, 53 - 94.

Hanns Ullrich (1998) (ed.), Comparative Competition Law: Approaching an International System of Antitrust Law, Baden-Baden 1998.

Roger Zäch (1999) (ed.), Towards WTO Competition Rules, Bern 1999.

Erich Vranes

Policy Lessons from Transatlantic Trade Disputes

I. Introduction

Few trade disputes have caught public attention to the same extent as the EU-US conflicts on bananas, hormone-treated beef, and US export subsidies through foreign sales corporations. These cases not only constitute precedent cases in WTO law but also highlight several structural deficiencies in WTO dispute settlement. In addition, they show the mutual relationships and spill-over effects of these and other trade disputes, and underline the intricate nexus of trade, domestic and foreign policy.

This chapter will focus on the above-mentioned three cases, while also delineating their implications for and connections to a series of other actual and emerging transatlantic trade conflicts. Section II. depicts the facts of these three cases; section III. describes the manifold political and procedural manoeuvres which led to the escalation of these disputes; finally, section IV. analyses the conclusions to be drawn both for WTO dispute settlement and for remedies to prevent future transatlantic "trade-wars".

II. The Facts in *Bananas*, *Hormones* and *FSC*

A. Stumbling Block One: The Bananas Case

The *bananas* case concerned the highly discriminatory banana import regime that the EC had established with the inception of the Internal Market in 1993. This import regime, just as the individual import regime of several Member States before, had already been condemned in GATT 1947 dispute settlement. However, the EC was able to block the adoption of these panel reports due to the principle of consensus that prevailed in GATT 1947.[1]

When the WTO came into force in 1995, the EC banana import regime was challenged again, this time by the US, Ecuador, Guatemala, Mexico and Honduras. This regime relied essentially on two quotas: A first quota of roughly 850,000 tonnes per year was reserved to twelve ACP countries which had traditionally supplied the EC with bananas in the past. Bananas coming under this quota could be imported free of tariffs. A second quota of 2.2 million tonnes which was autonomously increased by the EC to about 2.5 million tonnes was open for imports from third country bananas, as well as ACP country bananas that did not qualify for the first quota. Crucially, Latin American bananas and bananas traded by US undertakings thus came under this second quota. However, such bananas faced several obstacles. For example, a tariff of 75 Euro applied under this second quota; and parts of it were allocated to certain traditional ACP countries which therefore benefited from a guaranteed market share under this second quota. Moreover, a tariff preference was granted to ACP countries that profited from such allocations. Imports out of these quotas were only theoretically possible since prohibitive tariffs applied in this eventuality. It has to be added, in this regard, that the EC was required, by virtue of the

---

1 On this and the following see also *Cascante/Sander* (1999); *Salas/Jackson* (2000) 145 ff; *Komuro* (2000) 1 ff; *Vranes* (2002a).

so-called *Lomé* Convention concluded by the EC with almost 80 African, Caribbean and Pacific developing countries, to grant preferential treatment to imports from these countries. However, the waiver from GATT disciplines which the EC had obtained in 1994 in respect of its obligations under the *Lomé* Convention only covered MFN treatment. Hence, it was quite obvious that the other discriminations were in violation of WTO law.

Furthermore, and this is where the special interest of the US and American traders came in, these quotas were distributed to individual traders by means of licensing procedures that differed for both quotas. While it was relatively easy to fulfil the procedural requirements to obtain licenses for imports under the first quota, the respective procedures in respect of the second quota evidently were substantially more burdensome. A core issue was that 30 per cent of this quota were reserved to operators that had previously traded in EC and traditional ACP bananas (typically EC multinationals), while this share was taken away from traders that had previously imported third-country bananas (typically US multinationals and their German subsidiaries). It was clear that the EC traders would not be able to obtain amounts of bananas sufficient to use these additional licenses. However, the EC import regime made licenses tradeable between both groups of operators. Thus, US and German traders had to buy back the market share they had previously held from these EC traders thereby having to cross-subsidise the latter, an effect that the EC had indeed intended.[2]

It does not come as a surprise, therefore, that the US and Latin American countries sued the EC in 1996. Both the panel and the Appellate Body reports of 1997 declared that the EC import regime violated WTO law in several respects.[3]

---

2 Cf. the *bananas III* panel report, *EC - Regime for the Importation, Sale and Distribution of Bananas*, WT/DS27/R/ECU/GUA//HON/MEX/USA, adopted 25 September 1997, paragraphs IV.366, IV.390, 7.339 ff with further references to official EC documents.

3 The EC import regime was found to violate GATT Articles I:1, III:4, X:3, XIII:1, GATS Articles II and XVII, and Article 1.3 of the Licensing Agreement, cf. the panel report, *EC - Regime for the Importation, Sale and Distribution of Bananas*, WT/DS27/R/ECU/GUA//HON/MEX/USA, adopted 25 September 1997, and Appellate Body report, WT/DS27/AB/R, adopted 25 September 1997.

When these rulings had been handed down, it became clear very soon that the EC was not prepared to render its import regime WTO-consistent. This led to the notorious conflicts on the enforcement of the WTO decisions that were soon characterised as a "trade-war" which, in conjunction with the other transatlantic trade disputes discussed below, was seen as endangering the WTO system which had entered into force only some three years before.[4]

B. Stumbling Block Two: The Hormones Case

A second core dispute in transatlantic relations that had been running since the 1980s was also brought before the WTO in 1996, when the US and Canada challenged the EC import ban on hormone-treated beef. The Appellate Body found that the EC's import prohibition infringed WTO law because it was not based on a risk assessment in the sense of the WTO Agreement on Sanitary and Phytosanitary Measures, i.e. a risk assessment that was specific to the case at issue. While the Appellate Body held that the import ban was inconsistent with Article 5.5 of the SPS Agreement since the EC had instituted different levels of protection for various substances that risked inducing cancer, it reversed the panel's finding according to which this inconsistency had resulted in discrimination or a disguised restriction on international trade.[5]

With hindsight, it is surprising that the EC had not commissioned studies of the effects of hormones that would have qualified as sufficiently specific to the case in dispute, because it was clear since the Uruguay Round that the SPS Agreement had been concluded to deal with cases such as, in particular, the long-running controversy on the EC import ban.

When the AB decision had been adopted, the EC took the stance that it was required to carry out a specific risk assessment that would fulfil the conditions of the SPS Agreement as interpreted by the Appellate Body. However according to the US, the EC was required to lift its import ban. In view of the cautious attitude of EU citizens and the pronounced public attention this case had attracted,

---

[4] Cf. *The Economist,* 6 March 1999, 18 and 72; see also *Knox* (1999) 34 ff.

[5] Cf. the AB report EC - Measures concerning meat and meat products (hormones), WT/DS26/AB/R and WT/DS/48/AB/R, AB-1997-4, 16 January 1998, paragraphs 235 and 246; cf. also *Quick/Blüthner* (1999) 603 ff and *Pauwelyn* (1999) 641 ff.

it arguably appeared politically unthinkable that the EC abolish its import ban.

These conflicting standpoints naturally led to yet another severe enforcement dispute. The *bananas* and the *hormones* cases thus became the first ones to go through the novel enforcement stage in WTO proceedings in which implementation of WTO rulings by the losing party comes under multilateral scrutiny; and both were the first to reach the retaliation stage within the new WTO framework.

C. The "Revenge Case": Foreign Sales Corporations

Just one month after the AB *bananas* report had been handed down, and while the AB was still hearing the *hormones* appeal, the EC "countermoved" by starting another major case against the US, this time, however, as the complaining party in the so-called *FSC* case.

The EC argued that foreign sales corporations (FSCs) allow American-based undertakings to avoid taxation by channelling foreign income through offshore tax havens. This helps American firms save taxes as they would *otherwise* be liable for American tax on their foreign profits, because the US taxes world wide income. According to the WTO Agreement on Subsidies and Countervailing Measures, however, the foregoing of income taxes by the State that would otherwise be due constitutes the grant of a subsidy. Both the *FSC* panel and Appellate Body reports largely confirmed the EC's stance.[6]

Just as the *bananas* and *hormones* cases, the *FSC* dispute dates back to GATT 1947 where the EC had challenged the US tax scheme in the *DISC* case[7], upon which the US had introduced the FSC approach. However, although the new *FSC*, too, was in manifest breach of GATT law, the EC did not further pursue this case during the Uruguay Round. When the EC re-initiated it in 1997 threatening to impose retaliatory tariffs in the amount of US$4.043 billion, it was submitted that this breached a gentlemen's agreement according to which the EC and the US had agreed not to sue each other, before the WTO, on issues of taxation.[8] Moreover,

---

6 Cf. the panel report *US - Tax treatment for "Foreign Sales Corporations"*, WT/DS108/R, 8 October 1999, and the AB report, WT/DS108/AB/R, 24 February 2000.

7 *United States — Income tax legislation* (DISC), BISD 23S/98.

8 See *DeFazio*, Statement on Foreign Sales Corporations, H.R. 4986, The FSC Repeal and Extraterritorial Income Exclusion Act of 2000

many commentators speculated that this case was brought by the EC since it wanted to secure itself sufficient bargaining leverage in the *bananas* and *hormones* enforcement phase and in looming aircraft disputes concerning alleged subsidies to Airbus.[9]

III. Itinerary to Escalation

A. 1997-1998: Preparing the Ground

In 1997 and 1998, the Panel and Appellate Body reports were issued in the *bananas* and *hormones* proceedings. As indicated above, just one month after the AB *bananas* report had been handed down, and while the AB was still hearing the *hormones* appeal, the EC started the *FSC* proceedings against the US, arguably to increase its bargaining leverage in the *bananas* and *hormones* enforcement phase.

When the Appellate Body issued its *bananas III* report in September 1997, the notorious conflicts of the enforcement of the WTO decisions in the *bananas* case started. Having been granted a "reasonable period of time" for the implementation of the WTO rulings that was scheduled to end on 1 January 1999, the EC prepared amendments to its import regime during the first six months of 1998. While the complaining parties maintained that the proposals were again incompatible with WTO law, the EC refused to discuss them arguing that these were still in the drafting stage.

When the EC finally adopted the outlines of its new regime in July 1998[10], the complaining parties again requested consultations on the WTO consistency of these measures, submitting that most of

---

(address to the US House of Representatives, 12 September 2000, available at www.house.gov/defazio); see also *European-American Business Council* (2000); even if no such gentlemen's agreement had existed, however, it is quite obvious that there are linkages between *FSC* and the other disputes since the EC had not pursued the *FSC* case since the mid-1980s. A series of further indications and official statements by US officials and the former Commissioner Sir Leon Brittan (cf. *The Wall Street Journal,* 14 September 2000, B.4; *The Wall Street Journal*, 29 September 2000, A.17) point in the same direction; cf. in the following text.

9 See in the following for more details.

10 Council Regulation 1637/98 of 20 July 1998; see also Commission Regulation 2362/98 which implements the aforementioned regulation; for details see *Cascante/Sander* (1999); *Salas/Jackson* (2000) 145 ff; *Komuro* (2000) 1 ff; *Vranes* (2002a).

the violations determined in the 1997 WTO *bananas III* decisions were perpetuated in the envisaged regime. Upon this, in autumn 1998, the US Congress increased its pressure on the US Administration. This has been attributed to the fierce lobbying of *Chiquita* which has been reported to have granted financial assistance in electoral campaigns to both Democrats and Republicans after 1993, i.e. after the new EC banana import regime had been introduced.[11] Upon this, the US Administration announced that it would take action by 15 December if the EC had not by then implemented the WTO rulings, that is even before the time span granted to the EC by the WTO had elapsed. Having denounced the *unilateral* action envisaged by the US, the EC opened on 25 November 1998 an additional spin-off case by requesting consultations on the WTO consistency of a cornerstone of US trade law, namely Sections 301-310 of the Trade Act of 1974, arguing that these provisions forced the US to impose sanctions before the WTO itself had a chance to rule on the legality of such a unilateral action.[12]

The US, nevertheless, moved to publish a list of goods on which retaliatory 100 per cent *ad valorem* tariffs should be imposed. This action followed a unilateral determination by the US that the EC had not rendered its import regime WTO compatible. Moreover, the US expressed repeatedly and publicly that it was not prepared to submit its own subjective determination to the multilateral scrutiny of a WTO panel under Article 21.5 of the DSU.[13] This, in turn, incited yet another countermove by the EC which requested a panel under DSU Article 21.5 that should find that its implementing measures must be presumed to be WTO consistent unless a panel had found to the contrary under DSU Article 21.5. While the complaining parties opposed the establishment of this panel, only a few days later, on 18 December 1998, Ecuador too applied for the establishment of a

---

[11] Cf. *Neue Zürcher Zeitung* online, 19 April 2001 (available at www.nzz.ch, visited on 19 April 2001).

[12] The WTO panel decided, however, that the wording of section 301 gave the USTR enough discretion to go through WTO dispute settlement proceeding before imposing sanctions; cf. panel report, *US - Sections 301-310 of the Trade Act of 1974*, WT/DS/152/R, 22 December 1999, paragraphs 7.155 ff.

[13] Cf. especially the panel report WT/DS27/RW/EEC (recourse to Article 21.5 by the EC) at paragraphs 2.1 ff.

panel under Article 21.5 which should also examine the non-compliance of the EC's implementing measures.

B. 1999: Enforcement Impasses

On 12 January 1999, the DSB referred both Article 21.5 requests to the original panel, despite the US objection that the panel requested by the EC had become devoid of purpose in view of the fact that the panel requested by Ecuador had the same mandate.

Only two days later, the US put further pressure on both the EC and the WTO dispute settlement system by applying for authorisation for retaliation. This would have meant, in the view of the US, that authorisation to suspend tariff concessions would have to be granted *before* the panels just established under Article 21.5 had determined whether the EC implementing measures had in fact again violated WTO law. This move thus led to several delicate questions as regards the WTO enforcement system, among others the disputed relationship between Articles 21.5 and 22.6 of the DSU.[14]

Only after several blockades in the DSB[15], a compromise was reached at the DSB meeting on 29 January 1999: The EC requested arbitration on the appropriate level of retaliation under Article 22.6[16], which has the consequence that retaliation is not allowed for the time of the pertinent proceedings, and the DSB thus stayed its handling of the American application for authorisation of retaliation. Although the conflicting provisions of Articles 21.5 and 22.6 might arguably have been resolved by a teleological interpretation according to which the 22.6 arbitration procedure should have been initiated after the 21.5 panel had determined whether the EC's implementing were in fact contrary to WTO law,[17] the issue of how to reconcile these provisions was referred to DSU review. The DSB tried to find a way out of this dilemma by nominating the same three persons (the panellists of the original *bananas III* dispute) as panellists in the two 21.5 panels and as arbitrators in the 22.6 procedure, mandating them to "find a logical way forward" in this issue.

---

14 See in the following text.

15 The EC, together with St. Lucia, Dominica and Cote d'Ivoire blocked the adoption of the agenda of the DSB meeting at which the US request was to be dealt with on 25 January. This led to the suspension of the meeting. The DSB meeting was reconvened on 28 January, yet had to be suspended again.

16 WT/DS27/46.

17 This solution has been advocated by *Griller* (1999).

After a surprising procedural manoeuvre enabling them to prolong the arbitration proceeding, the panellists/arbitrators determined in three consistent decisions issued in April 1999 that the EC's implementing measures were still not in conformity with WTO law and that, therefore, the appropriate level of US retaliation amounted to US$191.4 million per year.[18]

On 19 April 1999, the DSB authorised the US to retaliate against the EC. This constitutes a "milestone" in the still short history of the WTO as it was the first instance in which retaliation was authorised by the WTO. The fact that sanctions were to be introduced by the US - as well the many manoeuvres by the EC and the US in the course of the enforcement proceedings - had considerably worsened the climate in transatlantic relations.[19] Moreover, the EU Member States were divided over the prospective amendments to the banana import regime, and private undertakings unrelated to banana trade but affected by US retaliatory tariffs started court proceedings against the EC.[20]

Just one month later, the US and Canada opened another "retaliatory front" by requesting WTO authorisation to impose tariffs in the *hormones* dispute. This authorisation was granted in July 1999.[21] Whereas the US maintained that the AB report mandated the EC to lift its import ban, the EC read this decision as merely requiring it to conduct a specific risk assessment in accordance with the SPS agreement. Arguably, as indicated above, it would have been politically impossible for the EC decision makers to take a different stance since lifting the import ban would have meant that the EC would have had to explain *inter alia* why it had not commissioned specific studies on the effects of hormones in meat before the *hormones* case was brought before the WTO.

It is worth noting, on a more general level, that the office of the United States Trade Representative, having sought public comment on the goods to be included on the list of goods to be targeted with prohibitive tariffs, was reported as having acknowledged that it was exceedingly difficult to find products to put on this list, since

---

18 For details see the contributions of *Griller* (2002) and *Vranes* (2002a) in *Breuss/Griller/Vranes* (2002).

19 Cf. e.g. *Wall Street Journal*, 29 November 1999, A:14; *The Wall Street Journal*, 23 December 1999, A, 2:2; *The Economist*, 13 May, 2000, 75-76;

20 Cf. *Schoißwohl* (2002).

21 Cf. WT/DS/26/21.

retaliatory tariffs would also hurt US institutional buyers and consumers.[22]

The EC, which clearly remained unwilling not only to withdraw its beef import ban but also to render its banana import regime conform to WTO disciplines, came under further pressure in the bananas context, when Ecuador applied for cross retaliation in November 1999. In yet another precedent decision, WTO arbitrators authorised Ecuador to suspend concessions and other obligations under GATT, GATS and TRIPS up to the amount of US$201.6 million per year, thus giving "green light" for the first cross retaliation granted under the auspices of the WTO.[23] Although it is questionable whether cross retaliations by small countries, and even more so small developing countries, constitute a "credible threat" sufficient to induce a change of import policies in large developed countries, Ecuador apparently was able to secure an *ersatz* victory in this case. According to trade insiders, the EC supported Ecuador in the reduction of its external debt in the *Club of Paris* in exchange for Ecuador's not implementing cross retaliation. One may speculate, however, whether this "settlement" was achieved due to the world-wide publicity that the bananas dispute had received rather than due to the effectiveness of the cross retaliation threat (see also below at IV.).

C. 2000: Negative Spill-Over Effects

Already in early 1999, observers maintained that the EC and the US were "testing the young Word Trade Organisation to breaking point" in *bananas* and *hormones*.[24] In 2000, however, the spiral in transatlantic disputes turned even faster, as, in the course of the year, the developments in both the *bananas* and the *FSC* cases came to a head. Moreover, in the US, presidential elections were imminent, and both sides of the Atlantic were suspected of increasingly "playing to the galleries"[25], since no one could risk losing face in these disputes that had attracted so much public attention and which involved considerable stakes and sensitivities, in especially as regards the *FSC* and *hormones* cases.

---

[22] Cf. *Wall Street Journal*, 12 March 2002; on this see also below.

[23] For a detailed discussion of this case and the cross retaliation device more generally cf. *Subramanian/Watal* (2000) 403 ff; *Vranes* (2001).

[24] *Economist,* 6 March 1999, 18 and 72; see also *Knox*(1999) 34 ff.

[25] *Economist*, 13 May 2000, 75-76.

Furthermore, it was clear that the EC would need a new waiver when the Fourth Lomé Convention and the pertinent WTO waiver expired on 29 February 2000. Seen from this perspective, it came "just in time" when the WTO Appellate Body confirmed that same week, on 24 February, that the American FSC scheme was in violation of WTO law. This, evidently, provided the EC with considerable leverage as regards the pressing problems of bananas and hormones, and the *Cotonou* waiver:

The EC had negotiated the *Cotonou* Convention as a successor agreement to the Fourth Lomé Convention. This complex and wide-ranging agreement, which has been applied provisionally since 1 March 2000, constitutes a central building block in the EU's external economic and development relations with 77 ACP countries, mostly former colonies of EU Member States. It provides for a preparatory period extending until the end of 2007, by the end of which new trading arrangements shall be concluded by the contracting parties.[26] In view of the preferential treatment of a series of products originating in ACP countries, it was clear that the EC would have to apply for a waiver from GATT disciplines to be granted by the WTO membership. And this is where another core trade (and foreign and development policy) problem of the EC came in, since it had to secure the support of the US, Latin American countries exporting bananas and other countries in order to achieve the three fourths majority required for waivers under WTO law[27]. With the transatlantic climate deteriorating due to *bananas*, *hormones*, *FSC* and other trade disputes, the outlooks looked quite uncertain. Moreover, it arguably caused ill-feeling on the US side that the EC should prolong its strategic economic and political partnership with almost 80 countries.

In May 2000, the tension rose even more when the US introduced the so-called "carousel" legislation in order to break European resistance in the bananas and hormones cases. This device was meant to require the US Administration to change the list of products targeted for retaliatory tariffs 120 days after their initial effective date, and every 180 days thereafter.[28] Evidently,

---

[26] Cf. e.g. *Matambalya/Wolf* (2001) 123 ff.

[27] Cf. Article IX para 3 of the WTO Agreement.

[28] Cf. e.g. the detailed information in *Office of the United States Trade Representative*, Press Release 00-41 of May 26, 2000, available at www.ustr.gov.

"carousel" sanctions were meant to render retaliation more compelling. Nevertheless, although the fundamental goal of WTO dispute settlement and sanctions is to induce compliance with WTO commitments, it is questionable whether carousel sanctions are consistent with WTO law since they undermine the fundamental principle of predictability in international trade that WTO law is meant to ensure. The EC almost immediately reacted by bringing a further WTO case in requesting consultations on the carousel legislation in June 2000.[29] However, the EC did not further pursue this case as it was able to employ the FSC case to deter the US from actually applying its carousel legislation.[30]

Still in May, a new case moved onto centre stage and proved to become yet another major source of conflict in transatlantic relations, namely the dispute on US import restrictions on steel products. These obstacles to trade were first dealt with by the WTO in the *British Steel* case in May 2000. According to the WTO rulings, privatisations, as had occurred in the EU steel industry, under competitive conditions and at a fair market price eliminated the benefit of earlier subsidies and therefore removed any justification for imposing countervailing duties.[31] As the US has not been willing to lower the tariffs it had imposed to protect its industry, the EC started another proceeding in the *steel* dispute before the WTO in November 2000 which is still pending today.[32]

Also in May 2000, the US threatened to file yet another WTO suit on alleged subsidies paid to Airbus. The EC was accused by some observers of intending to use the *FSC* case also to shield the EC Airbus undertaking and to inflict prospective retaliatory tariffs on Boeing aircraft and US military products. Thus, the FSC case,

---

29 *United States* - Section 306 of the Trade Act of 1974 and Amendments thereto, Request for Consultations by the EC, WT/DS200/1, G/L/386.

30 According to *The Wall Street Journal*, 2 October 2000, A.26, UK government officials intervened arguing that the *FSC* case might be easier to settle if the US did not issue its new retaliatory list, upon which the US pulled back the list, cf. ibidem; for the further developments in the *FSC* case see in the following.

31 *United States - Imposition of countervailing duties on certain hot-rolled lead and bishmuth carbon steel products originating in the United Kingdom*, WT/DS138/AB/R, 10 May 2000; see also *Bulletin Quotidien Europe*, No 7718 of 17 May 2000, 14.

32 Cf. the EC request for the establishment of a panel,WT/DS248/12, of 8 May 2002.

which initially may have been started to soften US pressures in *hormones* and *bananas*, spilled over even into defence issues.[33]

Finally, in autumn 2000, both the *bananas* and the *FSC* cases came to a head. As regards bananas, many wondered how the EC would manage to "square the circle" in reconciling the many diverging interests within the EC, and those of ACP countries, Latin American countries, the US and various traders. The key to the issue proved to be what, arguably, was a feint of the Commission in conjunction with the bargaining leverage it had accumulated in the *FSC* case. Having denounced the US implementing measures in the *FSC* case as overtly WTO inconsistent in May and September, the Commission announced its intention to administer the import quotas under the new *banana* import regime on the basis of a "first come first served" system. This would have meant that there was to be a pre-allocation of import licenses to traders while the vessels carrying bananas where still at a sailing distance from Europe in order to avoid discrimination against countries which are farther away such as Ecuador. The Commission itself admitted in the explanations to its proposal that the "first come first served" system might cause problems for a perishable good such as bananas, but declared that it was optimistic that the "first come first served" system might be tailored to deal with the specific challenge of ensuring regular import of bananas.[34]

While several traders and supporting countries maintained that this approach would have constituted a rather serious problem for them[35], it became increasingly clear that the Commission was using the option of the "first come first serve" system as a *bargaining chip* to soften US demands regarding the administration of the new import regime. The US, which originally had been in favour of the "first come first serve" system and had declared that it was WTO consistent[36], changed its view after consultations with *Chiquita*. It

---

33 On the background cf. e.g. *Defense Daily International*, 30 June 2000 Vol 1/Issue 13, 1.

34 COM(2000) 621 final, 4.

35 According to *Bulletin Quotidien Europe*, 25 November 2000, 16, and 7 December 2000, 12 about 60 European and Caribbean operators were opposed to the "first come first served system", just as several EU Member States, cf. *Bulletin Quotidien Europe*, 1 December 2000, 12.

36 See the interview with USTR special negotiator *Greg Frazier* of 17 October and the official summary provided by the US Mission to the

did so although *Chiquita's* main competitor and US number one trader, *Dole*, just as *Ecuador*, the world's largest exporter of bananas, had clearly favoured the "first come first served" system.[37] The US made it clear that they were in favour of a management of the quotas based on past trade by individual traders in the period before 1993, that is when *Chiquita* held the largest share (double its level in 2000) in the European market.[38] Only after having waited until after the EU-US summit of 18 December 2000, the EC clearly revealed that it might also settle for a historical reference period, however one *different* from that advocated by the US and *Chiquita* (see below).

At about the same time, in autumn 2000 and thus in the run-up to the EU-US summit, the EC and the US reached an agreement on how to proceed in the *FSC* case. This agreement had become necessary since the implementation of the WTO rulings, which was due - according to WTO arbitration - by 1 October 2000, was delayed in the US senate and the EC maintained that the envisaged amendments would not conform to WTO standards anyway. In this accord of 30 September the EC guaranteed that it would not unilaterally enact the US$4.043 billion sanctions it had announced it would impose, but would request the authorisation of sanctions in the WTO by 17 November that same year. Furthermore, it was agreed that the EC would request a compliance panel, while the US would request arbitration on the amount. The arbitration should be suspended pending the ruling of the compliance panel. This obviously was meant to avoid the dilemma of the conflicting pertinent DSU provisions that had caused problems in the *bananas* dispute.[39]

While this accord clearly took some steam out of this highly controversial dispute in the US election phase, the EC kept pressure on the US by obviously linking the FSC retaliation threat to the other looming *steel* and aircraft subsidies disputes in that it targeted iron and steel products, as well as aircraft and spacecraft products

---

European Union in Brussels, available at www.useu.be/issues, visited on 20 November 2000.

37 See e.g. *The Wall Street Journal*, October 9, 2000, A.22

38 Ibidem.

39 Cf. above.

in the indicative list of products on which retaliatory tariffs might be imposed.[40]

The 15th and last EU-US summit during President Clinton's term of office thus was confronted with the highly sensitive trade disputes in *EC - Hormones*, *EC - Bananas*, *US - FSC*, *US - Steel*, *Helms-Burton* and the prospective *Airbus* case. Already during the weeks before the summit it was expected that not even this meeting would be able to resolve these disputes[41], a view that was to prove correct: although trade issues were reported to have taken up a large part of the summit, none of the disputes could be settled.[42]

Following the summit meeting, the EC Agriculture Council decided on 20 December to introduce the "first come first served" system as of 1 April 2001, while giving the Commission the power to *defer* the entry into force to 1 July 2001. The EC Commissioner for Agriculture clearly signalled that the EC was willing to settle for a system of licenses distribution based on past trade volumes of banana traders if the US was able to agree with Central American exporting countries on such a "historic" reference period.[43]

D. 2001: FSC settles Bananas

As indicated, it was arguably this feint and the threat of retaliation in *FSC* which "helped" bring about a settlement of this high-profile trade dispute on 11 April 2001. According to this settlement, the new import regime has to start out on a transitional period based on import quotas until 2006. As of 2006, a tariff-only system will have to be introduced. During the initial phase, the import regime is to be based on past trade between 1994 and 1996, although this reference period had been found WTO-inconsistent in the 1999 arbitration award.

As was to be expected, Ecuador strongly criticised the agreement reached between the EC and the US, since it was not involved in the

---

40 Cf. the official documents (IP/00/1321, Memo/00/84) posted on the Commission trade website at www.europa.eu.int, last visited on 24 June 2002; on the spill-over to defence cf. also *Defense Daily International*, 3 November 2000 Vol 1/Issue 31, 1.

41 *Bulletin Quotidien Europe*, 14 December 2000, 8; *Bulletin Quotidien Europe*, 15 December 2000, 5; *European Report*, 16 December 2000, 1.

42 *Bulletin Quotidien Europe*, 20 December 2000, 10.

43 *Bulletin Quotidien Europe*, 21 December 2000, 14; *Bulletin Quotidien Europe*, 30 December 2000, 7.

negotiations although it is the world's largest exporter of bananas.[44] The EC however was able to come to an agreement with Ecuador on 30 April 2001 which paved the way for the introduction of the new banana import regime effective from 1 July 2001.[45]

Under WTO law, the new system necessitated two waivers, one from GATT Article XIII so as to make it possible for the EC to reserve the third quota to ACP bananas until 2006. A second one was needed for the time after 2006, since in the Cotonou Convention the EC has undertaken to give preferential access to bananas from ACP countries. In the agreement between the EC and the US, the US undertook to help achieve this waiver in the WTO.[46] Moreover, as a matter of considerable political importance, the EC commissioner for trade, Pascal Lamy, was reported as indicating on the day the agreement was signed that the US had also pledged to contribute to

---

44 Cf *Bulletin Quotidien Europe*, 3 May 2001; *Neue Zürcher Zeitung online*, 19 April 2001.

45 According to these compromises, three quotas (one quota for 2.2 million tonnes, a second one of 353,000 tonnes and a third one of 850,000 tonnes) will be introduced during a transitional period until 1 January 2006. There will be a customs duty of 75 Euro per tonne applicable to the first two quotas. Both quotas will be managed as one (Cf Commission Regulation 1442/93, Article 13). As of 1 January 2004, however, the trade volumes under the new import regime will be used as the new reference period This is a consequence of the agreement with Ecuador, cf the EU homepage europa.eu.int/comm/trade/dispute/understanding.htm (visited 9 May 2001).
Under the third quota there will be a tariff of Euro 300 (Cf Commission Regulation 216/2001, Article 18). As there will also be a tariff preference of 300 Euro for ACP bananas inside and outside all three quotas (Cf Commission Regulation 216/2001, Article 18 paragraph 4), this quota effectively guarantees access for ACP bananas. Of the 850 000 tonnes of the third quota, 100 000 tonnes had to be transferred to quota B by 2002. This corresponds to the wishes of Washington and Ecuador and reflects the fact that ACP trade in bananas never reached 850 000 tonnes but came close to 750 000 tonnes (Cf Inside US Trade, 17 November 2000 and 24 November 2000).

46 Cf. the outline of the agreement at the homepage of EU Delegation of the European Commission to the US (www.eurunion.org/news/press/2001027.htm, visited on 15 May 2001).

the gaining of a third WTO waiver needed for the Cotonou Agreement as such.[47] The waivers were granted by the WTO Ministerial Conference at Doha on 14 December 2001.[48]

As a direct consequence of these agreements, the sanctions which the US had imposed in the bananas dispute were lifted as of 1 July 2001. They were "definitively" lifted when the quotas had been adjusted and the relevant waiver had been granted by the WTO.[49]

E. 2002: New Developments

At the time of writing (i.e. at the beginning of July 2002), the arbitration award on the amount of sanctions to be imposed by the EC in the highly sensitive *FSC* case is still pending. Although its issuance had been postponed several times and was expected for 18 June 2002 at the latest, it has still not been handed down. It has been observed that it will be difficult for the EC not to impose sanctions in the *FSC* case due to the 30 per cent *steel* tariffs introduced by the US in March 2002. Both EU and US officials have been reported as having confirmed that the steel dispute, in which the EC has been joined by Japan, has considerably worsened the transatlantic political climate again.[50] It thus seems that both sides of the Atlantic are entrapped in the cross-purposes of domestic political dictates and their long-term trade interests: while the US Administration can hardly afford not protecting its domestic steel industry and thereby secure substantial amounts of votes, it is also expected to stand firm and defend its trade interests in the other trade cases it has been

---

47 Cf. Europe No 7944, 12 April 2001.

48 Cf. WT/MIN(01)/15 and WT/MIN(01)/16; technically speaking, the first waiver covers the Cotonou convention by waiving GATT Article I to the extent required until 31 December 2007; an annex introduces special procedural rules for banana imports from the ACP during 2006-2007. The second waiver covers the transitional banana import regime introduced until 2006 and waives the EC's GATT Article XIII commitments with respect to the above-mentioned third quota that has been reduced to 750,000 tonnes meanwhile. The Council has meanwhile taken the final steps to implement the new system, cf Council Regulation (EC) 216/01 of 29 January 2001.

49 Cf the homepages of the US Mission to the EU (www.useu.be/issues/bana0411.htm, visited on 15 May 2001) and the EU Delegation of the European Commission to the US (www.eurunion.org/news/press/2001027.htm, visited on 15 May 2001).

50 *The Wall Street Journal*, 12 March 2002, A.18.

pressing for so long. The EC, on the other hand, might undermine its own credibility if it does not take a firm stance not only in *steel* but also in *FSC*, although this case is prone to cause severe resentments across the Atlantic, since it has proved its major, if not only, credible trade threat so far.

IV. Policy Conclusions

As has become clear from the foregoing, the various transatlantic disputes can hardly be understood unless they are seen in their dynamic and multi-facetted interrelationships, as well as, more generally, in the context of a series of sometimes conflicting domestic and foreign policy concerns. Monocausal explanations of these disputes are thus almost impossible. While these disputes, their mutual influences and spill-overs to other policy fields would provide starting-points for a whole series of studies, this concluding section shall focus on four structural issues, namely the lack of a co-defendant status in WTO dispute settlement, problems surrounding waivers, the "credible threat" problem seen from a North-North and a North-South perspective; and possible strategies of conflict avoidance in transatlantic trade relations.

A. The Lack of Co-Defendant Status

One deficiency of the DSU, which has been particularly highlighted in the GATT/WTO *bananas* proceedings, is the lack of an opportunity for interested parties to join the proceedings as co-defendants. Whereas it is possible, under the DSU, for interested parties to join the complaining party in a dispute as co-complainants and enjoy full procedural rights, it is impossible for other WTO Members to join the respondent in a dispute in which they take an interest. This imbalance becomes all the more striking since a WTO Member can bring a claim as complainant if it merely has a potential trade interest[51] (and the same is true, by implication, for acquiring the status of co-complainant), whereas WTO Members actually affected by the outcome of a dispute cannot join the WTO Member denominated as the defendant by the complaining parties, nor can they appeal from an unfavourable panel decision. Thus, in *bananas*, those developing ACP countries that depend to a considerable extent on their bananas exports to the

---

[51] On the requirement of legal interest in WTO dispute settlement and the low threshold introduced by the AB in *bananas III* see the AB report in *bananas* WT/DS27/AB/R at paragraphs 132 ff.

EC and hence were directly affected by the outcome of the banana proceedings, were unable to intervene at the side of the EC in the various proceedings and had to rely on the handling of this dispute by the EC. Moreover, this deficiency entails the additional danger that WTO Members that are affected by a dispute but that are unable to join the responding party in WTO proceedings, lose considerable leverage in negotiations to prevent disputes in the first place as well as in amicable settlements of disputes that are already being heard before the WTO or that have reached the enforcement stage.

While this shortcoming of the DSU arguably may date back to dispute settlement under the GATT 1947 where the principle of consensus prevailed, it is all the graver under the WTO system where dispute settlement rulings cannot be blocked by affected WTO Members due to the doctrine of negative consensus. It is evident that this shortcoming of the DSU is not reconcilable with the command of procedural fairness and thus impinges on the legitimacy of WTO law and dispute settlement more generally.

B. Problems Surrounding Waivers

A further issue, related to a certain extent to the preceding one and raised in the WTO era in *bananas III* for the first time, is that of waivers. Waivers occupy a cardinal place in the WTO system as they serve, first, the purpose of exempting WTO Members from WTO disciplines in cases where this is preferable for economic and/or political considerations. Thereby, they secondly also serve the functions of increasing legal security and predictability in economic relations, avoiding disputes, and enhancing the legitimacy of the WTO framework as such. Finally, and this is where the status of third parties like the ACP countries in *bananas III* comes in again, waivers granted before disputes arise can mitigate the lack of a co-defendant status in WTO law.

Legally and institutionally speaking, however, there are two problems related to waivers in the WTO setting. First, there is the issue of how the dispute settlement organs interpret waivers and what degree of deference they apply to them. Once again, the *bananas* case is illustrative, since the EC had been granted the *Lomé* waiver that exempted EC banana trade with ACP countries from MFN disciplines. While the EC took the stance that the WTO Panel and Appellate Body should interpret the *Lomé* waiver by deferring to the underlying *Lomé* Convention and the understanding of the contracting parties as it ensued from the practice surrounding this convention, the AB took a distinctly non-deferential attitude reading the *Lomé* convention as if it were a part of WTO law, i.e. completely aloof from the practice of the contracting parties.[52] However, as *Howse* argues, the correct degree of deference cannot be abstractly defined, and absolute deference in *bananas III* would not have been appropriate, since third countries not parties to the *Lomé* Convention also had a legitimate stake in the interpretation of this convention.[53]

While the AB's approach of not completely deferring to the practice of the parties to the *Lomé* Convention arguably was legally correct therefore, there is a second problem concerning waivers which may even be more acute. According to Article IX:3 of the WTO Agreement, waivers can only be granted by a three quarters majority of the WTO membership. In view of the importance of waivers, the authorisation of which has been subjected to further disciplines in the WTO Understanding in Respect of Waivers, one may raise the question of whether the three quarters majority is not too high a threshold. It is telling in this context that it was quite uncertain until the EU-US banana settlement in 2001 whether the EC would be able to achieve this majority not only for the waiver in respect of the new banana import regime, but also for the waiver covering the *Cotonou* Convention; and it is difficult to dismiss the impression that the support of the US arguably was won due to the political linkings with the *bananas* settlement and the spectre of possible *FSC* retaliation.

C. The "Credible Threat" Problem

Transatlantic trade disputes so far show a propensity to go to the retaliation stage in which, since the inception of the WTO, the implementation by the losing party of WTO rulings comes under multilateral surveillance. *Bananas III* and *hormones* were the first two cases to have reached this phase, and the *FSC* case is about to draw level with them. While this characteristic of EU-US trade disputes can possibly be in part attributed to the sensitive subject matters in dispute in these cases (see below), it arguably also, in part, stems from the fact that WTO sanctions do not prove effective in many cases. Thus, both the US (in *hormones* and *bananas*) and

---

52 On this see also *Howse* (2000) 67-68; and *Weiss* (1999) 329 ff who criticizes the AB for the non-deferential attitude in *bananas* III.

53 *Howse* ibid.

the EC (in the indicative list it drew up in *FSC*) found it exceedingly difficult to find products suitable as "targets" for countermeasures, since retaliatory tariffs on many products would eventually also have had negative effects on domestic buyers and consumers.[54] Moreover, in *FSC*, while some European undertakings have been reported to favour retaliation[55], several others have opposed such action since they themselves benefit from the FSC system through subsidiaries established in the US.[56] Thus, even in the "North-North" context, between the world's two largest economies (which, moreover, rely on *internal* trade to a substantive extent), it has proven difficult to impose sanctions due to these economies' interdependencies.

This "credible threat" problem is all the more obvious in the "reverse" North-South context, i.e. when a small developing country tries to retaliate against a major industrialised country. A case in point is again *bananas III*, in which the WTO panel found that it would have been impossible for Ecuador to impose sanctions in the goods sector as well as under GATS: retaliatory tariffs on the importation of goods would have deprived the Ecuadorian economy of the necessary inputs for its domestic industry; and countermeasures under GATS would have risked seriously undermining the foreign direct investments climate. While Ecuador was therefore authorised by the WTO panel to suspend the protection of EC intellectual property, it is quite obvious that such cross retaliation would also hardly be practicable and effective, as there are too many practical constraints for implementing such countermeasures.[57] The arbitrators rightly stated in this case, that

---

54 Cf. *Wall Street Journal*, 12 March 2002. A.18.

55 Most notably *Airbus Industries*, which was reported as initially having backed the complaint as a means of attacking archrival Boeing Co.; however, Airbus, just as many other EU companies, changed its mind; cf ibidem.

56 Ibidem.

57 For example, economically speaking, it is highly questionable as to what extent suspension of intellectual property rights is practicable, since it is difficult to see to what extent that e.g. the retaliatory use of "European" geographical indications would actually benefit Ecuadorian business undertakings. As regards the suspension of protection of sound recordings, the problem manifestly arises that such works will usually include creative contributions of nationals of different states, often therefore of states which are not covered by the

one may ask whether the DSU's objective to induce compliance with WTO rulings "may ever be achieved in a situation where a great imbalance in terms of trade volume and economic power exists between the complaining party seeking suspension and the other party"[58].

The experiences of the EC and the US show, however, that this problem is also prevalent in the North-North context, and it is all the more so if a case involves sensitive issues, such as health protection in the *hormones* and taxation in the *FSC* cases.

D. Strategies of Conflict-Avoidance in Transatlantic Trade-Relations

This latter issue can be addressed from several inter-related perspectives besides the narrowly-focussed one of the effectiveness of sanctions. One could in particular raise the questions of whether it is the institutional setting of the WTO is prone to provoke escalations of conflicts and spill-overs to other disputes and other policy fields; whether it is the attitude of certain WTO Members towards WTO dispute settlement; or whether it is the specific nature of certain matters in dispute that provoke such escalations.

---

arbitrators' decision. This may also be the case, albeit more rarely, for industrial designs. But here just as in the other cases regarding suspensions under TRIPS at least two further problems emerge. First, the scope of the DSU authorization extends only to the applicant (Ecuador) and therefore, it can only be exploited on the Ecuadorian domestic market. Second, and this perhaps constitutes the greatest problem in practical terms, authorisation is granted only *provisionally*, i.e. until the EC as the non-complying party brings its measures into conformity with the DSU. This means that Ecuadorian undertakings would not be in a position to predict how long they could possibly benefit from the suspension of TRIPS rights, an obvious impediment for most investments and business decisions. Even if it were legally feasible to implement the sanctions satisfactorily, it remains doubtful whether the level of nullification or impairment suffered by Ecuador and implicitly determined by the arbitrators, i.e. US$ 201.6 million, could ever be reached on Ecuador's domestic market, given that the WTO authorization is confined to the Ecuadorian territory. For a detailed discussion of these issues see *Vranes* (2001); but see also the opposite view of *Subramanian/Watal* (2000) 403.

58 Cf. the arbitration report, WT/DS27/ARB/ECU, 24 March 2000, at paragraph 73.

Starting with the last issue, one can submit that there are of course "high-profile" cases, that is cases which inherently prove difficult to settle in the first place because they involve distinct national sensitivities such as the *hormones* case (concerning health protection and different societal values), *FSC* (taxation as a paradigm of sovereignty), *steel* (a core industry in crises), *Helms-Burton* (extra-territoriality) and so on. Yet, while it is clear that some cases will be perceived as more sensitive than others, it is difficult to argue that there are cases that the WTO is not apt to deal with at all, since almost any trade case will possess some potentially "sensitive" characteristics. However, it should be borne in mind that WTO dispute settlement often is only part of the picture when a trade issue is linked to other domestic, trade or foreign policy fields, as tends to be case ever more in today's increasingly interdependent world.

A comparison with the EU may be illustrative on this point. The EU/EC system, just as the WTO, establishes long-term goals whose pursuit should be mutually beneficial for all participants. But, on top of that, European integration relies on a *highly institutionalised* cooperation where all levels of government meet continuously, as opposed to "classic" international cooperation where heads of State meet quite infrequently (or never at all). Evidently, many other circumstances such as the relatively small number of EU Member States, comparatively great homogeneity of interests and values, the possibility to enact secondary law and so on also play an important role in this context. Moreover, through the direct applicability of EC law, complaints can be brought by private parties and are thus depoliticised.[59] Thus, disputes can normally be defused more easily in the EU.

Obviously the WTO institutional setting does not possess such features. How can one thus avoid situations in which one partner of the transatlantic relationship starts a WTO case which prompts the other party to bring a case in revenge so as not to have to comply with a WTO ruling? As regards the EC-US cases discussed here, it has sometimes been argued that, in particular, the *hormones* and the *FSC* cases should not have been brought at all. As regards

[59] It is, however, severely disputed whether direct effect of WTO law within the EC would be appropriate, at least in political terms, cf. e.g. *Griller* (2000); *Meng* (1995); *Petersmann* (1997); *von Bogdandy* (2001); *Eeckhout* (2002) all with extensive further references.

hormones, it has been submitted that it was clear that it would be impossible, *politically* speaking, for the EC to open its market for imports of hormone-treated beef. Seen from this perspective, there is a certain logic in the EC's countermove of bringing the *FSC* case, where it was also clear that compliance is almost impossible for the US, to shield against US enforcement pressures. This logic, however, compares to that of mutually assured destruction in cold-war politics. Moreover, it entails the danger of abuses as well as the risk that predominant trade powers as the US and the EC will undermine the WTO system by refusing compliance in a series of cases, or by moving disputes away from the WTO to other fora and alternative methods of dispute resolution.[60]

While it is evident that there is no simple nostrum to these multi-faceted problems, some remedial strategies shall be briefly addressed in this concluding section. Whereas there have been suggestions, in academic writing, aimed at improvements of the DSU[61], the following considerations shall concentrate on ways of *preventive* action open for WTO Members, in especially the EC and the US, i.e. strategies of avoiding trade disputes and escalatory spill-overs to other policy fields.

First, as indicated already, while it is clear, from a *legal* perspective, that e.g. the EC import ban on hormone-treated beef was illegal[62], that the FSC scheme was manifestly in violation of WTO law, and that both regimes were rightly condemned by the WTO once the cases were brought, it is a quite different question, from a *political* viewpoint, whether it was wise to sue in these cases at all and thus to consciously place the respective transatlantic trade partner in a Catch-22 situation. From the viewpoint of WTO law, each WTO Member retains complete discretion in deciding as to whether it should exercise diplomatic protection for its domestic producers by bringing a complaint and introducing sanctions against other WTO Members. A lesson to be drawn from the latest transatlantic disputes that created spill-over from *bananas* via *FSC* to e.g. aircraft products and thus defence issues, and even on the

60 This was actually proposed, in a speech to the EP, by the USTR *Robert Zoellick* under the impression of the FSC case, cf. *Bulleting Quotidien Europe*, 16 May 2001, 12.

61 Cf. e.g. *Horn/Mavroidis* (1999); *Hoekman/Mavroidis* (1999); *Jansen* (2000).

62 Cf. above.

transatlantic political climate more generally, is that, *politically* speaking, this discretion should be used with a view to long-term common interests and therefore with appropriate restraint in sensitive cases.

A *second* strategy is that of placing more emphasis on amicable settlements of disputes. Just as the first strategy, this requires appropriate filtering of cases to be brought and a weighing of the various short-term and long-term interests at stake which does not unduly cede to single-issue domestic lobbyist pressures. In this regard, appropriate use should be made of the bilateral confidential consultation phase provided for in the DSU. Although these consultations are mandatory in all WTO panel proceedings and a majority of cases is settled during this stage[63], there appear to be cases in which the parties seem to be pre-determined to go the whole way and where the consultation phase is not really utilised.[64] However, it would not be advisable to require WTO dispute settlement organs to actually review whether consultations have served certain "minimum functions" as the EC had argued in the *bananas* case[65], or to require closer involvement of WTO organs in this stage. This would again entail the risk that WTO Members not only consult confidentially before WTO proceedings are initiated (which as such will often be desirable), *but also* that disputes are moved away from the multilateral WTO system to other dispute settlement methods that are even less transparent and in which power politics play an even greater role than in the multilaterally surveyed WTO rules enforcement system.

A *third* alternative would build on bi- and multilateral negotiations on issues of common interest and on looming controversies. In EU-US relations, one can point to transatlantic initiatives such as the New Transatlantic Agenda, the Transatlantic Business Dialogue, the Transatlantic Environmental Dialogue and

---

63 Cf. *Busch* (1999).

64 Cf. *Cottier* (1999/2000) 181; *Vranes* (2002b); on the function of consultations more generally cf. *Hyun Chong Kim* (1999) 460 ff.

65 The EC argued that the consultations did not fulfil their minimum function of affording a possibility for arriving at a mutually satisfactory solution and a clear setting out of the different claims of which a dispute consists, cf. the *bananas III* panel report at paragraph 7.18.

the Transatlantic Consumer Dialogue.[66] Evidently, this approach risks having a bias in favour of business and elitist interests that are more easy to bundle and which attract more ample support in financial terms etc[67], just as it entails a plethora of problems in democracy, transparency and legitimacy terms. These complex issues can of course only be referred to in this concluding section. However, one should raise the question of whether such a cooperative approach, despite all the obvious drawbacks, does not constitute, in many cases, the solution to be preferred *faute de mieux* in today's increasingly interdependent, but unintegrated world, since the alternatives often are even more problematic: namely that of having to comply with an unfavourable WTO decision, having a ruling that the losing party cannot comply with, or worse still, having such a ruling which additionally incurs the danger of escalation and negative spill-overs as has been repeatedly the case in transatlantic trade relations in the first years since the inception of the WTO.

Such approaches, of which there are quite a few meanwhile[68], should involve a greater integration of foreign, trade, health, environmental and other policies, for example within the New Transatlantic Agenda, the TABD and the other dormant transatlantic dialogues that have to be reinvigorated. It should also comprise early warning and dispute prevention mechanisms and could involve "trade screening", i.e. preventive screening of regulatory measures within the EU and the US as well as within the framework of transatlantic partnership fora.[69] Such approaches

---

66 On the background of these initiatives see www.tabd.org, www.tiesweb.org, www.tacd.org.

67 It is striking in this context that the Transatlantic Business Dialogue which represents "united voice of American and European Industry" has usually been reporting successes, whereas the Transatlantic Environmental Dialogue had to be suspended after only two years since the US Government was unwilling to provide its share of financing (cf. www.tiesweb.org/taed, and the 2002 TABD mid year report, available at www.tabd.org).

68 Cf. the websites noted *supra*.

69 Cf. the ideas sketched out in *Taylor* (2001); *Johnson* (2001); *de Bièvre* (2001); *de Jonquières* (2001); *de Jonquières* also advocates stricter US campaign finance law to curb the influence of special interests over the initiation and escalation of trade disputes. As has been shown *supra* at

evidently evoke a multitude of novel issues in national and international governance. So far, there is sparse research on these strategies.[70] Since, however, these are being implemented already, academics should not stay behind.

Bibliography

Bibliography

de Bièvre, D. (2001), Re-designing the Virtuous Circle: Two Proposals for WTO Reform, essay submitted to the 2001 essay contest of the Robert Schumann Center Chair in Transatlantic Relation, European University Institute, available at www.iue.it/RSC/BP.

Bogdandy, A. von (2001), Rechtsgleichheit, Rechtssicherheit und Subsidiarität im transnationalen Wirtschaftsrecht; zur unmittelbaren Anwendbarkeit von Art. 81 Abs. 3 EG und des WTO Rechts, EuZW 2001, S. 357-365.

Busch, M.L. (1999), Democracy, Consultation, and the Paneling of Disputes Under GATT, Working Paper Series of the Center for International Development, Harvard University, 1999 (available at http://www.cid.harvard.edu/cidtrade/issues/disputepaper.html).

Cascante, J.C./Sander, G.G. (1999), Der Streit um die EG-Bananenmarktordnung, Berlin 1999.

Cottier, Th. (2000), Das Streitschlichtungsverfahren in der Welthandelsorganisation, in: *Müller-Graff*, Die Europäische Gemeinschaft in der Welthandelsorganisation, 2000, 179-189.

DeFazio, Statement on Foreign Sales Corporations, H.R. 4986, The FSC Repeal and Extraterritorial Income Exclusion Act of 2000

III., these influences were driving forces behind the *bananas* and *hormones* cases.

70 For a recent overview of publications on transatlantic governance cf. *Shaffer* (2002); see also the submissions, cited in the note *supra*, to the 2001 essay prize of the Robert Schumann Centre Chair in Transatlantic Relations, European University Institute, available at www.iue.it/RSC/BP.

(address to the US House of Representatives, 12 September 2000, available at www.house.gov/defazio)

Eeckhout, P. (2002), Judicial Enforcement of WTO Law in the European Union - Some Further Reflections, JIEL 2002, 91-110.

Griller, St. (1999), The Enforcement of WTO-Dispute Settlement Decisions, conference lecture the 1999 Vienna Conference "The WTO after the Seattle Ministerial Conference. Recent Developments and Future Perspectives", Vienna, December 9 and 10, 1999 (abstract available at http://fgr.wu-wien.ac.at/ecsa/wtoabstr.htm#griller).

Griller, St. (2000), Judicial Enforceability of WTO Law in the European Union. Annotation to Case C-149/96, *Portugal v Council*, JIEL 2000, 441-472.

Griller, St. (2002 forthcoming), Articles 21.5 and 22.6 and the Sequencing Problem under the Dispute Settlement Undertaking, in *Breuss, F./Griller, St./Vranes, E.* (eds.), The Banana Dispute. An Economic and Legal Analysis, Vienna - New York 2002 (forthcoming).

Hoekman, B.M./Mavroidis, P.C. (1999), WTO Dispute Settlement, Transparency and Surveillance, World Bank Policy Research Working Paper Series (available at http://www1.worldbank.org/wbiep/trade/papers_2000/dispute_settlement.pdf).

Horn, H./Mavroidis, P.C. (1999), Remedies in the WTO Dispute Settlement System and Developing Country Interests, Working Paper Series of the Center for International Development, Harvard University, April 11, 1999 (available at http://www.cid.harvard.edu/cidtrade/issues/disputepaper.html)

Howse, R. (2000), Adjucative Legitimacy and Treaty Interpretation in International Trade Law: The Early Years of WTO Jurisprudence, in *Weiler, J.H.H.* (ed.), The EU, the WTO, and the NAFTA. Towards a Common Law of International Trade, Oxford 2000, 35-69.

Hyun Chong Kim (1999), The WTO Dispute Settlement Process: A Primer, JIEL 1999, 457-476.

Jansen, B. (2000). Die Rolle der Privatwirtschaft in Streitschlichtungsverfahren der WTO, ZEuS 2000, 293-307.

Johnson, M.D.C. (2001), US-EU Trade Disputes: Their Causes, Resolution and Prevention, essay submitted to 2001 essay contest of the Robert Schumann Center Chair in Transatlantic Relation, European University Institute, available at www.iue.it/RSC/BP.

de Jonquières, G. (2001), How can transatlantic trade disputes be avoided? essay submitted to 2001 essay contest of the Robert Schumann Center Chair in Transatlantic Relation, European University Institute, available at www.iue.it/RSC/BP.

Knox, A. (1999), The World Trade Organization at a Crossroads, World Trade 1999, Vol. 12/Issue 10, October 1999, 34-42.

Komuro, (2000), The EC Banana Regime and Judicial Control, JWT 2000/Issue 5, 1-87.

Matambalya, F.A.S.T./Wolf, S. (2001), The Cotonou Agreement and the Challenges of Making the New EU-ACP Trade Regime WTO Compatible, JIEL 2001, 123-144.

Meng, W. (1995), Gedanken zur Frage unmittelbarer Anwendung von WTO-Recht in der EG, in *Beyerlin, U.* (ed.), Recht zwischen Umbruch und Bewahrung. Völkerrecht, Europarecht, Staatsrecht. Festschrift für Rudolf Bernhardt, Berlin et al (1995), 1063.

Pauwelyn, J. (1999), The WTO Agreement on Sanitary and Phytosanitary (SPS) Measures as Applied in the first three SPS Disputes, JIEL 1999, 641-664.

Petersmann, E.U. (1997), Darf die EG das Völkerrecht ignorieren?, EuZW 1997, 325 ff.

Quick, R./Blüthner, A. (1999), Has the Appellate Body erred? An Appraisal and Criticism of the Ruling in the WTO *Hormones* Case, JIEL 1999, 603-639.

Salas, M./Jackson, J.H.H. (2000), Procedural overview of the WTO EC - banana dispute, JIEL 2000, 145-166.

Schoißwohl, B. (2002), The ECJ's *Atlanta* Judgement: Establishing a Principle of Non-Liability?, in *Breuss, F./Griller, St./Vranes, E.* (eds.), The Banana Dispute. An Economic and Legal Analysis, Vienna - New York 2002 (forthcoming).

Shaffer, G. (2002), Managing US-EU Trade Relations through Mutual Recognition and Safe Harbor Agreements: "New" and "Global" Approaches to Transatlantic Economic Governance?, EUI working paper RSC No. 2002/28, available at www.iue.it/RSC.

Subramanian, A./Watal, J. (2000), Can trips serve as an enforcement device for developing countries in the WTO? JIEL (2000) 403.

Taylor, A. (2001), Economic Tensions between the European Union and United States: Underlying Causes and Possible Cures, essay submitted to 2001 essay contest of the Robert Schumann Center Chair in Transatlantic Relation, European University Institute, available at www.iue.it/RSC/BP.

Vranes, E. (2001) Principles and Emerging Problems of WTO Cross Retaliaton. Some Comments on a new Enforcement Precedent, EuZW 2001, 10-15.

Vranes, E. (2002a), From *Bananas I* to the 2001 Bananas Settlement: A Factual and Procedural Analysis of the WTO Proceedings, in *Breuss, F. / Griller, St. / Vranes, E.* (eds.), The EU Banana Dispute - A Legal and Economic Analysis, Vienna - New York 2002 (forthcoming).

Vranes, E. (2002b), The Banana Dispute: Fundamental Issues under WTO Law, in *Breuss, F. / Griller, St. / Vranes, E.* (eds.), The EU Banana Dispute - A Legal and Economic Analysis, Vienna - New York 2002 (forthcoming).

Weiss, Fr. (1999), Fishmeal of Bananas, in *Benedek, W./Isak, H./Kicker, R.*, Development and Developing International and European Law, Essays in Honour of Konrad Ginther on the Occasion of his 65th Birthday, Frankfurt am Main 1999, 329-335.

Other Resources

Bulletin Quotidien Europe, 1 December 2000, 12.

Bulletin Quotidien Europe, 14 December 2000, 8.

Bulletin Quotidien Europe, 15 December 2000, 5.

Bulletin Quotidien Europe, 16 May 2001, 12.

Bulletin Quotidien Europe, 20 December 2000, 10.

Bulletin Quotidien Europe, 21 December 2000, 14.

Bulletin Quotidien Europe, 25 November 2000, 16.

Bulletin Quotidien Europe, 30 December 2000, 7.

Bulletin Quotidien Europe, 7 December 2000, 12.

Bulletin Quotidien Europe, No 7718 of 17 May 2000, 14.

Defense Daily International, 30 June 2000 Vol 1/Issue 13, 1.

Economist, 13 May 2000, 75.

Economist, 6 March 1999, 18.

Economist, 6 March 1999, 72.

European Report, 16 December 2000, 1.

Inside US Trade, 17 November 2000.

Inside US Trade, 24 November 2000.

Neue Zürcher Zeitung online, 19 April 2001 (available at www.nzz.ch, visited on 19 April 2001).

Office of the United States Trade Representative, Press Release 00-41 of May 26, 2000, available at www.ustr.gov.

Wall Street Journal, 12 March 2002, A.18.

Wall Street Journal, 12 March 2002.

Wall Street Journal, 14 September 2000, B.4.

Wall Street Journal, 2 October 2000, A.26.

Wall Street Journal, 23 December 1999, A, 2:2.

Wall Street Journal, 29 September 2000, A.17.

Wall Street Journal, October 9, 2000, A.22.

Wall Street Journal, 29 November 1999, A:14.

Lukas von Lutterotti

The US Extraterritorial Sanctions of 1996 and the EU Reaction

I. Introduction

The enactment of the Helms-Burton Act and the Iran and Libya Sanctions Act by the United States in 1996, which both were designed to compel European companies to comply with unilateral US economic sanctions against the so-called "rogue States" put the EU-US relations to the test. Although it might have appeared to be one of the occasional trade disputes, the domestic and general foreign policy implications probably outweighed the actual trading interests at stake. These non-economic interests caused the ineffectiveness of the existing dispute settlement system until a political solution with a seemingly lasting interim solution was achieved by means of traditional bilateral diplomacy.

This dispute forced the EU to react on a broader basis and to take an approach that could not remain limited to trade policy but had necessarily to comprise traditional foreign policy. This contribution describes the central elements and mechanisms of the extraterritorial economic sanctions and the measures taken by the EU as a response.

II. The US Extraterritorial Economic Sanctions of 1996

A. The Liberty and Democratic Solidarity (LIBERTAD) Act of 1996

After the fall of Communist governments in the Soviet block in the early 1990s, some members of the US Congress were convinced that peaceful democratic change in Cuba could be brought about by increasing economic pressure on the country. As a response to Castro's attempts to open the Cuban economy to foreign investment, these circles were determined to deter international investments in Cuba, in particular since the Castro regime furthered foreign investment in property that had been expropriated without compensation by the Cuban Government and is still claimed by US citizens.

These considerations led to the development of the Liberty and Democratic Solidarity (LIBERTAD) Act, also known as the Helms-Burton Act, after its principal sponsors in Congress. Although the Clinton administration had previously criticised the bill and at the time was expected to veto it,[1] there was a change in opinion in February 1996 when Cuban MiGs shot down two US registered civil aircraft, which allegedly had violated Cuban airspace, with the resulting death of four Cuban exiles. To show his leadership in foreign affairs, President Clinton, who at the time was seeking re-election, signed the Helms-Burton Act into law on 12 March 1996, notwithstanding the foreseeable reaction of the EU to its extraterritorial effects.[2] The influences of the election campaign of 1996 were too obvious to be overlooked: "If this had not been an

---

1 *Lowenfeld* (1996) 419ff.
2 *Fidler* (1997) 297ff, fn. 14.

election year, LIBERTAD probably would have never been signed."[3]

The purposes of the Helms-Burton Act are reflected in its four Title headings:

Title I enforces and codifies the US embargo on trade and financial transactions that had been in effect since the Kennedy Administration and are embodied in the Cuban Assets Control Regulations. In 1992, the Cuban Democracy Act had imposed an outright prohibition on the issuance of export licenses for trade with Cuba which extended also to foreign affiliates of US firms.

Title II sets out a detailed scenario for Cuba's transition to democracy and America's ending of the embargo. According to these provisions, a "democratically elected government" is a government making "demonstrable progress in returning to United States citizens property taken by the Cuban government [...] or providing full compensation [...]." Critics of the Helms-Burton Act have cited this rather inflexible and unrealistic conditions as evidence for the assertion that the Act is not really aimed at the achievement of democracy and human rights in Cuba.[4]

Title III can be regarded as the centrepiece of the Helms-Burton law. It creates a cause of action against investors , so- called "traffickers", in earlier confiscated property in Cuba. The term "trafficking" stems from legislation to restrict trade in narcotics[5] and is probably meant to denounce investments in Cuba as criminal activity. According to the definition in Sec. 4 (13) LIBERTAD, it includes a wide range of commercial activity: Not only the actual selling and purchasing of confiscated property[6] or an interest

---

3 *Luciano* (1997) 4.

4 e.g. *Stern* (1997) 10, fn. 17.

5 *Lowenfeld* (1996) 425.

6 Sec. 4 (12): "(A) The term 'property' means any property (including patents, copyrights, trademarks and any other form of intellectual property), whether real, personal or mixed, and any present, future or contingent right, security, or other interest therein including any leasehold interest.
(B For the purposes of Title III of this Act, the term 'property 'does not include real property used for residential purposes unless, as of the date of the enactment of this Act –
(i) the claim to the property is held by a US national and the claim has been certified (...) and

therein, but all commercial activity that benefits from such property and any possible participation or management in relation to this is considered to be unlawful "trafficking".[7] Thus, not only firms that invest in Cuba, but also its managers are personally targeted by the sanctions.

Sec. 301 states the reasons why this specific remedy is retained appropriate: By providing financial means to the Cuban government, investors obviously undermine the US embargo policy. Furthermore „trafficking would complicate any attempt to return [the confiscated properties] to their original owners". The next paragraphs contain the Helms-Burton view of international law: On the one hand, it lacks "fully effective remedies for wrongful confiscation of property and for unjust enrichment" from the use of such property, while on the other hand, international law would allow national jurisdiction in cases where a conduct outside the territory has substantial effect within the territory. Thus, the United States claim an entitlement to protect their citizens against wrongful confiscation. The private remedies provided for in this act do, however, not only serve the purpose of providing due compensation to the victims of the Cuban expropriations, but they have also a punitive character, being designed "to deter trafficking

---

(ii) the property is occupied by an official of the Cuban Government or the ruling political party in Cuba."

7 Sec. 4 (13) As used in title III except as provided in subparagraph (b), a person 'traffics' in confiscated property if that person knowingly or intentionally –
(i) sells, transfers, distributes, dispenses, brokers, manages or otherwise disposes of confiscated property, or purchases, leases, receives, possesses, obtains control of, manages, uses, or otherwise acquires or holds an interest in confiscated property,
(ii) engages in a commercial activity using or otherwise benefiting from confiscated property, or
(iii) causes, directs, participates in, or profits from , trafficking (as described in clause (i) or (ii)) by another person, or otherwise engages in trafficking (as described in clause (i) or (ii)) through another person.,
without the authorization of any United States national who holds a claim to the property. "
The exceptions in subparagraph (B) refer to the trading of publicly traded securities, authorised travel to Cuba and transactions of Cuban nationals and residents who are not members of the Communist party.

in wrongfully confiscated property" and to "deny traffickers any profits [...]".

Sec. 302 regulates the civil action granted to any US national with claims to confiscated property against any person that "traffics knowingly or intentionally" in property after a 3-month period beginning on the date of the enactment of the Act. The latter is liable to the former for one of the following amounts:

- the amount certified with the Foreign Claims Settlement Commission plus interest or
- an amount determined by an expert appointed by the court,
- or the fair market value (current or at the time of expropriation plus interest).

The amount owed is increased to treble damages with a punitive character if the claim is certified by the Foreign Claims Settlement Commission or if the claim was notified to the defendant and he continues the "trafficking". To allow the action under Sec. 302, the Helms-Burton Act declares the inapplicability of the Act of State doctrine,[8] a doctrine developed by US courts which prohibits them to judge on the sovereign acts of a foreign State.

Sec. 306 contains the waiver authority of the President for reasons of national interest, each suspension being limited to six months. Since the enactment of the LIBERTAD act, given the international protests it has caused, President Clinton as well as President George W. Bush have continued to suspend the applicability of Title III. Therefore, no action under this Title has yet been brought to court and it is not very probable that this will be the case in the near future, since the EU has made it a condition that the US to suspend and eventually abolish the Title III action.[9]

Title IV requires the denial of entry visas to persons who, after 12 March 1996, confiscate or "traffic" in confiscated property in Cuba claimed by US nationals. As stated in Sec 401 LIBERTAD, the following persons are excluded from entering the United States:

- persons who, after the coming into force of the law, have participated in confiscation or have "trafficked" in expropriated property;
- corporate officers, principals, shareholders with controlling interest of an entity which has been involved in "trafficking";

---

8 Sec. 302 (6)

9 See: EU Unilateral Statement 18/5/1998, http://europa.eu.int/comm/dg01/0518uni.htm

- persons who are a spouse, minor child or agent of one of the above.

The State Department has set up a "Helms-Burton Implementation Unit" [10] within the Office of Cuban Affairs to collect and analyse information from all available sources on "trafficking" in property claimed by US nationals and to investigate persons who may be trafficking in confiscated properties in Cuba. When the evidence warrants, the US immigration authorities are instructed to exclude them from entry into the United States.

As there is no waiver authority for the President in respect to the Title IV provisions, they have been enforced on a number of occasions. To date, at least two European companies engaged in the Cuban tourist industry are known to have been blacklisted by the Helms-Burton Implementation Unit.[11]

B. The US Sanctions against Iran and Libya

The Iran and Libya Sanctions Act (ILSA) was signed into law on 5 August 1996, some months after the coming into force of the LIBERTAD Act, in presence of the families of the victims of the Lockerbie aeroplane crash caused by a Libyan terrorists' attack in 1988.[12][13] It sanctions foreign investments in the Libyan and Iranian petroleum industry since these investments could have a detrimental effect on the efficiency of US sanctions against those countries and could provide their governments with funds to foster world-wide terrorism.

Like the Helms-Burton Act, whose enactment pleased the Cuban-American lobby in Florida, the ILSA is not immune from domestic policy considerations. First of all, it was signed in times of presidential elections where there is less room for political compromise and much room for tough talking. This may explain the approval of President Clinton, who was seeking re-election and

---

10 US Department Of State 96/09/20 Statement: Helms/Burton Implementation Unit Established.

11 Speech of *Fraser Cameron*, European Commission Delegation to the US, before the American Chamber of Commerce of Cuba in the United States, 24/2/2000, at: http://www.eurunion.org/news/speeches/000224fc.htm

12 *Stern* (1997) 8.

13 The Iran and Libya Sanctions Act was devised by Senator Alphonse D'Amato and is therefore also called the D'Amato Act.

could well use a mean to underline his leadership qualities in international politics.

As Sections 101 and 102 LIBERTAD with respect to Cuba, Section 4 ILSA calls on the President to internationally promote a multilateral sanctions regime against Iran, including provisions to specifically limit its oil trade, and to report on this efforts. Section 4 (e) ILSA requires the President to submit reports to Congress on other countries' policy towards the target countries. Sec. 4(c) gives the President the option to waive the application of sanctions for investing in Iran with respect to nationals of a country that has itself enacted economic sanctions against Iran.

Sec. 8 of ILSA sets forth the conditions under which the sanctions shall be lifted, i.e. if the President determines that Iran does no longer acquire weapons of mass destruction and no longer supports international terrorism and that Libya has complied with the Security Council Resolutions. Sec. 13 (b) contains a so-called "sunset clause", which limits the validity of the Act to five years. However, in July 2001, President George W. Bush has extended the validity of the Act until 2006.

The sanctioned activity of the Iran and Libya Sanctions Act are investments in these countries of $20m or more (or a combination of $5m investments that exceed this amount in a one year period) that "directly and significantly" contributed to the enhancement of the target country's ability to develop its petroleum resources.[14] The persons against which the sanctions are to be imposed are the investors, their successor entities, their parent companies, subsidiaries and affiliates.

The sanctions provided for in ILSA are imposed by the President, who chooses two out of a list of seven (sec.6):

- Denial of assistance through the Export- Import Bank of the United States;
- denial of export licenses where required;
- prohibition of US financial institutions from providing loans and credits to those breaching the embargo;
- financial institutions that are themselves found in breach of the embargo can be prohibited as primary dealers in US Treasury bills or

[14] Sec.5 provides for amount of $40m and $10m respectively, but Sec.4 (d) lowers this threshold after an initial period of one year after the enactment (cfr. Sec.4(b)).

- may be denied to serve as a repository of government funds;
- exclusion from contracts of procurement with the US Government;
- import restrictions under the International Economic Powers Act (50 U.S.C. 1701 ff.).

Sec. 9 ILSA describes the procedure that is to be followed after that the President has determined an infringement of the ILSA sanctions regime under Sec. 5 by a foreign person: First, the President is asked to begin consultations with the "government with primary jurisdiction" and is given the option to delay sanctions on that behalf. Sanctions are not imposed if the foreign country has taken steps to effectively prevent the investment itself and can be further delayed if such actions are under way. The President can grant an individual waiver to a certain person for reasons of national interest under Section 9(c). If this is not the case, the President is obliged to impose sanctions of not less than two years. However, if the President can determine that the forbidden activities have ceased, he can limit the application of the sanctions to the minimum of one year.

In the bilateral negotiations conducted after 1996 by the EU and the US, the EU sought to obtain a general waiver granted under Sec. 4 c) for the whole EU with respect to the American embargo against Iran and a specific waiver under Sec. 9 (c) ILSA for EU companies with respect to Libya. However, at the time of writing, no permanent and general waiver under Sec. 4(c) has been granted and thus major investments in Iran and Libya remain subject to scrutiny by the US administration and can be blocked by imposing sanctions with respect to the investor. However, although guidelines for the implementation have been issued[15], the ILSA sanctions have never been implemented.

III. The Mechanisms of Extraterritorial Legislation

A. Extraterritorial Jurisdiction – Concept

Jurisdiction is an essential element of a State's sovereignty and comprises the power of a State to enact laws (jurisdiction to prescribe), to guarantee their application by virtue of its monopoly on the use of force (jurisdiction to enforce), and by providing a judicial system (jurisdiction to adjudicate).

---

[15] 61 Fed. Reg. 66067 (1996).

In short, extraterritorial jurisdiction can be defined as the setting and the enforcement of rules outside the territory of the regulating State.

In international law, extraterritorial jurisdiction is recognised in the form of (1) laws related to embassies, ships, aircraft or nationals abroad or (2) the authorised administration of another State's territory (e.g. customs matters). This is sometimes called extraterritorial jurisdiction in the strict sense and is characterised by the fact that essentially the scope of jurisdiction to enforce and to prescribe coincide. Moreover, the legislation of a State relating to its nationals abroad on the basis of their nationality has a long tradition as international customary law.[16]

As far as enforcement jurisdiction is more specifically concerned, one could think of the performance of sovereign acts abroad, as the arrest of a suspected criminal in another State, but also of the service of official documents, such as a writ of process.[17] These acts are strictly forbidden under international law, if carried out unilaterally.

In a wider sense, extraterritorial jurisdiction comprises also the establishment of rules that regulate behaviour beyond the reach of territorial supremacy, i.e. jurisdiction to prescribe with relation to an extraterritorial set of facts, without necessarily also enforcing it extraterritorially.[18] Instead, economically powerful States prefer to use the importance of their markets to foreign businesses which depend on these markets as a leverage, in order to create "incentives" for compliance with the extraterritorial rule, e.g. by threatening to seize their assets held within the regulating State's territory. Essentially, the price for market access is the compliance with the extraterritorial legislation, even if its content of the command is completely unrelated to the market access itself or the affected businesses activity in these markets.

With respect to matters of international trade, characterised by global interdependence, it is not unreasonable to adopt the broad concept of extraterritoriality, because the de facto regulation of a set of facts outside the territory should not be excluded from the

---

16 *Meng* (1987) 155.

17 *Mann* (1984) 38 ff.

18 *Meng* (1994) 74; *Mann* (1984) 33.

concept of extraterritoriality on the sole ground that enforcement is territorial.[19]

The territorial enforcement of rules regulating conduct abroad is also called "indirect enforcement jurisdiction".[20] In the case of economic sanctions, indirect enforcement jurisdiction forms the basis of so-called secondary boycotts. Indirect enforcement relies on a cost-benefit analysis operated by the addressee of the rule; the choice is between compliance, on the one hand, and non-compliance and avoidance of being subjected to the regulating State's enforcement jurisdiction, as a natural person and/or with one's assets or commercial interests, on the other hand. It becomes clear that this choice is not the same as with direct enforcement, where the choice is essentially between compliance and sanction, provided that evasion, most often on the basis of an inefficient judicial system, is not an option. With direct enforcement, i.e. enforcement of laws within the territorial jurisdiction of the regulating State, the potential for imposing sanctions is theoretically equal for all States, because, in theory, all of them have the monopoly on the use of force at their disposal.[21]

By contrast, indirect enforcement operates on the basis of factual differences between States in their economic and political power. As an example, a multinational corporation can afford to disregard a hypothetical extraterritorial law of a small Caribbean State and simply by avoiding holding assets within its jurisdiction; it can however not afford not to comply with an US law or an EC regulation that is applied extraterritorially, because it is likely to have relevant interests in both markets. In the global market for foreign direct investment, international investment decisions are taken also on the basis of the legal system of the State of

---

19 *Mann* (1984) 33.

20 *Mann* (1984) 47; *Puttler* (1989) 118.

21 For the purpose of this argument, the interesting discussion on the role of the efficiency of a State's enforcement and judiciary and the assessment of the risks related to the possibility for law breakers to go unpunished, has to be left aside. Suffice it to say that, if this possibility grows to a certain level and the number of unpunished criminals increases, there is the risk that organised crime gains a foothold in a society which establishes and mercilessly enforces its own rules , thereby largely replacing a State's monopoly of force. The present argument assumes that the State's monopoly of force is unchallenged and enforcement is more or less efficient.

investment. While poorer countries compete for badly needed foreign investment also with the attractiveness of their legal systems, only where there is a strong interest of foreign investors to be present in a particular market, States can afford to impose legal constraints without completely deterring these investments.

By affecting trading and investment interests of the foreign direct investor within the territorial jurisdiction of the regulating State, extraterritorial jurisdiction operates preventively with persuasion, often based on the threat of force or considerable economic disadvantage.[22] Therefore, sanctions need not be applied for the extraterritorial commands to be effective. It is sufficient to add an often weighty factor to the cost-benefit analysis of economic operators, in order for extraterritorial jurisdiction to have a substantial impact on the decision of foreign investors. The potential loss of or the detriment to the investment opportunity of foreign investors which influences the pattern of behaviour of multinationals is however also an indirect influence on the economy of the States of origin of these investing businesses. The regulation of this economy is obviously a sovereign right of the State concerned. If its economic interests are considerably affected, the State of origin of the exporting businesses feels obliged to protest against the exercise of extraterritorial jurisdiction. In this case, it often invokes its sovereign right to regulate its economy, which in its view is affected if its exporting and investment interests are curtailed by foreign legislative commands.

A special issue in this respect are restrictions on the market access for companies which do not comply with *domestic standards*, where the line of distinction is particularly hard to draw. The prime example in this respect is the case of environmental standards which are so strict as to completely prohibiting any import from certain countries. This was the case with the United States' Marine Mammal Protection Act which imposes dolphin – friendly fishing methods for tuna imports in the United States and Section 609 of Public Law 101-102[23] aiming to protect Turtles from being caught by the shrimp fishers' trawlers, which both caused the famous international trade disputes in the WTO arena.

---

22 For a detailed analysis of the persuasive aspect of extraterritorial jurisdiction, see *Meng* (1994) 82ff.

23 16 USC 1537.

By looking at the *formal* aspect of this import restricting legislation in general, scholars have cited prohibitive domestic standards as a case of territorial jurisdiction with extraterritorial effects[24], whereas the EU Commission and WTO panel report in the Tuna Dolphin case have used the expressions "extraterritorial" and "extrajurisdictional" to describe this legislation.[25] There can be no doubt that the regulation of a certain market and the access to that market, including provisions for the import of goods, capital and services fall within the domestic jurisdiction of a State, to which it is entitled as a sovereign, even though the effects of a provision in this field are predominantly outside the State's territory. Therefore, standards relating to imported goods and services as such can not be judged contrary to the principles of international law on jurisdiction.

If a provision however *substantially* establishes rules that regulate behaviour completely unrelated to the process of importation and if these rules are thus not functional to the regulation of the product's characteristics for the purpose of introducing it on a certain market, one has to conclude that the import restriction constitutes a hidden sanction for conduct abroad. This would therefore again be a case of indirect enforcement jurisdiction. I would suggest to take this teleological interpretation into account when qualifying the practice of restrictive domestic standards, thus including in the definition of extraterritorial jurisdiction the setting of prohibitive domestic standards for imported goods, if this is exclusively aimed at regulating conduct abroad.

B. International Law of Jurisdiction

The generally accepted international law principles of jurisdiction can be summarised with two basic rules:[26]

1) Jurisdiction to enforce within another State's territory is not allowed without the latter's consent.
2) Jurisdiction to prescribe may be asserted only where there is a sufficiently close contact.[27]

---

24 *Schwarze* (1994) 14; *Meng* (1994) 76.

25 Panel Report on "United States – Restrictions on Imports of Tuna", DS21/R, 3 September 1991.

26 *Bianchi* (1995) 442ff; *Meng* (1994) 496ff.

27 Other expressions have also been used: "substantial and bona fide connection", "genuine link" (*Brownlie* (1998) 313f), "sinnvoller

Rule one refers to jurisdiction to enforce, for which it is undisputed, given the general acceptance of the principle of non-intervention.

The second rule contains first of all the essential premise that the limiting function of international law extends also to the jurisdiction to prescribe.[28] This is important particularly in the cases of indirect enforcement jurisdiction, where jurisdiction to prescribe is applied extraterritorially whereas the enforcement is territorial. In fact, in his fundamental work on jurisdiction, F. A. Mann[29] has argued that a deliberate interference with another State's economic order infringes its sovereignty to regulate its economy, if not agreed upon beforehand, since the prescription is the prerequisite for enforcement, be it direct or indirect and "... it would be a most unattractive system of laws which would preclude a State from protecting its citizens against an international wrong before it is implemented." This argument seems convincing, since a legislative prescription always entails a threat of enforcement.[30] The existence in international law of basic rules limiting the jurisdiction to prescribe, possibly different from those governing the jurisdiction to enforce, is therefore conceivable in principle.

Secondly, rule two evokes a concept that in its basic idea is now widely accepted in scholarly debate and in State practice and therefore constitutes the starting point of every analysis on the international law of jurisdiction.

The theoretical development of what I summarised as rule two is primarily owed to the works of F. A. Mann, who described it as the "point of contact theory".[31] It states that there has to be a sufficiently close relationship of a State with a fact in order to subject it to its jurisdiction to prescribe.

The concept of the points of contact is derived from a common element of international private law systems, the factual relationship between the regulated fact and the regulating

---

Anknüpfungspunkt" (*Meessen* (1975) 101), "rattachement" (*Stern* (1986) 7ff). In fact, when asserting extraterritorial jurisdiction, it is common State practice to cite a close connection or genuine link of the underlying facts with the domestic legal order. *Bianchi* (1995) 446 f.

28 *Stern* (1986) 16f; *Meng* (1994) 485ff; *Bianchi* (1995) 41ff.

29 *Mann* (1984) 33.

30 See also *Bianchi* (1992) 427; *Brownlie* (1998) 313.

31 *Mann* developed his theses in two lectures held at the Academie de Droit International in The Hague: *Mann* (1964) 7 and (1984) 9.

jurisdiction.[32] In defining such a prerequisite, this concept, which has been further developed by scholarly writers as well as by State practice, overcomes the until then predominant approach that jurisdiction to prescribe was necessarily always limited to the territory of the regulating State, similar to the enforcement, with the only possible exception of jurisdiction over its nationals abroad.[33] Moreover, Mann's point of contact theory is expressly referred to legislative jurisdiction by distinguishing it from jurisdiction to enforce.[34]

In order to establish the existence of a point of contact or relevant link, several "bases of jurisdiction" have been identified, but no clear hierarchy has been established by State practice. The primary jurisdictional base that constitutes a point of contact is the territory, however nationality has always been accepted as a concurrent base and other links such as the effects within the regulating state's territory or the necessity to protect a state's continued existence have been successfully used to justify the exercise of prescriptive jurisdiction. Due to the evolutionary nature of international customary law, the number and types of accepted bases of jurisdiction may vary depending on the subject matter of the extraterritorial prescription.

Therefore, it is possible that more States have a relevant point of contact to a particular set of facts and claim jurisdiction (concurrent jurisdiction). Especially when both States adopt territorial enforcement measures, this can put single persons in a position where they are "caught between two masters" and any of their alternatives includes being sanctioned by one of the conflicting jurisdictions. In its original conception, the point of contact theory does not offer a indication how to resolve these conflicts within public international law, but requires the internal conflict of laws system concerned to make a choice between two systems each of which may claim to be closely connected with the issue at hand.[35]

The point of contact theory has considerable merits for overcoming the strict delimitation of prescriptive jurisdiction to the state's territory and adapting the theoretical framework of the international law of jurisdiction to the needs of a more interrelated

---

32 *Bianchi* (1995) 65ff.

33 *Mann* (1964) 24ff; *Bianchi* (1995) 48ff.

34 *Mann* (1964) 13ff and 128; cf. *Meessen* (1975) 102.

35 *Mann* (1984) 31ff.

economic and legal world order. Nevertheless, it leaves open the question how conflicts with concurrent jurisdiction are to be resolved within an exclusively international law framework in cases where no treaty settling the conflict for a particular field has been concluded.[36][37]

The detailed consequences of the point of contact theory on an international law level are therefore heavily disputed.

C. The Extraterritorial Scope of the Helms Burton Act

Essentially, the Helms-Burton Act results in an extraterritorial prohibition for foreign companies to invest in Cuba. The sanctions for violations of this prohibition are administered territorially and consist either in the damage claims by those private persons expropriated or in visa restrictions for managers and their families, administered by the immigration authorities.

The extraterritorial prohibition is not justifiable on the traditional grounds, as the LIBERTAD Act targets quite openly foreign persons, it cannot be based on the nationality of those concerned.[38]

The Helms-Burton Act expressly invokes the effects doctrine to justify its extraterritorial provisions.[39] This doctrine has been developed in international competition law and establishes jurisdiction in the presence of "direct, substantial and foreseeable effects" on the domestic economy. Several proponents of the Act, who follow this line of argument,[40] assert that the US citizens' claims, totalling - as certified by the State Department's Foreign Claims Settlement Commission - $6billion of present value, are substantially impaired by the "trafficking" operated by foreign investors, since it would complicate any restitution. Even when leaving out of consideration the fundamental difficulties in applying the effects doctrine to restrictions of trade and investment, i.e. in the field of economic sanctions,[41] it is hard to argue that foreign

---

36 In international taxation law a network of bilateral and multilateral treaties is established to solve similar conflicts.

37 See critical remarks by *Bianchi* (1995) 92 ff.

38 Sec. 301(11) LIBERTAD.

39 Sec. 301 (9) LIBERTAD.

40 *Clagett* (1996) 435ff.

41 The effects doctrine is commonly used in antitrust matters, but State practice showed considerable hesitance to accept it in circumstances of

investments in Cuba have "direct, substantial and foreseeable effects" in the US.

Neither can the extraterritoriality be justified with the need to protect national security, since foreign investments in Cuba are unlikely to impair national security in the United States.

Proponents of the Helms-Burton legislation assert that, in defending property rights as human rights, Title III gives effect to and thus strengthens the practice of international law governing the protection of property.[42]

This approach may allude to the US tradition of vindicating human rights before domestic courts on the basis of the Alien Tort Statute of 1789.[43] It relies, however, more on asserted standards of humanitarian law rather than on traditional international law concerning the treatment of aliens. In this area of international law, in fact, there is the tendency to subject *erga omnes* violations of international law to every State's jurisdiction.[44] Based on this trend, it could be argued that an extraterritorial measure, although not justifiable under general principles of jurisdiction, was a necessary reaction to violations of human rights as protected by the international community.[45] A similar argument has to be ruled out in the case of the Helms-Burton Act, since property rights cannot be qualified as universally agreed upon core values of the international community, as is the case with more fundamental human rights. Even if unlawful expropriations were prohibited by a human rights standard, this could hardly be said of a prohibition on the transfer of confiscated property to third parties as sanctioned by the Helms-Burton Act. This reflects the fact that issues of expropriation are still governed by the international regime on the treatment of aliens.[46]

---

export controls, which are similarly sensitive to foreign and security policy interests.

42 *Clagett* (1996) 438ff.

43 Filartiga v. Pena-Irala, US Court of Appeals, 2nd Cir., 1980, 630 F.2d 876 and Forti v. Suarez-Mason, US District Court, Northern District of California 1987, 672 F. Supp. 1531.

44 *Bianchi* (1995) 348ff. See in particular §703(2) Restatement: "Any state may pursue international remedies against any other state for a violation of the customary international law of human rights."

45 As suggested by *Bianchi* (1995) 353ff.

46 *Kress/Herbst* (1997) 640.

The Helms-Burton Act is, therefore, contrary to the international law principles of jurisdiction since it cannot be justified under any of the existing categories of jurisdictional links.

D. The Extraterritorial Scope of the US Sanctions against Iran and Libya

After its enactment in August 1996, the Iran and Libya Sanctions Act and its extraterritorial scope have been much less discussed in doctrine than the Helms-Burton Act. However, to European investors these provisions should be more important because of the close economic relations of the EU with the two target countries. This lack of scholarly attention may be attributed to ILSA's build-in waiver facility. However, although a permanent waiver under Sec. 4(c) for investments in Iran would be possible, until now only a waiver under Sec. 9(c) has been exercised on a case-by-case basis, which in effect allows US administration to control and possibly prevent any major investment in the petroleum industry of these countries.

As with Title IV LIBERTAD, which denies entry into the United States to foreign investors in Cuba, as well as to the managers and their families of investor companies, it has been asserted that the ILSA did not constitute an exercise of extraterritorial jurisdiction to prescribe and thus the international customary law principles on extraterritoriality were not applicable. This interpretation was largely based on a misconception of the territorial enforcement mechanism which deprives violators of rights accruing under treaty law or even of privileges not guaranteed under international law. This characterisation of the ILSA sanctions cannot be shared, because it disregards the underlying economic interrelations and the express purpose of the legislation.

Of particular interest is the case-by-case waiver technique adopted by the US administration under Sec. 9(c) ILSA, which allows the US to control every single major deal concluded by European investors in Libya or Iran. Compared with the waivers of the Helms-Burton Act, this method could be described as more sophisticated. The targeted transactions are not immediately prohibited and thus an attack of these provisions on the basis of treaty agreements is much more difficult, since there is considerable leeway for negotiations left once the provisions are applied in a given case. In general, the extraterritorial elements provide a trump card for the US position during these negotiations as they put the other party into a position from the beginning where it cannot walk away from the negotiating table without having achieved some sort of compromise. In contrast to the Helms-Burton Act's Title III, in the case of deals with Iran and Libya, negotiations have to be begun and concessions have to be made for each single deal. Therefore, the threat arising from the mere existence of this legislation to private investors, particularly those in the petroleum sector, should not be underestimated. In the case of ILSA, there is no prospect of justifying the US claim to jurisdiction on any of the traditional bases. Applying the strict interpretation of traditional international law concepts, a justification based on the protective principle would have to be denied since, *prima facie,* there is no sufficiently strong national security element to be *per se* found in foreign investment activities.

Following rather an approach of interest balancing, as suggested by a strong current of US doctrine of international law,[47] the case of ILSA sees European vital economic interests opposed to US foreign policy interests directed at the extraterritorial extension of the economic sanctions relating to the Iranian and Libyan petroleum industry. The outcome of a balancing of these conflicting interests would, therefore, largely depend on whether one assumes a purely economic perspective or admits considerations of US national security. In matters of national security, of course, it is hard to imagine how evidence would be valued by an independent court, if such evidence was produced at all by the parties.

VI. The EU Position

A. The EU Position on Extraterritoriality

On numerous occasions, the EU, and earlier the EC, has expressed its view on the United States' exercise of extraterritorial jurisdiction. Apart from various *aide-mémoires* concerning the extension of US jurisdiction to subsidiaries of US companies incorporated in the Community, the most comprehensive text on extraterritoriality was drawn up in 1982 as a reaction to the US pipeline embargo by a working group mainly consisting of Commission civil servants, but eventually adopted by the

---

47 American Law Institute, Restatement of the Law, The Foreign Relations Law of the United States, Chicago1986, §§401 ff, in particular §402 and §403.

COREPER.[48] This document, sometimes simply referred to as "the Comments", was submitted on behalf of the Community and its Member States to the US State Department in August 1982. The arguments presented therein consider the US export controls under international as well as under US law. It was the first time that the Community had taken such an explicit stance on a point of general customary law.[49] The line of argument can be broadly divided in two categories.

The first part argues that the measures taken by the United States lack a proper jurisdictional base, as the international law of jurisdiction would require. The Comments discuss the territoriality and the nationality principle as the generally accepted bases of jurisdiction and conclude that both cannot justify the exercise of US jurisdiction over companies incorporated in a Member State and with respect to activities taking place outside the US. Then, the protective principle and the effects doctrine are taken into consideration as principles "which have found less than general acceptance under international law"[50]. While the preconditions for the effects doctrine[51] are not deemed to be fulfilled, a possible reliance on the protective principle is excluded on the basis that the US had not invoked national security reasons in defending their trade restricting measures. The view adopted in the Comments would not exclude *a priori* the protective principle as a possible ground for the imposition of extraterritorial sanctions. In fact, in defending the Helms-Burton and the D'Amato Acts, the United States have taken up this hint and invoked national security as prime reason for their action.

The second line of argument alleges that the US measures, in addition, violate prohibitive principles of general international law. The interference in the trade relations of the EC with third countries is contrary to the principle of non-intervention. Moreover, according to the Comments, the United States' encouraging American companies to insert submission clauses in their licensing

---

48 European Communities: Comments on the US Regulations Concerning Trade with the U.S.S.R., reproduced in: 21 I.L.M. 891 (1982), hereafter: Comments. Commented in: *Kuijper* (1984) 94ff; *Bianchi* (1995) 261ff.

49 *Kuijper* (1984) 93.

50 Comments, supra fn. 48, p.896.

51 direct, substantial and foreseeable effects.

agreements with foreign enterprises would constitute an abuse of rights.[52]

Following the enactment of the Helms-Burton Act, the Presidency of the Council and the Commission, on behalf of the European Union, presented a diplomatic démarche in 1996, criticising the US legislation as "unacceptable as a matter of law and policy".[53] In particular, this note argues that the United States have no jurisdictional basis in international law to claim the right to regulate transactions abroad undertaken by non-US companies.

On a multilateral level, the presidency of the Council continuously takes this view within the UN General Assembly and each year supports the Resolution calling for an end of the Cuban embargo, "the extraterritorial effects of which affect the sovereignty of other States, the legitimate interests of entities and persons under their jurisdiction and the freedom of trade and navigation."[54]

The negative impact that extraterritorial economic sanctions have on international trade are discussed in the Commission's annual Report on US Barriers to Trade and Investment,[55] which states:

> "[Extraterritoriality] is a long-standing feature of the US legal system manifesting itself in - amongst others - the fields of the environment, banking, tax and export control. While the EU may share some of the objectives underlying such laws, it is opposed, as a matter of law and principle, to the extraterritorial application of domestic legislation

---

[52] i.e. clauses requiring the foreign licensee to submit to US export legislation.

[53] In fact, the Commission had already expressed its concerns in the run-up to the passing of the Helms-Burton bill. The respective letter of Vice-President of the Commission Brittan to the US Secretary of State Christopher, together with the démarche of March 1996 is reprinted in: 35 I.L.M. 397 (1996).

[54] See, e.g., Resolution adopted by the General Assembly on 9th November 2000, on the necessity of ending the economic, commercial and financial embargo imposed by the United States of America against Cuba, A/RES/55/20; cf. also the relative UN Press Release GA/9814 of 9/11/2000.

[55] European Commission, 2000 Report on US Barriers to Trade and Investment, July 2000, available at: http://europa.eu.int/comm/trade/pdf/usrbt2000.pdf

> insofar as it purports to force persons present in – and companies incorporated in - the EU to follow US laws or policies outside the US and to the extent that it serves only to protect US trade or political interests. In particular, the EU opposes the extraterritorial provisions of certain US legislation that hampers international trade and investment by seeking to regulate EU trade with third countries conducted by companies outside the US."[56]

The Helms-Burton and the D'Amato Act are specifically identified as "contrary to international law".[57]

A similar view on extraterritoriality was expressed in the EU amicus curiae brief in a recent case where a local State law containing extraterritorial economic sanctions was challenged before the US Supreme Court.[58]

From an international legal point of view, it can be concluded that the view continuously expressed by the EU on extraterritoriality is consistent with the well-established principle need of bases of jurisdiction. Although the most detailed legal opinion dates back to 1982, it can be inferred that the EU takes the view according to which all US measures criticised do in fact lack a recognised jurisdictional basis, with the general observation, of political rather than strictly legal nature, that the exercise of extraterritorial jurisdiction is inconsistent with the friendly bilateral relations.

As far as international relations are generally concerned, it emerges clearly that the EU strongly advocates a multilateral approach to the solution of problems at an international level, in particular, if the Union and its Member States themselves are not consulted; the EU is fundamentally opposed to the idea of one country imposing its will unilaterally.[59]

---

56 European Commission, 2000 Report on US Barriers to Trade and Investment, July 2000, p. 8.

57 European Commission, 2000 Report on US Barriers to Trade and Investment, July 2000, p. 10.

58 Crosby v. National Foreign Trade Council, US Supreme Court, 2000, amicus curiae brief in Support of Plaintiff National Foreign Trade Council, at: http://usaengage.org/resources/nftcbrief.html

59 For a detailed analysis of this aspect, see Fidler (1997) 297.

B. The EU Relations with Cuba, Iran and Libya

The framework of the EU foreign policy towards *Cuba* was defined in December 1996 in a Common Position within the CFSP.[60] In fact, Cuba has never been a natural trading partner for the EU, but the diplomatic tension over the Helms-Burton Act have shown the need for the EU to express its views on the situation in Cuba and to accordingly define a consistent strategy of foreign policy towards the regime of Fidel Castro.

In an approach labelled "constructive engagement"[61], the EU combines the concern for the human rights situation in Cuba with limited economic co-operation with Cuba which is to increase if progress towards democracy is achieved. The Common Position, in order not to increase the economic hardship for the Cuban people, expressly excludes coercive measures.[62] Besides, the EU provides humanitarian and emergency aid and supports regional co-operation programmes.[63] At the same time, the human rights are monitored by a human rights working group composed of the EU heads of mission in Havana and concerns are continuously voiced in bilateral contacts.[64]

The linkage between economic co-operation in return for the commitment to democratic values and human rights is, in fact, a constant in EU foreign policy, as demonstrated by the inclusion of human rights clauses in association agreements with the EU.

---

60 Common Position 96/697/CFSP, of 2 December, 1996, on Cuba, O.J. L322/1, 12/12/1996.

61 *Cameron* (European Commission Delegation, Washington D.C.), The European Union and Cuba, speech held at the Luncheon of the American Chamber of Commerce of Cuba in the United States, 24/2/2000, available at: http://eurunion.org/news/speeches/2000/000224fc.htm

62 The four elements lined out in the Common Position on Cuba are: 1) Concern for the human rights situation; 2) exclusion of coercive economic measures; 3) limited co-operation and political dialogue; 4) full economic co-operation is made conditional on improvements in human rights and political freedom. cf. Common Position 96/697/CFSP, of 2 December, 1996, on Cuba, O.J. L322/1, 12/12/1996.

63 *Cameron* (2000).

64 ibidem. Cf. also Statement by the Presidency on behalf of the European Union on Cuba, Pesc/99/65, 25 June 1999, 9408/99 (Presse 205), concerning the increased use of the death penalty following amendments to the Cuban Penal Code.

Recently, the requirement of the respect for human rights, democratic principles and the rule of law were inserted as "essential elements" in the new partnership agreement between the EU and the ACP countries.[65] Typically, Cuba participated as an observer to the negotiations of this new agreement, but eventually decided not to sign and as of today has not acceded to that partnership with the EU.[66]

The European diplomatic relations with *Iran* have long been very limited, but have opened up in recent years, discussing specific fields of possible co-operation such as environment, drug control, refugees and energy.[67] The EU has also raised the issue of human rights.

The trade relationship is dominated by the oil business; it accounts for more than 75% of EU imports from Iran, plants, machinery and equipment make up about 45% of EU exports to Iran.[68] As far as the issue of non-proliferation is concerned, Member States maintain national export controls on arms transfers to Iran,[69] transfers of dual use goods are subject to the Community dual use Regulation.[70]

The EU foreign relations with *Libya* have been characterised for a long time by the UN Sanctions imposed as a consequence of the alleged Libyan involvement of several terrorist attacks, in particular the Lockerbie bombing.[71] Accordingly, the EU has imposed economic sanctions against Libya, including an arms and a flight embargo, prohibition on exports of oil refinery equipment, a downsizing of diplomatic relations and, in 1993 a freeze of funds

---

65 EU-ACP Agreement, signed in Cotonou, Benin, on June 23, 2000, available at: http://europa.eu.int/comm/development/cotonou/index_en.htm

66 Agence Europe No. 7773, 5 August 2000, 3.

67 European Commission, The EU's relations with Iran – an overview, at: http://europa.eu.int/comm/external_relations/iran/intro/index.htm

68 ibidem.

69 e.g., Germany, Bundesamt für Wirtschaft und Ausfuhrkontrolle, formerly Bundesausfuhramt, BAFA Exportkontrolle - Kurzdarstellung, available at: http://www.bundesausfuhramt.de/informat/infod.html

70 Council Regulation 2000/1334/EC of 22 June 2000, setting up a Community regime for the control of exports of dual-use items and technology, O.J. L 159/1 of 30/06/2000.

71 UN Security Council Resolution 748 (1992), of 31 March 1992 and UN Security Council Resolution 883 (1993).

held abroad by the Libyan government.[72] However, neither the UN sanctions nor the relative measures of implementation taken by the EU extend these economic sanctions to the trade in oil, as did the sanctions imposed by the United States.

On 28 August 1998, the UN Security Council unanimously adopted Resolution 1192 that would suspend sanctions immediately if the Libyan authorities handed over the two suspects of the Lockerbie affair for trial in The Hague under Scottish jurisdiction. After a flurry of mediation efforts, Libya did deliver the suspects to the UN Secretary-General, who notified the Security Council by letter on 5 April 1999, so suspending the sanctions imposed under Resolutions 748 and 883.[73] Therefore, in 1999, the EU lifted the restrictive measures against Libya with the exception of the arms embargo.[74] In January 2001, the Scottish Court rendered the judgement which found the two Libyan agents guilty of the terrorist attack and thus implicitly attributed the responsibility to the Libyan government. As a result, at the time of writing, the United States have not yet lifted their economic sanctions, but neither have the UN and the EU decided to impose new sanctions.

---

[72] Council Regulation 92/945/EEC, of 14 April 1992, preventing the supply of certain goods and services to Libya, O.J. L101/53, 15/4/1992;
Council Regulation 93/3274/EC of 29 November 1993 preventing the supply of certain goods and services to Libya , O.J. L 295/1 , 30/11/1993;
Council Regulation 93/3275/EC of 29 November 1993, prohibiting the satisfying of claims with regard to contracts and transactions the performance of which was affected by the United Nations Security Council Resolution 883 (1993) and related resolutions, O.J. L 295/4 , 30/11/1993;
Common Position 93/614/CFSP, of 22 November 1993, reduction of economic relations with Libya O.J.L 295/7, 30/11/1993.

[73] Pursuant to Art. 8 UN Security Council Resolution 1192 (1998), UN Document S/1999/726.

[74] Council Regulation 1999/836/EC of 20 April 1999 suspending the application of Regulation (EC) No 3274/93, O.J. L 106/1, 23/04/1999;
Common Position 1999/261/CFSP of 16 April 1999, concerning Libya, O.J. L 103/1, 20/04/1999;
Common Position 1999/611/CFSP, of 13 September 1999, amending Common Position 1999/261/CFSP concerning Libya, O.J. L242/31, 14/09/1999 (deleting also the sanctions in diplomatic and consular contacts while upholding the arms embargo).

While complying with the UN economic sanctions, the EU has always entertained extensive trade relations with Libya, whose oil supply has been a crucial interest to the European countries. In fact, 90% of Libya's oil exports are directed to the EU, with Italy depending for 51% of its oil requirements on Libyan oil. Correspondingly, the half of all Libyan imports originates in the EU.[75]

After the end of the diplomatic sanctions in 1999, Libya has been invited to join the co-operation between the EU and the Mediterranean countries initiated in 1995 at a conference in Barcelona, from which Libya had been excluded because of the UN sanctions. As of today, Libya has however remained an observer to this partnership and has refused to fully adhere to its principles.[76]

To conclude, it is evident that the EU pursues a different foreign policy strategy than the United States. Its goal is to maintain and intensify trade relations with a view to supporting democratic changes by conceding trade opportunities in exchange for improvements in the human rights record. This strategy is not dissimilar from the policy pursued by the US with respect to China. With Iran and Libya, the differences become all the more evident when considering the diverging trading interests, given in particular the EU strategy to secure access to the oil reserves of both countries.

V. The EU Reaction

Already before the enactment of the Helms-Burton Act, the EU had protested against the extraterritorial reach of the law in two diplomatic notes.[77] Critical comments came also from the Council[78] and the European Parliament[79].

The Council[80] identified a series of measures, among them also travel restrictions for representatives of US companies and a watch list of US companies filing Title III actions. Eventually, the EU took the following steps:

---

75 European Commission, The EU's relations with Libya – an overview, at: http://europa.eu.int/comm/external_relations/lybia/intro/index.htm

76 Ibidem.

77 of March 5th and March 15th, 1996, in: 35 I.L.M. 397 (1996).

78 Council conclusions on the US Helms-Burton Act, Bulletin EU 7/8-1996, point 1.4.116.

79 Res. 24 May 1996, OJ 10/6/1996, C 166, p. 277

80 See fn. 79.

1) On 16 October 1996, the Representative of the European Communities requested the institution of a WTO panel on the matter of extraterritorial economic sanctions.[81]

2) The Council passed Regulation No. 2271/96 as a so-called "blocking statute" prohibiting the recognition of US court rules inside the EU and granting compensation to companies that were held responsible under Title III of the Helms-Burton act ("claw-back clause").

3) To integrate the blocking legislation, Joint Action No. 668/96/GASP of 22/11/1996[82] was passed calling on each Member State to take the measures it deems necessary to further protect the interests of persons affected by the extraterritorial application of laws of a foreign State.

4) Finally, in December 1996, the Council adopted a Common Position on Cuba that criticises the use of economic sanctions against Cuba and raises the matter of human rights, but gives priority to a "constructive dialogue" with Cuba.[83] This could be seen as a measure to further bilateral negotiations with the US on a settlement of the dispute.

A. Multilateral Steps

The EU, but also other trading partners of the United States like Canada and Mexico, have reacted in several ways to US extraterritorial trade legislation. The countries affected have presented diplomatic protests against the extraterritorial elements and against legislative unilateralism in general. In judicial proceedings, they appeared as amici curiae before US courts to argue against the extraterritorial application of US laws.[84] Steps have also been taken within the General Assembly of the United Nations, resulting, in general, in annual condemnations of the US policy against Cuba and, in particular, the extraterritorial economic

---

81 Statement by the Representative of the European Communities and their Member States before the WTO, as published at: http://www.eurunion.org/legislat/extrel/cuba/panel.htm

82 OJ 29/11/1996, L 309, p. 7

83 OJ 12/12/1996, L 322, p.1

84 In US antitrust cases it has been common for foreign governments to present their views in briefs of amici curiae.

sanction legislation.[85] A resolution within the Organisation of American States (OAS) has led to an Opinion of the Inter-American Juridical Committee criticising the Helms-Burton Act for its extraterritorial elements.[86]

Most importantly, the EU fought the extraterritorial economic sanctions within the WTO dispute settlement system which since the Uruguay round despite its shortcomings is by far the most elaborate and effective international system to resolve trade disputes.[87] According to the EC request for the establishment of a panel, the US economic sanctions against Cuba violate the provisions of both the GATT and the GATS, in particular, the prohibition of quantitative restrictions, the principle of non-discrimination. The denial of visas were criticised as inconsistent with the GATS Annex on the Movement of Natural Persons. Furthermore, the EC maintained that these legislative measures taken by the US constitute a nullification and an impairment of rights and benefits which the EC could expect to have accrued to it directly or indirectly under GATT and, respectively, the GATS in its trade relations with Cuba. Finally, according to the complaint, the US embargo impeded the attainment of the objectives of the GATT, notably the expansion of production and trade, the overall balance of rights and obligation between WTO Members, in particular the access to markets. The EC called also upon the general principle established in GATT jurisprudence according to which WTO Members should not try to force other Members to change their sovereign policies trough the use of trade sanctions.

The United States took the view that the issue was not to be dealt with within the WTO since it concerned vital US security interests. The US indicated that it intended to rely on the security exceptions of Art. XXI GATT and XIV bis GATS, defending the economic sanctions as "measures taken in time of war or other emergency in international relations."

Following bilateral negotiations with the US, the EU suspended its request for a panel. Although the EU has never formally relinquished its claims, to date the dispute has not been resumed.

---

85 G.A. Res. No. 54/21 of 18th November 1999 and precedents: 47/19 (1992), 48/16 (1993), 49/9 (1994), 50/10 (1995), 51/17 (1996), 52/10 (1997), 53/4 (1998).

86 Opinion of the Inter-American Juridical Committee, reprinted in: 35 I.L.M. 1322 (1996). Commented in: *Kress/Herbst* (1997).

87 WTO Doc. no. WT/DS38/2 of October 8th 1996.

Therefore, the WTO dispute settlement system has not yet yielded an authoritative pronunciation on conflicts on extraterritorial economic sanctions. This would support the hypothesis that the WTO system is not accessible to matters where foreign and security policy considerations outweigh traditional trade aspects. Problems of extraterritorial jurisdiction that are not burdened to the same degree by foreign policy implications have in fact already been dealt within the WTO system, e.g. in the realm of environmental law in the Tuna-Dolphin and Shrimps-Turtle cases.[88] Similarly, one recent panel has dealt with the indirect effects of Cuban expropriations in the US trademark law.[89] Although these trade disputes involved a high level of conflict, other than in the case of the Helms-Burton Act - neither party doubted that their object falls within the jurisdiction of the WTO dispute settlement system.

B. Blocking Legislation

The structure of the EU blocking statute, consisting of Regulation N.2271/96 and Joint Action 668/96, reflects this overlap of trading interests with traditional foreign and security policy. While it is discussed in a separate contribution to this book, the following paragraphs only consider briefly the mechanisms of blocking statutes and their effectiveness as a defence against extraterritorial jurisdiction.

The fundamental features of blocking statutes include the obligation imposed on local enterprises to notify any intrusion of a foreign authority and the prohibition to comply with it, a violation of which constitutes a punishable offence.

These constraints are contrary to the interests of businesses operating internationally. On the one hand, in the State enacting extraterritorial legislation, their operations are exposed to sanctions for non-compliance with the extraterritorial commands. On the other hand, if they chose to comply with the extraterritorial

---

88 i.e. Tuna/Dolphin II - *United States- Restrictions on the Imports of Tuna:* Report of the Panel GATT Doc. DS29/R and United States – *Import Prohibition of Certain Shrimp and Shrimp Products* – Panel Report WT/DS58/R.

89 WT/DS176/R Report of the Panel in *United States - Section 211 Omnibus Appropriations Act of 1998.* The incriminated provision prohibits the registration and enforcement of formerly expropriated Cuban trademarks in the US.

regulation, in the jurisdictions with blocking legislation, they are threatened by the sanctions of the blocking statutes.

As a result, enterprises have to choose between the lesser of two evils and are likely to decide based on the prospects of avoiding sanctions in one of the two jurisdictions. The logic of the blocking legislation counts on the United States' abandonment of the jurisdictional claim, based on the Foreign State Compulsion Doctrine, as developed by US jurisprudence. However, this concept does not necessarily apply to US administrative decisions, as related to customs, the denial of export licences and the imposition of entry restrictions for foreign persons. In any event, the process risk and the costs associated with the judicial proceedings are borne by the transnational corporation caught between the jurisdictions.

Two further instruments of blocking statutes include the express prohibition on the recognition of foreign judgements based on extraterritorial laws and the institution of private actions granting the recovery of costs incurred as a consequence of these judgements. The latter, a so-called "claw-back" provision, rests on the assumption that the persons who are interested in the enactment of extraterritorial legislation operate themselves internationally and thus have assets and interests also within the jurisdiction wanting to prevent the extraterritorial measures from taking effect. Only if this condition is fulfilled, the claw-back provisions influence the cost-benefit analysis of those private parties which promote the territorial enforcement of extraterritorial laws.

The blocking legislation works thus in a way that is similar to the exercise of extraterritorial jurisdiction. It is not designed to be put into practice, but to a large extent relies on the deterrence by raising the risks of cross-border transactions and influencing the cost-benefit analysis of international business, in order to deter foreign extraterritorial laws from being applied in the first place. Similarly to extraterritorial provisions, the blocking legislation is thus largely based on the interdependence of international trade relations.

While this combination of international trading interests is present in many antitrust cases, the application to matters of international trade with "rogue States" is problematic. Political pressure groups like the Cuban-American lobby in Florida, which is the main supporter of the US embargo against Cuba, are less sensitive to the threat of claw-back provisions than international businesses promoting anti-trust law suits.

The economic ineffectiveness of blocking statutes as a response to extraterritorial trade sanctions evidences that the enactment of blocking legislation is to a considerable extent motivated by the political wish to visibly react to the what is perceived an infringement of sovereignty and to safeguard of the State's sovereignty as expressed in the determination of foreign policy, rather than by the need to protect effectively the trading interests of the local enterprises.

Both the enactment of extraterritorial sanction laws and of countering them by blocking legislation corresponds to the traditional bilateral way of handling trade disputes in international relations, as opposed to the expectations of a more rule-oriented system of international trade law that were raised by the conclusion of the Uruguay round. Both legislative acts create situations of conflicting interests, leaving it to traditional bilateral diplomacy to negotiate the removal of the trade restrictions. As the existing regulatory and sanctioning mechanisms do not seem to be effective in dealing with non-economic and, in particular, political interests (foreign, domestic, or security policy), a State is rather encouraged to restrict international trade if these political interests outweigh the economic interests.

C. Bilateral Negotiations

The dispute between the EU and the United States on the extraterritorial sanctions was considerably cooled down, if not completely resolved, by bilateral negotiations. At the EU-US Summit in London in 1998, a document on the Transatlantic Partnership on Political Co-operation (TPPC) was agreed upon, setting out political commitments for the co-ordination of economic sanctions policy.

In this respect, it is important to distinguish the two moments in this process. First, concerning the specific issue on which there is open diplomatic controversy, negotiations are the principle instrument for resolving the dispute. In the present case, this ad hoc settlement is reflected in an Understanding reached in April 1997 and in a subsequent Understanding with Respect to Disciplines for the Strengthening of Investment Protection of May 1998.

The 1997 Understanding was essentially a commitment to continue negotiations under which the US agreed to further suspend Title III LIBERTAD actions in return for the EU suspending the case in the WTO. The 1998 Understanding, in its part I, sets out guidelines to discourage investment in what is deemed to be illegally expropriated property. In part II, it is made clear that these commitments are intended to be applied "on a policy basis", although it is also prospected to make a joint proposal on the issue to the project of a Multilateral Agreement on Investments (MAI)[90]. However, as specified in articles 4 and 5 of part II, the application is conditional on the success of the efforts of the US government to consult with Congress in order to insert a waiver provision for Title IV LIBERTAD and to amend the waiver of Title III, making it permanent. From an international law point of view, it may be observed that this text is a promise on behalf of the US government to conduct consultations, but it is no commitment, not even a political one, on behalf of the US as a sovereign. The action of a third party, i.e. the US legislator, constitutes thus a condition for the entry into force of the Understanding between the EC and the US, which has not yet been fulfilled as of the time of writing. The Understanding has therefore not entered into force. It seems however that as long as at least Title III LIBERTAD continues to be waived and the single case waivers under 9c of ILSA are granted, the EU is determined not to resume the WTO case.

Second, conscious of the detrimental effect of such political disputes, the EU and the US tried to preventively set up lasting mechanisms of mutual consultation concerning the future use of economic sanctions as laid down a document called Transatlantic Partnership on Political Co-operation. Consequently, precise mechanisms for a comprehensive co-operation and consultation on trade and investment-related matters as well as on issues of general foreign policy have been set up with the Declaration on an Early Warning Mechanism, released at the 1999 Bonn Summit.[91] However, the extension of the ILSA by the Bush Administration in July 2001 seems to have determined the failure of this consultation mechanism.

Given this experience it does not appear to be a realistic prospect of establishing a binding international regime on extraterritorial jurisdiction in the realm of export control and economic sanctions legislation.

---

90 Negotiations for the MAI have ended unsuccessfully. *Trebilcock/Howse* (1999) 357ff.

91 http://www.useu.be/SUMMIT/earlwarn0699.html

The bilateral negotiations have at least secured a semi-stable situation where waivers under the extraterritorial legislation are granted in return for political pledges by the other side. The need for both the EU and the US to co-operate in matters of foreign policy has led politicians on both sides of the Atlantic to leave open the resolution of the dispute, hoping that public attention would turn away from it. The 1998 Understanding was presented by both sides as a victory of their cause. While European Politicians announced that the other side would not enforce the extraterritorial trade sanctions, their US counterparts presented the agreement as the "internationalisation" of Helms-Burton, claiming they had convinced the Europeans to abstain from investments in Cuba.

For European multinational enterprises operating both in the US and countries targeted by its extraterritorial economic sanctions, a consistent practice of granting waivers as it seems to emerge from the bilateral contacts certainly reduces the political risk of being subjected to US sanctions. However, as long as the sanction legislation is in place and there is support from the US Congress to enact further laws, any major investment in the countries of political concern to the US will always be subject to the discretion of the US administration. Therefore, in these cases, preliminary co-operation with the EU Commission and a joining of lobbying efforts in bilateral contacts in order to ensure authorisation from the US authorities is probably the most promising strategy.

Bibliography

Bianchi, A. (1992), Extraterritoriality and Export Controls: Some Remarks on the Alleged Antinomy Between European and U.S. Approaches, GYIL 35 – 1992, 366.

Bianchi, A. (1995), L'applicazione extraterritoriale dei controlli all'esportazione – Contributo allo studio dei fenomeni di extraterritorialità nel diritto internazionale, Padova 1995.

Brownlie, I. (1999), Principles of International Law, Oxford[5] 1999.

Clagett, B.M. (1996), A Reply to Professor Lowenfeld, AJIL 1996, Agora: The Cuban Liberty and Democratic Solidarity (LIBERTAD) Act, 641.

Fidler, D.P. (1997); LIBERTAD v. Liberalism, An Analysis of the Helms- Burton Act from within Liberal International Relations Theory, Indiana Journal of Global Legal Studies, 2/1997, 297.

Howse, R.. / Regan, D. (2000), The Product/Process Distinction- An Illusory Basis for Disciplining "Unilateralism" in Trade Policy, EJIL vol.11, 2/2000, 249-289.

Jackson, J. (2000), Comments on Shrimps/Turtle and the Product/Process Distinction, EJIL vol.11, 2/2000, 303-308.

Jansen B. / Lugard, M. (1999), "Some considerations on Trade Barriers Erected For Non-Economic Reasons and WTO Obligations", JIEL 1999, 530.

Jansen, B. (2000), The Limits of Unilateralism from as European Perspective, EJIL, vol.11, 2/2000, 309-314.

Kress, C. / Herbst, J. (1997), Der Helms-Burton Act aus völkerrechtlicher Sicht, RIW 8/1997, 630.

Kuyper, J.P. (1984), The European Community and the US Pipeline Embargo: Comments on Comments, GYIL Vol. 27/1984, 72.

Lowenfeld, A.F., Congress and Cuba: The Helms-Burton Act, AJIL 1996, Agora: The Cuban Liberty and Democratic Solidarity (LIBERTAD) Act, 419.

Luciano, E. (1997), A Helms-Burton Act Analysis: Is this type of extraterritorial jurisdiction consistent with our treaty/agreements, customary international law & post-Cold War policy?, New England International & Comparative Law Annual 1997, 4.

Mann, F.A. (1964), The Doctrine of Jurisdiction in International Law, RdC 111, 1964 I, 7.

Mann, F.A. (1984), The Doctrine of International Jurisdiction Revisited After Twenty Years, RdC 186, 1984, 9.

Meessen K., (1975), Völkerrechtliche Grundsätze des internationalen Kartellrechts, Baden-Baden 1975.

Meng, W. (1987), Extraterritorial Effects of Administrative, Judicial and Legislative Acts, in: Bernhardt, R. (ed.), Encyclopedia of Public International Law, Instalment 10, 1987, 155.

Meng, W., (1994), Extraterritoriale Jurisdiktion im öffentlichen Wirtschaftsrecht, Berlin et al. 1994.

Puttler A. (1989), Völkerrechtliche Grenzen von Export- und Reexportverboten, Baden-Baden 1989.

Schwarze, J. (1994), Die Jurisdiktionsabgrenzung im Völkerrecht, Baden-Baden 1994.

Stern, B. (1986), Quelques observations sur les règles internationales relatives a l'application extraterritoriale du droit, Annuaire Francais de Droit International XXXII, 1986, 7.

Stern, B. (1997a), Can the United States Set Rules for the World?, JWT 1997, 10.

Stern, B. (1997b), Les lois Helms-Burton et D'Amato – une analyse politique et juridique (1997), in: *Ress, G., Stein, T. (eds.),* Vorträge, Reden und Berichte aus dem Europa- Institut, Nr. 363, Europainstitut der Universität des Saarlandes, 1997.

Trebilcock, M.J./ Howse, R. (1999), The Regulation of International Trade, London et al.[2] 1999.

Lukas von Lutterotti

The European Blocking Statute as an Attempt to Co-ordinate Simultaneous Action under the Three Pillars of the EU

I. Introduction

The European Blocking Statute was enacted in 1996 as a reaction to the extraterritorial economic sanctions imposed earlier that year by the United States on Cuba, Iran and Libya, to the detriment of European investors in these countries. Both the Helms-Burton Act (LIBERTAD Act)[1] and the Iran Libya Sanctions Act (ILSA)[2] were designed to extend the US embargoes against these "rogue states" internationally and threatened actual or potential foreign investors in Cuba, Iran and Libya with sanctions on the US market. The sanctions of the Helms-Burton Act included, besides traditional import restrictions, a provision that exposes foreign investors in Cuba, to damage law suits within the US, if they were determined to have an economic interest in formally expropriated property in Cuba.[3] Another provision denies entry visas to managers of companies investing in Cuba, as well as to their

---

1 Cuban Liberty and Democratic Solidarity (LIBERTAD) Act of 1996 (H.R. 927; S. 381)(enacted March 12, 1996, P.L. 104-114, 110 Stat. 785, 22 U.S.C. Sect. 6021ff. reprinted in (1996) 35 ILM 357.

2 Iran and Libya Sanctions Act of 1996 (H.R. 3107;S.1228 related)(enacted August 5, 1996, P.L. 104-172, 110 Stat. 1541, 50 U.S.C. Sect. 1701 note, reprinted in (1996) 35 ILM 1273. Also D'Amato Act or Kennedy-D'Amato Act, after its principal sponsors in Congress.

3 Title III LIBERTAD Act. In the language of Helms-Burton, this economic involvement is described as "trafficking" in unlawfully expropriated property.

families.[4] The ILSA threatened large foreign investors in the Iranian and Libyan petroleum industry with the denial of export and import licenses for the US market and the denial of access to the US financial market, on the grounds that substantial investments in those markets would further the ability of these countries to acquire weapons of mass destruction.

Both US sanction laws were staunchly opposed by the EU and its Member States, not only because they hurt European-based companies most, but also because they were viewed as an attempt to bring European foreign policy forcibly in line with US political goals. Amidst diplomatic controversy, the EU decided to take legislative action and adopted a so-called blocking statute, modelled on earlier British laws against extraterritorial US antitrust legislation, portraying it as a defence for the EU companies concerned.

Besides its implications for the transatlantic diplomatic relations at the time, the peculiarity of this legislation from the viewpoint of EU law consists in the fact that it is an apparently co-ordinated action under all three pillars of the EU, consisting of a Regulation under Community law[5] and a Joint Action under the powers of both the CFSP and third pillar, formerly labelled Justice and Home Affairs (JHA), today's Police and Justice Co-operation in Criminal Matters (PJC)[6].

As already dealt with in the other contributions of this book, the relationship of supranational Community law and intergovernmental EU law[7] is governed by the requirement of

---

4 Title IV LIBERTAD Act. The international legal and political implications of the extraterritorial US legislation are described in more detail in another contribution to this book.

5 Council Regulation (EC) No. 2271/96 of 22.11.1996, protecting against the effects of the extra-territorial application of legislation adopted by a third country , and actions based thereon and resulting therefrom, OJ L 309, 29.11.1996, p.1.

6 Joint Action (CFSP) No. 668/96 of 22.11.1996, adopted by the Council on the basis of Art J.3 and K.3 of the Treaty of the European Union concerning measures protecting against the effects of the extra-territorial application of legislation adopted by a third country, and actions based thereon and resulting therefrom, OJ L 309, 29.11.1996, p.7.

7 As it has become common in scientific debate, this paper uses the term "Union law" or "EU law" to describe the intergovernmental law of the

consistency of EU external action and the precedence of Community law over the law of the second and third pillars. The challenge for drafters of Union law is therefore not to erode but to complement the Community acquis, and at the same time fill the Union legal act with meaningful and operative provisions.

The potential intrusions of intergovernmental decision-making into the prerogatives of Community law can take two forms, viz., first, the setting up of conditions within the CFSP for an existing Community policy[8], and secondly, the choice of a legal base for a particular measure in the TEU rather than in the TEC, i.e. an intrusion into a potential, not yet exercised, Community competence.[9] The combination of legal acts chosen for the EU blocking statute could have constituted an example for the second type of infringements of Community prerogatives, since the attempt was made to fill with second and third pillar law "gaps" of Community law. If successful, this would have rendered the second and third pillar acts an intergovernmental alternative to Community decision-making which could be co-ordinated with the Community policies. This analysis shows that the attempt has failed due to the unlucky choice of the legal basis and the lack of political will to fill the CFSP action with any meaningful content.

II. The Regulation 2271/96

A. Content

The content of the Regulation (EC) No. 2271/96 is typical of a blocking statute and follows largely the example of earlier blocking legislation such as the British Protection of Trading Interests Act (PTIA).[10] Its main thrust is to counter and neutralise the effects of foreign court orders condemning a Community-based enterprise to pay compensation to foreign claimants, particularly those pursuant to Title III of the Helms-Burton Act. Similar to the PTIA, the

second and third pillar, as opposed to "Community law" within the first pillar of the EU.

8 Cf. the debate on the EU export control regime for dual use goods.

9 C-170/96 *Commission v. Council (Joint action regarding airport transit visas),* [1998] ECR I-2763.

10 Protection of Trading Interests Act, 1980, ch. 11 (Eng.), amended by Civil Jurisdiction and Judgments Act, 1982, ch. 27, and Statute Law (Repeals) Act, 1993, ch. 50, Sch. 1, pt. XIV. Reprinted in: 21 ILM (1982), p. 834. In the following: PTIA. Commented in *Lowe* (1981) and *Lowe* (1984) 54ff.

Regulation contains, as central elements, provisions on non-recognition of these extraterritorial foreign judgements, prohibitions on their enforcement as well as the facility for European companies of recovering any damages, including the legal costs, from US plaintiffs who have prevailed in the US courts invoking extraterritorial legislation (so-called "claw-back" clause).

Art 1 and 11 of the Regulation together define its scope, which has both a material and a personal aspect. As for the former, Art 1 refers to the Annex to the Regulation which contains a list of the targeted US extraterritorial legislation. Presently, it refers to the Cuban Democracy Act of 1992 and the Cuban Assets Control Regulations, the Helms-Burton Act (Titles I, III and IV) and the Iran Libyan Sanctions Act of 1996. This list can be modified by the Council or by the Commission, acting within a particular comitology procedure as provided for in Art 8 of the Regulation. Any application of these foreign laws, in particular actions based thereon and resulting therefrom, is subject to the provisions of the Regulation, and thus denied recognition and enforcement, in so far as it affects the interests of the persons protected by the Regulation.

The definition of the range of these persons is far more complicated. Not everyone having incurred damages due to the subjection to foreign extraterritorial laws is entitled to claim the recovery from the US plaintiffs and the denial of the recognition of the relative foreign court orders. In fact, Art 1 refers to persons "engaging in international trade and/or the movement of capital and related commercial activities between the Community and third countries." This limitation is closely linked to the delicate issue of the appropriate legal basis of the Regulation and will be discussed in the next sub-chapter. By contrast, the wording of Art 11 is not restrictive, but it encompasses a wide range of persons. Art 11 thus extends the protection of the Regulation not only to all legal persons incorporated within the Community and all natural persons being nationals of a Member State (resident within or outside the EC), but also to third country nationals resident or even only present within the Community, as long as they are acting in a professional capacity. By referring to Regulation (EC) No. 4055/1986, regulating the free provision of services concerning the maritime transport between Member States and between Member States and third countries, Art 11(3), also comprises shipping companies established outside the Community and controlled by nationals of a Member State, if their vessels are registered in that Member State in accordance with its legislation.

Art 2 of the Regulation imposes on any of these persons, whose economic and/or financial interests are affected by the laws referred to in the annex, the obligation to inform the Commission within 30 days after this effect has been noticed. If the person is a legal entity, this obligation applies directly to the management. Art 3 guarantees the confidentiality of the information provided pursuant to Art 2, prohibiting undue disclosure by the Commission.

The centrepieces of the Regulation are contained in Art 4, 5 and 6. Art 4 prohibits the recognition or enforcement within the Community of judgements and administrative decisions of foreign authorities giving effect, directly or indirectly, to the targeted extraterritorial legislation. Thus, it does not differ from other non-recognition clauses, such as Sec. 5 PTIA. Similar to these provisions, Art 4 of the Regulation is, to a considerable extent, merely declaratory, since judgements based on Title III LIBERTAD awarding damage payments to US claimants, would have to be denied enforcement in most legal systems on the grounds that it is contrary to public policy, both due to its political nature and its awarding of punitive damages.[11] However, the provision is not completely void of legal importance. It is conceivable that certain extraterritorial laws may in principle not be contrary to the *ordre publique* or to the public policy of a Member State's legal order and thus foreign court orders based thereon could be granted enforcement within the Community. In effect, Art 4 declares the extraterritorial laws listed in the annex as contrary to public policy by definition. Thus, the extraterritoriality of the legislation concerned can be said to constitute a "formal" rather than a substantial deficiency impeding recognition within the Community.[12]

Nevertheless, blocking provisions of the kind of Art 4 have inherent limitations. Although, contrary to the Commission's proposal, the final version of Art 4 contains a reference to decisions of foreign administrative authorities, it is questionable whether the extension of the non-recognition provision to these cases is a viable blocking provision at all. In fact, the denial of recognition and enforcement is an effective deterrent only to the extent that a

---

11 In this sense, *Reinisch* (1997) 902; *Glossop* (1998) 100.

12 *Reinisch* (1997) ibid.

foreign act needs the co-operation of the municipal authorities in order to take effect. As long as a law containing an extraterritorial command can be effectively enforced within the territory of the regulating State, there is no need for it to be recognised by foreign authorities. E.g., the denial of an export license, the cancellation of a credit facility by a US bank following a presidential order or the denial of a visa for entry into the United States pursuant to Title IV LIBERTAD unfolds its effects immediately from within the US legal order, affecting the foreign person "at the US border", assuming that it needs to enter the US market for economic reasons. In these cases, obviously, no particular recognition or enforcement is needed from a foreign legal system. Therefore, the inclusion of the reference to administrative decisions in Art 4 has to be deemed ineffective.

Art 5 of the Regulation expressly and comprehensively prohibits persons referred to in Art 11 from complying, actively or by deliberate omission, with any requirements resulting directly or indirectly from the targeted legislation, in particular "requests of foreign courts". Thus, the participation of a Community based enterprise in judicial proceedings according to Title III LIBERTAD is effectively barred. Moreover, a person may not "voluntarily" withdraw from operations in Cuba, Iran or Libya in order to protect its interests in the United States by avoiding the imposition of US sanctions. Apart from the difficulties to prove the underlying reasons for investment decisions, an all too obvious determination to comply with the requirements of the US legislation may thus lead to the imposition of sanctions under the EC Regulation. In this circumstance, it may be noted that Art 5 takes into account also the actions of subsidiaries and other intermediaries which would not per se be subject to the Regulation, if they act as agents of the Community-based person.

As regards the civil actions under Title III LIBERTAD, in the proceedings before a US court, Art 5 could constitute the basis for invoking the Foreign State Compulsion Doctrine. This doctrine, which has been developed in US courts and in reflected in §441 of the Restatement, avoids the extraterritorial application of US laws if a person is subject to diverging commands of the State with territorial jurisdiction. Its application has been made subject to several preconditions. First, the compulsion exercised by the foreign jurisdiction has to reach a certain intensity and, secondly, the person subject to it is required to show a bona fide conduct.[13] A successful reliance on Art 5 of the Regulation before US courts can be doubted, in particular concerning the first requirement. In fact, paragraph 2 of Art 5 provides for the possibility of the Commission authorising the persons subject to both the Regulation and the extraterritorial laws to fully or partially comply with the foreign laws „to the extent that non-compliance would seriously damage their interests or those of the Community". Moreover, US courts have made the application of the Foreign State Compulsion doctrine subject to the pondering of the foreign interests underlying the conflicting legislative commands.[14] In the case of laws of political nature, such as the Helms-Burton Act, the outcomes of such a balancing test operated by a US court can be deemed uncertain at best.[15]

Art 6 constitutes the "claw-back" clause of the Regulation. According to this provision, any person fulfilling the requirements of Art 1 and 11, having suffered damages from the application of one of the foreign extraterritorial laws listed in the annex, is entitled to claim recovery of these amounts before a court within the Community. Pursuant to Art 6(2), the persons from which such a recovery may be claimed are

- those natural and legal persons causing the damages resulting from the application of the targeted legislation,
- any other "entity" causing these damages,
- intermediaries and persons acting on behalf of the above.

Contrary to the Commission's first proposal, the final version of Art 6 refrains from holding liable EU subsidiaries of the US persons responsible for the damage, thereby refraining from "piercing the corporate veil" and respecting the separate legal personality of these

---

13 Société Internationale pour Participations Industrielles et Commerciales, S.A. v. Rogers, 357 U.S. 197, 211 (Compulsion through criminal sanctions) United States v. First Nat'l City Bank, 396 F.2d 897 (civil liability not qualified compulsion) Bona fide conduct: Eastern Railroad Presidents Conference v. Noerr Motor Freight, In., 365 U.S. 127 (1961); United Mine Workers of America v. Pennington, 381 U.S. 657 (1965) Commented in *Forwick* (1993) 115 ff.

14 United States v. First Nat'l City Bank, 396 F.2d 897, 903-04 holding that the need to enforce a U.S. subpoena outweighed German interests as expressed in its bank secrecy law.

15 The practicability of a judicial balancing test involving foreign sovereign interests as proposed by the Restatement remains doubtful.

subsidiaries. However, the interpretation of the scope of this provision in the present version implies several problems, in particular relating to the range of persons that can be subject to these claw-back claims.

The most important provision of Art 6 is its third paragraph. It establishes personal jurisdiction of a Member State court over the foreign defendant not only according to the general criteria of the law of conflicts,[16] but also in cases where the defendant simply holds assets in that Member State. The principles of the Brussels Convention, providing for the co-ordination of jurisdiction in civil and commercial matters between Member States, have extended to influence the systems of jurisdiction of Member States in this area, also in cases where relations with third countries are concerned.[17] According to the general principle of territoriality, jurisdiction is established in the State where the defendant is resident or domiciled or where he has an agent having the right to stay in court.[18] According to the principles of the European conflict law, as an exception, a person can be sued for damages arising from extra-contractual liability before the court of the Contracting State where the harmful event has occurred.[19] In the case of the Helms-Burton Act, assuming that the US person having acted under this Act is not resident or domiciled in the EU, it could neither be sued in a EU Member State on the basis of this exceptional provision, since the "harmful event" has occurred in the United States. Based on the general principles on jurisdiction to adjudicate, judges in most Member States would have to decline jurisdiction in this case. At this point, however, Art 6 of the Regulation operates a Community law extension of personal jurisdiction by establishing the presence

---

16 Cf. *Brussels Convention on Jurisdiction and the Enforcement of Judgments in Civil and Commercial Matters*, signed in Brussels, on 27 September 1968, by the Member States of the EEC, as amended by several accession treaties, consolidated version published in OJ 26.01.1998, C27. Now substituted *by Council Regulation (EC) No 44/2001 on jurisdiction and the recognition and enforcement of judgments in civil and commercial matters*, OJ 16.01.2001, L12.

17 e.g., in Italy, Art 3 (2) Law n. 218 of 31/5/1995, published in G.U. 3/6/1995, n. 128.

18 e.g., in Italy, Art 3 (1) Law n. 218 of 31/5/1995, Art 2 Brussels Convention, Art 2 Regulation (EC) 44/2001.

19 Art 5 (3) Brussels Convention, Art 5 (3) Regulation(EC) 44/2001.

of assets owned by the defendant in a Member State as a sufficient jurisdictional base for judicial action.

This derogation from the principles of the Brussels Convention is in accordance with Art 57(3) of the Convention which establishes the primacy of Community law over the provisions of the Convention. Also under Regulation 44/2001, Art 6 of the Blocking Statute continues to derogate from the general rules of jurisdiction, based on the *lex specialis* principle.[20] Art 6 takes obviously also precedence over all Member State legislation on jurisdiction, and thus any court in the EU would have to affirm its jurisdiction once the foreign defendant of a claw-back claim holds assets in its district.

A second area of concern of Art 6 is related to the fact that the exclusive reference to judgements has been given up in favour of a general reference to the "damages" caused, probably in order to extend the claw-back claim to disadvantages suffered by European companies from the application of extraterritorial legislation by administrative decisions. The central practical aspect of this issue would certainly concern the question whether the damages can be proven and a causal link can be established between the relative court order or administrative decision, on the one side, and the damage, on the other.

Only if these conditions were fulfilled, claims would be conceivable in practice, e.g. against persons who have initiated administrative proceedings under Title IV LIBERTAD which have led to the denial of visas to managers of EU companies.

In the case of ILSA, matters are even more complicated and this is not limited to the problem of providing proof on the damages suffered following the imposition of administrative sanctions by US administrative authorities under ILSA. In fact, a claw-back claim against the ILSA sanctions is completely impossible since there is no appropriate defendant. Although the term "entities"[21] has been added in the final version of Art 6 in order to cover also the eventualities of the ILSA sanctions, in order to be effective, it would have to be interpreted as allowing for court actions against the US Administration, despite the authorities having acted *iure imperii*. Obviously, such a far-reaching interpretation is not viable in practice, since it would be contrary to accepted standards of

---

20 Art 67 Regulation (EC) 44/2001.

21 "Stellen" in German.

international law.[22] Thus, the only meaning that can reasonably be attributed to the term in practice is that it covers non-governmental "entities" lacking legal personality, such as legal partnerships and associations, which can be possibly involved.[23] Nevertheless, the wording probably intentionally leaves uncertain the real scope of the provision, given that its aim is to deter extraterritorial laws from being applied in the first place rather than to be applied as a real remedy in practice.

Finally, Art 6 mentions a third group of potential defendants, i.e. "persons acting on behalf" and "intermediaries" of the ones having caused the damage. The meaning of these terms is completely obscure. The confusion on the wording "acting on behalf" increases, when comparing several language versions of the text. The variations range from the French "*agissant en nom*" to the Italian "*qualsiasi persona che agisca per suo conto*", and the German "*im Auftrag*". Thus, according to this provision, it could be possible to sue US lawyers owning assets in the EU who represent former owners of property in Cuba in any procedure in the United States, if their claim has lead either to action under Title III or to a determination under Title IV LIBERTAD.[24] Similarly, all natural persons acting, e.g. as authorised officers, on behalf of legal entities or partnerships promoting claims under the Helms-Burton Act could be subject to claw-back actions over the amount of the damages incurred by a foreign investor in Cuba due to the Helms-Burton Act, provided that these persons hold any kind of assets in the EU. This provision thus constitutes a parallel to the Helms-Burton Act's targeting of managers and shareholders of companies investing in Cuba.

To conclude, Art 6 creates a Community-law title of tort liability of questionable practicability. It certainly applies to all US sanctions which are enforced through private action in the courts, but only in a limited way to administrative decisions pursuant to Title IV LIBERTAD which are only indirectly based on the provision of information through private parties. Finally, Art 6 cannot provide protection against any US extraterritorial sanction

---

22 See e.g. *Neuhold/Hummer/Schreuer* (1997), paras 834 ff.

23 The fact that this term has been added in the preparatory work as shortly after the enactment of the ILSA and the German version of the term, "Stellen", however would suggest the former interpretation.

24 Cf. US Department of State Guidelines Implementing Title IV of the Cuban Liberty and Solidarity Act, 61 Fed. Reg., No. 117, 30655 ff.

imposed exclusively by the discretion of administrative authorities. What is more, neither the non-recognition of Art 4 is effective against these sanctions, as they do not need recognition for their enforcement. Therefore, companies subject to administrative sanctions such as those under ILSA or the Cuban Assets Control Regulations, are not effectively protected by the European "blocking statute". Instead, they are threatened by Art 5 with penalties if they choose to comply with the US legislative commands.

Art 7 to 9 of the Regulation contain provisions for the implementation. Art 7 assigns the central role to the Commission and also requires publication in the Official Journal of the specific judgements and decisions blocked on the basis of this Regulation. Art 8 lays down the details of the co-operation between the Commission and a committee composed of the COREPER regarding the amendments to the list of targeted legislation in the annex as well as for the waivers of Art 5.

Finally, Art 9 requires Member States to determine effective, proportional and dissuasive sanctions for breaches of the provisions of the Regulation.[25]

B. The Legal Basis for the European Blocking Statute

In order to assess the role of the Regulation in the overall framework which combines action under all three pillars of the EU, it is of pre-eminent importance to analyse its legal base. Since the Community acts "within the limits of the powers conferred upon it" and of the "objectives assigned to it" by the Treaty,[26] every legislative act of the Community has to be based on the powers that have been attributed to the Community. If the legal basis referred to in a given act of secondary law is logically consistent and legally correct, the mere existence and also the specific circumstances of the act conversely can support affirmations on the content and, possibly, the limits of the Community competence. If the case of the European Blocking Statute is to be analysed in the light of the complex relation between Community and Union law, the correct

---

25 The British Extraterritorial US Legislation (Sanctions against Cuba, Iran and Libya) (Protection of Trading Interests) Order 1996, states in this respect that any person violating the Regulation shall be guilty of a criminal offence and liable to a fine, not without expressly limiting its applicability to British territorial and personal jurisdiction.

26 Art 5(1) TEC.

assessment of the legal base of each act is critical. This inquiry will therefore yield first findings on the effective, as well as the potential, scope of the Regulation with respect to the Joint Action. After having assessed the legal background of the Joint Action, conclusions on the combination of the two legal acts will be drawn in chapter IV.

Whereas the Commission's proposal was based on Art 133 and 308 TEC, the final version of Regulation 2271/96 cites as legal bases Art 57, 133 and 308 TEC.[27]

It should be noted at this point that earlier considerations on the opportunity to enact blocking legislation had been voiced already in the 1980s on the basis of former Art 113 TEC.[28] By 1996, however, the scope of Art 133 had been limited by Opinion 1/94.[29] Nevertheless, the Commission's proposal chose Art 133 as a starting point, together with Art 308. After taking into account that the use of Art 133 would imply a limitation to the trade in goods, which in this case was not deemed sufficient, the Commission's proposal was revised to add Art 57 as a supplemental legal base, combining the Regulation with a Joint Action. As will be described below, a central consideration in this respect was the necessity to produce a legislative reaction within a short period of time, which made it mandatory to avoid a time-consuming involvement of the European Parliament (EP).[30] In fact, both acts were approved and enacted in November 1996, after Denmark's reservations on the use of Art 308 had been overcome, that were probably based on the Danish government's fundamental disapproval on a potential undue enlargement of Community powers.[31]

1. Art 133

Art 133 constitutes the basis of the EC's Common Commercial Policy(CCP).[32] It provides for a series of measures, which can be broadly distinguished in autonomous measures of commercial

---

27 Obviously, the text of the Regulation refers to Art 73c, 113 and 235 TEC-old, i.e. of the TEC in its version before the renumbering operated by the Treaty of Amsterdam, which entered into force in 1999.

28 *Kuijper* (1984) 94 ff.

29 Opinion 1/94, *WTO*, [1994] ECR I-5267.

30 *Huber* (1997) 305.

31 Agence Europe, No. 6838, 23 October 1996, 11.

32 former Art 113 TEC-old.

policy, on the one hand, and the conclusion of international commercial agreements, on the other. It would go beyond the scope of this chapter to discuss Art 133 in detail.[33] For the purposes of this analysis, it has to be considered whether the Regulation 2271/96 could be qualified as a measure within the autonomous commercial policy. This category comprises the power to fix tariff rates, the regulation of the imports and exports of the Community and the imposition of "measures to protect trade such as those to be taken in the event of dumping and subsidies"[34] granted by foreign States. An important instrument for the protection of trading interests of Community enterprises against unfair trading practices is Regulation No. 3286/94[35], the so-called Trade Barriers Regulation, which allows Member States, industry representatives and private parties to lodge a complaint with the Commission if they perceive obstacles to trade, i.e. "any trade practice adopted or maintained by a third country in respect of which international trade rules establish a right of action"[36], which has adverse trade effects on a Community industry, on a market within or outside the Community. The Commission then takes policy action on an international level, e.g. by instituting a WTO panel or, if necessary, by introducing duties and quotas.

There is, however, an important limitation to the scope of Art 133 as the basis of CCP. Since the Opinion 1/94, it has been clear that the Community competence under *Art 133 relates only to external trade in goods and a limited category of services, viz. those which do not imply the movement of persons across borders*.[37] The Community competence for the external trade in other services as well as in matters dealt with in the WTO under the TRIPS agreement had to be based on other Treaty provisions. This reasoning applies even more to measures of autonomous commercial policy. The implications of this distinction for the present case will be dealt with below in the next sub-chapter.

As a preliminary question, however, it has first to be asked whether the blocking Regulation can be qualified as a commercial policy safeguard measure at all, on the grounds that it protects the

---

33 See, e.g. *Bourgeois* (1992); *Hahn* (1999); *Müller-Ibold* (1999).
34 Art 133(1) TEC.
35 Regulation (EC) No. 3286/94, O.J. 1994, L 349/71.
36 Art 2(1) Reg. (EC) No. 3286/94.
37 *Opinion 1/94,* ECR [1995] I-5267, 5401.

Community's external trade in goods from interference through extraterritorial legislation. Unlike in the case of dumping and subsidies, there is no express reference to extraterritorial legislation in the text of Art 133. However, the wording "such as" suggests that these two cases are given only as specific examples of possible safeguard measures under Art 133 and that, in principle, they do not prevent other actions to protect trade from being taken. Both in doctrine and in jurisprudence, there have always been two fundamental approaches to the interpretation of Art 133, without the ECJ having shown a consistent preference for either of them.[38] Whereas under the instrumental approach, an act can be based on Art 133 if it constitutes an instrument for the regulation of international trade, according to a teleological interpretation, an act falls within the scope of Art 133 if it is aimed at the influencing of the volume or the flows of trade. Both approaches can be reconciled by comprising all measures expressly regulating trade relations with third countries as well as those acts which have the principle aim of influencing the volume or the flow of trade.[39]

It is quite obvious that the blocking provisions in Articles 4 to 6 of the Regulation do not constitute classic instruments of trade policy. Their impact on the volume and the flow of trade is incidental at best and cannot be said to constitute the main purpose of the Regulation. In particular, the central provision of Art 6, which derogates to the Brussels Convention and establishes personal jurisdiction based on the location of assets owned by the defendant, does not fall under the scope of Art 133.

Neither can this provision or the non-recognition of judgements be justified by a recourse to the doctrine of implied powers. Under this doctrine, which is derived from prior applications in general international law[40], where a Treaty provision confers a specific task on the Community, it is assumed to confer on the Community also "the powers which are indispensable in order to carry out that task".[41]Assuming that this task consists in the protection of Community interests against unfair trading practices, an instrument

---

[38] See, e.g., *Bourgeois* (1992) paras 3ff.

[39] *Bourgeois* (1992) para 5.

[40] *Reparation for Injuries Suffered in the Service of the United Nations,* ICJ Advisory Opinion, 11/4/1949, ICJ Reports 1949, paras 174ff.

[41] Joined Cases C- 281, C-283, C- 284, C-285 and C- 287/1985, *Federal Republic of Germany and Others v Commission of the European Communities (Migration policy)*, ECR [1987] I-3203, para 28.

which more properly belongs to the field of judicial proceedings and international private law can hardly be qualified an indispensable measure for the protection of international trading interests. In fact, it differs markedly from the measures provided in the Trade Barriers Regulation and the instruments adopted against dumping and subsidies.

By contrast, the obligations to provide information on trade interests affected by extraterritorial legislation could well be regarded as a measure of commercial policy in this broader sense. In fact, a similar obligation is somewhat parallel to the powers attributed to the Commission in Council Decision of 24/9/1998[42] which, based on Art 133, calls for a more systematic market access strategy of the Community, and requires the Commissions to assess existing trade barriers.

Similarly, Art 5 of the Regulation, which imposes the obligation on Community enterprises engaging in external trade of non-compliance with the foreign legislation, could be considered as covered by the Community powers implied in Art 133, even though it does not constitute a typical safeguard measure.

To conclude, Art 133 provides an insufficient legal base for the Regulation, not only because of its limitation to the regulation of the trade in goods, but also because the measures adopted under Art 4 and 6 of the Regulation are not specifically trade-related instruments.

2. Art 57 in Relation to Art 133

The most important limitation to Art 133 is its limitation to the trade in goods.

As a legal base for the Regulation 2271/96, the scope of Art 133 is therefore too narrow on two counts: First, as discussed in the preceding chapter, it does not cover some of the measures adopted in the regulation, viz. the claw-back provisions and those concerning the non-recognition of judgements and acts. Secondly – and this regards the whole Regulation – Art 133 does not cover all types of economic relations with third countries. In fact, since Opinion 1/94, it has been clear that the scope of Art 133, both in its Maastricht and in its Amsterdam version, extends only to trade in goods and to the trade in those type of services which does not require the movement of persons across borders.[43]

---

42 OJ 1998 L 265, 31.

43 Opinion 1/94, *WTO*, [1995] ECR I-5267.

As far as international agreements are concerned, the limitation of Art 133 to the trade in goods has finally been remedied to a certain extent by the amendments made to this provision by the Treaty of Nice in December 2000. The new paragraph 5 extends the scope of applicability of Art 133 "to the negotiation and conclusion of agreements relating to trade on services and the commercial aspects of intellectual property, insofar as they are not covered by [the preceding] paragraphs and without prejudice to paragraph 6". Paragraph 6 exempts the "trade in cultural and audiovisual services, educational services and social and human health services" from this rule. However, these amendments do not bring about any change for the autonomous measures of commercial policy. All measures other than the conclusion of international agreements, and therefore also the measures to protect trade, remain limited to the trade in goods, and those measures protecting the trade in services fall still under the powers implied by Art 47 and 49 TEC according to the *ERTA* doctrine; they are thus governed by the relative internal procedure of co-decision. Even before Opinion 1/94 authoritatively defined the scope of Art 133, autonomous measures of commercial policy relating to areas other than the external trade in goods could hardly be based on Art 133; instead, these measures would rather have been qualified as internal market legislation and would have been based on the more specific provisions, e.g. Art 57 and 59 TEC, but also Art 95 TEC. The amendments made in Nice to Art 133 do therefore not alter the problematic nature of Art 133 as the central legal base for a comprehensive blocking legislation.

A blocking regulation citing Art 133 as the only legal base would offer no protection to persons engaging in the provision of all other types of services[44], persons establishing subsidiaries in a third country and those making investments not directly related to the trade in goods. Therefore, most forms of foreign direct investment originating in the EU would not have profited from the blocking legislation in the Regulation. To remedy this situation, it would have been necessary to supplement Art 133 with other legal bases, notably Art 71 (the former Art 75 TEC) for the field of transport[45] and Art 57 for measures concerning the free movement

---

[44] i.e., those implying the movement of persons across borders.

[45] Consider, e.g. the restrictions on the transit of vessels through US ports, contained in the Cuban Assets Control Regulations, 31 CFR 515.207 (Revised as of July 1, 1999).

of capital to third countries. For services and the right of establishment, external action could have been justified by the implied powers according to the doctrine of parallelism between internal and external powers of the Community, based on Articles 47 and 49 (former Art 57 and 59 TEC).[46]

Except for Art 133, all of these possible legal bases are concurrent Community powers, which means that Member States retain their right to take separate action, as long as this does not impair the existing Community legal order. In particular, this implies the possibility for Member States to choose whether they wanted to take action at the Community or at the national level, possibly co-ordinated through an action under Union law. In this discussion, the procedural requirements implied by the various legal bases seem to have become decisive elements, since time consuming procedures with an extensive involvement of the EP were to be avoided due to the political necessity to react quickly.[47] Thus, an adoption of Art 71 which would have implied the co-operation procedure of Art 252 as well as the reliance on Art 47 and 49 which would have required the co-decision procedure of Art 251 were ruled out.

By contrast, Art 57(2) provides for measures to be taken by the Council on the proposal of the Commission. Therefore, Art 57 was chosen to supplement Art 133 as a legal base. As a result, the Regulation was adopted involving the EP only through the consultation procedure, as required by Art 308.

The "measures" mentioned in Art 57(2) relate to the "movement of capital to and from third countries involving direct investment – including investment in real estate – establishment, the provision of financial services or the admission of securities to capital markets." Art 57 thereby constitutes an exception to the general liberalisation of capital movements provided for in Art 56, which in principle extends also to capital movements to and from third countries ("erga omnes effect").[48] Whereas Art 57(1) allows for Member States' limitations to free movement of capital to third countries, the second paragraph of this provision concerns the respective actions on the Community level. Although their relationship to Art

---

46 *Huber* (1997) 305.

47 ibid.

48 cf. e.g., *S. Weber* (1992); *R. Weber* (1999); *Kiemel* (1992); *Freitag* (1997); *Bröhmer* (1999).

56 would imply that the measures envisaged under Art 57 are restrictive of capital movements, in Art 57 itself, they are not specified as necessarily being of either restrictive or liberalising nature. Therefore this provision has been interpreted as allowing for restrictions in the movement of capitals to and from third countries, e.g. for reasons of reciprocity, as well as for any further liberalisation, as long as they remain limited to the types of transfers mentioned in the provision.[49]

The provision only refers to those movements of capital which involve "direct investments, – including investment in real estate – establishment, the provision of financial services or the admission of securities to capital markets." This area of application largely reflects the exceptions already provided for under Art 7(1) of the Capital Movements Directive, but adds the notion of "direct investments including investments in real estate".[50] In this respect, it is particularly important to differentiate between portfolio investments which do not fall within the scope of Art 57 and any capital movement connected with forms of direct investment or establishment, as mentioned in this provision.[51] A definition of direct investments is provided by the expression used in the list in Annex I to the Capital Movements Directive of 1988, which emphasises the establishment and the maintenance of lasting economic links as central elements of direct investments.[52] Thus,

---

49 *Kiemel* (1992) 1601ff; *S. Weber* (1992) 565ff.

50 Directive 88/361/EEC, OJ 1988 L 178, 5.

51 *Kiemel* (1992) para 3; *S. Weber* (1992) 565ff; *Bröhmer* (1999) para 5.

52 Directive No. 88/361/EEC, OJ 1988 L 178/5. Annex I reads as follows: "I - DIRECT INVESTMENTS 1. Establishment and extension of branches or new undertakings belonging solely to the person providing the capital, and the acquisition in full of existing undertakings.
2. Participation in new or existing undertaking with a view to establishing or maintaining lasting economic links.
3. Long-term loans with a view to establishing or maintaining lasting economic links.
4. Reinvestment of profits with a view to maintaining lasting economic links."
The explanatory notes to the Annex further specify:
"Direct investments - Investments of all kinds by natural persons or commercial, industrial or financial undertakings, and which serve to establish or to maintain lasting and direct links between the person providing the capital and the entrepreneur to whom or the undertaking

the following constitute "direct investments": the establishment of branches and subsidiaries, the participation in foreign companies through the acquisition of shares which grant the effective participation in the management of the company, the granting of long-term loans establishing lasting economic links and the reinvestment of profits. By contrast, portfolio investments are made exclusively for the purpose of earning dividends or interest, i.e. without effectively participating in the control of a legal entity.

While the expressions "establishment" and "financial services" used in Art 57(2) take up the general meanings of these notions in the Treaty, it has to be emphasised that legal acts based on Art 57(2) can regulate the exercise of these activities only to the extent that a *strong relationship with the movement of capitals to and from third countries exists*. In other words, Art 57(2) does not provide a basis for the general regulation of the external aspects of the right of establishment and of activities in the financial services sector.[53]

Therefore, some important trading activities of Community-based enterprises are not covered by the Regulation, notably the

---

to which the capital is made available in order to carry on an economic activity. This concept must therefore be understood in its widest sense. The undertakings mentioned under I-1 of the Nomenclature include legally independent undertakings (wholly-owned subsidiaries) and branches. As regards those undertakings mentioned under I-2 of the Nomenclature which have the status of companies limited by shares, there is participation in the nature of direct investment where the block of shares held by a natural person of another undertaking or any other holder enables the shareholder, either pursuant to the provisions of national laws relating to companies limited by shares or otherwise, to participate effectively in the management of the company or in its control. Long-term loans of a participating nature, mentioned under I-3 of the Nomenclature, means loans for a period of more than five years which are made for the purpose of establishing or maintaining lasting economic links. The main examples which may be cited are loans granted by a company to its subsidiaries or to companies in which it has a share and loans linked with a profit-sharing arrangement. Loans granted by financial institutions with a view to establishing or maintaining lasting economic links are also included under this heading."

Case law using this list as a reference: C-203/80, *Casati,* [1981] ECR I-2614, Joined Cases C- 163/94, C-165/94 and C-250/94, *Sanz de Lera and Others*, [1995] ECR I-4821.

53 *Kiemel* (1999) para 4; *Bröhmer* (1999) para 5.

provision of services implying a movement of persons across borders and the transport sector. One need just think of European consultants, architects or building enterprises which want to extend their business activity to Cuba. They would almost inevitably become "traffickers" under Title III of the Helms-Burton Act and thus be subject to the sanctions. Presently, the Regulation No. 2271/96 would not apply to them.

3. Art 308 TEC

Given that other Treaty provisions do not cover the specific instruments adopted with Articles 4 and 6, the Regulation cites the general clause of Art 308 TEC as a remedy. However, it is clear that this Article is not a catch-all legal base, which would run counter to the enumerative principle of Community powers as laid down in Art 5 TEC. In particular, it cannot create powers which are not attributed to the Community under specific Treaty provisions.[54] Moreover, Art 308 cannot be employed as a substitute for existing Treaty provisions, in order to circumvent their procedural requirements.[55] In brief, several preconditions have to be fulfilled for the use of Art 308 as a legal base:[56]

a) Necessity

First, Art 308 can only be used if it is "necessary to attain, in the course of the operation of the common market one of the objectives of the Community." These objectives can be either general objectives pursuant to Art 2 TEC, as specified in Art 3 and 4 TEC, but also specific goals set out in other provisions of the Treaty. In the case of Regulation 2271/96, its considerations cite the objectives mentioned in Articles 131, 133 and 57 TEC, namely the harmonious development of world trade, the progressive abolition of restrictions on international trade and the free movement of capital between Member States and third countries. It has been argued, on the one hand, that it is not the Community objective of international trade and the free movement of capital which is protected by the Regulation, but rather the specific persons which engage in specific trade relations.[57] On the other hand, EU trade

---

54 Opinion 2/94, *ECHR,* [1996] ECR I- 1759, para 30.

55 Art 308 TEC: „... and this Treaty has not provided the necessary powers..." *Rossi* (1999) para 41.

56 *Kapteyn/Verloren van Themaat* (1998) 233; *Rossi* (1999); *Röttinger* (1999).

57 *Reinisch (*1997).

relations could be said to be indirectly protected by acting in a way that also corresponds to the interests of the persons engaged therein.

A challenge to the legal base of Art 308 would rest primarily on the fact that Art 6 of the Regulation provides for new tort liability. Following a strictly instrumental interpretation of Community competence, such a measure which is unprecedented in Community law would not find a legal base in the Treaty.

However, the claw-back provision is typical for any blocking legislation. Therefore, Art 6 constitutes rather a further emphasis and a logical consequence of the general prohibition on the enforcement of foreign judgements. In this circumstance, it might be also indicative that the Community had already employed similar measures before. In fact, the prohibition to comply with foreign judgements and similar orders and the non-recognition of foreign claims had been accidental elements of Community economic sanctions against Iraq,[58] Libya,[59] Haiti[60] and Yugoslavia[61].

Taking a teleological rather than an instrumental approach, the provision of Art 6 can therefore be considered as a measure of international private law.

In matters of international private law, there is undoubtedly an interest of the common market in the compatibility of national conflict rules in order to ensure a common demarcation of jurisdiction with respect to third countries. Diverging national blocking legislation with respect to a specific foreign act would in fact arbitrarily discriminate among market participants within the Community which are engaged in external trade. Therefore, several provisions providing protection against the choice of law of a third country have been based on Art 95 TEC in order to safeguard the legal framework of the Internal Market.[62] A similar choice however would have required the much more time consuming co-decision procedure and thus Art 95 was not even adopted as a supplementary legal base.[63] Thus, the problem is not the complete lack of fundamental objectives in the Treaty, but rather whether Art 308 is appropriate where Art 95 could have been used instead. Due to its

---

58 Regulation (EC)3541/92 of 7/12/1992, OJ 1992, L 361, p.1.
59 Regulation (EC) 3257/93 of 29/11/1993, OJ 1993, L 295, p.4.
60 Regulation (EC) 1264/94 of 30/5/1994, OJ 1994, L 139, p.4.
61 Regulation (EC) 1733/94 of 11/7/1994, OJ 1994, L 182, p.1.
62 *Basedow* (2000) 696.
63 *Huber* (1997) 305.

character of subsidiarity with respect to other legal bases in the Treaty, Art 308 cannot be chosen as an alternative legal base, only because its use would facilitate the legislative procedure.[64] In practice, the Community legislator has developed several rules on the conflict of laws within the Internal Market for various, but limited fields, such as consumer protection, which were based predominantly on Art 95, but also on other provisions, including Art 308; some of them also refer to the conflict with the laws of a third country.[65] It could thus be argued that Art 95 would have been the more appropriate legal base for the purpose of regulating the recognition of judicial and administrative acts of a third country and the jurisdiction of the Member State courts for damage suits. However, the approximation of laws is arguably not the main purpose of the Regulation 2271/96. There is therefore still a good case for the use of Art 308. Ultimately, this issue reflects a fundamental problem of private international law in the Community legal system in general.

b) The Operation of the Common Market

Art 308 also requires the achievement of this goal to integrate itself into "the course of the operation of the common market". The interpretation of this part of Art 308 is relatively controversial as to the exact scope of the term "common market".[66] Furthermore, the phrase, which in French reads "dans le fonctionnement du marché commun" has been interpreted as circumscribing the finality of all applications of Art 308 in the sense that they must be directed to the improvement of the common market.[67] The prevailing opinion, however, seems to be that this phrase has to be interpreted as simply requiring any act based on Art 308 not to run counter to the objective of the Common Market.[68] Adopting the latter

---

64 C-350/92, *Spain v. Council*, [1995] ECR I-1985 para 40.

65 See e.g, Art 6(2) of *Council Directive 93/13/EEC of 5 April 1993 on Unfair Terms in Consumer Contracts*, OJ 1993 L 95/29, based on Art 100a TEC-old, i.e. Art 95 TEC.

66 Overview in *Rossi* (1999), para 23.

67 E.g., *Tomuschat* (1976) 60ff; *Dashwood* (1996) 123.

68 *Schwartz* (1992) para 62; *Kapteyn/Verloren-van Themaat* (1998) 233; *Rossi* (1999) paras 24ff; *Röttinger* (1999) para 9.

interpretation, this precondition presents no obstacle to Art 308 as a legal basis for Regulation 2271/96.[69]

c) Subsidiarity

As a final condition for the use of Art 308 as a legal base, the respective powers must not be provided for by other Treaty provisions. In 1996, this was not the case, as the above analysis has shown. Besides, it was impossible to rely on Art 301[70] which provided the legal base in the economic sanction legislation just mentioned, as the blocking provisions are not only accidental to a general interruption of reduction of economic relations with a third country, but central to the Regulation 2271/96, which obviously does not intend to reduce economic relations with the United States.

Due to the requirement of subsidiarity, Art 308 cannot be relied upon to extend the scope of the Regulation to services and the transport sector. Therefore, *the addition of Art 308 as a legal base leaves the limited personal scope of the Regulation unaltered.*

As for the content of the Regulation, however, the recourse to Art 308 as a legal basis was indispensable to cover the specific measures taken in Art 4 and 6 of the Regulation.

4. Conclusion

The above analysis has shown that Art 133 and 308 alone would have been insufficient as the sole legal bases of the Regulation, since this would have significantly limited its scope to the activities related to the trade in goods.

The addition of Art 57 remedies this problem to some extent by extending the scope to capital movements, thereby covering many of the investment activities targeted by Helms-Burton and D'Amato. Nevertheless, neither Art 57 nor Art 308 can remedy the exclusion of services and transports from the Regulation, as determined by the limited scope of Art 133. To include these sectors, a recourse to the proper foundations in the Treaty, such as e.g. Art 43 ff, Art 49 and Art 71 TEC would have been necessary.

However, the overall construction of the Regulation, in particular the use of an annexed list, would suggest that it was

---

69 The argument presented by *Huber* (1997) 306, according to which the Regulation removes discrimination between European investors investing in Cuba and those investing in other countries is rather artificial. With the broader interpretation of Art 308 adopted above, it is however unnecessary. In this sense, *Reinisch* (1997).

70 Art 228a TEC-old.

intended as a more general instrument, comprising also the business activities of the service sector. A focussing on the immediate causes of the blocking legislation, as reflected in the legal bases eventually adopted, does not exactly correspond to this intention.

As it will become clear from the overall construction of the Blocking Statute, the foreign trade in services not covered by the Regulation, as a concurrent Community competence, was intended to be regulated by the Member States, to the extent that they consider necessary any further protection of Community-based economic operators.

III. The Joint Action

A. Content

The Joint Action (CFSP) 668/96 contains a single substantial provision:

„Article 1 – Each Member State shall take the measures it deems necessary to protect the interests of any person referred to in Art 11 of Regulation (EC) No 2271/96 and affected by the extra-territorial application of laws including regulations and other legislative instruments referred to in the Annex to Regulation (EC) No 2271/96, and actions based thereon or resulting therefrom, insofar as these interests are not protected under that Regulation.“[71]

The content of this provision is rather vague, in particular due to the phrase "measures it deems necessary". Despite its vagueness, the measures provided for in the Joint Action can be distinguished in two groups, according to its two legal bases, former Art K.3 TEU-old and former Art J.3 TEU:

1. Given that former Art K.3 TEU has been chosen as a legal basis, it emerges clearly that this wording refers to measures discussed as a response which would have mirrored the sanctions under Title IV LIBERTAD, such as entry restrictions for managers of black-listed companies or the requirement of any US citizen entering EU territory to declare that he was not involved in a Helms-Burton law suit.[72] At the time, an appropriate action

---

[71] *Joint Action 96/668/CFSP of 22/11/1996*, concerning measures protecting against the effects of extra-territorial application of legislation adopted by a third country, and actions based thereon and resulting therefrom, [1996] OJ L 309/7.

[72] Agence Europe, No. 6821, 28.September 1996, p. 7.

concerning visas under Community law was precluded, since former Art 100c TEC provided only for the imposition of a general visa requirement for third country nationals, which was politically not adequate.[73] Before Amsterdam, the preconditions for entry were designed as "matters of common interest" under former Art K.1 TEU, and the relative co-operation was to be organised under the procedure pursuant to former Art K.3 TEU, including the adoption of joint actions. Any common measure below the threshold of a general visa requirement for US citizens, such as the proposed declaration on Helms-Burton was therefore an action within the third, and not within the Community, pillar.

After the entering into force of the Treaty of Amsterdam, all decisions related to visas fall within the Community competence of Art 62 TEC. In particular, the Council is now also responsible for establishing standards and procedures to be followed by the Member States in carrying out checks on persons at the external borders and the establishing of procedures and conditions for issuing visas by the Member States.[74] [75] In this respect, it is necessary to signal the fact that Denmark, the United Kingdom and Ireland do in principle not take part in the adoption of all measures pursuant to Title IV TEC, i.e. those relating to visa, asylum and immigration.[76] However, these States have preserved the right to join the other Member States with respect to the whole title or limited to single measures.[77] Therefore, at the present stage, a blocking statute wanting to introduce rules limiting the entry of a

---

[73] Agence Europe, No. 6821, 28.September 1996, p. 7.

[74] Art 62 (2) TEC, sub-paragraphs a and b(ii).

[75] According to Art 67 TEC, the consultation procedure is to be followed for measures both under Art 62(2)a and 62(2)b(ii), with the Council acting by unanimity. After May 2004, acts under Art 62(2)b(ii) will by governed by co-decision, for those under Art 62(2)a there is a option to switch to this procedure. The Treaty of Nice, despite its amendments to Art 67 TEC, has not changed the situation for these particular provisions. *Griller et al.* (2000) 469 ff.

[76] *Protocol (No.4) on the Position of the United Kingdom and of Ireland*, Annex to the TEC; *Protocol (No.5) on the Position of Denmark,* Annex to the TEC.

[77] Although there could be some doubts on the right of Denmark to take part in single measures under Title IV TEC, see: *Griller et al.* (2000) 469f.

certain category of third country nationals to the Union could in principle be based on Community law.

Since the Joint Action was also conceived as a measure within the second pillar, based on former Art J.3 TEU, it implied also further measures. These are closely linked to the definition of its scope of application, since this second type of measures under CFSP is rather implicitly added by the phrase "insofar as these interests are not protected under the Regulation", and is therefore intimately related to the limitation of the scope of the Regulation to trade in goods and capital movements. In fact, the Joint Action makes a reference only to Art 11 of the Regulation 2271/96, which provides for a wide personal scope of application, extending to all persons doing business in the Community, and to the Annex which determines the targeted foreign legislation, but not to Art 1 of the Regulation. This implies that the Joint Action has, in principle, the same wide personal and material scope as the Regulation, *but it does not follow the latter's limitation of the Regulation to persons engaging in international trade and movement of capital,* pursuant to Art 1 of the Regulation.

It has, therefore, to be concluded that the Joint Action aims at the protection of the interests of those persons who would in principle be included in the Regulation, but could not claim protection under the Regulation due to the latter's limitation to trade in goods and capital movement. Thus, persons engaged in the international trade in services and the transport sector, were thought to be protected by Member State measures. The Joint Action does not define the content of these measures and leaves it to the discretion of each Member State. Consequently, the powers of CFSP under former Art J.3 TEU have not been employed to take particular measures of general foreign policy on EU level, but, apparently, to oblige Member States to supplement the Regulation with other measures for enterprises in the transport and services sector which were to be defined as need would arise and to confer to them the respective powers. The law of the second pillar thereby assumes a vicarious role with respect to Community law, rather timidly attempting to co-ordinate Member State action in matters falling within the concurrent competence of both the Community and the Member States, but in which respect no Community action had been taken.[78] It will have to be analysed whether a similar use of intergovernmental EU law as a compromise solution between Community law and separate Member State acts can be reconciled with the provision of Art 47 TEU. In any event, in this particular case, due to the developments in bilateral EU-US negotiations, the Member States have not decided on measures implementing the Joint Action within their jurisdiction.

B. The Legal Base

It can reasonably be doubted that the legislative technique adopted by the Joint Action meets the requirements of the TEU for similar measures, formerly under J.3 TEC-old, and now under Art 14(1) TEU.

The new provision, introduced by the Treaty of Amsterdam, does not fundamentally alter the characteristics of this instrument of CFSP. Both the old and the new version require a joint action to lay down the objectives pursued, the scope and the means necessary, the conditions for the implementation and, if necessary, the duration of the joint action. Other than former J.3 TEU however, Art 14(1) TEU contains a reference to the specific situation where the instrument of a Joint Action shall be employed, viz. "where operational action by the Union is deemed to be required".[79] This is to distinguish it more clearly from common positions, which are rather intended to "define the approach of the Union to a particular matter of a geographical or thematic nature".[80] Since the Joint Action (CFSP) 668/96 has to be considered with respect to the standard of Art J.3 TEU-old, it could not be reproached for the fact that it would contain general declarations of foreign policy instead of a particular "operational action by the Union". Moreover, so far the practice does not seem to give too much weight to this distinction. In fact, decisions under the CFSP concerning economic sanctions have continued to be taken as Common Positions, although the adoption of Joint Action might have been more

---

78 As described above, a Community legal act on the basis of Articles 47, 49 and 71 would have required the co-operation procedure and was considered to be too time-consuming.

79 Art 14(1) TEU.

80 Art 15 TEU. See: *Griller et al.* (2000) 385ff; *Pechstein/König* (1998) 147ff; *McGoldrick* (1997) 149ff; *Münch* (1996); *Fink-Hooijer* (1994).

appropriate.[81] It has also to be conceded that, as regards the possible content, Joint Actions do have a broad variety of possible applications, as the practice has demonstrated.[82]

However, whatever the content, the main purpose of a Joint Action has always been an action or operation within the common Union framework, e.g., concerning the EU administration of Mostar[83], the observation of elections[84] or the nomination of special envoys[85]. In the present case, the reference to the Union framework is considerably limited. There is no other case where the Member States are demanded in similar general terms to take any action they deem necessary. This does not simply leave a wide margin of discretion to each Member State, probably including the possibility of not taking any measure at all, it also proofs a lack of co-ordination between the single measures. In fact, the determination of the scope, the means and the conditions for implementation are so vague that the requirements of former Art J.3(1), second sub-paragraph do not seem to be fulfilled. In this respect, two aspects have to be criticised. First, the scope of application of the Joint Action is defined with a negative reference to Regulation 2271/96 and thus essentially remains unlimited.[86] Secondly, the measures to be taken are completely left to the discretion of the Member States and no conditions for the implementations are set out.[87]

---

81 cf., e.g., *Common Position of 10 May 1999*, concerning additional restrictive measures against the Federal Republic of Yugoslavia, 1999/318/CFSP, in 1999 OJ L123, p.1. see also: *Münch* (1996) 418, fn. 15.

82 cf. overview in: *Münch* (1996) 417ff, 427ff.

83 e.g., *Joint Action 96/476/CFSP*, July 26, 1996 on interim arrangements concerning the phasing out of the European Union Administration of Mostar, [1996] OJ L195/1.

84 e.g., *Joint Action 96/406/CFSP*, of June 10, 1996 concerning action by the Union to support the electoral process in Bosnia and Herzegovina, [1996] OJ L168/1.

85 e.g., *Joint Action 96/676/CFSP*, of November 25, 1996, on the nomination of an EU special envoy for the Middle East peace process, [1996] OJ L315/1.

86 See chapter IV.

87 e.g., Germany was assured that it needed not take action with respect to visas, Agence Europe No.6843, 30 October 1996, p. 6.

C. Relation between the Joint Action and the Law of Member States

It could be asked whether the Joint Action 668/96 requires Member States to take any implementing measure at all. In principle, Member States are under an obligation to align their international conduct and the positions they adopt to the provisions of any Joint Action. Art 14 TEU, as well as the former Art J.3 TEZ, clearly provides that "joint actions shall commit Member States". This obligation is however only binding under international law and notably is not subject to the jurisdiction of the ECJ.

In Joint Action (CFSP) 668/96, the binding, or rather co-ordinating, effect is counteracted by granting a very wide margin of discretion to Member States on its implementation to the extent that it is also possible not take any action at all.[88] This underlines the fact that the Joint Action was not the appropriate legal instrument for the objective pursued. As far as the binding effect of third pillar joint actions under former Art K.3 TEU is concerned, the Treaty text has never defined their binding effect. It thus depended on the content of each single act and the circumstances of its adoption.[89] Consequently, a precise obligation of Member States cannot be deferred from the text of the Joint Action.

The same level of co-ordination of blocking legislation on the level of the Member States could have been reached without any action within the Union framework. Since the EC powers in all of the matters concerned by the Regulation 2271/96 except those under Art 133 are considered a concurrent Community competence, Member States preserve their responsibilities to the extent that the Community has not legislated in the relative sector and the national measure therefore do not run counter to existing Community law. Moreover, the obligation to co-ordinate matters of general interest within CFSP under Art 16 TEU could have been complied with by other means. Neither the adoption of the Joint Action nor the thereby implied obligation of Member States to co-ordinate possible national blocking legislation based on Art 14(5)[90] add a significant level of additional co-ordination, given that the enactment of

88 "whenever it deems necessary".

89 *Pechstein/König* (1998) 132.

90 *Bianchi* (1998) 374.

blocking statutes is in any event a "matter of foreign policy of general interest" under Art16 TEU.[91]

The Joint Action was obviously not necessary to render legitimate under EU or Community law the existing blocking legislation of single Member States, such as the British PTIA and the 1992 Order. To the extent that the scope of existing national blocking statutes is covered by the Regulation 2271/96, they are superseded and rendered inapplicable by the adoption of the Community legal act due to the primacy of Community law. The other parts of the national legislation, as matters of concurrent Community competence, remain applicable without the need to justify their existence, provided that they are not contrary to existing Community law. Therefore, besides limiting the application of the PTIA where it is superseded by the Regulation, the British PTIA Order of 1996 could have expressly extended the obligations of non-compliance and information of sections 1 and 2 PTIA, to the persons affected by the Helms-Burton and D'Amato Acts to the extent that they are *not* protected by the Community blocking legislation.[92]

Of course, such an extension, concerning the relation between Community and Member State law, would not have required the passing of a Joint Action under former Art J.3 TEU. It is further evidence of the unworkability of the Joint Action that the British Order is not concerned with accompanying national measures, as prospected in the Joint Action, but only with the express limitation of the PTIA with respect to the Regulation.

Due to its lack of content, the Joint Action, albeit formally binding, is not able to impose on Member States any specific

---

91 This assumption is justified by the fact that the Regulation 2271/96 has been enacted on Community level and the case was an issue in EU-US diplomatic contacts. It is thus likely that additional measures adopted by single Member States are of "general interest" and affect the foreign policy of the Union.

92 Cf. Art 3(1) of the British *Extraterritorial US Legislation (Sanctions against Cuba, Iran and Libya) (Protection of Trading Interests) Order 1996*, Statutory Instrument 1996 No. 3171, which states that the relevant sections of the PTIA "shall not apply in respect of any matter to the extent that Art 5 of the EC Counter-measures Regulation applies in respect of it." Accordingly, Art 3(2) provides for the recovery of damages under Section 6 PTIA, to the extent that Art 6 Regulation 2271/96 applies.

obligation of conduct. The Joint Action with its present content, therefore, constitutes an inappropriate instrument for the co-ordination within the Union legal framework of potential blocking measures at the national level, since the same effect could have been achieved without taking any measure within the intergovernmental pillars at all.

IV. The European Blocking Statute as an "Integrated System"

The European Blocking Statute, in taking double action both under intergovernmental as well as under supranational EU law, implies the co-ordination of three levels of lawmaking: intergovernmental second pillar EU law, Community law and Member State law.

The relationship between the latter two in the field of external relations has been defined by the jurisprudence of the ECJ, which basically distinguishes the powers vested on the EC by the Treaty in concurrent and exclusive Community powers. Member States may thus only take external action in matters of concurrent Community competence, but only to the extent that this field is not already regulated by the Community and that the Member State action would conflict with the Community policy.

The relationship between sources of intergovernmental EU law and Member State law are defined by the TEU. As the TEU institutes, for the second and third pillar, an international and not a supranational treaty regime, Member States are bound by second pillar law in general, and in particular by joint actions, according to the rules of general international law.

The relationship between EC law and intergovernmental EU law is defined by Art 47 TEU, according to which nothing of the intergovernmental provisions of the TEU shall affect Community law. The analysis of this provision constitutes the purpose of the analysis below. Preliminarily, it is here remarked that the analysis of Art 47 TEU and the relationship between supranational and intergovernmental EU law has to be separated from the relationship between Community law and Member State law. The categories elaborated by the jurisprudence and doctrine for the division of external powers between the EC and the Member States can therefore not have a direct effect on the interpretation of Art 47 TEU. The fact that a Community competence is deemed exclusive with respect to Member States may be evidence that certain measures under the second pillar may also be excluded on the basis of Art 47 TEU. In principle, however, with respect to the Communities, the external powers attributed by the TEU to the Union may be different in both their scope and their nature than those still retained by the Member States.

Similarly, the intergovernmental Union law's binding effect on Member States does not necessarily imply a binding effect on the Communities. In principle, it is, therefore, possible that a measure of second pillar law has a binding effect with respect to Member State action, but this effect does not extend to Community legal acts.

A. Intergovernmental Second Pillar Law or Community Law – an Alternative?

Prior to the entry into force of the Treaty of Amsterdam, matters of immigration were generally regulated within the third pillar, with the exception of former Art 100c TEC, which concerned the decision on the list of third countries whose nationals had to be in possession of a visa upon entry into the Community. The requirement of entry visas for a particular group of US nationals, as it was considered as a reaction to the Helms-Burton Act, as opposed to a general visa requirement for all US citizens, would not have been covered by this provision and, therefore, a common measure had to be taken as a measure under former Art K.3 TEU.

It has, however, to be examined to what extent the measures envisaged on the basis of former Art J.3 TEU are compatible with the provision of Art 47 TEU. They do obviously not infringe upon the Community acquis, on the grounds they predetermine an act under EC law, as in the case of export controls of dual use goods, because the Joint Action expressly exempts the Regulation from its scope of application. It is rather the question whether it constitutes a violation of the acquis that, in the case of the European Blocking Statute, a legal base under intergovernmental law is employed instead of an existing potential legal base under Community law.

Since the legal bases of the Regulation deliberately restrict its scope of application, excluding the trade in services, it does not guarantee the universal application to all external trade relations with third countries, although such a universal scope would have been possible by employing other legal bases in Community law. Given that the scope of the Joint Action expressly covers all relevant trading interests not covered by the Regulation, this includes those potential Community powers concerning external trade which have deliberately not been employed in the Regulation, creating a conflict of powers between second pillar law and potential Community law. It is the express reference to the scope of applicability of the Regulation made in the text of the Joint Action which leads to the conclusion that the Joint Action, and particularly its reference to Art J.3 was TEU-old, was intended as a substitute measure for all cases where the Regulation had not sufficient political support or could not provide suitable instruments which could cover the whole range of possible trading interests affected by the US legislation.[93]

Moreover, since not all Member States fully agreed with the measure under Community law,[94] it was probably also intended to leave it to the discretion of Member States to take any further action. The passing of a Joint Action also on the basis of former Art J.3 TEU was obviously aimed to create the appearance of EU co-ordinated action, while at the same time leaving as much discretion as possible to Member States for specific action as need would arise.

This sets an interesting precedent. In matters having some aspect of foreign policy it probably occurs quite often that Community procedural requirements seem too strict or are not feasible within a short period of time and an universal agreement among Member States cannot be achieved. In these cases, it could be tempting to employ the instruments of the second pillar as a way to co-ordinate Member State action, either effectively or apparently, as in the case of the blocking statute. A similar strategy would add an additional option to the use of a Community legal base, which reinforces the role of the Council as the main actor in foreign policy to the detriment of the Commission which would effectively loose the monopoly of initiative in all matters being somehow related to foreign policy and lending themselves to treatment within the second pillar.

---

93 Irrespective of any measure under the third pillar concerning immigration!

94 In particular Denmark had proposed to limit EU action to measures within intergovernmental EU law. Cf. Agence Europe, No. 6838, 23 October 1996, p. 11.

B. The Precedent: The Joint Action Regarding Airport Transit Visas

Unlike in the cases of the export regime of dual use goods,[95] in the case at issue it is not the question whether the second or third pillar legal act actually pre-determines an already existing act of Community law, but whether an intergovernmental act can be adopted at all in matters where there is a valid potential legal base in Community law. In the Commission's action for annulment against the Joint Action Regarding Airport Transit Visas, the ECJ has already examined a similar set of facts to arrive a controversial finding.[96]

At the time of the enactment of the Joint Action 96/197/JHA, concerning the transit of third-country nationals on the airports within the territory of the Community[97], matters of visa policy and immigration were still subject to intergovernmental regulation under Title VI TEU, but, under former Art 100c TEC, the visa policy already fell within the powers of the Community, in particular, the determination of those third countries whose nationals must be in possession of a visa when crossing the external borders of the Member States, a task which was fulfilled by Council Regulation (EC) No. 2317/95.[98] These first powers of the Community concerning visa policy were, however, concurrent with the powers of the Member States, since former Art 100c TEC did neither expressly nor implicitly exclude the enactment of Member State law in this field.

On 4 March 1996, the Council passed the aforesaid Joint Action, based on former Art K.3 TEU, regulating the transit of nationals of third countries through the international zones of airports in the Member States, including the issue of transit visas by the Member State consular authorities to nationals of a list of third countries. The Commission brought an action for annulment maintaining that the Joint Action violated the powers of the Community under

---

95 See *Birgit Weidel's* contribution on dual-use goods in this volume.

96 C-170/96 *Commission v. Council (Joint action regarding airport transit visas),* [1998] ECR I-2763.

97 Joint Action of 4 March 1996 adopted by the Council on the basis of Art K.3 TEU on airport transit arrangements, OJ 1996 L 63, p.8.

98 Council Regulation (EC) No. 2317/95 of 25 September 1995, O.J. 1995, L 234, p.1. See also, albeit far less controversial, on the adoption of a uniform visa format: Council Regulation (EC) No. 1683/95 of 29 May 1995, OJ 1995, L 164, p.1.

former Art 100c TEC, since it would have been possible to regulate the matter under Community law.

The most interesting aspect of the case was the preliminary question whether the Court had jurisdiction to annul such an act, which at its face was an act of secondary Union law. In this matter, Advocate General *Fennelly* endorsed the Commission's argument that the Joint Action constituted, in effect, an act of the Council under its Community powers, which had erroneously been adopted under the intergovernmental procedure of third pillar law. The Advocate General held that the act had to be judged not on the base of its denomination, but according to its content and that, therefore, the Court had jurisdiction to entertain the annulment action, since Art 230 allowed the Court to review the legality of "acts of the Council".[99] According to this view, the Court's review of the joint action would in any event not be based on its validity under the TEU.

In substance, the Court shared this conclusion, but it based its reasoning rather on the preservation of the Community acquis under Art 47 TEU, which according to Art 46 TEU falls within the Court's jurisdiction.[100] Thus, any act of the Council, also those under the intergovernmental pillars, could be reviewed in the light of a possible affection of the Community acquis, which had to be prevented under Art 47. The approach taken by the Court was "to ascertain whether the Act affects the powers of the Community under that provision and *to annul the Act if it appears that it should have been based on Art 100c of the EC Treaty*."[101]

Ultimately, however, the Court rejected the request for annulment in the merits, opting for a narrow interpretation of the scope of former Art 100c TEC. According to the ECJ, this provision concerned only those cases where third country nationals in fact crossed the external borders of the Community. Since this was not the case with the mere transit on airports, the case was dismissed.

This judgment has been interpreted in the sense that it would support the controversial conclusion that the Council is pre-empted

---

[99] C-170/96 *Commission v. Council (Joint action regarding airport transit visas),* [1998] ECR I-2763, Opinion of AG Fennelly, para 15.

[100] C-170/96 *Commission v. Council (Joint action regarding airport transit visas),* [1998] ECR I-2763, paras 14ff.

[101] ibidem, para 17.

from taking any action under Union law, if the Treaty gives powers in a particular matter to the Community, since action "should be based" on the Community legal base. This preemption would apply even if the Community power is only concurrent with respect to Member States.[102] Accordingly, there would remain no option for legislators to take a particular measure under intergovernmental EU law, if the TEC provided any legal base for this measure.

According to this radical view, in the case of the European Blocking Statute, the attempt to employ a second pillar legal act as an alternative to an act under Community law, would have to be excluded.

C. Prospected Solution: Differentiation According to the Regulatory Content and the Form of the Second Pillar Legal Act

Such a radical reduction of applicability of second pillar law has – quite rightly - been heavily criticised, because it would induce Member States to take action in a particular matter even outside the structure of the Treaties, if there was no majority for a solution under Community law and this would be contrary to the object and purpose of Art 47 TEU.[103]

However, looking more closely on the scarce wording of the judgment, it seems that it does not necessarily imply this radical statement on the relationship of intergovernmental and supranational law, but leaves enough spaces for intermediate solutions. In the view of the author, while there may be good reasons to exclude the adoption of certain intergovernmental acts in matters of concurrent and not yet exercised Community powers, the Court's argument does not necessarily lead to the conclusion that any legal act under EU law is pre-empted by a potential EC competence.

The passage of the judgment is, in fact, very short and, as an *obiter dictum*, does not further set out its arguments in detail. It has to be borne in mind that the Court simply states that the matter in consideration falls within its jurisdiction, proposing to "annul the act if it appears that it should have been based on Art 100c TEC"[104]. The fact that the ECJ finds that it has jurisdiction over acts which potentially affect Community law should not be too surprising,

---

[102] *Griller* (1999) 57ff.

[103] ibid.

[104] C-170/96 *Commission v. Council (Joint action regarding airport transit visas),* [1998] ECR I-2763, para 17.

given Art 46 and 47 TEU. However, the Court does not specify which criteria it would apply in order to decide the question whether a particular act should have been based on the TEC rather than on a provision under the TEU. Since the judgment finds that, in this particular case, it was not even possible to base the act on Art 100c, it does not specify on the choice between two possible legal bases.

If ever invested again by a similar question and if this question should prove decisive for the final verdict, there is reason to suggest that the Court would not take this radical position without further examination. This examination may consist in a distinction according to the specific ability of the intergovernmental act at issue to limit or infringe upon Community powers. This specific ability, on the one hand, certainly depends on the *regulatory content* of the particular second pillar legal act whose determination would require an examination of the particular act in its merits.

However, the formal aspect of the examination should not be neglected. First, from the form of the intergovernmental legal act[105] and thus from its legal base in the TEU[106], conclusions could be drawn as regards its specific potential to infringe and limit the Community policies in the matter concerned and the existing and potential Community legal acts. The form of the intergovernmental legal act would thus constitute an element for a more in-depth examination of the potential repercussions on Community law of the particular act concerned.

Secondly, a *formal distinction* according to the particular instrument employed for action under the intergovernmental second pillar may also constitute *in itself* a valid alternative to clearly distinguish between second and third pillar legal acts which can be adopted in matters which potentially fall within Community competence and those which would amount to a violation of Art 47 TEU.

This approach presupposes an integrated view of the EU legal order, as it may lead to different conclusions according to the type of the intergovernmental legal act and does not once and for all define relationship between intergovernmental EU law as such, on the one hand, and Community law, on the other. It is thus incompatible with a concept of intergovernmental EU law and EC

[105] Common Strategy, Common Position, Joint Action

[106] Art 13, 14, 15 TEU.

law as two monolithic masses of law which cannot be co-ordinated at all and are mutually exclusive in their use. In this respect, the solution proposed draws a great deal from the concept of second and third pillar law as "*Nebengemeinschaftsrecht*" or peripheral Community law, as characterised by *Pache*, who in turn builds on earlier works of *Hilf*.[107] It characterises intergovernmental Union law as a continuously evolving corpus of law, distinct from general public international law, which is developed in strong relationship with Community law, with the option to integrate larger or smaller parts of it into Community law. In very vivid terms, *Pache* describes intergovernmental EU law as "Community law in vitro". This concept is likely to apply not only for matters of the third pillar, but also for the second pillar. There is already an authoritative line of argument, headed by Commission President *Prodi*, which sustains that a truly Common Foreign and Security Policy can only be achieved by introducing the Community method also in this sector, although a political change in this sense may still be very far.[108]

1. The Instruments of the European Council: Principles of CFSP, Guidelines and Common Strategies

In principle, the obligation to safeguard the Community body of law applies also to cases where the Community policy makes part

---

[107] *Pache*(1995) para 16, with further references.

[108] Speech by *Romano Prodi*, An Enlarged and more united Europe, a Global Player - challenges and opportunities in the new century to the College of Europe, Bruges, 12th November 2001:
"But Europe [...], will not succeed in contributing to peace and stability in the world, nor will it be able to fill a political role that matches its economic stature, or indeed be accepted in such a role, unless it is united in its actions.
This problem will be resolved once and for all only if the necessary adjustments are made and the entire foreign and security policy of the Union is brought inside the Community system. I have no doubt that one day this will come about, notwithstanding the current resistance and reluctance. Resistance and reluctance are of course understandable, because this is the conclusion of a long and difficult journey, similar to that which led to the single currency.
It is, however, a process that is already under way and one which we must move forward patiently and pragmatically, as we have always done when taking the tricky and important steps towards integration."

of an overall approach, which is presented to the international community by the Council Presidency or General Secretary. Consequently, on the basis of Art. 47 TEU, the Council has to fully respect Community law and the existing Community policies when formulating its statements and positions, in order not to alter or affect them in any way and it has the obligation to co-operate with the Commission for that purpose. The obligation for Council and Commission to co-operate is expressed in Articles 3(2) and 18(4) TEU. The latter "fully associates" the Commission in the task of representing the EU foreign policy: Furthermore, the Commission's power, albeit it is shared with the Member States, to make proposals to the Council pursuant to Art 22 TEU is also an expression of this obligation. The Treaty does however not define the details of this co-operation and they are left to inter-institutional practice. In any event, the role of the Council as the shaper of general foreign policy and as the speaker of the EU and the Commission's leading role in the definition of the specific external relations of the Community in matters such as development aid and trade make a strong relationship of co-operation indispensable.

Such a co-ordinated approach can be envisaged when aimed at the production of any declaration or measure which takes a comprehensive approach to external relations. This is undoubtedly the case with the principles and common guidelines defined by the European Council which are included in the Conclusions of the Presidency.

Another instrument of European Council for laying down the general lines of foreign policy are the common strategies, which according to Art 13(3) second subparagraph TEU are recommended by the Council. So far, only three Common Strategies, regarding respectively the EU relationship with Russia, the Ukraine and the Mediterranean Region, have been adopted.[109] They line out a vision of the EU for the specific region, set objectives for the EU policy, define comprehensively all areas where action is needed. In contemplating the instruments and means, the common strategies provide that all EU institutions and bodies shall implement the strategy, "each acting within the powers attributed to them by the

---

[109] Common Strategy of the European Union on Russia, OJ L157/1 of 24.06.1999; Common Strategy of the European Union on Ukraine, OJ L331/1 of 23.12.1999; Common Strategy on the Mediterranean Region 2000/458/CFSP, OJ L183/5 of 22.07.2000.

Treaties, and in accordance with the applicable procedures under those Treaties."[110] In this light, it seems recommendable that also the Commission should take part in the preparation of common strategies, since their content regards also Community action under the responsibility of the Commission. The binding effect of common strategies on the Communities operates certainly more in a political than in a legal way. Pursuant to Art 13 TEU, the Council shall ensure the unity, consistency and the effectiveness of the action by the Union; accordingly, the common strategies require the Council to review EU action and report at least annually to the European Council on their implementation; with the Commission contributing within its competence.[111] Since Art 13 is not subject to the review of the ECJ, it is not possible to seek the annulment of a particular measure taken by the Commission in violation of a Common Strategy. Therefore, the only means to ensure consistent implementation of these strategies are the periodical reports and recommendations by the Council to the European Council.

It is, therefore, not conceivable that the global approach taken in the basic documents of the European Council, which is their very purpose, would constitute an infringement of Art 47 TEU. The participation of the Commission President may be regarded as an expression of the fact that the European Council sets out the principles for the EU as a whole, comprehensive of all three pillars. It could thus be argued that legal acts of the European Council because of their very nature do not lend themselves to a review under Art 47 TEU. There is no need to limit these type of acts as regards content and to exclude matters falling within EC competence from being treated in these documents on the grounds that an inclusion would constitute an infringement of the Community acquis.

2. Joint Actions

An infringement of Art 47 is much more likely with the more specific legal instruments of the EU foreign policy, i.e. the instruments adopted within the second pillar by the Council.

This problematic relationship between a global approach by the CFSP and the preservation of the Community acquis becomes evident in the case of joint actions, which, according to Art 14

---

[110] cf., e.g., Art 24 of the Common Strategy on the Mediterranean Region 2000/458/CFSP.

[111] Ibid. Art 33.

TEU, "shall address specific situations where operational action by the Union is deemed to be required". Since these acts constitute the basis for specific EU action, their content would be likely to violate the prerogatives of the Community policies if they covered subject matters within the responsibility of the Community. It is, in fact, not possible to imagine a joint action within the realm of Community powers, whose content fulfils the requirements of Art 14 by addressing specific situations with operational action and does at the same time not enter in conflict with Community powers in the form of existing or potential legal acts under Community law.

The adoption of a joint action, fulfilling the Treaty's requirements of addressing specific situations and taking operational action, does not only infringe upon Community prerogatives, if the application of Community law is made conditional upon a determination within intergovernmental EU law. The adoption of a joint action in matters of potential Community competence *instead of an act of EC law* may be criticised for its choice of the wrong legal base.[112] Such an undue recourse to intergovernmental decision mechanisms, bypassing already existing Community powers, certainly would "affect" the Community treaties and could be regarded a violation of Art 47 TEU.

In the light of the principle of the preservation of the Community acquis, it is, in fact, not likely that the TEU intended to expressly provide an intergovernmental alternative to practically every existing EC competence in matters charged with foreign policy interests, thus allowing to substitute supranational with intergovernmental procedures. Not only would this be contrary to the goal of building an "ever closer Union"[113], there was not even a need for such a provision, given that Member States have always been free to adopt traditional instruments of international law also in matters of concurrent Community competence. The Schengen process has demonstrated that traditional intergovernmental acts can perfectly be formally build up outside of the EU framework, and then subsequently, be integrated into it. The subsequent practice in the Treaties of Amsterdam and Nice, in the view of the enlargement to a Union of 27 Members, has shown the tendency to

[112] C-170/96 *Commission v. Council (Joint action regarding airport transit visas),* [1998] ECR I-2763, Opinion of AG *Fennelly.*

[113] Art 1 TEU.

increase supranational decision-making and reduce the intergovernmental aspects of the EU framework.[114]

Moreover, the solution to admit any intergovernmental act on the basis that there is a lack of political will for supranational decision-making and foreign policy interests are somehow involved, does not seem feasible neither from a political point of view. The EU trade and foreign policy has shown that there are many issues in international economic law which can suddenly acquire a foreign policy aspect which they had not had before, one just needs to think of the tighter controls on international finance in the wake of the bombings of 11 September 2001. Would these change in circumstances suddenly justify the adoption of a joint action instead of a regulation on tighter banking laws or, yes, visa controls in airports? Furthermore, also in the light of the above analysis of the Blocking Statute, which found its substantial unworkability, it has not yet been proven that intergovernmental EU legal acts are better suited than supranational acts to regulate delicate matters of EU foreign trade.

It is therefore here suggested that the need to safeguard the Community acquis, according to Art 47 TEU, precludes a joint action from determining or influencing Community action in any way, be it in relation to existing legal acts of Community law[115] or in relation to potential Community powers.

3. Common Positions

Other than joint actions, common positions, in defining the approach of the Union to a particular matter of a geographical or thematic nature, need not regard a specific situation or be immediately operative.[116] A common position, could therefore co-ordinate Member State action in a particular matter falling within concurrent Community competence, without thereby necessarily infringing Community powers, although it remains bound by the obligation of Art 47 TEU.

---

[114] E.g., integration of justice co-operation in civil matters, Art 65 TEC.

[115] C-70/94 *Fritz Werner Industrie- Ausrüstungen GmbH v. Federal Republic of Germany*, ECR [1995] I-3189; C-83/94 *Criminal Proceedings against Peter Leifer and Others*, ECR 1995, I-3231. See also *Birgit Weidel's* contribution on the pillar construction in this volume.

[116] Art 15 TEU.

Although common positions can occasionally also provide for specific measures on the level of the EU[117], in defining the approach of the EU to a particular matter, they rather have a co-ordinating and strategic function. These functions could not be fulfilled by a Community legal act as well and it is, therefore, possible to imagine common positions in matters falling within Community powers of which it could not be said that "they should have been based" on a legal base of the TEC, because a Community measure would not be able to fulfil the same function.

The nature of common positions, as defined in Art 15 TEU, other than the character of joint actions, is thus not *per se* in contrast with a potential Community legislation in the same matter. The strategic and planning function of common positions allows them to merely take account of measures to be implemented by the EC and lay down principles to be observed by the Member States, without having a binding effect upon the Communities.[118] If a particular matter requires co-ordinated action both on the level of EC, the intergovernmental pillars of the EU and by the Member States, a common position would appear suited to define the role of the latter starting out from the primacy of the former.

Concerning the binding effect of common positions on the Communities, the Council and the Commission have therefore agreed to a *mode d'emploi*, which was acknowledged by the Council in its meeting of March 6, 1995.[119] This agreement accepts in principle the possibility that common positions also cover the full scope of external action by the EU, including matters falling within Community competence. It emphasises, however, the need to respect the Commission's exclusive right of initiative within EC law and the impossibility for common positions to require the Commission to act in a certain way; instead, a common position can only take note of the Commission's intentions.

Timmermans therefore suggests to restrict these references to the recital and to avoid mentioning them in the operative part of a

---

[117] Such specific measures would have to be tested for their compatibility with Art 47 TEU.

[118] *Timmermans* (1996) 66 ff.

[119] *Council Document 5194/95*. The full text is unpublished, but its content is discussed in *Timmermans* (1996). References also in *Kaufmann-Bühler* (1998), paras 9ff.

common position, in order not to infringe Community prerogatives.[120]

4. Declarations

An instrument of CFSP, which is not specifically mentioned in the TEU, but which is important in practice, are the declarations made on behalf of the EU by the representatives of its institutions in the day-to-day management of foreign policy. These declarations are the typical instruments of communication and presentation of foreign policy, but do not directly imply legal obligations within international law. The declarations are presented by the Presidency either as declarations of the Presidency on behalf of the EU or as declarations of the EU.

Although there is certainly a need to co-ordinate the communication of foreign policy between the Council (High Representative, Presidency) and the Commission (President, Commissioner for external relations), a comprehensive presentation of EU foreign policy legally does not infringe upon the prerogatives Community policy, since it does not imply substantial measures.

5. Conclusion

To sum up, the preclusive effect of Art 47 TEU in matters of potential Community competence is different according to the type of intergovernmental legal act adopted, because each of these instruments has a different effect on Community policies.

The instruments adopted by the European Council are given by the Treaty a co-ordinating function, obliging all institutions of the EU, albeit in a rather political than legal way, since it is impossible to annul an act for its incompatibility with a common strategy. In these cases, the need for co-ordination and collaboration between institutions of both intergovernmental (Council) and supranational (Commission) nature outweighs the need for safeguard of the Community acquis; a limitation of these instruments on the basis of Art 47 TEU would therefore not be justified.

Political declarations have no binding effect on the Communities and can, therefore, not be deemed to infringe upon the Community acquis in violation of Art 47 TEU.

By contrast, joint actions and common positions can contain specific provisions which can constitute a limitation of Community powers and thus an infringement of Art 47 TEU. This is, in

---

[120] *Timmermans (*1996) 69.

particular, the case for joint actions, since, if its content fulfils the requirements defined in Art 14 TEU, it implies "operational action", which, in most cases, could have been taken under Community competence as well. According to the approach of the ECJ in the ATV case, such a joint action in matters of Community competence is therefore in violation of the principle of preservation of the Community acquis of Art 47 TEU, even if the Community has not yet taken action in the specific matter affected.

Other than for joint actions, the content of common positions is not as narrowly defined by the Treaty. It seems, therefore, possible that common positions, other than joint actions, lay down the EU approach to a certain matter in broader terms, merely taking note of actions under Community law, and binding only Member States, without thus providing for actions that "should have been based" on a legal base in Community law.

D. Application to the Case

If this rationale is applied to the case of the Blocking Statute, the adoption of the Joint Action, to the extent that it is based on former Art J.2 TEU and that it provides for protective measures for the European trading interests in the trade in services, an infringement of Community law under Art 47 TEU, on the grounds that the measure is founded on an intergovernmental legal base where a Community legal base would have been available.

Substantially, however, the specific provisions presently contained in Joint Action 668/96/CFSP themselves do not constitute a concrete infringement of Community powers, because the Joint Action completely omits to take any "joint action" under the second pillar at all and is completely devoid of factual content. Even the "transfer" of powers to the Member States operated by the Joint Action, by assigning to them to take action insofar as this had not been done by the Regulation, was completely unnecessary. In fact, since the respective EC competence is not exclusive, the Member States already disposed of these powers! In the present case, therefore, the Joint Action rather violates the requirements of Art 14 TEU[121] than the obligation to safeguard the Community acquis of Art 47 TEU.

It could now be asked whether it would have been possible at all adopt a meaningful second pillar action as an alternative to a

[121] i.e., if it had been taken after the entering into force of the Treaty of Amsterdam which introduced the specifications to Art 14 TEU.

Regulation with a broader legal base and in any case as a supplement to the Regulation and, without at the same time infringing upon the Community acquis.[122]

Based on the approach lined out by the ATV case and taken up in this paper, a joint action for CFSP as an alternative to action under Community law is not viable, because it is based on the wrong legal base. Speaking with the ECJ in the ATV case, it appears that the Joint Action, insofar as it is designed to extend the blocking legislation to the international trade in services, should have been based on the legal bases under Community law.

Other second pillar instruments with different formal requirements could avoid binding commands for EC. A co-ordination of the single national measures, as required in its simplest form by Art 16 TEU, could have been achieved within the Union framework by systematic informal co-operation, consultation and information, pursuant to former Art J.2 TEU or Art 16 TEU. If the purpose, however, was to take a strong and visible stance against the US use of extraterritorial laws, political declarations, as have effectively been made both by the Commission and the Presidency of the Council, would have been sufficient.

Considering more specifically the possibility of a common position of the Council as the intergovernmental part of the Blocking Statute, instead of the Joint Action, this would seem a valid alternative, not only because this would allow a more meaningful content, but also for its better compatibility with Community law. A common position defining the EU stance on extraterritoriality, and taking only note of the measures taken within Community law, would probably have achieved a higher degree of co-ordination and could have contained the principles of EU action in greater detail without thereby necessarily infringing upon the Community acquis.

In any event, both for a common position or a joint action, be they based solely on former Art K.3 TEU or also on former Art J.3 TEU, a better wording should have been chosen, expressing at least some common denominator on the Union level. This could have been achieved by referring to any common measure envisaged, such as, e.g., certain procedural pre-conditions imposed on US citizens entering the territory of a Member State.

---

122 At the time of adoption (1996), absent a Community competence in this matter, the recourse to Art K.3 was justified.

V. Conclusion

In international trade and, in general, matters having implications for the external relations of the EU, the adoption of joint actions under the second pillar of the EU does not constitute an *alternative* to the use of legal instruments of Community law. These acts would affect the powers of the Communities as laid down in the TEC and should be annulled by the ECJ on the grounds that they violate Art 47 TEU.

However, this does not imply that any other legal act under the second pillar is precluded in matters falling within Community powers. The analysis of the instruments of CFSP according to their content and form shows that only the adoption of joint actions, due to their nature as defined in Art 14 TEU, appear to be *a priori* excluded if the subject matter of the act falls within Community competence. Other instruments of CFSP, however, fulfil different functions which can in principle be co-ordinated with Community powers without constituting a predetermination of or an alternative to Community law. This is certainly true for all acts of the European Council, but possibly also for common positions, as long as they are limited to "taking note of" Community policies.

The European Blocking Statute has, therefore, to be deemed a failed experiment to the extent that the Joint Action is used as a substitute for Community action. It is only the Joint Action's unlawful lack of content that avoids a tangible infringement of Community powers. However, the combination of acts of supranational and intergovernmental EU law is not completely impossible and it would be feasible to employ other instruments of CFSP in order to co-ordinate EU external action.

Bibliography

Basedow, J. (2000), The Communitarization of the Conflict of Laws Under the Treaty of Amsterdam, CMLRev. 2000, 687.

Bianchi, A. (1998), Le recenti sanzioni unilaterali adottate dagli Stati Uniti nei confronti di Cuba e la loro liceità internazionale, Riv. Dir. Int. 2/1998, 313.

Bourgeois, J. (1999), Art 113, in: *von der Groeben, H. /Thiesing, J./Ehlermann, C.D.* (eds.), Kommentar zum EWG Vertrag, Baden-Baden[5] 1999, 812.

Bröhmer, W. (1999), Art 56, in: *Calliess, C./Ruffert, M.* (eds.), Kommentar des Vertrages über die Europäische Union und des Vertrages zur Gründung der Europäischen Gemeinschaft, Neuwied 1999, 738.

Dashwood, A. (1996), The Limits of European Community Powers, ELRev 21 (1996), 113.

Fink-Hooijer, A. (1994), The Common Foreign and Security Policy of the European Union, EJIL 2/1994, 173.

Forwick, C. (1993), Extraterritoriale US-amerikanische Exportkontrollen, Heidelberg 1993.

Freitag, R. (1997), Mitgliedstaatliche Beschränkungen des Kapitalverkehrs und Europäisches Gemeinschaftsrecht, EWS 1997, 186.

Glossop, P. (1998), Canada's Foreign Extraterritorial Measures Act, International Lawyer 1/1998, 93.

Griller, S. (1999), Die Unterscheidung von Unionsrecht und Gemeinschaftsrecht, EuR Beiheft 1 1999, 45.

Griller, S./Droutsas, D./Falkner, G./Forgó, K./ Nentwich, M. (2000), The Treaty of Amsterdam- Facts, Analysis, Prospects, Vienna 2000.

Hahn, M. (1999), Art 133, in: *Calliess, C./Ruffert, M* (eds.), Kommentar des Vertrages über die Europäische Union und des Vertrages zur Gründung der Europäischen Gemeinschaft, Neuwied 1999, 1282.

Huber, J. (1997), .La réaction de l'Union Européenne face aux lois américaines Helms-Burton and D'Amato, RMU 1997, 305.

Kapteyn, P.J.G./VerLoren van Themaat, P. (1998), Introduction to the Law of the European Communities – From Maastricht to Amsterdam, London, The Hague, Boston 1998.

Kaufmann-Bühler, W. (1998), Art. J.2. EUV, in: *Grabitz E./Hilf, M.* Das Recht der Europäischen Union, 12th instalment, München 1998.

Kiemel, W. (1999a), Art 73b, in: *von der Groeben, H./Thiesing, J./Ehlermann, C.D* (eds.), Kommentar zum EWG Vertrag , Baden-Baden[5] 1999, 1560.

Kiemel, W. (1999b), Art 73c, in: *von der Groeben, H./Thiesing, J./Ehlermann, C.D* (eds.), Kommentar zum EWG Vertrag, Baden-Baden[5] 1999, 1601.

Kuijper, J.P. (1984), The European Community and the US Pipeline Embargo: Comments on Comments, GYIL Vol. 27 (1984), 72.

Lowe, V. A. (1981), The British Protection of Trading Interests Act 1980, AJIL 1981, 257.

Lowe, V. A. (1984), International Law Issues Arising in the Pipeline Dispute: the British Position, GYIL 1984, 54.

MacGoldrick, D. (1997), International Relations Law of the European Union, London 1998.

Müller-Ibold, T. (1999), Art 133, in: *Lenz, C.-O.* (ed.), EG Vertrag, Köln[2] 1999, 1074.

Münch, L. (1996), Die gemeinsame Aktion im Rahmen der GASP: Inhalt, Rechtsnatur und Reformbedürftigkeit, EuR 4/1996, 415.

Neuhold, H./Hummer, W./Schreuer, C. (1997), Österreichisches Handbuch des Völkerrechts, Wien 1997.

Pache, E. (1995), Art M EUV, in: *Grabitz, E./Hilf, M.* (eds.) Das Recht der Europäischen Union, 8th instalment, München 1995.

Pechstein, M./ Koenig, C. (1998), Die Europäische Union, Tübingen 1998.

Reinisch, A. (1997), Blockiermaßnahmen der EU gegen extraterritoriale Rechtsakte, ecolex 1997, 900.

Rossi, M. (1999), Art 308, in: *Calliess, C./Ruffert, M.* (eds.), Kommentar des Vertrages über die Europäische Union und des Vertrages zur Gründung der Europäischen Gemeinschaft, Neuwied 1999, 2187.

Röttinger, M. (1999), Art. 308, in: *Lenz, C.-O.* (ed.), EG Vertrag, Köln[2] 1999.

Schwartz, I. (1999), Art 235, in: *von der Groeben, H./Thiesing, J./Ehlermann, C.D* (eds.), Kommentar zum EWG Vertrag, Baden-Baden[5] 1999.

Timmermans, C.W.A. (1996), The Uneasy Relationship Between the Communities and the Second Union Pillar: Back to the 'Plan Fouchet'?, Legal Issues of European Integration 1996, 61.

Tomuschat, C. (1976), Die Rechtsetzungsbefugnisse der EWG in Generalermächtigungen, insbesondere in Art 235, EuR, Sonderheft 1976, 60.

von Hoffmann, B. (ed.) (1998), European Private International Law, 1998.

Weber, R. (1999), Art 56, in: *Lenz, C.-O.* (ed.), EG Vertrag, Köln[2] 1999.

Weber, S. (1992), Kapitalverkehr und Kapitalmärkte im Vertrag über die Europäische Union, EuZW 1992, 561.

Anita Lukaschek

Economic Sanctions and the European Union's Legal Framework

I. Introductory Remarks

Where matters which touch upon the very core of national sovereignty are deemed to be covered by exclusive Community competence, things aren't supposed to be easy. Where a Union is not a unity and common is not common, things aren't supposed to get any easier.

These are possible remarks made at the outset of a closer evaluation of the European Community's and European Union's attitude towards a text book example of linkage between foreign policy and external trade: Economic sanctions, generally defined as trade restricting discriminatory measures, imposed by one authority against another subject of international law in pursuance of a foreign policy objective, namely to alter the conduct of the target State[1].

The measures may have considerable impact on both "worlds": Apparently, their imposition is of highly sensitive nature as to a country's foreign policy and diplomacy. Considering moreover, that in the case of a total trade embargo, trade flows with an entire foreign market get blocked, there may be considerable economic effects not only (as intended) as to the sanctioned State, but also

---

1 On the definition of the notion "economic sanction" and related terms, compare in particular *Schneider* (1997) 27 f; In the present survey the term "embargo" is for reasons of variety synonymously used, although this is, strictly spoken, not correct, since embargoes are usually construed as restrictions on trade of goods only; ibid. 35.

regarding the economy of the "sanctioner", who is knowingly accepting such self-damaging effects. If trade embargoes are disparately applied within the internal market, there is of course a manifest risk of distorting effects on the common market.

Even though there is an undeniable need for uniform, rapid and thus effective implementation and application of embargo measures within the Community which can be accomplished best by way of Community legislation, there is also a sort of reluctance on the part of some Member States to hand over that sensitive foreign policy instrument to the Community.

The first part of this paper briefly surveys the first approximation towards a "Common Sanctions Policy" in order to subsequently assess the legal value of the sanctioning practice established thereby taking into account the relevant ECJ case law. The outcome of this evaluation is not just of merely historical interest, as the second part of the paper, dealing with the post-Maastricht-period and the present legal situation, proofs. The Maastricht Treaty substantially altered the legal framework for the imposition of sanctions without, however, eliminating the fundamental problem: dualism in external relations within the Union. The initial ambiguous project of creating a genuine political Union has not been realised. With the Maastricht Treaty the Member States created a so-called Common Foreign and Security Policy (CFSP), "supplementing"[2] the traditional Communities. The dualism in external relations continued, with a new competitor though, namely the European Union acting under Title V of the Maastricht Treaty concerning the CFSP. The second part of this brief survey intends to examine the potential consequences of the altered legal framework for the taking of hybrid acts such as in particular economic sanctions.

Eventually, I shall conclude with some suggestions on desirable improvements of the *status quo* and observations on possible future developments respectively.

---

2 See Article 1 TEU.

II. Pre-Maastricht Sanctions Policy at the European Level

A. European Embargo Practice Before the Entry into Force of the Maastricht Treaty

When first confronted with the inseparable fusion of an economic instrument and a foreign policy tool and the ensuing competence problem in the context of implementation of mandatory UN Security Council resolutions, a multitude of Member States favoured the view – in line with the Council's position – that former Article 224 TEEC (now Article 297 TEC)[3] provided for the adequate legal basis for the taking of national measures following consultations and co-ordination[4].

This sometimes called "Rhodesia doctrine"[5] may be put down to a goal-focused concept of a Common Commercial Policy (CCP) (a so-called subjective or purposive approach[6]), which prevents embargo measures from falling within the CCP's scope because of the foreign policy objectives they pursue. Member States and the Council construed ex Article 224 EEC Treaty (now Article 297 TEC) as genuine reserve of sovereignty precluding the existence of a parallel Community competence[7].

---

3 If not (as here) indicated otherwise, the numbering in the present contribution gives the recent numbering as amended by the Amsterdam Treaty.

4 See Written Questions No 526/75 and No 527/75 by Mr. Patijn to the Council and the Commission respectively, OJ C 89 of 16.4.1976, 6 f, as well as Written questions No 68/65 and No 5/73 by Mr. Vredeling to the Commission, OJ C 14 of 25.1.1966, 199, and OJ C 57 of 17.7.1973, 27.

5 Denominated after the sanctions against Rhodesia (where the white minority regime of premier Ian Smith had against Rhodesia unilaterally proclaimed independence), taken that way, in implementation UN SC Res. 232 (1966) and 253 (1968) respectively; See *Kuijper* (1975) 231 and *Koutrakos* (2000) 1345; The same procedure was chosen when implementing the sanctions decided on by the UN Security Council against Iran on the occasion of the seizure of the US embassy in Teheran; See *Nuttall* (1987) 223.

6 See at 329 ff.

7 See *Vedder* (2001) para 69 with further references; By contrast, interpreting that provision as a safeguard clause, which "merely" enables the Member States to derogate from Community law in specific situations (e.g. "in order to carry out obligations the Member State has accepted for the purpose of maintaining peace and

In the course of time, however, ex Article 113 (now Article 133 TEC) increasingly gained practical recognition as possible legal basis for the imposition of Community sanctions against third countries and, in particular, for the implementation of UN Security Council resolutions at the Community level. However, such Community measures adopted on the basis of ex-Article 113 TEC were regularly preceded by consultations within the framework of European Political Cooperation (EPC).

Ex Article 113 EEC Treaty served for the first time as legal basis for embargo measures in 1980, when the EEC decided on measures intended to ensure the effectiveness of the US grain embargo against the USSR (imposed on occasion of the Soviet invasion in Afghanistan), and subsequently in 1982 when the Community adopted the first autonomous embargo based on ex Article 113 EEC[8]. On the very same day, however, it adopted a second regulation exempting Greece from the application of the former on grounds of ostensible "particular difficulties for that Member State's trade and economy"[9]. The exemption, however, was more likely a concession offered to disapproving Greece in order to prevent it from relying on the so-called Luxembourg compromise[10].

An example illustrating that some Member States still considered themselves unconstrained by Community measures are the sanctions taken on occasion of the Falklands crisis, where the Community imposed an import embargo against Argentina following the same two-step procedure (consultation and consensus in EPC plus Community regulation based on ex Article 113 EEC

---

international security" as provided for in Article 297 TEC third case), would have led to the result that the Member States would in fact have been enabled to take national measures by virtue of that provision (and provided for that one does not interpret Article 297 TEC as not applying to cases where all Member States are concerned by the situation provided for therein, such as in particular the existence of a mandatory UN SC Resolution; See *Koutrakos* (2000) 1345.

8 Council Regulation 596/82 of 15 March 1982, OJ L 72, 15.

9 Council Regulation 597/82 of 15 March 1982, OJ L 72, 19.

10 See *Stein* (1995) 80; *Garçon* (1997) 52 with further references; *Zemanek* (1990) 149. Also Denmark initially opposed the measures but eventually consented. One year later, however, it unilaterally suspended the measures without prior Community authorisation; See *Garçon* (1995) 53.

Treaty[11]) developed and exercised before in context with the Poland embargo. The preamble of the regulation, however, also referred to consultations among the Member States under ex Article 224 EEC Treaty (now Article 297 TEC) upon the taking of unilateral measures of the United Kingdom pursuant to this provision. In this case, a parallel application of the two provisions (ex Article 113 and 224 EEC Treaty) had been accepted, and also the coexistence of two different consultation fora in pursuance of different aims: the EPC, providing for the framework for foreign policy coordination, and consultation within the Community cadre in accordance with the provision of ex Article 224 EEC Treaty with the objective of avoiding distorting effects on the common market. Subsequently some Member States (Denmark, Ireland, Italy) raised objections as to the first prolongation of the embargo by invoking fundamental considerations or domestic policy reasons.

Albeit with a slim majority and even without preceding EPC consultations, prolongation measures had been finally adopted[12], yet the initially opposing countries refused to apply them properly[13].

Subsequently, however, the "combined approach", i.e. EPC consensus plus Community measure based on former Article 113 EEC Treaty, was applied in a number of cases[14] and eventually it was fundamentally accepted and acknowledged by the Member States. The mere fact of a practice being employed, however, does not necessarily entail its legitimacy.[15]

---

11 Council Regulation 877/82 of 16 April 1982, OJ 1982 L 102, 1.

12 Council Regulation 1176/82 of 18 May 1982, OJ 1982 L 136, 1; Council Regulation 1254/82 of 24 May 1982, OJ 1982 L 146, 1.

13 See e.g. *Ress* (2000) 202 ff.

14 Council Regulation 3302/86 of 27 October 1986, OJ 1986 L 305, 11, suspending imports of gold coins originating in the Republic of South Africa (which does not expressly cite Article 113 though); Council Regulation 2340/90 of 8 August 1990, OJ 1990 L 213, 1preventing trade by the Community as regards Iraq and Kuwait,; Council Regulation 1432/92 of 1 June 1992, , OJ 1992 L 151, 4, prohibiting trade between the EEC and the Republics of Serbia and Montenegro.

15 See e.g. Opinion 1/94, *WTO*, [1994] ECR I-5267, para 52, referring to its judgment in Case 68/86, *United Kingtom v Council*, [1988] ECR 855, para 24.

B. *The Allocation of Community Embargo Competence*

1. The Existence Question[16]

a) Economic Sanctions and the Scope of CCP Viewed in Goal-Orientated and Subject-Orientated Perspectives Respectively

The present contribution does not go into the details of the long-lasting debate concerning the scope of the Community's competence in the field of common commercial policy but confines itself to a brief summary of the relevant contravening points of view supplemented by a more profound evaluation of the ECJ's approach towards the subject-matter.

To these ends, two different aspects potentially delimiting the scope of CCP shall be distinguished[17]: firstly, a goal-focused demarcation of this policy's confines (which objectives are covered?), and secondly a subject-orientated delimitation regarding the several policy instruments (which instruments are covered?)[18].

Both issues are likewise controversial and both aspects are likewise essential in order to ascertain if and to which extent Article 133 TEC constituted (or constitutes) an adequate legal basis for the imposition of economic sanctions. Although it appears convenient to structure the scope discussion in the suggested way, it shall be acknowledged that both aspects bear mutually conditional elements.

aa) The Goal-Orientated Perspective: "Objective" v. "Subjective" Approach

As regards the first aspect, the main arguments and contravening positions of the long-standing debate may be categorised as follows: An "objective" approach – traditionally advocated by the Commission - conceives CCP as covering all measures objectively

---

16 The distinction between «existence question», dealing with the question of attribution of powers to the Community, and «exclusivity question», evaluating the nature of acknowledged Community competence, has been suggested in the Introduction to *Dashwood/Hillion* (2000) V, in context with EC's external relations competence.

17 Which shall not be confused with the two different approaches within the goal-orientated scope, namely the "subjective" or "purposive" approach versus the "objective" or "instrumental" approach though, see below aa).

18 See e.g. *Vedder* (2001) paras 26 ff ("Gegenständlicher Geltungsbereich").

influencing trade, regardless of the ends they pursue. By contrast, a "subjective" or "purposive" concept – favoured by the Council and a multitude of Member States likewise – confines the scope of CCP to actions which are exclusively aimed at influencing the volume and pattern of trade[19].

Consequently, the latter theory repudiated the existence of an embargo competence under Article 133 EC Treaty (ex Article 113 TEEC) on grounds that such measures (exclusively) pursue foreign policy aims, whereas the instrumental approach conceived them as covered by the scope of CCP for they are affecting trade flows by making use of "classical" trade policy instruments (mainly restrictions on trade).

The Court had been called upon to deal with the question whether a measure could be excluded from the scope of CCP on the sole ground that it pursues objectives other than traditional aspects of foreign trade (in the case at issue: development policy objectives) already in its *Opinion 1/78 ("Natural Rubber")*[20]: It stressed the dynamic element inhering in a common commercial policy and maintained that it would no longer be possible to carry on any worthwhile common policy if the Community was not in a position to avail itself of more elaborate means with a view to furthering the development of international trade. Hence ex Article 113 EEC Treaty (Article 133 TEC) must not be interpreted in such a way as to restrict the CCP to the use of instruments intended to have an effect only on the traditional aspects of external trade. Implementation of CCP required a non-restrictive interpretation of that concept in order to avoid disturbances in intra-Community trade by reason of the disparities which would then exist in certain sectors of economic relations with non-member countries.[21]

In line with that reasoning the Court acknowledged in the *Generalized Tariff Preferences* case that the Treaty takes into account possible changes in the concept of international trade relations (such as the progressive strengthening of links between trade and development policy)[22].

---

19 On the diverging views of the Community institutions see e.g. their reasoning before the Court in Opinion 1/78, *International Agreement on Natural Rubber*, [1979] ECR 2871, paras 38 f.

20 Ibid.

21 Ibid., para 45.

22 Case C-45/86, *Commission* v *Council*, [1987] ECR 1493.

Regarding the specific linkage "trade policy measure – foreign policy goal", the two landmark judgments are *Werner* and *Leifer*[23]. Both concerned the export regime for so-called dual-use goods, i.e. goods that may serve for civil and military purposes likewise and the question whether national measures restricting the export of such goods were still permissible in view of the exclusive Community competence in the field of CCP[24].

The Court seemed to entirely come down on the "instrumentalist" side of the fence when it reiterated its reasoning in Opinion 1/78, namely that CCP demanded a non-restrictive interpretation[25], and stated moreover that "a measure (...), whose *effect* is to prevent or restrict the export of certain products, *cannot be treated as falling outside the scope of the common commercial policy on the ground that it has foreign policy and security objectives*"[26]. "The nature of those products cannot take them outside the scope of the common commercial policy"[27]. Rules restricting exports of dual-use goods from third countries fell therefore within the scope of ex Article 113 EEC Treaty (now Article 133 TEC) and since in this matter the Community enjoyed exclusive competence, a parallel competence of the Member States is excluded save where the Community grants them specific authorization[28].

These judgments may certainly be considered as the final acceptance of the instrumental approach in the Court's

---

23 Case C-70/94, *Werner*, [1995] ECR I-3189 and Case C-83/94, *Leifer*, [1995] ECR I-3231.

24 Already an earlier case, namely Case C-367/89, *Aimé Richard*, [1991] ECR I-4645, dealt with "goods described as strategic materials"; AG Jacobs maintained in his Opinion [1991] ECR I-4635, paras 15 to 29, that since the case concerned a restriction on exports to a third country, it fell within the scope of the Export Regulation (and thus within the scope of CCP). The Court, however, chose another path by considering the facts from a purely internal transit perspective and avoided thus to pronounce itself on the status of export controls in Community law. See in particular *Govaere/Eeckhout* (1992) 941 ff.

25 See Case C-70/94, *Werner*, [1995] ECR I-3189 and Case C-83/94, *Leifer*, [1995] ECR I-3231, para 9.

26 Case C-70/94, *Werner*, [1995] ECR I-3189, para 10; Italics added by the author.

27 Case C-83/94, *Leifer*, [1995] ECR I-3231, para 11.

28 Ibid, para 13.

jurisprudence. The significance of this judgment also for the kindred field of economic sanctions is plain. Economic sanctions and provisions governing trade with dual use goods are both trade restricting measures in pursuance of foreign policy goals[29]. The major difference lies in the situation-centred and punctuated nature of economic sanctions, usually directed against one specific target State with the purpose of changing the conduct of the latter, whereas the rules governing the export of "dual-use" goods are regularly of a more permanent, continuous nature, following more general (although foreign and security policy) objectives.

In proceedings concerning the lawfulness of a unilateral trade embargo imposed by Greece against the Federal Republic of Macedonia, the Advocate General again stressed that "the decisive element is not the purpose of the embargo but its effects", a view which can hardly be misconceived as concerns its preference for either of the two theories[30].

Not long after the *Werner* and *Leifer* judgments, the Court was referred to another case concerning the question whether commercial policy instruments could be lawfully embraced by the Community's competence as to CCP when pursuing foreign policy aims. In *Centro Com*[31], however, sanctions measures, namely those imposed against the Federal Republic of Yugoslavia, were at issue. The plaintiff, the Italian company Centro Com, was permitted to export consignments of pharmaceutical goods to the Republics of Serbia and Montenegro with the approval of the UN Sanctions Committee and the prior authorisation of the Italian authorities, in accordance with the relevant provisions of the EEC Sanctions Regulation providing for the possibility of exempting such transactions. Payments for these exports were to be made from an account held by the National Bank of Yugoslavia by a bank in the United Kingdom. The United Kingdom, however, adopted national

---

29 Occasionally the term «embargo» is also used for describing export control measures as to dual use goods.

30 Opinion of AG Jacobs in Case C-120/94, *Commission v. Greece*, [1996] ECR I-1514, para 42, delivered on 6 April 1995, thus only few weeks after his Opinion in the Werner and Leifer cases. The Court, did not adjudicate on that matter, since the case was removed from the register when Greece and Macedonia concluded a temporary agreement and Greece lifted the embargo: Order of the President of the Court of 19 March 1996, [1996] ECR I-1535.

31 Case C-124/95, *Centro-Com*, [1997] ECR I-80.

measures allowing payments for such exports to be made only if the exports took place form its own territory and were authorised by its own competent authorities. Relying on this national act, the Treasury thus refused to authorise the transfer of funds for the exports made by Centro Com. The question referred to the Court concerned the compatibility of the UK's national measures with Community law. The case raised several interesting issues, such as the question whether measures pursuing foreign policy aims are covered by the CCP, and the issue of the instrumental boundaries of such measures since payments are at issue. The judgment features some interesting statements on the relationship between measures of foreign and security policy, which will be subject of the next section of the present contribution. The Court maintained that it was indeed in the exercise of their national competence that the Member States had expressly decided to have recourse to a Community measure, namely a regulation based on ex Article 113 (now Article 133) TEC. Even if the national measures adopted were not measures of CCP, they had to respect the Community rules adopted under the CCP.

The Court's attitude towards the "finalistic" scope of CCP may be summarised as follows: Although its statements in this case were not as manifest and proclamatory as those in *Werner* and *Leifer*, it can nevertheless clearly be inferred from them that the Court regards economic sanctions as falling within the scope of CCP (*argumentum*: "the common commercial policy (...) *as implemented by* (the Sanctions Regulation)"[32]. Moreover, it referred to its reasoning in *Werner* by reiterating that "the Member States cannot treat national measures as falling outside the scope of CCP on the ground that they have foreign and security objectives"[33].
In a recent judgment regarding a claim for embargo damages, the Court of First Instance unreservedly maintained that the imposition of trade embargoes is a measure of CCP, and fell thus within the exclusive competence of the Community.[34]

It shall be marginally noted that the Maastricht Treaty was not yet applicable in all cases cited. However, from the cases *Werner* and *Leifer* onwards it is not completely unreasonable to consider

32 Case C-124/95, *Centro-Com*, [1997] I-80, para 53; Italics added by the author.
33 Ibid, para 26; Case C-70/94, *Werner*, [1995] ECR I-3189, para.
34 Case T-184/95, *Dorsch Consult*, [1998] ECR II-667, para 74.

that although the Maastricht Treaty was not yet in force at the material time of the cases and thus not directly applicable to them, the Court's findings were nevertheless inspired by the spirit of the new legal framework and the newly introduced provisions.

bb) The "Instrumental" Perspective Demarcating the Subject-Matters of Regulation

The second aspect of the scope discussion concerns the equally controversial issue of measures and instruments falling within the ambit of CCP.

It is established that the enumeration of topics in Article 133 TEC (e.g. changes in tariff rates, the conclusion of tariff and trade agreements, the achievement of uniformity in measures to protect trade) shall not be conceived as exhaustive[35].

The other areas that fall within Article 133 TEC were mainly unclear, in particular the question whether ex Article 113 EEC Treaty (Article 133 TEC) also embraced services, transport and transport services.

Some clarification as to this question could be inferred from Opinion 1/94, the Court's renowned seminal WTO Opinion, which eliminated to a certain extent the obscurities as to the provision's field of application. The Court held that the CCP embraces the whole field of trade in goods, but only to a limited extent trade in services (so-called "cross-frontier" services) and intellectual property[36].

The Treaty of Amsterdam[37] and – even more recently – the Treaty of Nice[38] introduced some innovations offering ground for a potential extension of the instrumental scope of CCP confined to the field of conventional measures though.[39]

The limited "instrumental scope" of ex Article 113 EEC Treaty (Article 133 TEC new) was likewise a major problem for the Community making recourse to this provision: Economic sanctions, and in particular those prescribed by the UN Security Council, frequently exceed these limits, for they also embrace restrictions on

---

35 See Opinion 1/78, *International Agreement on Natural Rubber*, [1979] ECR 2871, para 45.

36 See e.g. *Griller* (1995), 269; *Burnside* (2000) 152 f.

37 See Article 133 para 5 TEC.

38 See Article 133, amended para 5 and newly introduced Articles 6 and 7 TEC, Treaty of Nice, OJ C 80 of 10.3.2001.

39 On the new version of Article 133 TEC see *Vedder* (2001).

the exchange of services, transport services, financial services, air transport and capital.

Nevertheless, there are some embargo regulations adopted by the Community on the basis of ex Article 113 EEC Treaty, containing prohibitions on the provision of services, transport and transport services likewise[40]. In Opinion 1/94 (the „WTO-Opinion"), the Commission cited examples in support of its view that the transport services fell within the EC's competence in the field of CCP, an argument which was rejected by the Court on the basis that those precedents were not conclusive for export and import embargoes could not be effective without simultaneous suspension of transport services, which is in fact 'a necessary adjunct to the principal measure[41].

Also in case *Centro-Com* concerning payments, the Court – although pointing out that for the case at issue it was not essential whether payments are covered by the CCP or not[42] – apparently falls back on the "necessary-adjunct-method" when it describes the payments at issue as an "essential element of the export transaction".

b) Conclusions

It shall be submitted – in line with a purposive concept – that embargo measures are, irrespective of their manifest foreign policy goals, covered by the goal-defined scope of CCP, being limited as to its "instrumental" range though, which embraces measures regarding in particular services, transport, transport services, restrictions on capital movements, only up to a very limited extent, namely as "necessary adjuncts" ensuring the effectiveness of the principal measure.

2. The Exclusivity Question

On the basis of this finding, namely acknowledging a Community embargo competence under Article 133 EC Treaty (ex Article 113 EEC Treaty), the answer to the question about the nature of the Community powers in the field might appear plain, for

---

40 See *MacLeod/Hendry/Hyett* (1996), 353.

41 Opinion 1/94, *WTO*, [1994] ECR, I-5267, para 51.

42 Case C-124/95, *Centro-Com,* [1997] I-80, para 32: "(E)ven if such measures do not constitute measures of commercial policy, they may nevertheless be contrary to the common commercial policy, as implemented in the Community, if and insofar as they contravene Community legislation adopted in pursuance of that policy".

it is well established by the Court's case law that full responsibility for commercial policy had been transferred to the Community by former Article 113 EEC Treaty (now Article 133 TEC)[43], and that in view of this exclusive Community competence national measures are permissible only if authorized by the Community[44].

The Court reiterated these fundamental statements in its *Werner* and *Leifer* judgments and hence made sufficiently clear that the fact that matters of foreign and security policy are concerned may not affect the Community's exclusive powers as to common and commercial policy: "The specific subject-matter of commercial policy, which concerns trade with non-member countries and, according to (ex) Article 113 (Article 133), is based on the concept of a common commercial policy, requires that a Member State should not be able to restrict its scope by deciding freely, in the light of its own foreign and security requirements, whether a measure is covered by Article 113."[45]

Regrettably, the message is less plain in its *Centro Com* judgement. The paragraphs on the "relationship between measures of foreign and security policy and the common commercial policy", give the impression that the Court recognized a parallel competence of the Member States resulting from their "retained national competence in matters of foreign and security policy" when it states that it had been "indeed *in exercise of their national competence in matters of foreign and security policy* that the Member States expressly *decided to have recourse to a Community measure*". "Even where measures as those in issue in the main proceedings have been adopted *in the exercise of national competence in matters of foreign and security policy*, they must respect the Community rules adopted under the common commercial policy"[46]. This reasoning seems to grant the Member States the margin of discretion which has been expressly excluded in the *Werner* judgment as incompatible with the concept of CCP[47].

---

43 Opinion 1/75, *Local Cost Standard*, [1975] ECR 1355, at paras 1363 f

44 Case 41/76, *Donckerwolcke*, [1976] ECR 1921, para 32; Case 174/84, *Bulk Oil*, [1986] ECR 559, para 31.

45 Case C-70/94, *Werner*, [1995] ECR I-3189, para 11; Compare also AG Jacobs in Case C-120/94, *Commission v Greece*, [1996] ECR I-1513, paras 40 f.

46 Case C-124/95, *Centro-Com,* [1997] I-80, paras 28 f; Italics added by the author.

47 Case C-83/94, *Leifer*, [1995] ECR I-3231, para 13; see above at 331.

The above statements might be interpreted restrictively, insofar as the Court addressed the leeway the Member States enjoy by virtue of the Treaty's safeguard clauses, or, in the specific case, the derogation clause contained in the Export Regulation (Article 11), which also referred to public security reasons as ground for justification. However, in the relevant passages there is no indication that the Court in fact intended such a restrictive interpretation and did not consider a general parallel national competence.

A similar concept of parallelism has been suggested by *Govaere/Eeckhout* in context with strategic export controls after the *Aimé Richardt* judgment[48]. For this field, however, the Court had made it sufficiently clear in the *Werner* and *Leifer* cases that national acting is excluded because of Community's exclusive competence.

There is no reasonable ground why this should be otherwise in the case of economic sanctions. The fact that economic sanctions adopted under ex Article 113 EEC Treaty (Article 133 EC Treaty) have in practice been regularly subject to a prior (but not binding) decision within the EPC cadre may not change the system of competencies of the Treaty. A corresponding custom law principle has not been established[49].

Consequently it shall be submitted that the Community's embargo competence under Article 133 EC Treaty (ex Article 113 EEC Treaty) is of unreservedly exclusive nature[50]. Member States may rely on foreign and security prerogatives only within the bounds set by the Community law order, e.g. by invoking the safeguard clauses of the Treaty or if authorised by the

---

48 *Govaere/Eeckhout* (1992); another theory which aims to explain the alleged coexistence of competences is the "*acte-mixte doctrine*", taking as a model the conclusion of so-called "mixed agreements", i.e. international agreements on subject-matters which lie partly within the (exclusive) comptence of the Community, partly within the Member States' competence sphere ("shared comptence") and to which both, Community and Member States are parties; see in particular *Mestmäcker/Engel* (1991).

49 See *Ress* (2000), 138 f with further references.

50 Opinion of AG Jacobs in Case C-124/95, *Centro-Com*; [1997] ECR I-81; Case T-184/95, *Dorsch Consult,* [1998] ECR II-667.

Community[51]. This at first glance seemingly narrow leeway for national action, turns out to provide a rather remarkable room for manoeuvre, taking into account, first, the broad concept of "security" ultimately inspiring the interpretation of security exemptions, considering an inclusion of the security of the international community in general[52], and second, the jurisprudence's cautious approach as to issues involving a foreign and security policy estimation[53].

III. Economic Sanctions within the European Union's Legal Framework

A. Introductory Remarks

The pillar structure of the European Union as introduced by the Treaty of Maastricht has from the moment of its establishment attracted the attention of political and legal doctrine. The general tenor has undergone an evolution from an initial general outcry, in particular, on the part of the integrationists[54], to a sort of general acceptance of a structure which is not likely to be completely abandoned in foreseeable future. While fundamental maintenance of the structure is predictable for a while, slight and silent changes in its substance are, however, attestable with a view to changes introduced or envisaged by the Amsterdam and Nice Treaty

---

[51] In particular Article 11 "Export Regulation", authorising measures taken by the Member States on the ground of public security, See Cases C-70/94, *Werner*, [1995] ECR I-3189 and C-83/94, *Leifer*, [1995] ECR I-3231, and also Case C-124/95, *Centro-Com,* [1997] I-80.

[52] See Case C-70/94, *Werner*, [1995] ECR I-3189, paras 26 and 27, and Case C-83/94, *Leifer*, [1995] ECR I-3231, paras 27 and 28, where the Court noted that 'it is becoming increasingly less possible to look at the security of a State in isolation, since it is closely linked to the security of the international community at large, and of its various components. So, the risk of a serious disturbance to foreign relations or to peaceful coexistence of nations may affect the security of a Member State' citing AG Jacobs who maintained that "the notion of security should be understood as extending to the security of the international community in general".

[53] Opinion of AG Jacobs in Cases C-70/94, *Werner,* and C-83/94, *Leifer*, para 42 and 45; Opinion of AG Jacobs in Commission v. Greece, [1996] ECR I-1513, para 67.

[54] See e.g. *Curtin* (1993) 17 – 69.

respectively, namely an increasing approximation of structures between the two predominantly intergovernmentally organised pillars and the supranational Community pillar, by way of gradually introducing small doses of the méthode communautaire (e.g. qualified-majority voting, jurisdiction of the Court) to the two Union pillars[55]. Another symptom of "lingering communitarisation" is the shift of powers from the intergovernmental pillars to the Community, as it was the case when a multitude of former third pillar matters have been inserted into the first pillar by the Treaty of Amsterdam.

These welcome developments shall not, however, obscure the fact that there are significant differences in the functioning of the different pillars, and e.g. the separation of external affairs management of the European Union persists, with all ensuing problems, be it on the internal (e.g. interinstitutional), be it on the external level (representation) are far from being resolved.

B. The Second Pillar – A Common Foreign and Security Policy Being Out of Common?

Due to the predominantly intergovernmental nature of the second Union pillar the CFSP lacks - notwithstanding its denomination - the essential elements which are characteristic for formulation of the common policies within the Community pillar (CCP, CAP,...). Apparently within the Union's framework some policies are more common than others.

For the purposes of this survey it is essential to ascertain the author of acts adopted within the non-Community-pillars, by asking whether the latter constitute mere coordination for a for the Member States' national policies or is it the European Union defining e.g. its genuine foreign and security policy within the second pillar. The latter assumption presupposes that the European Union had legal personality - another hotly debated question, which had been initially categorically denied, but is now – in particular in view of the amendments made by the Nice draft Treaty[56] – fundamentally acknowledged by doctrine[57].

---

[55] See *Griller/Droutsas/Falkner/Forgó/Nentwich* (2000) 59 f; *De Witte* (1998) 56.

[56] Article 24 TEU; See, moreover, the Agreement concluded between the European Union and the Federal Republic of Yugoslavia (FRY) on the activities of the European Union Monitoring Mission (EUMM) in the

Although Article 1 TEU, when addressing the non-Community pillars, merely speaks of "policies and forms of cooperation", Article 11 TEU stipulates that it is "the Union" that "shall define and implement a common foreign and security policy"[58]. Without going into the depth of this controversy, it is submitted here that it is indeed the European Union as such which defines its own foreign and security policy.

This means, however, for the field of economic sanctions, that the Community is confronted with a new combatant, which might claim prerogatives as to the definition of a common foreign and security policy.

C. The Scope of CFSP, the Concept of Consistency, the Acquis Communautaire *and Other Inter"pillar"ities*

Article 11(1) TEU, first article of Title V TEU governing the CFSP, provides that "(t)he Union shall define and implement a common foreign and security policy covering all areas of foreign policy"[59]. The wording gives the impression of a broad-ranging, if-not-to-say overarching scope of the Union's common foreign and security policy. Potential limits as to the Union's powers may, however, arise from the frequently addressed dualism of the Union's external relations competencies. In other terms this concerns the question whether the Union may globally act also in areas which come within the province of the first pillar[60] ("Community criterion"[61]). The enumeration of objectives in Article 11 TEC possibly serves as point of reference for a qualification and delimitation of the CFSP's scope, but it does not, however, settle the question whether economic aspects (for which the instruments of action must be found in the EC Treaties) are covered.

FRY on the basis of Article 24 TEU, Council Decision 2001/352/CFSP published in OJ 2001 L 125, 1.

57 See *Weidel* in this volume at 38ff with further references.

58 Version as amended by the Amsterdam Treaty; Compare, however, its predecessor, former Article J.1: "The Union *and its Member States* shall define and implement a common foreign and security policy, (...)"; Italics added by the author.

59 Italics added by the author.

60 Possible overlaps with the third Union pillar will not considered here, although being likewise thinkable; see *Neuwahl* (1994) 233.

61 *Neuwahl* (1994) 231; *Timmermans* (1996) 62.

In my view, the answer to that question is a qualified yes. It is neither possible nor desirable to completely eliminate subject-matters bearing first pillar features from the second pillar's panoply. Being a major economic force in the global play it is essential for the functioning and effectiveness of the EU's CFSP to bring that powers at stake. Or, as the Council once phrased it: CFSP cannot be reduced to the field of "pure politics"[62]. Considerations with "Community flavour" cannot and shall not be entirely subtracted from the Union's powers under Title V TEU.

Nonetheless, the serious, frequently addressed and occasionally manifested risk of what is variably called "CFSP overflow"[63], repatriation of Community power under the guise of transfer of Community policies to the intergovernmental pillars[64], or intergovernmentalism invading the Community sphere[65] and encroaching on Community competence needs to be acknowledged. The autonomous role of the Community as to the economic external relations and the state of integration reached in this field needs to be respected.

The drafters of the Union Treaty, and, in particular, those advocating the integrationist way, were apparently aware of the risks inhering the system they established and the difficulties arising from the dualism of the EU external relations, since they introduced a number of provisions, with the objective of ensuring consistency and coherence in the Union's external activity and the still superior objective of preserving the state of integration already reached.

Accordingly, Article 3 TEU provides for that consistency and continuity shall be ensured, in particular, the consistency of the Union's external activities as a whole in the context of its external relations, "while respecting and building upon the *acquis communautaire*".

Article 2, fifth indent, declares the maintenance and upgrading of *the acquis communautaire* to one of its basic objectives, and finally Article 47 TEU stipulates that nothing in this Treaty (safe

---

62 Legal Note from the Council's legal service, cited in "EUROPE" No 6351 of 5. 11.1994, 4.

63 Legal Note from the European Commission on the Common Position regarding Rwanda, cited in "EUROPE" No 6351 of 5.11.1994, 4.

64 *Obradovic* (1997) 68.

65 *Dehousse* (1994) 11 f.

the provisions amending the Community Treaties and the final provisions of the Union Treaty) shall affect the Community Treaties. The Court – enjoying only very limited powers outside the Community pillar - is by virtue of Article 46 TEU competent to scrutinise the respect of Article 47 TEU[66]. The consistency commitment does not form part of the final provisions, however, and thus (as moreover indicated in Article 3 TEU) it does not entail any commitments on the Community which would in effect encroach on the autonomous exercise of its competencies conferred upon it by the Community Treaty[67].

Hence it shall be submitted that the Community is not bound by decisions taken within the second pillar, for accepting such a binding effect would be incompatible with the provision of Article 47 TEU[68].

The interrelationship between the first in second pillar is marked by a general preference to the EC pillar, involving a denial of free political choice between pillars, wherever the EC pillar provides for an adequate legal basis for action[69] and eventually by an ensuing fundamental supremacy of Community law over Union law[70]. As already pointed out, any unauthorised intrusion of Union law into the Community sphere can be made subject of the Court's scrutiny.

It appears thus that the Community and its competencies are sufficiently shielded against CFSP invasion by the Union legal order. In practice, however, the Community cocoon is not always sufficiently respected[71].

---

66 See again Case C-170/96, *"Airport Transit Visa"*, [1998] ECR I-2763.

67 See, however, *Pechstein* (1995) 247 ff, who maintains that Article 47 TEU does also refer to implicit amendments of the EC Treaty, such as, in particular, the concept of consistency, which would otherwise lack effectiveness.

68 The decisions may have a binding effect on the Member States in international law though; See *Stein* (1995) 69; Maastricht Decision of the German Bundesverfassungsgericht, paras 17 ff, published in CMLRev. 1994, 57 ff.

69 *Weatherhill* (1998), 153-178.

70 See *Griller* (1999) 56 ff.

71 For examples see in particular, *Timmermans* (1996) 61 ff.

D. Article 301 TEU – Bridge Over Troubled Waters of CFSP or Cuckoo's Egg within the Community Nest?

What has been observed in a general context in the last chapter is particularly true for the specific case of economic sanctions: Bearing in mind their importance as genuine foreign policy instruments a common foreign and security policy not having them at its disposal would appear as an (even more) toothless tiger. On the other hand, as it cannot be ignored that they operate by means of CCP, and thus implementation comes within the province of the first pillar.

Even though it was submitted in the last section that the European Union acting under Title V TEU may – in very restricted terms though - also address matters fundamentally falling within the realms of the Community pillars, it was also stressed that several provisions of the Union Treaty prevent the Community from being bound by such acts. Whether and how such decisions are effectuated within the first pillar, depended (at least hypothetically) on the good will of the institutions acting within the Community framework, in particular on the Commission to submit a corresponding proposal.

As concerns the imposition of economic sanctions, however, the Treaty on European Union itself precluded this consequence by establishing an express link between the two pillars for the specific case of economic sanctions, by introducing Article 301 (ex Article 228 a) into the Community legal order. The provision reads as follows:

> "Where it is provided, in a common position or in a joint action adopted according to the provisions of the Treaty on European Union relating to the common foreign and security policy, for an action by the Community to interrupt or to reduce, in part or completely, economic relations with one or more third countries, the Council shall take the necessary urgent measures. The Council shall act by a qualified majority on a proposal from the Commission."

By amending the EC Treaty, the Treaty on European Union established an express exemption to the general rule that Union law may not have any binding effect for the institutions acting under the first pillar: In this special case, they are, moreover, obliged, by virtue of Community law, to implement the second pillar act, i.e. a common position or joint action. With Article 301 TEC, the concept of consistency had been enshrined in the Community legal order, and thus exceptionally commits within the limited scope of that provision the Community to the observance of Union law[72].

This does not mean, however, that this exceptional possibility of a CFSP act to be determinative for Community action is unconfined. The Union acting within the second pillar is nonetheless committed to the general requirement of consistency and accordingly it shall take into account existing Community legislation when considering the adoption of embargo measures and, moreover, respect the Community's competence as to external commercial policy. Accordingly, it shall confine itself to the adoption of the political decision on principle that and to which extent the economic relations with a third country shall be interrupted or reduced for reasons pertaining to the ambit of foreign policy, whereas the Community's primary task is to determine how this interruption and reduction of economic relations shall take place by concretising the "necessary and urgent" commercial policy measures which shall be taken to achieve these ends. Accordingly the Commission will be regularly obliged to submit a proposal[73] but still disposes of sufficient margin of manoeuvre to consider Community concerns.

Some authors, however, conceive economic sanctions taken under Article 301 as pure foreign policy measures[74]. Practical usage of this Article, reducing the Community part of the procedure to a pure implementation function, has indeed been criticised by the Commission[75] which considered its role degraded to a implementing body of second pillar decisions.

---

72 See *Garçon* (1997) 11 ff: "gemeinschaftliche Verankerung des Gebotes horizontaler Kohärenz".

73 See e.g. *Gilsdorf/Kuijper* (1997) Art 228 A, para 4, who maintain that only in an "extreme case" (e.g. a change of circumstances) the Commission shall be permitted to refrain from submitting a proposal.

74 See *Lasok* (1998) 436; *Fouwels* (1997) 292, 297 and 300, who even refers to economic sanctions as third policy instrument which figures – together with common positions and joint actions – "legally within the remit of CFSP"; *Karagiannis* (1999) 375, who describes Article 301 as "le bras séculier de la PESC" and speaks of a "communautarisation partielle de la PESC" introduced by Article 301 TEC.

75 See European Commission, Rapport sur le Fonctionnement du Traité sur l'Union Europeenne (1995), para 132: «L'adoption de certaines positions communes a en effet conditionné, par le biais de l'unanimité

1. The Scope and Nature of Article 301 EC Treaty: Substantial of Procedural Attribution of Powers?[76]

Apart from establishing an express link between first and second pillar and thus introducing the concept of consistency to the Community legal order the new provision followed a further motive, namely the one of creating a legal basis for comprehensive economic sanctions, i.e. sanctions which exceed the Community's powers as regards CCP. This is of particular relevance to the implementation of UN Security Council Resolutions which frequently encompass prohibitions on the provision of services, transport, transport services, financial services, etc. As considered in the first part of this survey, prior to the TEU these fields appeared to be covered by Community measures, only if and insofar as they were ancillary to measures falling within the scope of CCP[77]. Viewed from this angle, the broad wording Article 301 TEC seems to extend the Community's embargo power compared to the prior situation[78]. Article 301 TEC is not a genuine empowering provision, however, for it does not enable the Community to act in fields which do not already fall within the Community's competence sphere, albeit only in the internal sphere[79]. The scope of the embargo competence is thus confined to fields in which the Community legislator is authorised to act, but exists independently of the enactment of internal legislation in this field by virtue of Article 301 TEC. The Community thus acquired express horizontal, situational external competence without, however, gaining new substantial competencies.

---

requise, le contenu des sanctions. (...). Ainsi, la contagion du processus intergouvernemental propre à la cooperation politique qui s'était manifestée par le passé s'est poursuivie, 'les organes de la politique étrangère et de sécurité commune tendant à devenir le véritable contre de gravité de la mise en œuvre des nouvelles dispositions.»

76 Distinction made by *Dashwood* (2000) 121.

77 See above at 335.

78 Irrespective of the potential possibility to base embargo measures exceeding the scope of CCP on ex Article 235 (now Article 308) TEC; See Council Regulation (EEC) No. 3541/92 (OJ 1992 L 361, 1) prohibiting the satisfying of Iraqi claims with regard to contracts and transactions (...), which is based on ex Article 235 EEC Treaty.

79 *Karagiannis* (1999) 374.

Therefore, and because of its specific "cross pillar" function, it cannot be simply qualified as procedural norm either, although a systematic interpretation could possibly suggest such an understanding[80], being inserted directly after the prototype of a non-substantial provision, Article 300 TEC (former Article 228 TEC)[81].

2. The Exclusivity Question

In accordance with what has been just said about its specific nature, Article 301 TEC respects the repartition of powers between the Community and the Member States in the subject-matters concerned[82]. That means that "classical" trade sanctions, falling within the substantive realm of CCP, are likewise exclusive, whereas e.g. in the field of service and transport (provided that there are no exclusive implied external powers) the embargo power is a concurrent one[83]. For efficiency reasons one might also consider a general exclusive embargo competence.

Within the Union's legal framework, the exclusivity question has assumed dichotomy: it is not confined to the interplay between the powers of the Community and the Member States, but moreover it concerns the relationship between Community action and the European Union acting under Title V TEU.

As regards the latter, it needs to be recalled what has been submitted above, namely that the powers of the Community do not in principle preclude the Union (acting under Title V TEU) from considering economic aspects, for which the instruments are found within the first pillar. Article 301 TEC supports that view: Assuming that the European Union acting within the second pillar were not allowed to consider subject matters coming within the first pillar's province at all, would not it be the very Article 301 TEC

80 See *Schmitter* (1995) 726 ff. Recent doctrine almost unanimously conceives Article 301 TEC as substantial norm without further considering that issue though.

81 It shall be noted, however, that sanctions regulations are regularly based on the sole Article 301 TEC (and Article 60 TEC respectively) without citing any further legal bases.

82 *Karagiannis* (1999) 375.

83 Consequently the principle of subsidiarity applies. See *Karagiannis* (1999) 375 ff (who conceives Article 301 TEC as *lex specialis* in relation to Article 5/2 TEC, wherever urgency of action is given). Generally, a preference for Community action will be given in respect of the objective of the measures and their particular need of effective and rapid enforcement.

which establishes an exemption to that rule and thus created a CFSP competence? Article 301 TEC, however, shall not be construed as a provision conferring powers on the Union acting within the CFSP cadre.

The parallel power is subject to a twofold restriction though: first, the concept of consistency obliges the institutions acting within the CFSP pillar to pay sufficient regard to action made or to be made within the Community pillar, and second, several Treaty provisions are aimed at safeguarding the *acquis communautaire*, at hence the independence of the institutions acting within the first pillar.

Another and final question arising from the triangle relationship between Community, Member States and Union, is whether the Member States – in the limited fields where they are allowed to impose national embargo measures (e.g. an arms embargo by virtue of Article 296 TEC) – are obliged to consult the CFSP cadre. This question concerns, in effect, still another exclusivity question, namely the exclusivity of the CFSP pillar as to foreign and security issues.

Although exclusivity is considered with regard to single procedures governed by Union law[84], the Member States' foreign policy activities demonstrate, however, that a general exclusiveness of the Union's legal framework in general, and of Title V governing the CFSP in particular, cannot be assumed. Some EU Member States (in particular the Benelux countries) criticised the fact that some EU members were acting outside the Union's framework, and questioned the compatibility of such acting with the Union Treaty[85], when in context with the Bosnian war a coalition of States, the so-called "Contact Group", made up of representatives of the USA, Russia, the UK, Germany and France issued a number of statements and recommendations on the Balkans situation including agreements on embargo measures[86]. By introducing the possibility

---

84 See *Schorkopf* (2001) para 31, who maintains that Article 7 TEU in the version of the Nice Treaty, stipulates exclusive procedural rules in case of a serious breach by a Member State of principles mentioned in Article 6(1) TEU (i.e. principles of liberty, democracy, respect for human rights and fundamental freedoms, and the rule of law) occurs.

85 See "EUROPE" No 7210 of 29 April 1998, 3.

86 See e.g. Contact Group Statement on Kosovo of 9 March 1998, London; Contact Group Statement on Kosovo of 31 March 1998, Bonn; Contact Group Statement of 29 April 1998, Rome.

of enhanced cooperation in the field of CFSP, the Treaty of Nice revives the question of compatibility of such *ad hoc* arrangements with the Treaty's provisions governing the CFSP: the fact that it now expressly regulates the conditions required for the establishment of enhanced cooperation entails that any other form of cooperation of a smaller group of countries is not permissible anymore[87]. Even though the possibilities to proceed by enhanced cooperation are very limited (namely to the implementation of a joint action or a common position), this does not entail that Member States are free to set up coalitions in any other case. Such an understanding would render the provisions almost idle. The aim of the provisions was to establish a legal framework for enhanced cooperation in matters of foreign and security policy which preserves the rights of the non-participating countries. An exclusivity of the provisions concerning enhanced cooperation as to matters of foreign and security policy shall thus be considered (just as some do for the Article 7 TEU procedure[88]).

For CFSP matters in general, it shall be noted that Article 16 TEU stipulates an obligation for the Member States to "inform and consult one another within the Council on any matter of foreign and security policy *of general interest* in order to ensure that the Union's influence is exerted as effectively as possible by means of concerted and convergent action."[89] Regardless of the question, which matters are deemed to be of general interest within the meaning of the cited article and the question, how the obligation enshrined therein can be enforced, it shall be noted that the leeway of action given to the Member States on the basis Article 296 and 297 TEC cannot be curtailed by that provision[90]. The coordination procedure prescribed by Article 297 TEC (to prevent the functioning of the common market from being affected) follows aims different from those of concerted and convergent action within the cadre of the second pillar, and shall thus not be substituted by or merged with the latter.

87 Compare *Regelsberger* (2002) 227-232.
88 See above at 347.
89 Italics added by the author.
90 Compare again Article 47 TEU.

3. The Speciality Question – Article 301 EC Treaty and its Relation to other Treaty Provisions

a) Article 133 EC Treaty: Autonomous Community Trade Embargoes

As submitted above, Article 301 TEC provides for concerted and convergent action within the Union by tying action under Title V TEU with a Community instrument in a specific field, thus introducing an exceptional Community law obligation for the latter to respect and moreover implement the former. In certain areas, it infers express external competencies, although limited to the specified field of economic sanctions and conditional on the existence of a common position or joint action adopted under the provisions of Title V TEU, from existing internal powers

The speciality of Article 301 TEC is characterised by and confined to its specific cross pillar dimension. In other words, it is special only insofar as a common position or joint action taken within the second pillar, being the indispensable prerequisite for its applicability, is available.

Wherever there is no such CFSP initiative, however, the Community is in principle free to act on its own initiative under the powers conferred on it. Article 301 TEC shall not be interpreted as meaning that it was intended to abolish these powers.

It is questionable whether there is an obligation of the Commission to initiate action within the second pillar[91], which prevents it from directly submitting a proposal for Community action under Article 133 TEC. Such an obligation could potentially arise from Article 3 TEU, making the Commission (together with the Council) responsible for ensuring consistency of the Union's external action. Again it must be submitted, however, that Article 47 TEU, which may not be overruled by Article 3 TEU, is opposed to an interpretation restricting the Commission's rights under the Community Treaty and Article 301 TEC cannot be read as meaning that the Commission meets an obligation to consult the CFSP cadre, nor does unsuccessful initiative within the second pillar preclude Community action. Otherwise those Member States being in favour of sanctions measures (e.g. all of them save the dissenting one) would (if the conditions which permit national action under Article

[91] Article 22 (1) TEU.

297 TEC are not fulfilled) not be allowed to act on the national level where Community embargo competence is exclusive. The Community, however, would be paralysed too.

The existence of a Community embargo adopted on the basis of Article 133 TEC does in principle not prevent the Union from dealing with the same subject-matter later on. Article 301 TEC moreover obliges the Community to adjust its former measures in accordance with the decisions taken in the framework of CFSP.

b) Article 60 EC Treaty: Financial Sanctions

Notwithstanding the broad horizontal scope of Article 301 TEC, the Maastricht Treaty introduced by means of Article 60 (ex Article 73 g) a specific legal basis for the taking of financial sanctions which provides for that in the cases envisaged in Article 301 and according to the same procedure "necessary urgent measures on the movements of capital and on payments" may be taken. As already mentioned above, the Community's embargo power under ex Article 113 (now Article 133) TEC was in principle conceived as not embracing the movement of capital or payments.

Financial sanctions have played an extremely important role in recent sanctions policy for they are central piece of a targeted sanctions strategy[92]. Because of the high speed with which financial assets can be transferred, effective financial sanctions require rapid action.

In contrast to the wording in Article 301 TEC ("the Council (...) *shall* take the necessary urgent measures"), Article 60 uses the word "may" in this context, which could be interpreted as conceding the Council a certain margin of manoeuvre as to the implementation of the CFSP decision.

Unlike Article 301 TEC, the specific provision for financial embargoes expressly regulates the repartition of powers between Community and Member States: Paragraph 2 provides that without prejudice to Article 297 TEC and as long as the Council has not taken measures pursuant to paragraph 1, a Member State may take unilateral measures for serious political reasons and on grounds of urgency. In such a case the Commission and the other Member States shall be informed at the latest by the date on which the measures enter into force. The Council, acting by a qualified majority on a Commission's proposal, may decide that the Member

---

92 *Cortright/ Lopez* (2000) 240 ff.

State concerned has to amend or abolish the measures, the European Parliament shall be informed of that decision.

It is remarkable in this context that, by governing the limited possibilities where Member States shall be allowed to act on the national level, the Treaty gives an express statement on the nature of Community competence in the field.

c) Article 300 para 2 EC Treaty: Suspension of Agreements as Economic Sanctions

Economic sanctions with third countries particularly involve the suspension or termination of existing trade agreements with such countries.

The suspension of an agreement will usually be the first reaction to a third country's "misbehaviour" [93]. Regularly such a suspension or termination will be a precondition for the taking of further sanctions, such as e.g. a full trade embargo, which would otherwise contravene with the Community's obligations under the trade agreement.[94]

Such measures seem to be covered by the scope of Article 301 TEC since they will usually entail a reduction of economic relations with a third country.

However, another Treaty provision – Article 300 para 2 in the Amsterdam version – governs the procedure to suspend the application of agreements in general, irrespective of the grounds and objectives underlying its suspension.

---

93 In context with the Yugoslav crisis: Decision 91/586/ECSC/EEC, OJ 1991 L 315, 47; Council Regulation (EEC) No 3300/91 and Council Decision 91/601/EEC of 25 November 1991 (OJ No L 325 of 27 November 1991, 23); "EUROPE" of 9 November 1991: immediate suspension and later termination of the Cooperation Agreement with Yugoslavia

94 See, however, Council Regulation (EEC) No 1608/93 of 24 June 1993 (OJ L 155 of 26 June 1993, 2), introducing an embargo concerning certain trade between the European Economic Community and Haiti: The Community did not suspend the application of the ACP-EEC Convention, but merely considered in the preamble of the Regulation that "(w)hereas the Security Council has (...) decided that (the) restriction shall apply notwithstanding the existence of any rights or obligation conferred or imposed by any international agreement or any contract (...), and therefore the fourth ACP-EEC Convention, to which the Community and Haiti are parties, does not pose an obstacle to the implementation of the said Security Council decision."

During the last decade the European Community usually included a so-called "human rights clauses" in agreements it concluded with third countries. The insertion of such a clause enables the Community to unilaterally suspend the application of the agreements, should human rights and democratic principles be violated by the other party. In absence of such a clause suspension is possible only within the narrow limits provided for by the international law of the Treaties (by e.g. invoking the *clausula rebus sic stantibus*[95]).

Article 302 para 2 TEC viewed in relation to Article 301 TEC provides for the more specific procedural provision regarding the suspension of trade agreements. Following the logic of the *actus contrarius* concept, regarding the suspension of a treaty as the reverse of its conclusion, suspension of an agreement shall be possible to the extent the Community was entitled to its conclusion. In other words: if the Community is authorised to include a human rights clause – an issue which is, however, not completely beyond question[96] – it shall not be restricted in relying on it. The suspension of a Treaty by one party as an reaction to its breach by the other party does not necessarily exercise a coercive or even punitive function, but of corrective nature, insofar as it re-establishes the equilibrium between the Treaty partners[97].

The suspension of trade agreements as an economic sanction, following a corrective aim, namely a change of conduct on the part of the target State, can consequently take place without any CFSP involvement. It can, however, be subject of a CFSP "umbrella" act.[98] As noted at the outset, moreover, further economic sanctions would possibly be in breach of existing trade embargoes, wherefore the prior suspension is necessary for their imposition. The suspension of trade agreements falls within the ambit of "necessary urgent measures restricting trade with third countries" by virtue of Article 301 TEC.

---

95 Compare Case C-162/96, *Racke,* [1998] ECR I-3655.

96 See *Fierro* (2001) 41 ff; *Riedel/Will* (1999) 723 ff.

97 See *Sicilianos* (1993) 341 ff. It is questionable, however, to which extent such an equilibrium existed at the time of the conclusion of the agreement.

98 See *Riedel/ Will* (1999) 751, who suggest to draw up a general human rights report on all countries within the framework of CFSP, which should cover both, measures taken by the EC as well as such within the CFSP.

Accordingly, wherever the suspension of a Treaty is subject to a common position or a joint action, a combined application of the two provisions is suggested: On the one hand, the (stricter) procedural requirements of Article 300 para 2 shall be met, i.e. unanimity-voting by the Council, where unanimity is required because of the substantial legal basis underlying the agreement or the provision of the agreement to be suspended, and, furthermore, the involvement of the European Parliament, which shall be immediately and fully informed of such a decision. By stipulating a mere right to information the necessities of urgency are sufficiently merited. On the other hand, the exceptional predominance of Union law over Community law by virtue of Article 301 TEC, commits the institutions acting within the first pillar's framework to the suspension of the agreement being a necessary urgent measure within the meaning of that provision.

As regards the suspension of so-called mixed agreements, the participation of the Member States is necessary. A CFSP act envisaging suspension imposes a corresponding obligation under international law.

E. Overcoming Dualism – The Concept of a Single Sanctions Act

It is doubtful whether the present sanction practice is a practicable way of external relations dualism management within the European Union. The somehow cumbersome procedure is of enhanced problematic bearing in mind the necessities of urgency inhering the measure: Two different Council instruments following different procedural rules are needed, likewise two initiative acts are requested.

In order to facilitate the imposition of embargo measures the idea of a single sanctions act combining a CFSP instrument (i.e. joint action or common position) with the Community measure might appear seductive. Such an integrated approach presupposes the unity of the EU's legal system as advocated by the exponents of a unitarist EU model[99]. It is doubtful whether the imposition of such hybrid acts is feasible within the European Union's legal system[100]. Considerable difficulties, in particular as regards the justiciability of such measures, could arise.

---

[99] *BogdandyNettesheim* (1996) 267 ff.

[100] *Timmermans* (1999) 69, who dissuades from applying an integrated approach: "(I)t is difficult to unite what the Treaty and its what the Treaty and its authors so clearly wished to separate".

Some authors, however, advocate the possibility of a single initiative act, i.e. a Commission proposal of the Community regulation submitted before the adoption of a CFSP instrument in order to avoid the time lag caused by a Commission proposal submitted between the two Council decisions[101].

IV. Final Remarks

The present EU sanctions procedure is an undesirable but nonetheless inevitable result or side-effect of the dualism in the Union's external activities.

While Article 301 TEC may be an adequate means of dualism management, it is, at any rate, not a perfect solution. Many of the problems are caused by the Union's pillar structure and the separation of external activities and are thus likely to exist as long as this structure is retained. Irrespective of gradual integration progresses gained in the field of foreign and security policies, it is still arguable whether and to which extent the integration process will proceed in the 'high-politics' areas[102].

Eventually, it shall be noted that political realities do not always correspond with legal potentialities. This is particularly true in policy areas as sensitive as the one at issue.

---

[101] *Schneider* (1996) para 9; *Osteneck* (2000) para 1; See the termination of the economic sanctions against Haiti: Proposal for a Council Regulation COM/94/433final of 12 October 1994, based on Article 228 a (now Article 301) TEC and on Common Position „94/.../CFSP", forwarded on 13 October 1994 to the Council. The Common Position 94/681/CFSP, however, was adopted only on 14 October 1994 (Council Decision concerning the Common Position defined on the basis of Article J.2 TEU regarding the termination of the reduction of economic relation with Haiti; OJ 1994 L 271, 3), and implemented on the basis of the above mentioned Commission proposal by Council Regulation (EC) 2543/94 of 19 October 1994 (OJ1994 L 271, 1).

[102] See *Falke* (2000) 139 f.

Bibliography

Bogdandy, A./Nettesheim, M. (1996), Ex Pluribus Unum: Fusion of the European Communities into the European Union, ELJ 1996, 267-289.

Burnside, A., (2000) The Scope of the Common Commercial Policy Post Opinion 1/94: Clouds and Silver linings, in: *Dashwood, A./Hillion, C.* (eds.), The General Law of E.C. External Relations, London 2000, 152-159.

Cortright, D./Lopez, G. A. (2000), The Sanctions Decade. Assessing UN strategies in the 1990s, Boulder et al. 2000.

Curtin, D. (1993), The Constitutional Structure of the Union: A Europe of Bits and Pieces, CMLRev 1993, 17-69.

Dashwood, A. (2000), The Attribution of External Relations Competence, in: *Dashwood, A./Hillion, C.* (eds.), The General Law of E.C. External Relations, London 2000, 115-138.

Dashwood, A./Hillion, C. (eds), The General Law of E.C. External Relations, London 2000.

De Witte, B. (1998), The Pillar Structure and the Nature of the European Union: Greek Temple or French Gothic Cathetral?' in: *Heukels, T./Blokker, N./Brus, M* (eds.), The European Union after Amsterdam. A Legal Analysis, The Hague 1998, 51-68.

Dehousse, R..(1994), From Community to Union, in: *Dehousse, R.* (ed), Europe after Maastricht. An Ever Closer Union?, München 1994, 5-15.

Falke, A. (2000), The EU-US Conflict over Sanctions Policy: Confronting the Hegemon, EFARev. 2000, 139-163.

Fierro, E. (2001), Legal Basis and Scope of the Human Rights Clauses in EC Bilateral Agreements: Any Room for Positive Interpretation? ELJ 2001, 41-68.

Fouwels, M. (1997), The European Union's Common Foreign and Security Policy and Human Rights, NQHR Vol. 15/3 (1997), 291-324.

Garçon, G. (1997), Handelsembargen der Europäischen Union auf dem Gebiet des Warenverkehrs gegenüber Drittstaaten, Baden-Baden 1997.

Gilsdorf, P./Kuijper P. J. (1997), Article 228A, in: von der *Groeben, H./Thiesing, J./Ehlermann, C.D.* (eds.), Kommentar zum EU/EG-Vertrag, 5th edition, Baden-Baden: 1997.

Govaere, I./Eeckhout, P. (1992), On Dual Use Goods and Dualistic Case Law: The Aimé Richardt Judgement on Export Controls, CMLRev. 1992, 941-965.

Griller, S. (1995), The Common Commercial Policy Instruments after the Uruguay Round – with some Implications for Austria, in: *Breuss, F.* (ed.), The World Economy after the Uruguay Round, Vienna 1995, 296-338.

Griller, S. (1999), Die Unterscheidung von Unionsrecht und Gemeinschaftsrecht nach Amsterdam, EuR 1999, Beiheft 1, 45-72.

Griller, S./Droutsas, D./Falkner, G./Forgó, K./Nentwich, M. (2000), (eds.) (2000), The Treaty of Amsterdam. Facts, Analysis, Prospects, Vienna 2000.

Karagiannis, S. (1999), Sanctions internationales et droit communautaires, RTDeur 1999, 363-394.

Koutrakos, P (2000), Is Article 297 EC a „Reserve of Sovereignty"?, CMLRev. 2000, 1339-1362.

Kuijper, P. J. (1975), Sanctions against Rhodesia, CMLRev. 1975, 231.

Lasok, D. (1998), The Trade and Customs Law of the European Union, London et al. [3] 1998.

MacLeod, I./Hendry, I. D./Hyett, S. (1996) The External Relations of the European Communities, New York 1996.

Mestmäcker, E.-J,/Engel, C. (1991), Das Embargo gegen Irak und Kuwait, Entschädigungsansprüche gegen die Europäische Gemeinschaft und gegen die Bundesrepublik Deutschland, Baden-Baden 1991.

Neuwahl, N. (1994), Foreign and Security Policy and the Implementation of the Requirement of "Consistency" under the

Treaty on European Union, in *O'Keeffe, D./Twomey, P. M.* (eds.), Legal Issues of the Maastricht Treaty, London et al. 1994, 227-246.

Nuttall, S. (1987), Interaction between European Political Co-operation and the European Community, YEL 1987, 211-249.

Obradovic, D. (1997), Repatriation of Powers in the European Community, CMLRev. 1997, 59-88.

Osteneck, K. (2000), Artikel 301, in: *Schwarze, J.* (ed.), EU-Kommentar, Baden-Baden 2000, 2371-2379.

Pechstein, M. (1995), Das Kohärenzgebot als entscheidende Integrationsdimension der Europäischen Union', EuR 1995, 247-258.

Regelsberger, E. (2002) Die Gemeinsame Außen- und Sicherheitspolitik nach „Nizza" – begrenzter Reformeifer und außervertragliche Dynamik in der ESVP, in *Griller, S./Hummer, W.* (eds.), Die EU nach Nizza. Ergebnisse und Perspektiven, Wien 2002.

Ress, H.-K. (2000), Das Handelsembargo, Heidelberg 2000.

Riedel, E./Will, M. (1999), Human Rights Clauses in External Agreements, in: Alston, P. (ed.), The EU and human rights, Oxford 1999, 723-754.

Schmitter, C. (1995), Article 228 A, in: *Constantinesco, V./Kovar, R./Simon, D.* (eds.) Traité sur l'Union Européene. Commentaire article par article, Paris 1995, 757-766.

Schneider, H. (1996), Artikel 228a, in: *Grabitz, E. /Hilf, M. Grabitz, E./Hilf, M.* (eds.), Das Recht der Europäischen Union, 9th instalment, München 1996.

Schneider, H. (1999) Wirtschaftsanktionen. Die VN, EG und Bundesrepublik Deutschland als konkurrierende Normgeber beim Erlaß paralleler Wirtschaftssanktionen, Berlin 1999.

Schorkopf, F. (2001), Art. 7 EUV, in: *Grabitz, E./Hilf, M.* (eds.), Das Recht der Europäischen Union, 17th instalment, München 2001.

Sicilianos, L.–A. (1993), The Relationship Between Reprisals and Denunciation or Suspension of a Treaty', EJIL 1993, 341.

Stein, T. (1995), Das Zusammenspiel von Mitgliedstaaten, Rat und Kommission bei der Gemeinsamen Außen- und Sicherheitspolitik', EuR 1995/Beiheft 2, 69.

Timmermans, C. (1996), The Uneasy Relationship Between the Communities and the Second Union Pillar: Back To The Plan Fouchet?, Legal Issues of European Integration 1996, 61-70.

Vedder, C. (2001), Art 133 EGV, in: *Grabitz, E. /Hilf, M. Grabitz, E./Hilf, M.* (eds.), Das Recht der Europäischen Union, 17th instalment, München 2001.

Weatherill, S. (1998), Safeguarding the acquis communautaire, in: *Heukels, T./Blokker, N./Brus, M.* (eds.), The European Union after Amsterdam. A Legal Analysis, The Hague 1998, 153-178.

Zemanek, K. (1990), Austria and the European Community, 1990 GYIL, 130-165.

Peter Hilpold

Human Rights Clauses in EU-Association Agreements

I. Introduction

The systematic introduction of human rights clauses in association agreements concluded by the EC with third countries has become a much publicized feature of the Community's foreign relations. While many industrialized countries attributed high priority to human rights issues the approach chosen by the EC is – considering its smoothness, flexibility and proactive nature – without doubt unique.[1]

---

[1] In this sense see also the Communication from the Commission to the Council and the European Parliament – The European Union's Role in promoting Human Rights and Democratisation in Third Countries, COM (2001) 252 final.

The main thrust of this essay is to examine whether the high reputation of these clauses can effectively live up to the far-reaching expectations they engender in consideration of their nature and the particular setting in which they have to operate in the meantime. Conditionality as it is practised by the European Union at present is the result of a long learning process which has dramatically changed the appearances of this instrument over the years. One of the most important changes brought about by this process was the passing over from a result oriented approach to a process oriented one. In the past the aims of conditionality had to be realized through an immediate approach: The respect for certain human rights standards was imposed. In the meantime, however, sensibility has grown for the fact that respect for human rights can be assured only within a democratic system with broader constitutional guaranties. Therefore, in the last years attention concentrates on this latter field and the assumption is that the former aim will be achieved as a natural consequence of ”good governance”. The exact interrelations between these aims have, however still to be explored and even the meaning of “good governance” is – as will be shown – not yet fully understood. This problem leads us to more fundamental issues referring to the ultimate interests pursued with these measures and whether the pursuit of these interests influences the attainability of the officially declared goals.

Finally, it should never be forgotten that the EU cannot put in place a policy of conditionality disregarding similar experiments in other regions. On the contrary, these experiments are rather strongly interconnected and success or failure of these efforts in one place will necessarily influence the shape of related endeavours in the other site.

II. The Basis of the Conditionality Issue in the European Union's Foreign Relations

A. The Relevance of the Historical Perspective

The multi-faceted issue to be dealt with here and even the basic challenges the human rights clause-approach is faced with at present cannot be fully understood if we do not pay sufficient attention to the way this whole topic has developed over the years. Perhaps contrary to the appearances the present development of this instrument is not the result of a long-term strategy but rather the outcome of a costly – and still ongoing – trial-and-error process. To adopt a dynamic rather than a static view means also to gain better insight in the causes and the conditions which characterize this process whereby we should be enabled to draft tentative scenarios for the further development of this issue. Finally, this process-oriented view can bear evidence of the fact that the different settings in which these clauses are intended to operate runs counter to any attempt for an over-generalization of their meaning and possible effects.

B. Conditionality and Development Policy

Usually, the origins of the human rights clause are traced back to the development regime between the EC and an ever-growing number of developing countries in Africa, the Pacific and the Caribbean. While this trade regime was already established in 1975 it was not before 1989 that the topic of the human clauses came to the forefront. This change of policy was rendered possible by the flexible fabric of the Lomé-Convention system which was renewed in a 5 years rhythm.[2]

The need for special instruments to suspend or to terminate the Lomé cooperation regime was already felt while Lomé I was in force. In 1977, when the human rights violations committed by Uganda's dictatorial ruler *Idi Amin* became rampant, the EC had to take notice of the fact that no adequate instruments were at their disposal to interrupt the flow of aid to this country in order to exercise pressure on the government. While on the factual level it was possible to attain this

2 As it is known, the single steps in this process were designed with Roman numerals. The Lomé I Convention of 1975 was followed in 1980 by Lomé II and in 1985 III became operative. In 1990 Lomé IV entered into force. Although this Convention was intended to remain in place for a ten years period it was substantially modified on the occasion of the mid-term review process which gave birth to the so-called Lomé IV-bis Convention which entered into force in 1995. In spring 2001 the Lomé Convention system definitely expired and was substituted by the Cotonou agreement now in place. For an exhaustive account of this development with special regard to the human rights issue see *Arts* (2000). See also *Hoffmeister* (1998); *Pippan* (1999) and *Hilpold* (2002a). With regard to the Cotonou agreement see *Hilpold* (2002b).

aim[3] this result could not satisfy on a juridical level. On the contrary, it bore evidence of a serious flaw in the system which proved not easy to be eradicated as the negotiations for Lomé II showed. Victim of both the conflict between East and West and North and South the human rights issue was not a suitable matter to find a consensus between the parties. Not only was an agreement lacking on the precise nature of the human rights to be protected but the third world countries were basically against any conditionality in the development policy of the EC. Only by the Lomé III Convention a timid opening towards conditionality was tried and achieved. While this consensus was not yet strong enough to find expression in the main text of the Convention,[4] in Annex I an explicit reference to human rights was placed,[5] although this statement is strongly interrelated to the development issue and it does not seem clear, in which relationship human rights and development stand and whether both aims enjoy the same status or whether one objective becomes instrumental to the other.

When the end of the Cold War became apparent the adoption of a more unbiased approach was possible and the human rights issue could

---

3 See the decision of the EEC Council of Ministers of 21 June 1977, 10 Bull. EC no. 6, 1977, 92-93.

4 Only Article 4 of the Convention made an indirect reference to human rights by underscoring the necessity to respect people's dignity.

5 "1. The Contracting Parties hereby reiterate their deep attachment to human dignity as an inalienable right and as constituting an essential objective for the attainment of the legitimate aspirations of individuals and of peoples. They reaffirm that every individual has the right, in his own country or in a host country, to respect for this dignity and protection by the law.
2. The Contracting Parties proclaim that ACP-EEC co-operation must help eliminate the obstacles preventing individuals and peoples from actually enjoying to the full their economic, social and cultural rights and that this must be achieved through the development which is essential to their dignity, their well-being and their self-fulfilment.
3. In this respect the Contracting Parties reaffirm their obligation and their commitment under international law to fight for the elimination of all forms of discrimination based on ethnic group, origin, race, nationality, colour, sex, language, religion or any other situation. They proclaim their determination to work effectively for the eradication of apartheid which constitutes a violation of human rights and an affront to human dignity."

be faced more squarely. Article 5 (1) of the Lomé IV Convention seemed to leave no doubt on the priority to be attributed to human rights in respect to development, or, to put it an other way, that the respect for human rights is prerequisite and final end of development at the same time:

"Cooperation shall be directed towards development centred on man, the main protagonist and beneficiary of development, which thus entails respect for and promotion of all human rights. Cooperative operations shall thus be conceived in accordance with the positive approach, where respect for human rights is recognized as a basic factor of real development and where cooperation is conceived as a contribution to the promotion of these rights.

In this context development policy and cooperation are closely linked with the respect for and enjoyment of fundamental human rights. The role and potential of initiatives taken by individuals and groups shall also be recognized and fostered in order to achieve in practice real participation of the population in the development process in accordance with Article 13".

The way up to the mid-term review during the early 90s left enough time and opportunities to take the changes of 1989 into full account. The result was not only a human rights clause which deserved properly this characterization but also a respect-demanding attempt to set the human rights issue in an adequate frame. It was recognized that it was not possible to assure the respect of a certain human rights standard without providing for broader guarantees in the single constitutional systems. This new approach was an implicit acknowledgement of the fact that it would be illusionary to concentrate the whole attention only on human rights while disregarding the prerequisites which are indispensable to attain this aim.[6]

As a consequence, Article 5(1)(3) of the Lomé IV-bis Convention reads as follows:

"Respect for human rights, democratic principles and the rule of law, which underpins relations between the ACP States and the Community and all provisions of the Convention, and governs the

---

6 See *Hilpold* (2002b).

domestic and international policies of the Contracting Parties, shall constitute an essential element of the Convention."

This provision stands in close connection with Article 366a(2) of Lomé IV-bis, the so-called non-compliance clause:

"2. If one Party considers that another Party has failed to fulfil an obligation in respect of one of the essential elements referred to in Article 5, it shall invite the Party concerned, unless there is special urgency, to hold consultations with a view to assessing the situation in detail and, if necessary, remedying it.

For the purpose of such consultations, and with a view to finding a solution:

- the Community side shall be represented by its Presidency, assisted by the previous and next Member States to hold the Presidency, together with the Commission;
- the ACP side shall by represented by the ACP State holding the Co-Presidency, assisted by the previous and next ACP States to hold the Co-Presidency. Two additional members of the ACP Council of Ministers chosen by the Party concerned shall also take part in the consultations.

The consultations shall begin no later than 15 days after the invitation and as a rule last no longer than 30 days.

3. At the end of the period referred to in the third subparagraph of paragraph 2 if in spite of all efforts no solution has been found, or immediately in the case of urgency or refusal of consultation, the Party which invoked the failure to fulfil an obligation may take appropriate steps, including, where necessary, the partial or full suspension of application of this Convention to the Party concerned. It is understood that suspension would be a measure of last resort.

The Party concerned shall receive prior notification of any such measure which shall be revoked as soon as the reasons for taking it have disappeared."

At this juncture, conditionality had reached a degree of maturity where the structure of the relevant provisions resembled very much that of present instruments. As will be shown below, recent human rights clauses in EC association agreements commonly consist of an "essential element" clause defining the aims of the clause, or, to put it in another way, containing the material part of the clause, and the so-called "non-compliance" clause containing the procedural steps to be taken in case an essential element had been disregarded or violated.

The last stage of this special, development related field of human rights clauses was reached by the Agreement of Cotonou of 23 September 2000. Here conditionality reaches a sophistication unmatched before not only within the EC but in worldwide perspective. The road taken by the Lomé IV-*bis* Convention was further followed and with regard to early attempts to draft a meaningful human rights clause, the focus had perceptibly shifted.

Article 9 of the new Partnership Agreement between the African, Caribbean and Pacific States on the one part, and the European Community and its Member States, on the other part, reiterates the plethora of aims to be achieved by this cooperation regime between North and South which have developed over the years setting at the same time new priorities. Paragraph 1 of Article 9 points out that co-operation shall be directed towards sustainable development which requires the respect for all human rights and fundamental freedoms, including respect for fundamental social rights, democracy based on the rule of law and transparent and accountable governance. The wording of this provision differs conspicuously from that of earlier attempts to describe the ultimate purpose of development cooperation. In fact, it is no longer required to obey only "fundamental" human rights but respect for "all" human rights is demanded. In addition, "fundamental freedoms" are also mentioned whereby the drafters of this Convention made sure that the vast area of social and economic rights, usually also considered as human rights (of the so-called "second generation") cannot be disregarded. This choice reflects a compromise in the long-running conflict between industrialized and developing countries where the first saw political and civil rights as paramount, the second social and economic rights. Now, an all-encompassing approach was adopted, while, at the same time, in order to counter excessive demands, it was made sure, that only fundamental social rights could be claimed.

Furthermore, within this clause, a distinction was drawn between essential elements and fundamental elements. To the first category, the respect for human rights, democratic principles and the rule of law was counted, while good governance was defined as the (only) fundamental element.

At first glance, it seems that good governance has now become centre-stage. It constitutes a necessary, albeit not sufficient condition for the respect of human rights. Good governance forms the foundation on which a democratic society committed to the respect of human rights and the rule of law can be build.[7] In para 3 of Article 9 of the Cotonou Agreement good governance is defined as follows:

"In the context of a political and institutional environment that upholds human rights, democratic principles and the rule of law, good governance is the transparent and accountable management of human, natural, economic and financial resources for the purposes of equitable and sustainable development. It entails clear decision-making procedures at the level of public authorities, transparent and accountable institutions, the primacy of law in the management and distribution of resources and capacity building for elaborating and implementing measures aiming in particular at preventing and combating corruption."

Defined in this way, good governance becomes an all-encompassing criterion which can easily be adapted to new needs, which allows for punctual interventions and from which the respect of all the other elements should result as a natural consequence. On the other hand, the vagueness of this concept cannot be overseen[8]. Too many details remain unclear to base conditionality solely or primarily on the concept of good governance. On the other hand, however, it would be unfair to dismiss this new approach as pure political rhetoric. It is rather likely that the new concept of good governance set cornerstones for all future discussions on a strengthening of conditionality in the EC's external relations. As a result, it can be said, that for the time being the concept of good governance is far from being void of content. Its relevance is, however, mainly of a political nature as it is directed at influencing the future negotiation process on this issue without prejudicing its results. Reliance on good governance gives expression to a process-oriented

---

7 For an account on the development of this concept see *Arts* (1995), *Ginther/de Waart* (1995) and *Nherere* (1995).

8 For a detailed critic of this concept see *Hilpold* (2002b). See also *van Boven* (1995), at 311, for whom this concept constitutes more a general term identifying a set of legal principles than a rule or principle of international law *per se*.

approach while it means at the same time that responsibility for the respect of human rights falls back on governments in a result-oriented way. It follows also that the relevant standards have to be applied according to their actual meaning and a specific obligation lasts on the government to look continuously for any change in this meaning. In sum, while the *essential elements* as defined by the Cotonou agreement comprise the results of the past conditionality discussion which has been running for almost a quarter of a century, good governance as a *fundamental element* is future oriented and shall give new impetus to the whole endeavour directed at giving substance to the conditionality issue. This varying degree in the clarification of the two concepts is also reflected in the non-compliance provisions at the articles 96 subs. of the Cotonou Agreement. In fact, according to Article 96, the violation of obligations stemming from essential elements gives rise to a procedure regulated in all details. Where consultations do not lead to a solution of the controversy or appear unfeasible or in case of special urgency "appropriate measures" can be taken. These are defined as "measures taken in accordance with international law, and proportional to the violation".[9] On the other hand, the Cotonou Agreement contains no specific "non-compliance" provision in case of violations of the good governance obligation. Only where this violation finds expression in the specific form of corruption an analogous procedure is foreseen in Article 97 of the Cotonou Agreement. It appears therefore fair to say that the fundamental element clause which seems conceptually to be the most comprehensive one is operative only in a small field. In consideration of the vast potential for interventions the concept of "good governance" offers it is probably not surprising that the beneficiaries of development cooperation are opposing any further extension of the applicability of this concept.

Without doubt, the area of development policy was the most prominent field in which conditionality and, in particular, human rights clauses, could develop. Two aspects made the development policy particularly well-suited for experiments of this kind. First of all, the degree basic human rights were guaranteed in the EC and in the APC countries differed generally in a very pronounced way. In the presence

---

9 See Art 96 para 2 lit. (c) of the Cotonou Agreement.

of manifest human rights abuses States or International Organizations imposing conditionality could rightly argue they were acting out of *erga omnes*-obligations without being accused of being intervenors. The second aspect which created fertile ground for conditionality in the EC-ACP relations is to be seen in the fact that the main function of the Lomé framework, development cooperation, has given life to an uneven relationship where the EC was automatically in a good position to make aid and trade concessions conditional on the respect for certain standards of legitimacy. These two factors paving the way for conditionality contributed, however, at the same time to discredit it. The different attitudes towards human rights could be seen - and were in part actually thus defined - as the result of deliberate choices rather than as the expression of a development gap. To impose certain "Western" values could be felt as an act of cultural imperialism. This impression was further reinforced by the dependency of the receiver countries from aid and trade concessions. To make trade cooperation conditional on the acceptance of these values was widely perceived as a further act of exploitation in the best tradition of colonial rule. On the contrary, from the viewpoint of the developing countries, the colonial past had given rise to a right to development cooperation. It can, therefore, not surprise that after the promising beginnings conditionality in the EC-ACP relations brought only mixed results after years of various experiments. Much of that what had been achieved in the EC-ACP relations since 1975, the year Lomé I entered into force, had been made possible by changes unfolding outside this specific framework. It was not lest the fact that the EC itself had undergone profound changes that has permitted conditionality to acquire the importance it can claim at present.

C. The Protection of Human Rights within the European Union

It cannot be denied that the EC had been handicapped in its attempts to impose a human rights clause on its trading partner by her rather tentative and ambiguous handling of the human rights on its own internal level. As it is known, originally, the EEC treaty did not mention human rights. It was only by the way of the ECJ jurisprudence that the question whether human rights were part of the EC law even without explicit competence in this field was answered in the affirmative.[10] In view of the ever growing numbers and weight of the EC competences this situation could, however, not satisfy. Voices within the EC which required this institution to declare itself explicitly with regard to this issue were mounting. Various alternatives were discussed, amongst it the integration of human rights provisions into the primary law or the adherence to the European Human Rights Convention. An important step was set by the Treaty of Maastricht. By Article F of the Treaty of the European Union for the first time a reference to human rights was integrated into primary law, even though this provision was a rather cautious one:

"2. The Union shall respect fundamental rights, as guaranteed by the European Convention for the Protection of Human Rights and Fundamental Freedoms signed in Rome on 4 November 1950 and as they result from the constitutional traditions common to the Member States, as general principles of Community law." The Member States stopped short from the adoption of a Charter of Fundamental Rights or from an adhesion to the ECHR.[11]"

To this provision, another one was added by the Treaty of Amsterdam - now in Art. 6 of the Treaty on European Union - which gave further impetus to considerations of legitimacy on which the whole action of the Union should be based:

"1. The Union is founded on the principles of liberty, democracy, respect for human rights and fundamental freedoms, and the rule of law, principles which are common to the Member States."

As the ECJ regarded an adhesion of the EC to the ECHR as irreconcilable with existing EC law[12] and because, on the other hand, the factual protection of human rights on a more or less equivalent level as

---

[10] In the "*Stauder*" case (Case 29/69, [1969] ECR 419), the ECJ qualified the fundamental individual rights as general principles of the Community legal order without however specifying the legal basis for such a qualification. In the years after the ECJ became more specific; first by reference to the common constitutional traditions of the Member States (Case 11/70, *Internationale Handelsgesellschaft*, [1970] ECR 1125), than as well as to the treaties for the protection of human rights concluded by the Member States (Case 4/73, *Nold*, [1974] ECR 491). See *Kingreen* (1999) 58.

[11] See *Hilf* (1995) 20.

[12] See Opinion 2/94, *ECHR*, [1996] ECR I-1759.

it is guaranteed through the ECHR system was not considered as sufficient an instrument, it was looked for a new way whereby this new commitment towards human rights could be officialized without enlarging substantially the obligations so far undertaken in this field. The solution to this problem was the EU Charter on Fundamental Rights proclaimed at the Nice Summit on 7 December 2000. This non-binding document summarizes much of the human rights *acquis* within the European Union and gives only very cautiously a new - and progressive - formulation to the single rights. Nonetheless it gives the European Union a totally different standing in the human rights clause issue. While it could be hardly maintained for the past that the protection of human rights within the European Union was insufficient this protection materialized along a much too indirect way and therefore it was difficult for the Union to take advantage of its achievements in this field on the international bargaining table. The European Charter of Fundamental Rights, on the contrary, is intended not only to lay a new, transparent basis for the ever-intensifying efforts to improve the human rights standards applicable within the European Union but it is also - to a very large degree - directed outwardly. It is true that the very legal nature of this Charter is not totally clear and it is also true that efforts are underway to solidify and strengthen the legal character of this instrument. Nonetheless, already by materializing into a written document which can be considered as an expression of the common consent on this matter within the European Union - and not only as a political declaration of the organs of the EC like previous documents - this Charter will strengthen considerably the position of the Union when she requires respect for certain human rights standards.

D. Conditionality as a Structural Element of the European Union's Foreign Policy and Legal Order

Conditionality as applied by the European Union may have received its most prominent expression in the framework of the EC-ACP development cooperation as described above. This is, however, by far not the only feature of this instrument. On the contrary, the European Union (or, respectively, the European Community) has used this instrument in many different ways in order to achieve certain standards of legitimacy in their international relations.

First of all, the recognition practice of the EC Members following the break-up of the Federal Yugoslav Republic has to be mentioned in this respect.[13] On 16 December 1991 the Foreign Ministers of the EC Member States agreed on a catalogue of criteria to be followed for the recognition of the States which have come into being on the former territory of Yugoslavia.[14]

On this occasion, it seemed that the traditional criteria for Statehood (people, territory and government) had lost their primary importance while legitimacy - as defined by the EC with reference to international documents - had become paramount. When these conditions were set, it was clear that several entities aspiring for recognition did not yet fulfil them, at least not in all detail. The function of these conditions was therefore not to exclude single pretenders but to make sure they obeyed criteria which were regarded as indispensable parts of the European Public Order. In fact, as a consequence of these conditions, the constitutional order of several pretenders was adapted. This future-oriented, proactive connotation of the recognition policy is typical for conditionality as applied by the EC.[15] With regard to human rights

---

13 See *Hilpold* (1993) 387 ff.

14 This declaration was issued together with a Declaration on the Guidelines on Recognition of New States in Eastern Europe and the Soviet Union. The Declaration on Yugoslavia is reprinted in the European Journal of International Law, Vol. 4, 1993, p. 73.

15 See the Communication from the Commission to the Council and the European Parliament - The European Union´s Role in Promoting Human Rights and Democratisation in Third Countries, COM(2001) 252 final, at 9:
"[...] the EU's insistence on including essential elements clauses is not intended to signify a negative or punitive approach. They are meant to promote dialogue and positive measures, such as joint support for democracy and human rights, the accession, ratification and implementation of international human rights instruments where this is lacking, as well as the prevention of crises through the establishment of a consistent and long-term relationship. The dialogue on human rights that they enable should be a two-way one, with the EU also agreeing to discuss human rights and democratisation issues within its own borders."

clauses this orientation becomes an outright necessity when a backfiring effect of conditionality is to be avoided.[16]

A further field where conditionality has become a structural element is the Generalised Scheme of Tariff Preferences (GSP), a bundle of autonomous, unilateral trade preferences adopted by industrialized countries to the benefit of developing countries. The latest GSP of the EU took effect in 1995[17] and will last until 2004. The most innovative element of this scheme was - together with the "graduation" of preferences according to the degree of development of the single developing countries - the introduction of a pronounced incentive structure for receiver countries which adapted their legal system to a vast number of standards of legitimacy in fields such as human rights, social clauses or protection of the environment. On the other hand, it was also provided for a system of "negative" incentives - or traditional sanctions - for countries which violated some fundamental legitimacy standards. All in all this system brought conditionality to its highest perfection by implementing it through positive as well as negative measures. It should, however, also be mentioned that the recourse to such an elaborated form of conditionality was rendered easy by the extreme dependence of large parts of the receiver countries from the concessions granted by the EU.[18]

In practice for a long time the application for membership to the EC has been conditional on the basis first of Article 237 EEC and afterwards of Article O of the Union Treaty.[19] This practice was again set on an official legal basis by Article 49 introduced by the Treaty of Amsterdam which links the application for membership to the respect for the principles set out in Article 6(1) of the Treaty, which asks, *inter alia*, for the respect of human rights and fundamental freedoms.

---

16 In fact, it is not only known that sanctions are often of limited value to guarantee the respect for human rights but they can give way to a downward spiral in which measures and countermeasures lead to an overall worsening of the situation. Conditionality should not be perceived as a possibility to inflict unilaterally a suffering but rather as a stimulant to improve the human rights situation.

17 See Regulation No. 3281/94, OJ L 348 of 31. 12. 1994, p. 1.

18 For an overview of the new GSP of the EU see *Hilpold* (1996) 98 ff.

19 See *Hilf* (1995) para 21.

This form of conditionality has become of special importance through the Eastern enlargement process, and, in particular, through the so-called Europe Agreements, "a framework within which [the candidates] are preparing for membership".[20] The Member States specified the criteria for admission through the so-called Copenhagen criteria of 1993 which are again distinguished in a political criterion, an economic criterion and the requisite to be able to adopt the Community *acquis*. According to the political criterion only those candidates can become members that have achieved stability of institutions, guaranteeing democracy, the rule of law, human rights, respect for and protection of minorities. These Copenhagen criteria are the benchmark in the screening process through which the Commission examines the progress achieved by the candidates in their approximation efforts and allow for a very thorough evaluation of the single countries. Although it would prima facie seem that the economic criteria are more important for the approximation to the European Union than the political ones, it appears that the Commission has attributed in the past a very prominent role to the latter.[21] In order to foster and to coordinate the process of approximation through aid measures special Accession Partnerships were concluded wherein particular attention could be given to the question whether the Copenhagen criteria had been respected.

A last field for which conditionality has become of central importance is that of the sanctions mechanism against Member States in case of a "serious and persistent breach [...] of principles mentioned in Article 6(1)" of the Union Treaty. This sanction mechanism is contained in Article 7 of the Treaty of the European Union and had been introduced by the Treaty of Amsterdam. Here conditionality operates clearly in a preventive way. The mere existence of this mechanism shall make sure that the fundamental principles of the European Public Order as they are spelled out in Article 6 (1) of the Union Treaty remain untouched.

---

20 See http://europa.eu.int/comm/enlargement/pas/europe_agr.htm. See also *Williams* (2000) 601 and *Lenaerts* (2000) 594 ff.

21 See *Voina-Motoc* (2000) 110.

III. Human Rights Clauses as "Essential Elements"

As we have seen above, conditionality in EU law can assume various expressions. Human rights clauses are only special instruments, albeit usually very effective ones, to achieve that very goal. Implanted in development instrument they attained much of their effectiveness through the natural discrepancy in the power structure between donor countries and beneficiaries. Up to the case Portugal v. Council[22] and in the follow-up to Opinion 2/94 which set a clear limit to the external powers of the EC in the field of human rights agreements it was unclear whether the EC had the competence to insert human rights clauses in binding agreements. This legal basis was found by the ECJ in Article 177(2) of the EC Treaty as amended by the Treaty of Amsterdam.[23] Still open remained, however, the question of the legal basis for such clauses outside the field of development cooperation. Although it can be assumed that Article 6 of the Treaty of the European Union may constitute a sufficient legal basis for human rights clauses in association agreements even if they cannot be considered as a development instrument[24] this question will be definitely settled by Article 181a, as it will be inserted in the EC treaty by the Treaty of Nice.[25]

---

[22] C-268/94, *Portugal v. Council*, [1999] ECR I-6177.

[23] See *Fierro* (2001) 44. For Advocate General La Pergola there was even an obligation to insert clauses of this kind. See point 29 of the Opinion of the Advocate General.

[24] See *Ferris* (2001) 45 f.

[25] Paragraph 1 and 2 of Article 181a shall read as follows:
"Without prejudice to the other provisions of the Treaty, and in particular those of Title XX, the Community shall carry out, within its spheres of competence, economic, financial and technical cooperation with third countries. Such measures shall be complementary to those carried out by the Member States and consistent with the development policy of the Community.
Community policy in this area shall contribute to the general objective of developing and consolidating democracy and the rule of law and to the objective of respecting human rights and fundamental freedoms."

With regard to their structure, human rights clauses were subject to a longer development.[26] Over the years, those clauses have grown in substance and detail and they are displaying in the meantime a very high degree of refinement.[27] As a very impressive example the Articles 9 and 96subs. of the recent Cotonou Agreement already referred to above can be cited. While in Article 9 the single essential elements are cited, the Articles 96 and 97 contain the "non-compliance"-clause. These articles are mainly of a procedural nature and refer to the "appropriate measures" to be taken in the case a violation of an essential element is claimed.[28] The Cotonou Agreement is, however, also a good example for the fact, that human rights clauses are difficult to be isolated from other conditions if conditionality is to be effective in practice. The requirement to respect human rights comes together with a whole array of further conditions which are strongly interrelated. The single conditions assume a different weight depending from the nature of (and the parties to) the relevant cooperation instrument. The human rights clauses may play a more prominent role in the Europe Agreements than in the ambit of (recent) development agreements. At first glance, this may seem odd but there are reasons that can explain this situation. As already shown,[29] development cooperation within the Lomé system has revealed the limits of a purely or mainly human rights oriented conditionality approach. On a longer run, the protection of human rights can be guaranteed only in the presence of a solid constitutional framework while punctual interventions in legal environments where basic democratic conditions cannot be guaranteed

---

26 This process is analyzed by *Riedel/Will* (1999) 723 ff. On this issue see also the Communication on the inclusion of respect for democratic principles and human rights in agreements between the Community and third countries (COM(95) 216 final).

27 In 1995 the Council approved a model clause.

28 Such appropriate measures can be, for example, the suspension of high level contacts or changes to cooperation programmes, including the postponement of new projects. See Communication from the Commission to the Council and the European Parliament - The European Union's Role in promoting Human Rights and Democratisation in Third Countries, COM(2001) 252 final.

29 See also *Hilpold* (2002b).

are usually condemned to show only ephemeral effects. While a significant number of beneficiaries of development cooperation measures have insufficient democratic structures the case of the accession candidates is different as serious democratic deficits would have excluded them from becoming candidates for membership in the first place. Even in that case where the Accession Partnerships has given the opportunity to the European Union to bring forward detailed criticism with regard to the respect of the rule of law and democracy,[30] this criticism referred to situations which could be corrected internally through the normal democratic process. Furthermore, it has to be mentioned that the accession process is characterized by a series of measures directed at harmonizing essential elements of the legal systems of accession candidates with those of the Member States. By this way conditionality can be restricted to core legitimacy criteria. A comparable phenomenon is lacking with regard to development association. Finally, it has to be mentioned that development association is characterized by two aspects: On the one hand the industrialized countries dispose over significant leverage as they have more bargaining power than the developing countries. On the long run, every concession can be withdrawn or not be renewed. On the other hand, developing countries are usually very wary of their sovereignty and resent strictly every interference in their internal matters to which human rights are often counted even if this does not appear to be justified from an international law perspective. The human rights issue has therefore to be couched into broader terms which are accepted to be "politically correct" in the international relations if the European Union is to use her leverage successfully.

IV. What Future for Conditionality in the Human Rights Sphere?

During the last quarter of a century the human rights clause has taken a dramatic evolution. The main experimental field has been the

---

[30] This was the case of Slovakia. On the occasion of the first round of opinions issued by the Commission it was criticized that the rule of law and democracy was not sufficiently rooted in political life and that the protection of minorities was insufficient.

area of development association but in the meantime conditionality has been both generalized and specialized. Would it be true that the degree of evolution of the human rights clause issue was always a few steps ahead with regard to the general development of this subject then it could be argued that human rights clauses in their strict sense have already lost part of their appeal as they are now only one element of broader requirements of legitimacy wherein the requisite of "good governance" is gaining continuously more ground. If we consider, however, the above mentioned fragmentation of the developments in this field, we have to recognize the paramount importance of human rights clauses in the ambit of the accession association.

The area of human rights is probably the most delicate one for official redress in the international relations. In times when the respect for human rights has become an aim every State purports to follow in principle and when the end of the conflict between East and West has considerably enlarged the common ground in the definition of human rights States will resent it very much if they are accused of negligence in this field. The European Union had therefore to adopt a general, all encompassing approach which should make sure that the defence and the promotion of human rights was the consequence of an unbiased, principled attitude where no distinction was made between the single cooperation partners on the basis of larger political considerations. It can be no doubt that a conditionality approach gaining continuously more importance in the external relations the human rights element is predominant and this will be the same or even more so in the future. The Cotonou Agreement may, however, indicate the adoption of a partly new approach: While the language is very general and seems to require the trading partner to respect all-encompassing criteria of legitimacy on which probably everyone can agree, this vagueness of the wording allows, at the same time, for very detailed interventions. This broadly defined interest of the European Union for legitimacy in the ambit of development cooperation is, however, unlikely to stir up much of controversy as the whole policy followed in this field is primarily proactive. "Non-compliance" should be the absolute exception and should it happen this would be an implicit admission of (at least partial) failure of the Community policy. Should the worst case scenario of non-compliance become reality the abstractness of the conditionality provisions as described above should allow for interventions on the level most suited for and at the same time this should happen in a very diplomatic fashion. The suspension of concessions should therefore become in any case a measure of last resort as stated in Article 97 of the Cotonou Agreement. On the other hand, in the accession context, or - even more so - among the Member States within the European Union the question of the respect for human rights is addressed more squarely and with less diplomatic restraint.[31]

As already mentioned in the introduction a critical examination of conditionality has also to look at the forces behind this phenomenon. Why is human rights conditionality more pronounced in agreements to which the EC is part of than elsewhere? Why had the EU taken such a strong stance in favour of human rights clauses while other important players on the international scene had been far more reluctant to embrace this cause? The answer is to be found in the strong influence exercised on this issue both by several EU organs acting out of self-interest as by the public opinion. Among the EU organs having influenced this process the European Parliament deserves first to be mentioned. This institution has been (and still is) the most fertile ground for discussions on human rights issues and for the drafting of special documents. On the basis of this confrontation with the human rights issue stood partly a genuine interest for this cause by the single MEPs. In part, however, other reasons seem to have been the determining forces. First of all, the human rights issue was a welcome pretext for the European Parliament to look for more clout in external economic relations and to have a say also on future developments of association agreements entered already into force. In special cases even the existence of a protectionist bias cannot be excluded. This is specifi-

---

[31] This was very well exemplified in the attempt carried in 2000 by 14 EU Member to impose sanctions on Austria because of alleged deficits with regard to the guarantee of fundamental human rights and democratic principles as a consequence of the establishment of a new coalition government with the participation of the Freedom Party. Although these actions were politically motivated and had finally to be withdrawn as they were unjustified they evidenced a very high sensibility for questions of legitimacy. See *Pernthaler/Hilpold* (2000).

cally true for those cases of conditionality in which particular importance is attributed to labour standards.

Also other EU organs showed a notable amount of self-interest when engaging in human rights affairs. As has been recently pointed out in the literature[32] the Commission and the Council follow a different approach with regard to the implementation of human rights conditionality. While the Commission - eager as it is to preserve the justification for its bureaucratic structure - favours a positive approach and the continuation of cooperation over a disruption, the interests of the Council are different. It favours "negative" measures with an immediate impact on public opinion as for its Members the internal political support is often of crucial importance. Negative measures are often more perceptible than positive ones and therefore in this sense of a greater political value for politicians dependent from a continuous political support from their constituencies.[33] Notwithstanding these differences, however, both institutions rely on human rights issues for their particular goals.

It can therefore be said that human rights clauses are at least as much inward oriented as they are directed at the promotion of the ideals they are purported to realize[34]. They allow for cooperation with countries that do not fulfil the high standards of the European Union and make sure that the European Union cannot be accused of levelling down international human rights standards. On the contrary, by this way the Union can claim to actively promote human rights and at the same time counter the critics who accuse the European Union of a democratic deficit.

This "selfish" aspects of conditionality do not, however, jeopardize the potential efficacy of this instrument as long as it is applied in a coherent manner. These forces have rather set forth a self-accelerating and reinforcing process whereby the public opinion expects this policy to be a success story and where a failure will necessarily bear internal political consequences at least on the long run. A comparison of the

---

32 See *Fouwels* (1997) 314 f.

33 *Ibid.*

34 For a critical view of these „internal effects" see, however, *Williams* (2000) 616 ff.

relevant EU documents on conditionality reveals over the years an ever-increasing ambition which has caused a corresponding increase of the expectations by the informed public. Even if conditionality in the first stages of its development had much the nature of a political expedient by now this is now longer the case and expectations for practical consequences of this policy run high.

One drawback of this development cannot, however, be overseen: The handling of foreign relations becomes highly political even in "technical" areas such as economic cooperation not characterized *per se* by a predominant political nature. This increases the danger that discretionality gains undue weight in the balancing of the interests concerned in this field.

In sum, it can be said, that human rights conditionality is here to stay and with the proclamation of the Charter of Fundamental Rights at the Conference of Nice the European Union and its Member States can follow this attempt in future on an even more solid basis. Ultimately, however, the success of this policy will depend in a large measure from the development of conditionality in a global perspective. The European Union is in this sense both an actor which influences the development of criteria and procedures of conditionality as subject of broader developments which create the specific environment for the adoption of such policies. In view of its central contributions to the standard-setting process with regard to the conditionality issue it was therefore more than appropriate that the European Union has continuously revised its respective policies in order to come up to its responsibilities not only within their own bilateral relations but also on a global level.

References

Philip Alston (ed.) (1999), The EU and Human Rights, Oxford 1999

Karin Arts (1995), European Community, development cooperation, human rights, democracy and good governance: at odds or at ease with each other?, in Konrad Ginther et al. (ed.), Sustainable development and good governance (1995), 259-273.

Karin Arts (2000), Integrating Human Rights into Development Cooperation: The Case of the Lomé Convention, The Hague et al. 2000.

Barbara Brandter/Allan Rosas (1999), Trade Preferences and Human Rights, in Philip Alston (ed.), The EU and Human Rights, Oxford 1999, 699-722.

Elena Fierro (2001), Legal Basis and Scope of the Human Rights Clauses in EC Bilateral Agreements: Any Room for Positive Interpretation?, ELJ 1/2001, 41-68.

Martine Fouwels (1997), The European Union's Common Foreign and Security Policy and Human Rights 3/1997, 291-324.

Konrad Ginther et al. (ed.), (1995), Sustainable development and good governance, The Hague et al. 1995.

Meinhard Hilf (1995), Artikel F, in: Eberhard Grabitz/Meinhard Hilf, (eds.), Kommentar zum EWG-Vertrag, München 1995, 1-14.

Peter Hilpold (1993), Die Anerkennung der Neustaaten auf dem Balkan, Archiv des Völkerrechts 4/1993, 387-408.

Peter Hilpold (1996), Das neue Allgemeine Präferenzschema der EU, EuR 1/1996, 98-114.

Peter Hilpold (2002a), Konditionalität in den Beziehungen zwischen der EU und den AKP-Staaten: Menschenrechte, Demokratie, Rechtsstaatlichkeit und verantwortungsvolle Regierungsführung ZEuS 2/2002, 239-245.

Peter Hilpold (2002b), EU development cooperation at a crossroads: The Cotonou agreement of 23 June 2000 and the principle of good governance, EFARev. 2002, 53-72.

Frank Hoffmeister (1998), Menschenrechts- und Demokratieklauseln in den vertraglichen Außenbeziehungen der Europäischen Gemeinschaft, Heidelberg et al. 1998.

T. King (1997), Human Rights in the Development Policy of the European Community: Towards a European World Order?, NYIL Vol. XXVIII (1997), 51-99.

Thorsten Kingreen (1999), Artikel 6, in Christian Calliess/Matthias Ruffert (ed.), Kommentar zu EU-Vertrag und EG-Vertrag, Neuwied 1999, 49-119.

Koen Lenaerts (2000), Fundamental rights in the European Union, in E.L.Rev. 2000, 575.

Pearson Nherere (1995), Conditionality, human rights and good governance: a dialogue of unequal partners, in Konrad Ginther et al. (ed.), Sustainable development and good governance (1995), 289-307.

Manfred Nowak (1999), Human Rights "Conditionality" in Relation to Entro to, and Full Participation in, the EU, in Philip Alston (ed.), The EU and Human Rights, Oxford 1999, 687-698.

Peter Pernthaler/Peter Hilpold (2000), Sanktionen als Instrument der Politikkontrolle - der Fall Österreich, Integration 2/2000, 105-110.

Christian Pippan (1999), Demokratie durch Völkerrecht? Zu den Menschenrechts- und Demokratieklauseln in den Verträgen der Europäischen Gemeinschaft mit Drittstaaten am Beispiel des Lomé-Abkommens, in Wolfgang Benedek et al. (ed.), Essays in Honour of Konrad Ginther, Frankfurt am Main et al. 1999, 473-500.

Eibe Riedel/Martin Will (1999), Human Rights Clauses in External Agreements of the EC, in Philip Alston (ed.), The EU and Human Rights, Oxford 1999, 723-754.

Bruno Simma/Jo Beatrix Aschenbrenner/Constanze Schulte (1999), Human Rights Considerations in the Development Co-operation Activities of the EC, in Philip Alston (ed.), The EU and Human Rights, Oxford 1999, 571-626.

Theo van Boven (1995), The emerging right to good governance, in NQHR 3/1995, 304-311.

Iulia Voina-Motoc (2000), Les critères politiques dans le partenariat avec les pays d'Europe Centrale et Orientale, in Marie-Francoise Labouz (ed.) (2000), Le Partenariat de l'Union Européenne avec les Pays Tiers, Bruxelles 2000, 103-123.

Andrew Williams (2000), Enlargement of the Union and human rights conditionality: a policy of distinction?, E.L.Rev. 2000, 601.

Bernd Martenczuk*

Cooperation with Developing and Other Third Countries: Elements of a Community Foreign Policy

---

* Member of the Legal Service of the European Commission. The article expresses the personal views of the author only.

I. Introduction

Many of the contributions contained in the present volume are concerned with the Community's common commercial policy, and in particular the relation between foreign policy and foreign trade. However, this does not mean that the commercial policy is the only policy area of the Community which may have foreign policy implications. On the contrary, the Community's external competences are wide and varied. Some of these competences are explicitly foreseen in the Treaty, others may be implicit, following in particular the progress of internal legislation. Overall, the Community's external competences cut across most areas of international relations, making the Community an increasingly important actor in international affairs.

One important area of the Community's activities in the field of external relations is development cooperation and cooperation with other third countries. The Community's cooperation policies cover, in varying degrees, all areas of the globe. Since the Maastricht Treaty, the EC Treaty provides an explicit legal basis for cooperation measures with developing countries. In addition, the Community has established cooperation policies with third countries which are not developing countries. The purpose of the present contribution is to examine the Community's cooperation policies from a legal point of view, and to establish to what extent they may be considered to constitute elements of a Community foreign policy. On this basis, the article will examine the relationship between Community cooperation policy, the European Union's Common Foreign and Security Policy (CFSP), and the bilateral cooperation policies of the Member States.

II. Historical Background

The Community's policy of cooperation with developing and other third countries has developed gradually.[1] The Treaty of Rome

---

[1] For a historical overview of Community development cooperation, see *McMahon* (1998) in particular 1 – 27, and *Zimmermann/Martenczuk* (2000a) notes 1 - 5.

in its original version did not contain any specific legal basis for Community development cooperation, or cooperation with other third countries. The only pertinent provisions were contained in Part IV of the Treaty, concerning the association of the Overseas Countries and Territories. However, with the process of decolonization and the resulting accession of most of these territories to independence, Part IV of the Treaty gradually lost its importance.

The Community was thus faced with the necessity to define its relationship with the newly independent countries, in the beginning in particular in Africa. For this purpose, the Community concluded already in 1964 the Yaoundé Convention with 18 mainly French-speaking African countries. The Yaoundé Convention, which was renewed once, was eventually replaced by the successive Lomé Conventions, which applied to developing countries in Africa, the Caribbean and the Pacific (ACP). Today, the Community's relationship the ACP countries, the number of which has risen to 77, is defined by the ACP-EC Partnership Agreement signed in Cotonou on 23 June 2000.[2]

While relations with the ACP countries have constituted an important part of Community development cooperation, the Community has gradually extended its activities to developing countries in other regions of the world. For instance, in 1992 the Council adopted a regulation governing financial and technical assistance and economic cooperation with the developing countries of Latin America and Asia (ALA).[3] In the context of the Barcelona process, the Community also developed close relations with the countries of the North Africa and the Middle East (MEDA), some of which can be considered as developing countries.[4] However, it was only the Treaty of Maastricht which, with the introduction of Articles 3 r and 179 - 181 EC (ex-Articles 130u - 130y), defined development cooperation formally as an area of Community policy, and

---

2 OJ L 317, 15.12.2000, p. 1. For more detail on the Cotonou Agreement and its historical background, see *McMahon*, supra note 1, 31 – 93; *Martenczuk* (2000) 461.

3 Regulation 443/92, OJ L 52, 27.2.1992, p. 1.

4 Regulation 1488/96, OJ L 189, 30.7.1996, p. 1, as last amended by Regulation 2698/00, OJ L 311, 12.12.2000, p. 1. On the difficult question of the legal basis of the Meda regulation see infra III.1.

established a specific legal basis for the adoption of Community measures in this field.

The Community has also established close cooperation with countries which are not considered as developing countries. Since 1989, this has been the case particularly for the countries of Eastern and Central Europe, which were covered by the Community's PHARE Programme, and which are by now candidates for accession to the EU.[5] Specific programmes have also been established for the countries of the former Soviet Union and Mongolia (TACIS),[6] and for the countries of the former Yugoslavia and Albania (formerly OBNOVA, now CARDS).[7] Finally, the Community has adopted cooperation measures with third countries outside Europe, including industrialised OECD countries.[8] In the absence of a more specific legal basis, such cooperation measures had to be adopted on the basis of Article 308 (ex-235) EC. However, the Treaty of Nice,[9] once it enters into force, will introduce a new Article 181a into the EC Treaty, covering "Economic, Financial and Technical Cooperation with Third Countries".

III. Development Cooperation

The present section will examine Community development cooperation by focusing on three aspects: its geographical coverage,

---

5 Regulation 3908/89, OJ L 375, 23.12.1989, p. 11. The ten countries currently covered by PHARE are Bulgaria, the Czech Republic, Estonia, Hungary, Latvia, Lithuania, Poland, Romania, Slovenia, and Slovakia.

6 Currently regulation 99/00, OJ L 12, 18.1.2000, p. 1. The regulation does not apply to the Baltic countries, which as candidates for accession fall under the PHARE regulation.

7 Regulation 2666/00, OJ L 306, 7.12.2000, p. 1. The Regulation covers Albania, Bosnia and Herzegovina, Croatia, the Federal Republic of Yugoslavia, and the Former Yugoslav Republic of Macedonia. The Regulation does not apply to Slovenia, which as a candidate for accession falls under the PHARE regulation.

8 See Council regulation 382/01 concerning the implementation of projects promoting cooperation and commercial relations between the European Union and the industrialised countries of North America, the Far East and Australasia, OJ L 57, 27.2.2001, p. 10.

9 OJ C 80, 10.3.2001, p. 1.

its substantive scope, and the measures and instruments available to the Community for its implementation.

A. Developing Countries

Article 177 (1) EC, which defines the objectives of Community development cooperation, repeatedly uses the term "developing countries". Accordingly, Community development cooperation does not concern all third countries, but is geographically limited to cooperation with the developing countries and regions of the world. However, the Treaty does not contain a definition of the term developing countries, let alone a list of countries which are to be considered as developing. Therefore, the geographical scope of development cooperation must be determined by other means.

Given the absence of a Community definition, some guidance might be expected from international practice. In fact, several international organisations have attempted to define the term "developing country" by categorising countries according to various criteria, in particular gross national income (GNI) per capita.[10] However, these lists are not always coherent, and will necessarily reflect the needs and policies of the organisation maintaining them. While they may provide useful orientations, they are in no way binding for the Community. The Community institutions must autonomously define which countries they regard as a developing, taking into account the objectives of Community development cooperation.

The notion of "developing country" under Community law can not be defined with respect to one single criterion, such as GNI per capita. The institutions may take into account a wide range of criteria, including economic and social development, structural factors, as well as geographic and political considerations, for

---

10 The World Bank classifies countries in income groups according to gross national income per capita (http://www.worldbank.org/data/databytopic/class.htm). The Development Assistance Committee (DAC) of the OECD maintains a list of developing countries based essentially on aid flows; the DAC treats the transition economies as a group separate from developing countries (http://www.oecd.org/dac/htm/daclst2000.htm). The United Nations Conference on Trade and Development (UNCTAD) maintains a list of least-developed countries (LDCs) including currently 49 countries (http://www.unctad.org/en/pub/ldcprofiles2001.en.htm).

defining which countries are to be regarded as "developing".[11] For this purpose, the Community institutions enjoy a considerable margin of appreciation in determining the geographic reach of Community development cooperation. This allows them to take into account changes taking place in the economic, social or political situation of a country, which may justify a revision of the qualification of certain countries.

The practical reach of Community development cooperation can most easily be defined with reference to the regulations adopted on the basis of Article 179 (1) EC establishing Community cooperation programmes with specific developing countries or regions. Developing are in particular the 77 ACP states which are parties to the Cotonou Agreement, which is an association agreement within the meaning of Article 310 EC. Even though cooperation with these countries has a specific legal basis in the Cotonou Agreement and financial assistance is provided separately through the European Development Fund (EDF) established by Internal Agreements concluded by the Governments of the Member States,[12] for all other purposes these countries are consistently being regarded as falling under the scope of Community development cooperation. This also includes South Africa, which enjoys a qualified status under the Cotonou Agreement, and in particular does not benefit from financial assistance of the EDF.[13] However, South Africa benefits from assistance under the European Programme for Reconstruction and Development (EPRD), which was adopted on the basis of Article 179 (1) EC, and is financed by the Community budget.[14] Also covered by Community development cooperation are the developing countries of Asia and Latin America, which are covered by the ALA regulation.[15] This regulation, which was adopted before the entry into force of the Maastricht treaty on the basis of Article 308 (ex-235) EC, refers specifically to cooperation with the

---

11 See in this sense the Commission's communication on Community Development Cooperation, COM (2000) 212 final, p. 5.

12 For the financing and admininstration of Community aid under the Cotonou Agreement, see Internal Agreement of 23 June 2000, establishing the 9th EDF (OJ L 317 of 15.12.2000, p. 355).

13 See Protocol No. 3 to the Cotonou Agreement, concerning the status of South Africa.

14 Regulation 1726/00, OJ L 198, 4.8.2000, p. 1.

15 Supra note 3.

"developing countries of Latin America and Asia"; since the entry into force of the Maastricht treaty, it has to be considered as falling within the scope of the Community's development cooperation.

In contrast, cooperation with the countries of Central and Eastern Europe, the Balkans as well as the countries of the former Soviet Union and Mongolia is currently governed by the PHARE, Cards and TACIS regulations,[16] all of which have been adopted on the basis of Article 308 EC. Although some of these countries might be regarded as similar to developing countries in terms of their economic and social development, they have not been regarded as developing countries by the Community. This illustrates clearly the importance of structural and political factors in the classification of countries as developing or not. Another interesting case is the MEDA regulation,[17] which covers the countries of North Africa and the Middle East bordering the Mediterranean, including Israel and until recently also Cyprus, Malta, and Turkey. Given the specific characteristics of the latter countries, and notwithstanding that the regulation covers also countries whose characteristics may be more similar to that of developing countries, it was decided to base the MEDA regulation not on the provisions concerning development cooperation, but on Article 308 EC.[18]

It should be noted that treatment of a country in one area of Community policy does not necessarily prejudge its status under another area of Community policy. For instance, most of the countries covered by the TACIS, Cards and MEDA regulations benefit from trade preferences under the Community's regulation on the general system of preferences (GSP), through which the

---

[16] See supra under II.

[17] See supra note 4.

[18] In its last recital, the regulation justifies this legal basis as follows: "whereas the measures under this Regulation go beyond the framework of development assistance and are intended to apply to countries only in part classifiable as developing countries; whereas, therefore, this Regulation cannot be adopted other than on the basis of the powers provided for in Article 235 of the Treaty". This justification may be less valid today, given that Cyprus, Malta and Turkey as accession candidates no longer fall under the MEDA regulation, but under cooperation instruments specific to them.

Community grants trade preferences to developing countries.[19] However, this does not mean that the Community institutions are obliged to treat these countries as developing for the purposes of the Community's development cooperation policy.[20]

Overall, there is clearly a measure of uncertainty and unpredictability with respect to the classification of third countries as developing. This situation is unsatisfying, given particularly the important procedural differences between Articles 179 EC, which provides for the procedure of codecision, and Article 308, according to which the Council decides by unanimity after consulting the European Parliament. The distinction between developing and non-developing third countries may also hinder the formulation of coherent Community policies on a global scale, an aspect to which we shall return when examining the Community's cooperation with non-developing third countries.

B. The Objectives of Development Cooperation

The objectives of development cooperation are defined in broad terms in Article 177 (1) EC. These objectives include the sustainable economic and social development of the developing countries, and more particularly the most disadvantaged among them; the smooth and gradual integration of the developing countries into the world economy; and the campaign against poverty in the developing countries.

The description of these objectives is relatively wide, and therefore leaves the Community a margin of appreciation for the definition of the actual content of its cooperation with developing countries. Such cooperation may often involve financial and technical assistance, but is not necessarily limited to these aspects. Cooperation measures may also concern areas which internally fall under other fields of Community policy. However, as the Court has said for a cooperation agreement with India based on Article 181 EC, cooperation agreements must not impose on the Community "such extensive obligations concerning the specific matters referred to that those obligations in fact constitute objectives distinct from

---

19 Currently Regulation 2501/01, OJ L 346, 31.12.2001, p. 1. The list of beneficiary countries is contained in Annex I to the Regulation.

20 It would not even seem excluded that in exceptional cases, a country might be considered as developing for certain aspects, but not for others. For an example with respect to Turkey, see infra note 71.

those of development cooperation".[21] In concrete terms, this means that whereas the Community can provide funding and assistance to developing countries in all fields relevant for their development, be they economic, social, cultural, or political, the Community could not, through cooperation measures, affect internal legislation in fields other than that of development cooperation.[22]

It should be noted that under Article 177 EC, development cooperation is not limited to questions of economic or social development. Rather, Community development cooperation may address all the causes of poverty and under-development, including questions related to the political system of the developing countries. The importance of political considerations for development cooperation is illustrated by Article 177 (2) EC, which provides that Community policy in this area "shall contribute to the general objective of developing and consolidating democracy and the rule of law, and to that of respecting human rights and fundamental freedoms". The Court of Justice held on this basis that the inclusion of a human rights clause in the cooperation agreement with India was in accordance with the objectives of Community development policy.[23] In fact, by now most Community cooperation agreements include provisions which permit the suspension of the agreement in case of the violation of essential elements such as democracy, the rule of law, and human rights.[24] Moreover, in 1999, the Community adopted a regulation enabling the Community to provide technical and financial aid to "development cooperation operations which contribute to the general objective of developing and consolidating democracy and the rule of law and to that of respecting human rights and fundamental freedoms".[25]

However, not all measures that are motivated by considerations relating to development cooperation must necessarily be based on the legal bases in this field. In fact, Article 178 EC provides that the Community must take the objectives of development cooperation into account in all its policies which are likely to affect developing countries. This is particularly important for the delimitation

---

[21] Case C-268/94, Portugal v. Council, [1996] ECR I-6177, para. 39.
[22] Cf. *Peers* (2000) 100, 112.
[23] Case C-268/94, Portugal v. Council, [1996] ECR I-6177, para. 29.
[24] On this, see *Brandtner/Rosas* (1998) 473 ff and *Hoffmeister* (1998).
[25] Regulation 975/99, OJ L 120, 8.5.1999, p. 1.

between development cooperation and the common commercial policy. The Community traditionally provides for trade preferences benefiting developing countries, particularly through the regulation on the Generalised System of Preferences.[26] As the Court has confirmed, even though the GSP regulation also pursues objectives in the field of development cooperation, it had to be based on Article 133 (ex-113) EC concerning the Common commercial policy.[27] This conclusion, which is in accordance with Article 180 EC, means that where the Community adopts a measures regulating international commerce, this measure must be adopted on the basis of Article 133, even if it is intended to benefit developing countries.

C. Measures and Instruments

Measures adopted for the implementation of Community development cooperation may take the form of international agreements or of autonomous measures.

1. International Agreements

Under Article 181 (1) EC, the Community and the Member States within their respective sphere of competence shall cooperate with third countries and with the competent international organisations. The arrangements for Community cooperation may be the subject of agreements between the Community and the third parties concerned. Such agreements shall be negotiated and concluded according the general procedures applicable for Community agreements contained in Article 300 EC. This means that such agreements are usually concluded by the Council acting by qualified majority upon a proposal from the Commission and after consultation of the Parliament.[28]

---

26 See supra note 19.

27 Case 45/86, Commission v. Council, [1987] ECR 1493, para 20. See also Opinion 1/78, International Agreement on Natural Rubber, [1979] ECR 2871, para 45.

28 Unanimity in Council is necessary where this is required for the adoption of internal rules, or in the case of association agreements; the assent of Parliament is required for association agreements, other agreements establishing a specific institutional framework by organising cooperation procedures, where the agreement has important budgetary implications, or where the agreement entails amendment of an act adopted under the co-decision procedure.

Cooperation agreements concluded on the sole basis of Article 181 (1) EC must remain within the limits of development cooperation as described in Article 177 EC. As a consequence, in practice only few agreements have been concluded on the basis of Article 181 (1) EC alone.[29] More frequently, provisions on financial or technical cooperation are found in bilateral cooperation agreements with third countries that also cover other areas of Community policy, in particular trade. In this case, the conclusion of the international agreement will have to be based not only on Article 181 (1), but on all the substantive legal bases required by the content of the Agreement.[30] Occasionally, recourse to Article 181 (1) may also be necessary for multilateral agreements dealing with horizontal matters such as environmental policy, where such agreements also pursue the objectives of development cooperation.[31]

Finally, in certain cases the Community has concluded association agreements within the meaning of Article 310 EC with developing countries. Pursuant to Article 300 (2) and (3) EC, association agreements are concluded by the Council deciding by unanimity upon a proposal from the Commission, and after having

---

29 Two examples are the Food Aid Convention 1999 (OJ L 163, 4.7.2000, p. 37), and the Convention between the EC and the United Nations Relief and Works Agency for Palestine Refugees (UNRWA) concerning aid to refugees in the countries of the Near East, for the years 1999 to 2001 (OJ L 261, 7.10.1999, p. 36).

30 Examples of such agreements abound: see e.g. the Cooperation Agreement with India, OJ L 223, 27.8.1994, p. 161; the Cooperation Agreement with Laos, OJ L 334, 5.12.1997, p. 14; the Cooperation Agreement with Yemen, OJ L 72, 11.3.1998, p. 17; the Framework Cooperation Agreement with Chile, OJ L 42, 16.2.1999, p. 46; the interregional Framework Cooperation Agreement between the EC and Mercosur, OJ L 112, 29.4.1999, p. 65; the Economic Partnership, Political Coordination and Cooperation Agreement between the EC and its Member States and Mexico, OJ L 276, 28.10.2000, p. 44; or the Cooperation Agreement with the Member States of the Gulf Cooperation Council, OJ L 54, 25.2.1989, p. 1 (still concluded before the entry into force of the Maastricht Treaty on the basis of ex-Articles 113 and 235 EC).

31 See e.g. the UN Convention to combat desertification in countries seriously affected by drought and/or desertification, particularly in Africa, OJ L 83, 19.3.1998, p. 1.

obtained the assent of the European Parliament. Even if association agreements contain provisions on development cooperation, separate recourse to the legal basis of Article 181 (1) EC is unnecessary. The most important association agreement with a development component is the Cotonou Agreement with the ACP countries. The Cotonou Agreement in fact contains a financial protocol, which sets out the amount of financial assistance of the Community to the ACP countries for the period from 2000 to 2005, and contains the conditions and procedures for the implementation of this assistance. Association Agreements with a development component have also been concluded with South Africa[32] and with several countries of North Africa and the Middle East.[33]

2. Autonomous Measures

According to Article 179 (1) EC, the Council may adopt the measures necessary to further the objectives of Community development cooperation. Since the Treaty of Amsterdam, such measures are adopted according to the codecision procedure set out in Article 251 EC. Measures adopted under Article 179 (1) EC may take the form of any of the acts mentioned in Article 249 EC. In practice, regulations have been the most common form for measures of development cooperation.[34]

The measures adopted in the field of development cooperation follow a similar structure. In general, they first establish the objectives and the content of the cooperation measures to be promoted, define the conditions and modalities for the implementation of the measures, and provide for decision-making procedures for the approval of individual projects or programmes. The responsibility for the taking of decisions on projects and programmes is generally held by the Commission, where necessary acting in consultation with a committee composed of

---

32 This agreement is being provisionally applied on the basis of Articles 310 and 300 (2), first paragraph; see OJ L 311, 4.12.1999, p. 1.

33 See e.g. the Agreements with Algeria (OJ L 263, 27.9.1978, p. 1); Egypt (OJ L 266, 27.9.1978, p. 1); Jordan (OJ L 268, 27.9.1978, p. 1); Lebanon (OJ L 267, 27.9.1978, p. 1); Morocco (OJ L 70, 18.3.2000, p. 1).

34 However, decisions can occasionally also be found; see e.g. Decision of the Parliament and the Council concerning the Community contribution to the Global Health Fund, OJ L 7, 11.1.02, p. 1.

representatives of the Member States.[35] In terms of their content, two types of cooperation measures can be distinguished. On the one hand, the Council has adopted a number of regional instruments, covering measures of cooperation with a specific country or region; on the other hand, there are numerous "thematic" or "horizontal" instruments, which cover cooperation in certain areas with all developing countries.

In terms of geographic instruments adopted on the basis of Article 179 (1) EC, the main cases to be mentioned are the ALA regulation and the South Africa regulation.[36] In contrast, cooperation with the biggest group of developing countries, the ACP countries, is primarily governed by the Cotonou Agreement. Article 179 (3) EC states in fact that "this Article shall not affect cooperation with the African, Caribbean and Pacific countries in the framework of the ACP-EC Convention". However, this curiously worded provision does not mean that Community development cooperation does not apply to the largest group of developing countries. In fact, the ACP countries have consistently been regarded as falling under development cooperation, and are covered by all the thematic instruments of development cooperation adopted on the basis of Article 179 (1) EC. Article 179 (3) EC must be understood as referring to the specific status of the EDF, which is not a part of the Community budget, but is established by Internal Agreements of the Member States. With respect to the situation

---

35 These procedures are now modulated for a number of instruments by the recently adopted "rapid reaction mechanism" (Regulation 381/2001, OJ L 57, 27.2.2001, p. 5). According to Article 3 (1) of the Regulation, which was adopted on the basis of Article 308 EC, the mechanism applies "when in the beneficiary countries concerned there occur situations of crisis or emerging crisis, situations posing a threat to law and order, the security and safety of individuals, situations threatening to escalate into armed conflict or to destabilise the country and where such situations are likely to jeopardise the beneficial effects of assistance and cooperation policies [...]". In this case, the Commission may take action without recourse to any committee; it is however required to inform the Council before taking a decision, and must "duly take into account the approach adopted by the Council, in the interest of the cohesion of EU external activities" (Article 4 [2] of the Regulation).

36 See supra notes 3 and 14.

before the entry into force of the Treaty of Amsterdam, the Court had already confirmed the compatibility of this situation with the Treaty.[37] It must be assumed that the intention underlying Article 179 (3) EC was to preserve the possibility to maintain the extra-budgetary status of the EDF even beyond the entry into force of the Maastricht Treaty.[38]

Thematic instruments adopted on the basis of Article 179 (1) EC are numerous. Adopted on this basis was the regulation on humanitarian aid, which constitutes the basis for the Commission's humanitarian activities world-wide.[39] Closely related is the regulation on food aid, which is equally based on Article 179 (1) EC.[40] Outside this area, there is a regulation concerning rehabilitation and reconstruction in developing countries.[41] More recently, a regulation concerning operations of development cooperation which contribute to the general objective of furthering democracy, human rights, and the rule of law has been adopted.[42] Finally, an increasing number of instruments concern more specific topics of development cooperation such as cofinancing of NGO activities in the field of development,[43] decentralised cooperation,[44] conservation of tropical forests,[45] the integration of the environmental dimension into the development process,[46]

---

37 Case C-316/91, Parliament/Council, [1994] ECR I-625. On this case, see *Ward* (2000) 46-47.

38 Cf. with further references *Zimmermann/Martenczuk* (2000b) note 8. This is also confirmed by declaration no. 12 to the Maastricht Treaty, according to which the Conference agreed "that the European Development Fund will continue to be financed by national contributions in accordance with the current provisions".

39 Regulation 1257/96, OJ L 163, 2.7.1996, p. 1.

40 Regulation 1292/96, OJ L 166, 5.7.1996, p. 1.

41 Regulation 2258/95, OJ L 306, 28.11.1996, p.1.

42 Regulation 975/99, OJ L 120, 8.5.1999, p. 1.

43 Regulation 1658/98, OJ L 213, 30.7.1998, p. 1.

44 Regulation 1659/98, OJ L 213, 30.7.1998, p. 6.

45 Regulation 2494/00, OJ L 288, 15.11.2000, p. 6. This regulation was based also on Article 175 (1) EC.

46 Regulation 2493/00, OJ L 288, 15.11.2000, p. 1. This regulation was based also on Article 175 (1) EC.

population policies,[47] HIV/Aids,[48] or the integration of gender issues in development cooperation.[49]

IV. Cooperation with Non-Developing Third Countries

This section will examine the Community's cooperation policy with non-developing countries by focusing on threes aspects: the legal basis and procedures for the adoption of such measures, the measures and instruments adopted by the Community in this area, and the new legal basis to be introduced by the Nice Treaty for such cooperation measures.

A. Legal Basis and Procedures

Unlike for cooperation with developing countries, the EC Treaty still does not contain any specific provisions concerning the cooperation with non-developing third countries. However, the Community has needed to build relations also with such countries, some of which are, due to their economic and political importance or their geographical proximity, of great importance for the Community's external relations. In the absence of a specific legal basis, and to the extent that such measures did not fall under other areas of Community policy, such measures had to be based on Article 308 EC.

Whereas the possibility of basing cooperation with non-developing countries on Article 308 EC has generally been accepted,[50] recourse to this provision can nonetheless cause considerable practical difficulties. Unlike under Article 179 (1), according to which measures are adopted by the Parliament and the Council acting under the codecision procedure, measures under Article 308 EC are adopted by the Council acting unanimously and after consultation of the Parliament. The requirement of unanimity constitutes a considerable hurdle for the adoption of cooperation measures, without this being justified by any specific characteristics of non-developing countries.

Additional difficulties are created where cooperation measures, due to their horizontal or thematic character, should apply both to developing and to non-developing countries. Under the case law of

---

47 Regulation 1484/97, OJ L 202, 30.7.1997, p. 1.

48 Regulation 550/97, OJ L 85, 27.3.1997, p. 1.

49 Regulation 2836/98, OJ L 354, 30.12.1998, p. 5.

50 Cf. *Bungenberg* (2000) 884 – 888.

the Court,[51] it would be inappropriate to combine the legal bases of Articles 179 (1) and 308 EC, since the procedures applicable under these provisions are not compatible, particularly with respect to the rights of Parliament. Therefore, in accordance with the Court's case law, where a measure applies both to developing and to non-developing countries, it needs to be determined which aspect is predominant, and the act must be adopted on the corresponding legal basis. An example of a case where the legal basis for development has been retained is the humanitarian aid regulation, which covers assistance to "people in third countries, particularly the most vulnerable among them, and as a priority those in developing countries".[52] Another example is the rehabilitation regulation, which includes among its definition of "developing countries" also the countries of the Mediterranean, of the Caucasus and of Central Asia, which are not traditionally considered as developing countries.[53] Examples where Article 308 EC has been retained as the predominant legal basis are the MEDA regulation, covering a group of countries exhibiting in varying degrees the characteristics of developing countries,[54] or the recent regulation on the rapid reaction mechanism, which covers the reaction to crises both in developing and in non-developing countries.[55] Finally, where it is not possible to make out such a centre of gravity, it may be necessary to adopt two separate acts, one based on Article 179 (1), the other on Article 308 EC. This approach was followed in the field of human rights, where a separate regulation covering non-developing countries, but otherwise identical to the regulation covering developing countries, was adopted.[56] However, such a

---

51 Case C-300/89, Commission v. Council, [1991] ECR I-2867, para. 17 - 21.

52 Article 1 of Regulation 1257/96 (supra note 39).

53 Article 1 (2) of Regulation 2258/96 (supra note 41).

54 See supra III.A.

55 See supra note 35. The emergency procedures contained in this regulation are applicable to all the instruments listed in its annex, which includes both instruments applicable to developing countries and instruments applicable to other third countries.

56 Regulation 976/99, OJ L 120, 8.5.1999, p. 8. The same approach has been followed for two recently adopted regulations concerning action against anti-personnel landmines; see Regulation 1724/2001, OJ L 234,

"splitting" of acts is not helpful for the efficiency and coherence of the Community's action, and moreover does not remove the requirement of unanimity for the adoption of the act applicable to non-developing countries.

B. Measures and Instruments

As for developing countries, measures adopted for the implementation of Community cooperation with non-developing countries may take the form of international agreements or of autonomous measures.

1. International Agreements

There is currently no specific legal basis equivalent to Article 181 (1) EC for the conclusion of international agreements providing for cooperation measures with third countries. The absence of such a legal basis is unproblematic where the Community has concluded association agreements based on Article 310 EC with non-developing third countries. This is the case particularly for the ten candidate countries from Central and Eastern Europe, with which the Community has concluded "Europe Agreements" based on Article 310 EC.[57] Association agreements also bind the Community with the three Mediterranean candidate countries Cyprus, Malta, and Turkey.[58] An association agreement is also the Agreement establishing the European Economic Area (EEA), which includes Iceland, Liechtenstein, and Norway.[59] A package of seven agreements with Switzerland, which together will be based on Article 310 EC, is currently in the course of conclusion.

Outside the field of association agreements, where an international agreement contains provisions on cooperation measures that do not fall under other areas of Community

---

1.9.01, p. 1 (applicable to developing countries) and Regulation 1725/2001, OJ L 234, 1.9.01, p. 6 (applicable to other third countries).

57 See e.g. the Europe Agreement with Bulgaria, OJ L 358, 31.12.1994, p. 1. For more background on the legal relationship between the EC and the countries of central and eastern Europe, see *Evans* (1996) and *Maresceau/ Montaguti* (1995).

58 See OJ L 133, 21.5.1973, p. 1 (Cyprus); OJ L 61, 14.3.1971, p. 1 (Malta); OJ L 217, 29,12.1964, 3685 (Turkey). With Turkey, the association also includes a customs union (see decision 1/95 of the EC-Turkey Association Council, OJ L 35,13.2.1996, p.1).

59 OJ L 1, 3.1.1994, p. 1.

competence, conclusion of the Agreement may require recourse to Article 308 EC. Whereas there seem to be no agreements exclusively based on Article 308 EC, recourse to Article 308 EC has been frequent in the context of general cooperation agreements with third countries simultaneously covering other policy areas, in particular trade. Examples for such agreements are the cooperation agreements which the Community has concluded with most countries of the former Soviet Union and Mongolia, which were all based, along with other provisions, on Article 308 EC.[60] A similar example in the area of the former Yugoslavia is the cooperation agreement with the Former Yugoslav Republic of Macedonia.[61] Finally, the Community has also concluded cooperation agreements with certain industrialised third countries, in particular Canada and South Korea.[62]

In all these cases, the recourse to Article 308 EC has a similar function as recourse to Article 181 (1) EC for developing countries: it covers provisions on economic, financial or technical cooperation for which no legal basis can be found elsewhere in the Treaty. However, recourse to Article 308 EC also implies that the conclusion of the agreement, even if for all other areas qualified majority would suffice, has to be decided by unanimity.

2. Autonomous Measures

On the basis of Article 308 EC, the Community has also adopted a number of autonomous instruments governing economic, financial and technical cooperation with non-developing third countries. Most of these instruments have a regional focus. There are only few "thematic" or "horizontal" instruments covering specifically non-developing third countries, with the exception of those that "mirror" a parallel instrument applicable to developing countries, as in the case of the Human Rights regulations.[63]

---

60 See e.g. the decision for the conclusion of the Cooperation Agreement with Russia, OJ L 327, 28.11.1997, p. 1.

61 OJ L 348, 18.12.1997, p. 1. A Stabilisation and Association Agreement is currently in the process of conclusion. In the meantime, the Council has already decided the conclusion of an interim agreement on trade and trade-related matters, which partially replaces the cooperation agreement with this country (OJ L 124, 4.5.2001, p. 1).

62 OJ L 260, 24.9.1976, p. 1 (Canada); OJ L 90, 30.3.2001, p. 45 (Korea).

63 See supra under I.

With respect to the candidate countries of Central and Eastern Europe, the general instrument for the provision of assistance is the PHARE regulation.[64] Originally adopted to cover only Poland and Hungary, this instrument now applies, after several amendments, to all 10 candidate countries from Central and Eastern Europe. These countries are also covered by two further instruments, the first one establishing an "Instrument for Structural Policies for Preaccession" (ISPA)[65], the second concerning pre-accession measures for agricultural and rural development.[66] The objectives and conditions of the "accession partnership" with each candidate country is established by the Council upon a proposal from the Commission, acting on the basis of a further regulation adopted on the basis of Article 308 EC.[67] As regards the three Mediterranean candidate countries, all of which used to be covered by the MEDA regulation, Cyprus and Malta are now covered by a specific financial instrument concerning the implementation of a preaccesion strategy.[68] With respect to Turkey, there is a regulation concerning the establishment of an accession partnership.[69] With respect to specific financial assistance, there is a regulation regarding the implementation of measures to intensify the EC-Turkey customs union,[70] and a further regulation concerning the implementation of measures to promote economic and social development in Turkey.[71]

---

64 See supra note 5.
65 Regulation 1267/99, OJ L 161, 26.6.1999, p. 73.
66 Regulation 1268/99, OJ L 161, 26.6.1999, p. 87.
67 Regulation 622/98, OJ L 85, 20.3.1998, p. 1.
68 Regulation 555/00, OJ L 68, 16.3.2000, p. 3.
69 Regulation 390/01, OJ L 58, 26.2.2001, p. 1. On the basis of this regulation, the Council has decided on the principles, priorities and objectives of this partnership; see decision 2001/235, OJ L 85, 24.3.2000, p. 13.
70 Regulation 764/00, OJ L 94, 14.4.2000, p. 6.
71 Regulation 257/01, OJ L 39, 9.2.2001, p. 1. Curiously, this regulation is based on Article 179 (1), and not on Article 308 EC. It is not entirely clear whether this choice of legal basis results simply from the fact that the candidate status of Turkey was not yet taken into account, or whether the classification of Turkey as a developing country for the purposes of this regulation was a conscious choice. An indication in the latter sense could be the 13th recital of the regulation, which provides that "projects and programmes financed with this support

Furthermore, a regulation based on Article 308 EC on pre-accession financial assistance to Turkey has recently been adopted.[72]

Assistance to the countries of the former Yugoslavia - with the exception of Slovenia, which as an accession candidate falls under the PHARE instrument - and Albania are now covered by the recently adopted CARDS regulation.[73] The Council has, on the basis of Article 308 EC, also established the European Agency for Reconstruction, to which the Commission may delegate the implementation of Community assistance under the CARDS regulation.[74] This creation of an agency with legal personality and responsibility for implementation constitutes a new approach towards the implementation of Community assistance. Whether this constitutes a precedent or will be limited to the specific situation of post-conflict reconstruction in former Yugoslavia remains to be seen. Also on the basis of Article 308 EC, the Council has approved a Community contribution to the UN Mission in Kosovo (UNMIK) and the office of the High Representative of the OECD in Bosnia-Herzegovina.[75] The follow-up of financing decisions taken for this purpose may equally be delegated to the Agency for Reconstruction.[76]

Support to the countries of Eastern Europe and Central Asia is covered by the TACIS regulation, which was most recently renewed in 1999. This regulation, which is valid until 2006, covers measures to promote the transition to a market economy and to strengthen democracy and the rule of law. Cooperation with the countries of North Africa and the Middle East is governed by the MEDA regulation, equally adopted on the basis of Article 308 EC.[77]

Finally, the Council has recently adopted a regulation "concerning the implementation of projects promoting cooperation and commercial relations between the European Union and the industrialised countries of North America, the Far East and

---

must benefit above all the population affected by Turkey's development lag".

72 OJ L 342, 27.12.01, p.1.

73 Supra note 7.

74 See Article 1 of Regulation 2667/00, OJ L 306, 7.12.2000, p. 7.

75 Regulation 1080/00, OJ L 122, 24.5.2000, p. 27.

76 Article 2 (4) of Regulation 2667/00.

77 See already supra III.A.

Australasia".[78] This regulation, which covers particularly cooperation measures to promote access of European business to the Japanese market, is partially based on Article 133 EC. However, to the extent that the regulation covers cooperation measures not directly linked to commercial matters, e.g. promoting links in the field of culture, academia, research or civil society,[79] it was deemed necessary to base the regulation also on Article 308 EC. This regulation is interesting since it shows that Community cooperation policy is not limited to developing or transition countries, but can in fact apply to all third countries regardless of their level of economic and social development.

C. The Nice Treaty and Cooperation with Non-Developing Third Countries

The frequent recourse to Article 308 EC for cooperation measures with non-developing third countries clearly shows that the legal bases provided by the EC Treaty in its current form are not adequate to the objectives and activities of the Community in the field. In order to redress this situation, and in accordance with the general objective to reduce the incidence of unanimity voting in the Council, the Nice Treaty contains a new Title XXI concerning "Economic, Financial and Technical Cooperation with Third Countries". This new Title will consist of one single article (future Article 181a EC), which will, once the Nice Treaty has entered into force, provide a new legal basis for cooperation measures with third countries reading as follows:

> "1. Without prejudice to the other provisions of this Treaty, and in particular those of Title XX, the Community shall carry out, within its spheres of competence, economic, financial and technical cooperation measures with third countries. Such measures shall be complementary to those carried out by the Member States and consistent with the development policy of the Community.
>
> Community policy in this area shall contribute to the general objective of developing and consolidating democracy and the rule of law, and to the objective of respecting human rights and fundamental freedoms.

---

[78] Regulation 382/01, L 57, 27.12.2001, p. 10.

[79] See Article 4 of the Regulation.

2. The Council, acting by a qualified majority on a proposal from the Commission and after consulting the European Parliament, shall adopt the measures necessary for the implementation of paragraph 1. The Council shall act unanimously for the association agreements referred to in Article 310 and for the agreements to be concluded with the States which are candidates for accession to the Union.
3. Within their respective spheres of competence, the Community and the Member States cooperate with third countries and the competent international organisations. The arrangements for Community cooperation may be the subject of agreements between the Community and the parties concerned, which shall be negotiated and concluded in accordance with Article 300.
The first subparagraph shall be without prejudice to the Member States' competence to negotiate in international bodies and to conclude international agreements."

1. Objectives and Scope

The new provision will entitle the Community to carry out, within its sphere of competence, economic, financial and technical cooperation measures with third countries.

The new provision applies "without prejudice to the other provisions of this Treaty, and in particular those of Title XX", concerning Community development cooperation. Accordingly, Article 181a EC does not apply to cooperation with developing countries. The residual character of the provision means that its geographical scope is identical with that of the countries and regions for which previously recourse to Article 308 EC was necessary. In fact, the central objective of Article 181a EC was not to create a new Community competence, but to provide for a simpler procedure for the exercise of a Community competence that was previously exercised on the basis of Article 308 EC. For this reason, the Community's practice of cooperation with non-developing third countries until the signature of the Treaty of Nice provides a useful point of reference for the interpretation of the new Article 181a.

The "economic, financial and technical cooperation measures" are not further described in the new Article. The first subparagraph of the Article provides that "such measures shall be complementary to those carried out by the Member States and consistent with the development policy of the Community". This reference to Title XX means that where the economic, social and structural characteristics of the country concerned are comparable to those of a developing country, the objectives of development cooperation set out in Article 177 may also provide inspiration for cooperation with non-developing third countries. However, cooperation with third countries on the basis of Article 181a may also take on substantively different content from development cooperation. For instance, Article 181a would seem to permit the Community to adopt cooperation measures regarding industrialised third countries, as it has already done in the regulation concerning relations with North America, the Far East and Australasia.[80] Of course, to the extent that such measures fall under the scope of other Community policies, in particular the common commercial policy, the more specific legal basis will prevail.

It should be noted that like development cooperation, the new Article 181a is not limited to questions of economic relations. Rather, cooperation with third countries may include all questions relevant in relations with third countries, including political matters. This is in fact illustrated by the second subparagraph of Article 181a (1), which in terms identical to Article 177 (2) EC provides that Community policy in this area shall contribute to the general objective of developing and consolidating democracy and the rule of law, and to the objective of respecting human rights and fundamental freedoms. In concrete terms, this means that regulations like the human rights regulation applicable to non-developing countries could in the future be based on Article 181a.

Article 181a does not limit the type of the measures falling under it. Whereas it certainly covers classic financial and technical assistance, more innovative measures of cooperation would not seem excluded. Therefore, it does not seem excluded that instruments such as those concerning Community support to MINUK or the creation of the European Agency for Reconstruction may in the future - at least partially - be based on Article 181a.

2. Measures and Instruments

The legal basis for the adoption of internal acts will be Article 181a (2), which provides that the Council, acting by a qualified

---

80 See supra note 78.

majority on a proposal from the Commission and after consulting the European Parliament, shall adopt the necessary measures. This provision, which is the functional equivalent of Article 179 (1) for developing countries, should make recourse to Article 308 EC in the future unnecessary for cooperation with third countries. The main improvement achieved by this provision is that the Council decides by qualified majority and no longer by unanimity, as necessary under Article 308 EC. However, an important procedural difference remains in the fact that under Article 179 (1), the Council decides in co-decision with the Parliament, whereas under Article 181a, the Parliament will merely have to be consulted. Since the procedures of Article 179 (1) and 181 (a) are still not entirely compatible, it is not clear whether acts could be based on both provisions simultaneously.[81] This is regrettable, since it implies that the unsatisfying distinction between developing and non-developing countries for the adoption of internal measures, resulting sometimes in the adoption of two separate acts, will have to continue for some time.

A legal basis for the conclusion of international agreements concerning the arrangements for Community cooperation will in the future be provided by Article 181a (3), which is drafted in terms identical to those of Article 181. Such agreements shall be negotiated and concluded according to the procedures of Article 300, which means that the conclusion is usually decided by the Council acting upon a proposal from the Commission by qualified majority and after consultation of the Parliament. This new legal basis will normally make reference to Article 308 EC unnecessary for the conclusion of cooperation agreements with non-developing third countries, which will therefore most frequently be concluded by qualified majority.

However, this advance seems to be partially contradicted by the second sentence of Article 181a (2), which provides that the

---

81 It should be noted that in case C-300/89 (supra note 51), the Court based its conclusion regarding the incompatibility of the procedures in question primarily on the fact that under Article 308 EC, the Council had in any case to decide by unanimity. Since this requirement no longer applies under Article 181a, it is not excluded that the Court might today reach a different result regarding the possibility to combine Articles 179 (1) and 181a.

Council "shall act unanimously for the association agreements referred to in Article 310 and for the agreements to be concluded with the States which are candidates for accession to the Union". From a systematic point of view, it is already unclear why this provision is inserted in paragraph 2 of Article 181a, which deals with the adoption of internal measures, and not in paragraph 3, which deals with the conclusion of international agreements. As for the reference to Article 310 EC, the provision is moreover superfluous, since it already follows from the first subparagraph of Article 300 (2) that the Council shall act unanimously with respect to association agreements. The only innovation contained in this sentence seems therefore to be the requirement of unanimity for "agreements to be concluded with the States which are candidates for accession to the Union".[82] On a first reading, this provision might seem to require that all international agreements to be concluded with candidate countries would have to be concluded by unanimity, even where other provisions of the Treaty, e.g. in the field of trade, would normally permit conclusion by qualified majority. However, such an interpretation would contradict the objective of the Treaty of Nice, which was to promote and not to restrict the use of qualified majority voting in the Council. Moreover, it would also result in a discrimination of the candidate countries, which would be subject to stricter procedural requirements than all other countries. For this reason, the reference to "the agreements" with candidate countries must be read to refer to such agreements which in scope and function are equivalent to association agreements, i.e. general trade and cooperation agreements. In this reading, the second phrase of Article 181a (2) becomes largely irrelevant, since all present candidate countries already have association agreements with the Community, to which the unanimity requirement applies.

Overall, Article 181a is a useful addition to the Treaty, which will permit qualified majority voting for most matters, and thereby reduce the procedural differences between Community cooperation with developing and non-developing countries. It is regrettable, however, that this harmonisation of procedures is not complete,

---

[82] It may be noted that this is the first time that the Treaty uses the term "candidate for accession" and attaches legal consequences to this status.

particularly with respect to the role of Parliament. It must also be criticised that the drafting of the provision is unsystematic and unclear. It scope is therefore difficult to discern unless recourse is had to the Community *acquis* of cooperation measures with third countries already existing on the basis of Article 308 EC.

V. Community Cooperation Policy, CFSP and Member States

The present section will examine the relationship of Community cooperation policy with CFSP, and with the Member States' remaining competence in the field of cooperation with third countries.

A. Community Cooperation and CFSP

As was shown in the preceding sections, Community cooperation policy - in particular cooperation with developing countries - is not limited to addressing the symptoms of poverty and underdevelopment. Rather, Community cooperation policy increasingly follows a "deep" approach, which permits the Community to address the underlying causes of poverty and underdevelopment, such as political and social instability, lack of adequate institutional and administrative structures, and insufficient respect for democratic principles, human rights and the rule of law.[83] The most prominent horizontal instrument for Community measures in this respect are the human rights regulations, which permit the Community to carry out a wide range of activities promoting democracy, the rule of law and human rights in developing and non-developing third countries.[84] Most regional instruments of development cooperation equally permit the Community to contribute to actions in the fields of administrative and institutional reform, democracy, human rights, and the rule of

---

83 See the Commission's communication on the Community's development policy, which defines institutional support, good governance and rule of law as a priority area for Community development cooperation (COM [2000] 212 final, 30-31).

84 For a detailed description of possible measures, see Article 2 of Regulation 975/99 (OJ L 120, 8.5.1999, p. 1), and Article 3 of Regulation 976/99 (OJ L 120, 8.5.1999, p. 8).

law, and even conflict prevention and resolution.[85] Another illustration are the human rights clauses which the Community has introduced into most of its cooperation agreements, and which in the case of violations of democratic principles, human rights or the rule of law may give rise to the suspension of cooperation.[86] A particularly striking example is finally the regulation on the Rapid Reaction Mechanism, which provides for simplified decision making procedures for the application of Community cooperation instruments in case of "situations of crisis or emerging crisis, situations posing a threat to law and order, the security and safety of individuals, situations threatening to escalate into armed conflict or to destabilise the country and where such situations are likely to jeopardise the beneficial effects for assistance and cooperation policies".[87]

Inevitably, many Community measures in this area may also have political implications. Therefore, the question of the relationship of Community cooperation policy with the CFSP arises. In particular, the question might arise whether, where the Community has a competence to adopt a particular measure or carry out a particular action, the Council is still free to adopt the same or a similar measure acting within the framework of CFSP. A concrete example would be electoral observation, which is now explicitly covered by the human rights regulations.[88] Another example would be the sending or support of facilitators and mediators in situations of internal conflict in a third country, actions which are now equally covered by the human rights regulations.[89] It should be noted that the distinction between Community competence and CFSP has important institutional implications. Under most Community instruments, it is the Commission, where appropriate after consultation of a committee composed of

---

85 See Article 2 (2) of Regulation 1726/00 (South Africa); Article 1 of Regulation 443/92 (ALA); Article 2 (2) of Regulation 2666/00 (Cards); Article 2 (2) and Annex II to Regulation 99/00 (TACIS); Articles 9 and 11 of the Cotonou Agreement.

86 See supra note 24.

87 Supra note 35.

88 See in particular Article 2 (2) (f) of Regulation 975/99; Article 3 (2) (f) of Regulation 976/99.

89 See in particular Article 2 (3) (c) of Regulation 975/99; Article 3 (3) (c) of Regulation 976/99.

representatives of the Member States, which approves the measures to be taken. In exchange, it is the Council who decides on actions in the context of CFSP in accordance with the requirements of Article 23 EU.

The central provision governing the relationship between the Community and CFSP is Article 47 EU, which provides that nothing in the EU Treaty shall affect the EC Treaty.[90] In concrete terms, this means that no measure adopted in the context of the 2nd (or 3rd) pillar may affect the competences of the EC under the EC Treaty. However, Community competence would necessarily be affected the Council were to adopt an act or measure which could also have been adopted on the basis of the EC Treaty. As a consequence, the 2nd pillar has a residual character: only where action is not possible on the basis of the EC Treaty may recourse be had to CFSP instruments. Concretely speaking, this means that at least since the entry into force of the Human Rights regulations, electoral observations mission must be adopted exclusively on the basis of the relevant Community instruments, and not through CFSP action.[91] The same applies to the support for mediation and facilitation efforts,[92] and any other measure of support to democracy, human rights and the rule of law covered by the Human Rights regulation.[93] It should be noted that this applies also where the Commission, for reasons of political opportunity, has decided not to take action under the relevant Community instrument.

---

90 On the relation of Community competence and CFSP, see in more detail *Wessels* (1999) 56-58.

91 In this sense, see the Commission's communication on EU Election Assistance and Observation, COM (2000) 191 final, 11.

92 Legally doubtful is therefore Council decision of 14.5.2001, concerning a European Union contribution to a mission to facilitate dialogue in Togo (OJ L 132, 15.5.2001, p. 7). However, at the time of the adoption of this decision, it was agreed that this decision would remain exceptional, and any continuation of the mission would take the form of special representatives of the Council pursuant to Article 18 (5) EU.

93 To this extent, the human rights regulations have partially superseded the Common Position of 25 May 1998 concerning human rights, democratic principles, the rule of law and good governance in Africa (OJ L 158, 2.6.1998, p. 1).

The gradual evolution of Community cooperation policy has therefore important implications for the scope of the second pillar. In fact, given the subsidiary character of CFSP, the adoption of specific legal basis for Community cooperation measures can be regarded as leading to a corresponding "communitarisation" of matters previously falling under CFSP. It should be noted that the distinction between Community competence and CFSP is not merely theoretical, but is also amenable to judicial review. As the Court has already held, Article 46 EU does not exclude its competence to interpret the final provisions of the EU Treaty, including the provision of Article 47 EU, concerning the relationship between the Community and the second and third pillar.[94] As a consequence, were the Council acting within the framework of CFSP to adopt an act falling under Community competence, the Court would have jurisdiction to review such an act under Article 230 EC.

B. Community Cooperation and Member States

Unlike other areas of Community policy, for instance the common commercial policy, Community cooperation policy is not an exclusive Community competence. For the situation before the entry into force of the Treaty of Maastricht, this was already recognised by the Court of Justice.[95] It is now explicitly confirmed in Article 177 (1) EC, according to which Community policy in the sphere of development cooperation "shall be complementary to the policies pursued by the Member States". Article 181 (1) EC further provides that "within their respective spheres of competence, the Community and Member States shall cooperate with third countries and with the competent international organisations", whereas Article 181 (2) provides that the Community's competences in the field remain "without prejudice to Member States competence to negotiate in international bodies and to conclude international agreements". Identical principles also apply for cooperation with non-developing third countries, as confirmed by the future Article 181a EC.

---

94 Case C-170/96, Commission/Council, [1998] ECR I-2763, para 14 - 17.

95 Joined cases C-181/91 and C-248/91, European Parliament v. Council and Commission, [1993] ECR I-3685, para 16; case C-316/91, European Parliament v. Council, [1994] ECR I-625, para 26.

If therefore there is no doubt that development cooperation constitutes a shared competence of the Community and its Member States, this does not mean that Member States may ignore the Community framework in the conduct of their bilateral cooperation policies. Indeed, the Court has repeatedly stated that where the Community and its Member States act jointly in international fora or in the context of international agreements, they are under a duty of close cooperation.[96] This duty of cooperation, which can already be deduced from Article 10 EC, is further specified for the field of development cooperation in Article 180 (1) EC, according to which "the Community and its Member States shall coordinate their policies on development cooperation and shall consult each other on their aid programmes, including in international organisations and during international conferences. The same principles must be considered to apply also with respect to non-developing third countries."[97] This requirement of coherence in the external action of the Community and its Member States also follows from Article 3 (2) EU, according to which the Union shall ensure "the consistency of its external activities as a whole in the context of its external relations, security, economic and development policies".

As a consequence, both the Community and its Member States must, in the conduct of their cooperation policies, take due account of each other's policies. This means in particular that individual Member States may not with their bilateral policies contradict or adversely affect cooperation measures that have been adopted by the competent Community institutions. For instance, where the Community has decided to suspend its cooperation with a particular third country, e.g. due to human rights abuses in this country, a Member State may not at the same time decide to make new assistance available for such a country. Similarly, where the Community is putting in place cooperation measures in a particular country, e.g. an electoral observation mission, Member States may

---

[96] Ruling 1/78 IAEA Convention [1978] ECR 2151, para 36; Opinion 2/91 Convention no. 170 of the International Labour Organization [1993] ECR I-1061, para 36; Opinion 1/94 WTO [1994] ECR I-5267, para 108.

[97] It must be noted that the future Article 181a EC does not contain a provision equivalent to Article 180 EC. However, this cannot exclude the applicability of the duty of cooperation, which already flows from Article 10 EC, in this area.

not without the agreement of the competent Community institutions individually carry out a competing observation mission.

Finally, it should be added that the competences of the Member States in the field of development cooperation are limited to the conduct of their bilateral cooperation policies. Coordinated action at the European level must therefore take place exclusively through the appropriate Community mechanisms, or, where the action in question does not fall under Community competence, through CFSP. Accordingly, the competences of Member States in the field of development cooperation would not entitle Member States to act jointly outside the Union framework, thereby possibly also affecting Community competences.

VI. Conclusion

For a long time, the European Community was regarded as a primarily economic organisation. Even though it disposed of important competences with respect to third countries, in particular in the field of the common commercial policy, these competences were regarded as functionally limited. Foreign policy as such was regarded as being outside the ambit of the Community, and remained the prerogative of the Member States. This understanding clearly underlies the Treaty of Maastricht, which organised the Common Foreign and Security Policy as a separate pillar of the Union outside the framework of the Community.

Cooperation with developing and other third countries clearly shows that this distinction between the three pillars of the Union, and in particular between Community competence and CFSP, is becoming increasingly outdated. By now, Community cooperation policy covers potentially all countries of the world, and pervades, subject to the other provisions of the EC Treaty, all areas of cooperation with third countries, including economic, social, and political aspects. By their very nature, measures of Community cooperation are also political instruments, and are used in accordance with political objectives. Community cooperation policy can therefore be regarded as a component of a Community foreign policy, which the Community conducts, within the framework of the Union, on the basis of the various competences it has in the external field. In exchange, due to its residual character, CFSP is becoming increasingly focused on areas in which the Community does not yet have competence, in particular the security and defence area.

In the long run, the question must be asked whether the separation between Community foreign policy measures and CFSP can be maintained. The distinction between foreign policy formulation, supposedly taking place in the CFSP context, and the use of instruments of foreign policy, most of which fall under Community competence, is becoming increasingly artificial. There is no doubt that the coherence and efficiency of the European Union's external action would be increased if all its external activities were brought under one common legal framework. It is submitted that Community cooperation policy shows that the European Community would be perfectly well adapted for providing such a framework.

References

Barbara Brandtner/Allan Rosas (1998), Human Rights and the External Relations of the European Community: An Analysis of Doctrine and Practice, EJIL 9 (1998), 468-490.

Marc Bungenberg (2000), Dynamische Integration, Art. 308 und die Forderung nach dem Kompetenzkatalog, EuR 6/2000, 879-900.

Andrew Evans (1996), The Integration of the European Community and Third States in Europe. A Legal Analysis, Oxford 1996.

Frank Hoffmeister (1998), Menschenrechts- und Demokratieklauseln in den vertraglichen Außenbeziehungen der Europäischen Gemeinschaften (= Beiträge zum ausländischen und öffentlichen Recht und Völkerrecht Vol. 132), Berlin/Heidelberg/New York 1998.

Marc Maresceau/Elisabetta Montaguti (1995), The Relations between the European Union and Central and Eastern Europe, CMLRev. 1995, 1327-1367.

Bernd Martenczuk (2000), From Lomé to Cotonou: The ACP-EC Partnership Agreement in a Legal Perspective, EFARev. 2000, 461-487.

Joseph A. McMahon (1998), The Development Cooperation Policy of the EC, London et al. 1998.

Steve Peers (2000), Fragmentation or Evasion in the Community's Development policy? The Impact of Portugal vs. Council, in: Alan Dashwood/Christophe Hillion (eds), The General Law of E.C. External Relations, London 2000, 100-114.

Angela Ward (2000), Community Development Aid and the Evolution of the Inter-Institutional Law of the European Union, in: Alan Dashwood/Christophe Hillion (eds), The General Law of E.C. External Relations, London 2000, 42-47.

Ramses A. Wessel (1999), The European Union's Foreign and Security Policy, The Hague 1999.

Andreas Zimmermann/Bernd Martenczuk (2000a), Artikel 177, in Jürgen Schwarze (ed), EU-Kommentar, Baden-Baden 2000, 1691-1701.

Andreas Zimmermann/Bernd Martenczuk (2000b), Artikel 179, in Jürgen Schwarze (ed), EU-Kommentar, Baden-Baden 2000, 1701-1709.

Birgit Weidel

The Community Export Control System for Dual Use Goods – A Story of Reconquering Lost Grounds?

I. Introduction

Since the end of the Second World War, restrictions and controls on exports of arms and strategic goods have become an essential component of national security policy. Despite the significant economic dimension of such trade restrictions, no attempts have been made for decades to establish a coherent legal regime at the level of the European Community. Constituting core elements of security policy, matters touching on defence and armament have been regarded as an unimpeachable reserve of national sovereignty. This assumption excluded any action on the part of the European Community, which was perceived as a purely economic organisation. At the beginning of the 70s, the governments of the EC Member States nevertheless started to coordinate questions of "high politics" informally in the framework of European Political Cooperation. The Treaty on European Union (TEU) gave a new political and legal quality to this informal cooperation. By establishing a Common Foreign and Security Policy (CFSP), the so-called second pillar of the European Union, it has created an official forum explicitly designed to deal with foreign policy and security issues. However, action in the framework of CFSP differs significantly from action under the Treaty establishing the European Community (TEC). Due to the intergovernmental structure of the second pillar, which ensures a high level of individual national influence, acts adopted under CFSP do not have the same legal quality in terms of enforceability and effectiveness as the law generated under the TEC. These significant structural differences are subject to legal tensions as soon as competences between the TEC and CFSP are not clear-cut.[1]

This is exactly the case for export controls on military or dual-use goods, as trade in strategic goods is allocated at the interface of commercial policy, an EC competence, and foreign and security policy. It thus serves as an excellent example for the difficulty to determine the borders between external EC and CFSP competences. Economic and political aspects are inextricably linked in measures restricting trade with third countries for reasons of security policy considerations. This duality was reflected in the structure of the first EU export control regime for dual-use goods established in 1994, which was based on both the first and second pillars. This cross-pillar was implicitly rejected by two judgments of the European Court of Justice (ECJ). Coherently this system has been replaced by a regime exclusively based on the TEC. This essay will re-examine the background of competence distribution with regard to trade in dual-use goods and analyse whether the control system established under Community law actually lives up to a common export policy in this area.

II. International Export Control Regimes for Dual-Use Goods

National and European export control regulations are strongly influenced by arrangements at international level. For a comprehensive understanding, it is illuminating to look at the export control mechanisms developed at the international plane. Without going into the details of the different regimes, this section provides a short overview on the existing initiatives.[2]

The most influential and effective control regime was certainly set up by the Coordination Committee for East West Trade Policy (CoCom). Founded in 1949 at the instigation of the US, CoCom's main objective was to prevent the arming of Warsaw Pact states with Western technology and armaments. The Committee elaborated three different lists of products and technologies, which were subject to export restrictions. The "munitions list" included arms and munitions, whereas the "nuclear list" contained nuclear substances. The third list, the so-called "industrial list", referred to

---

[1] See *Weidel* in this volume, 26ff and 49ff.

[2] For a detailed presentation with further references see *Karpenstein* (1998) 154ff.

dual-use goods. Despite working only on an informal basis, the export control system developed in CoCom led to a harmonisation of Western European national export controls, since it was not only adopted by its members[3] but also by other Western-oriented states.

Although, CoCom was dissolved in 1994 following the end of the Cold War, its work is now continued in the framework of the Wassenaar Arrangement (WA) founded in 1996. Contrary to its predecessor, however, the WA is not directed against any state or group of states and presently consists of 33 participating countries, including former Warsaw Pact states.[4] According to its "Initial Elements", the arrangement aims to contribute to regional and international security and stability, by promoting transparency and greater responsibility in transfers of conventional arms and dual-use goods and by complementing and reinforcing the existing control regimes for weapons of mass destruction and their delivery systems. Efforts shall be made to prevent the acquisition of armaments and sensitive dual-use items for military end-uses, if the situation in a region or the behaviour of a state raises serious concerns on part of the participating states.[5] States have undertaken to control the export of goods enumerated either in the "Munitions List" or in the "List of Dual-Use Goods and Technologies", which largely correspond to the lists established by CoCom, and to notify transfers and denials of export authorisations. Like CoCom, the WA is an informal forum not entailing binding effects for the participating states.

Whereas CoCom and subsequently the WA are certainly of particular importance for the Communitarian dual-use control system, other international regimes have also influenced the identification of dual-use goods. The Treaty on the Non-Proliferation of Nuclear Weapons requires the parties to control transfers of material and equipment intended for the use, manufacture or processing of certain nuclear substances. Restrictions on exports of biological and chemical substances arise from the Chemical Weapons Convention of 1997 (CWC) and the

---

3 Members of NATO (except Iceland), Japan and Australia.

4 Inter alia the Russian Federation and the Ukraine.

5 Pt. I of the Initial Elements published under http://www.wassenaar.org/.

Biological Weapons Convention of 1972.[6] Apart from these legally binding agreements, further control regimes have been set up by informal bodies like the Nuclear Suppliers Group[7] or the Missile Technology Control Regime.

III. Definition, Nature and Strategic Importance of Dual-Use Goods

The term "dual-use goods" generally refers to products which can be used for both civil and military purposes.[8] This legal definition deployed in the former dual-use regulation offers no real clarification what is to be understood by dual use goods. The new legal framework no longer simply refers to "goods", but "items, including software and technology, which can be used for both civil and military purposes, ... includ[ing] all goods which can be used for both non-explosive uses and assisting in any way in the manufacture of nuclear weapons or other nuclear explosive devices".[9] These descriptions fail to provide precise criteria allowing the delineation of dual-use products from military or civil goods. Taken literally, almost every product would qualify for a dual use good or item, since virtually every product can somehow be used for military purposes. Hence the mere aptitude for military purposes cannot be the decisive factor.[10] Equally, goods mainly serving specific military purposes, like tanks, munitions, but also explosives, are generally not considered as dual use goods, although in exceptional cases, they might be also be deployed for civil purposes like disaster operations.[11] Items identified to serve dual-

---

6 The texts of both agreements are available under http://disarmament.un.org/TreatyStatus.nsf.

7 On the nuclear non-proliferation policy of the EU in the context of international regimes see *Rosa* (2001).

8 See Art 2 (a) of Council Regulation 3381/94 setting up a Community regime for the control of exports of dual-use goods, OJ L 367, 31. 12. 1994, 1.

9 See Art 2 (a) of Council Regulation 1334/2000 setting up a Community regime for the control of exports of dual-use items and technology

10 The fact that a good is actually used for military purposes does not automatically entail its qualification as dual use good. See for example *Kreuzer* (1997) 308.

11 *Egger* (1996) 65.

use purposes are mainly high-tech products, technologies, software or industrial equipment.

For a better understanding of the specific nature of theses goods, one has to look at the developments of the last decade in the field of international foreign and military policy. In the period of Cold War the main focus of technological research was devoted to the armaments industry. Due to enhanced investment, new technological developments and inventions mainly originated from the military sector. As a consequence, one could observe a technology transfer from the military to the civil sector. New techniques, originally developed for purely military purposes, proved to be useful and operational for other purposes as well. The situation was completely reversed by the end of the East-West conflict. The shortening of defence budgets led to a breakdown in turnovers of armaments enterprises and forced the latter to switch to new markets and to adapt their production to the needs of the civil sector. Significant technological progress was now achieved in the more competitive civil sector and the results were subsequently also applied in military production. Consequently a clear distinction between products determined for military uses and products determined for purely civil purposes can no longer be drawn precisely.[12]

In practice, the issue has been solved by the establishment of descriptive lists, aligned to the "International Industrial List" elaborated in the framework of CoCom. This list has identified "strategic goods", which increase the military strength of armed forces by either strengthening their capabilities in conventional missions or permitting the construction or deployment of powerful arms like weapons of mass destruction. The selection of these products did not only depend on a product's features accounting for its potential use for military purposes. Such a decision involved further strategic considerations concerning the level of technological development or the availability of these products in countries of the Warsaw pact based on secret service information, military observation reports and strategic prognosis. Hence the political and ideological background played an important role for the identification of dual use products. After the end of the Cold War, additional focus was put on the actual end-use of the product. Export controls have been extended to the supply of goods, which

---

12 See *Karpenstein* (1998) 112ff; *Egger* (1996) 1.

were actually intended for military uses. On the one hand, controls thus depend on the subjective knowledge of the exporter or the authorities of the exporting country about the end-use of the product. On the other hand, the necessity of an authorisation is also determined by objective criteria like the consignee or the country of destination, the aim of which is to prevent consignments to unstable or unreliable states or companies.[13]

IV. Distribution of Competence and the Question of the Legal Base

A. The Need for a Community Regime

For a small group of chemicals the Community has already laid down a requirement for export authorisations in 1989.[14] Until 1994, however, global export control regimes on dual-use products existed only at national level. However, national border controls effectuated in order to verify the implementation of these control systems were incompatible with the concept of the Single Market which required the total suppression of internal border controls. Of course, the efficient implementation of national control systems was significantly impeded by the abolition of physical checks. Taking advantage of the lack of systematic border controls and the differences in national export policies, exporters could effectuate their exports from those Member States with the least restrictive regulations. Since this practice of "licence shopping" clearly undermined the efficacy of more rigorous national export control regimes, additional need was felt to establish a common system ensuring a Community-wide control based on uniform standards that substituted national checks by controls at the external borders of the Community.[15]

In 1992, the Commission thus submitted a proposal for the establishment of a Community control system. From the beginning discussions on the proposal were characterised by vehement disagreement on the question whether the Community actually enjoyed competence to regulate the export of dual use goods. Given the fact that such a system mainly involves considerations of

---

13 *Karpenstein* (1998) 112ff; *Egger* (1996) 65ff.

14 Council Regulation 428/89 concerning the export of certain chemical products, OJ L 50, 22. 2. 1989, 1. It has been repealed by the dual-use regulation of 1994.

15 *Kuijper* (1993) 398ff; *Emiliou* (1996) 61.

security policy, an area reserved to the intergovernmental sphere, be that individually or in the framework of CFSP, considerable resistance against a far-reaching harmonisation lead to a rather moderate outcome, representing merely a first step towards the establishment of a complete and consistent common export control system.[16]

B. The "Integrated System" of 1994

The most striking feature of the export control system set up in 1994 was its hybrid or "cross-pillar" nature. In fact, the export regime was composed by a regulation based on ex-Art 113 (now 133) TEC and a joint action adopted pursuant to ex-Art J.3 (now Art 14) TEU[17]. According to Art 1 of the joint action, these instruments jointly formed an "integrated system involving, in accordance with their own powers, the Council, the Commission and the Member States".

Whereas the regulation contained details on the authorisation and customs procedure, administrative cooperation and control measures, the crucial and politically sensitive aspects were incorporated in the CFSP decision. In particular, this concerned the list of goods requiring an export authorisation (Annex I), the list of countries for exports to which a general export authorisation could be granted (Annex II) and the criteria guiding the decision of national authorities whether to authorise an export or not (Annex III). By withdrawing these issues from the scope of the regulation, Member States managed to safeguard their unimpaired influence on these delicate questions of foreign and security policy, since decisions in this respect were subject to unanimous vote and furthermore not amenable to judicial review.

---

[16] Cf. Consideration 7 of Council Regulation 3381/94 setting up a Community regime for the control of exports of dual-use goods, OJ L 367, 31. 12. 1994, 1.

[17] Council Decision 94/942/CFSP on the joint action adopted by the Council of the basis of Article J.3 of the Treaty on European Union concerning the control of exports of dual-use goods, OJ L 367 , 31. 12. 1994, 8.

C. The Community's Competence to Control the Export of Dual-Use Goods

1. The Application of the TEC to Dual-Use Goods

The doubts raised with regard to the Community's competence to create an export regime for dual-use goods have been linked to the strategic nature of dual-use goods. Rather as a matter of fact than due to legal constraints, matters touching on security policy have long been considered to fall outside the scope of the TEC. Consequently the entire military sector has de facto been excluded from EC legislation. Legal arguments put forward to defend this point of view have been founded on Art 296 (ex-Art 223) TEC. According to para 1 (b) of this provision, Member States may take measures considered necessary for the protection of the essential interests of their security which are connected with the production of or trade in arms, munitions and war material. These measures may not adversely affect the conditions of competition in the Common Market regarding products which are not intended for specifically military purposes. For a long time Member States have interpreted this security proviso as a reserve of sovereignty which per se precludes the application of Community law to military goods.[18]

In 1999, the ECJ has confirmed the opinion generally defended in literature[19], according to which Art 296 TEC does not constitute a general exemption from the scope of the TEC, but merely a possibility for Member States to derogate from Community law under certain circumstances. In the case at issue, the defendant (Spain) had invoked ex-Art 223 TEC to justify a measure contravening secondary Community law. Recalling its narrow interpretation of security derogations[20], the ECJ required Member States relying on a safeguard clause to prove that the limits laid down in these provisions are respected by the unilateral measure

---

18 *Trybus* (2000) 663.

19 See for example *Kuijper* (1992) 399; *Gilsdorf* (1994) 18; *Emiliou* (1996) 59; *Eikenberg* (2000) 119.

20 In *Johnston* the ECJ purported that ex-Arts 36, 48, 56, 223 and 224 TEC concerning derogations from the TEC related to public safety deal with exceptional and clearly defined situations. According to the ECJ, it is not possible to infer from these provisions a general security proviso inherent in the Treaty. Case C-222/84, *Johnston*, ECR [1986] 1651, para 26.

concerned. The ECJ has thus not only implicitly dismissed the preclusive character of Art 296 TEC, but furthermore established a necessity to explicitly invoke and justify a national measure founded on this security proviso.[21]

The implications of these findings are far-reaching. The judgment should have resolved all remaining legal doubts on the general applicability of Community rules to strategic goods and the existence of a Community competence to establish a Common Market for defence goods.[22]

The question whether dual-use goods fell within the scope of the TEC has already been answered in the affirmative in a slightly different context by the ECJ in its *Richardt* judgment [23]. The case concerned a French company's delivery of certain dual-use goods to its contracting partner in the former Soviet Union. The company had obtained the necessary export licence from the French authorities. Due to the cancellation of the flight from France to Moscow, the goods were transported to the airport of Luxembourg on the initiative of the airline. Since the goods were not accompanied by a special transit licence required under Luxembourg law, the Luxembourg authorities confiscated the goods. This act was challenged on the grounds that it was incompatible with Community law. Whereas AG Jacobs proposed to evaluate the situation in the light of the export regulation[24], the ECJ considered the goods to be in transit and examined the compatibility of the measure with the Community transit regulation[25] and ex-Art 36 (now Art 30) TEC. The ECJ stated that the transit regulation covers all goods irrespective of their possible strategic nature. Subsequently, it went on to examine whether the measure could be justified by recourse to Art 36 TEC, recalling that the purpose of ex-Art 36 TEC is not to reserve certain matters to the jurisdiction of the Member States but merely to allow national legislation to derogate from the principle of free movements of

---

21 Case C-414/97, *Commission v. Spain*, ECR [1999] I-5585, at paras 21-24. See also *Trybus* (2000) 663 and 666.

22 In respect to the latter aspect see *Trybus* (2000) 667ff.

23 Case C-367/89 *Aimé Richardt*, ECR [1991] I-4621.

24 Council Regulation 2603/69 establishing common rules for exports, OJ L 324, 27. 12. 1969, 25 .

25 Council Regulation 222/77 on Community transit OJ L 38, 9. 2. 1977, 1.

goods.[26] In this way, the ECJ confirmed the general applicability of Community law to dual-use goods. However, it considered the national measure to be justified under the public security proviso contained in ex-Art 36 TEC.

2. The Legal Base – Security Policy and Trade

The construction of the integrated system has to be regarded as an attempt to cope with the twofold nature of the dual-use control regime. Laying down export controls and restrictions for certain goods, the measure pursues the immediate aim of regulating and thus influencing trade between the Community and third countries. In this respect, the act clearly constitutes a commercial policy instrument. However, the overall objective of the integrated system was undoubtedly not inspired by trade policy considerations but mainly by reasons of security policy. The problem arising here is the difficult question of evaluating the legal base of a trade policy instrument pursuing a non-commercial objective. The issue lies at the heart of a fundamental dispute concerning the scope of the Community's Common Commercial Policy (CCP).[27]

a) The Applicability of Art 133 TEC

It was exactly with respect to this fundamental difference of opinion relating to dual-use goods that the ECJ delivered two important preliminary rulings. The *Werner*[28] case concerned the refusal of German authorities to grant an export licence for the delivery of a vacuum-induction smelting and cast oven and induction spools to Libya. Meanwhile, the *Leifer* case concerned criminal proceedings against German exporters who delivered plant parts and chemical products to Iraq without the necessary export licences[29]. In both cases the ECJ was asked to rule on the compatibility of national export restrictions concerning dual-use goods in the light of Community law. Since the Community export system on dual-use goods was not in existence at the time at question, the references had to be answered in the light of the legal situation existing before 1995. The ECJ first examined the question whether the national export restrictions were covered by the scope of CCP. In *Werner* it held that a measure the effect of which is to

---

26 Case C-367/89 *Aimé Richardt*, ECR [1991] I-4621, paras 16-19.

27 Compare *Lukaschek/Weidel* in this volume at 130ff.

28 Case C-70/94, *Werner*, ECR [1995] I-3189.

29 Case C-83/94, *Leifer*, ECR [1995] I-3231.

prevent or restrict the export of certain products cannot be treated as falling outside the scope of CCP on the ground that it has foreign policy and security objectives. The concept of CCP requires that a Member State should not be able to restrict its scope by freely deciding, in the light of its own foreign policy or security requirements, whether a measure is covered by ex-Art 133 (now 133) TEC.[30] In *Leifer*, the ECJ even pronounced on the (ir)relevance of the strategic character of dual use goods, stating that the nature of these products cannot take them outside the scope of CCP. Recalling the exclusivity of CCP, the ECJ came to the conclusion that rules restricting exports of dual-use goods to non-member countries fall within the exclusive competence of the Community, which excludes national measures save where specific authorisation is granted by the Community.[31]

Half a year after the entry into force of the "integrated system", the ECJ thus confirmed an exclusive competence of the Community to regulate the export of dual-use goods.

b) The Ample Derogation Possibilities

Having established the applicability of Art 133 TEC to export controls on dual-use goods, the ECJ went on to examine whether the national measures could be justified by a specific Community authorisation. Similar to Art 30 (ex-Art 36) TEC, Art 11 of the Community export regulation provides for an exemption inter alia on the grounds of public security. In this respect the Court referred to its interpretation of public security in ex-Art 36 (now 30) TEC set out in the *Richardt* case[32], according to which the concept of public security covers both the internal and the external security of a Member State. The same concept has to be applied in the context of the export regulation. The ECJ pointed out the difficulty to distinct precisely between foreign-policy and security-policy considerations and observed that the security of a state can no longer be regarded in isolation, since it is linked to the security of the international community. For these reasons, it acknowledged that the risk of serious disturbance to foreign relations or to the peaceful coexistence of nation may affect the security of a Member State. The decision whether the national measures could be justified pursuant to Art 11 of the export regulation was left to the appraisal

30 Compare Case C-70/94, *Werner*, ECR [1995] I-3189, paras 10 and 11.

31 Case C-83/94, *Leifer*, ECR [1995] I-3231, paras 11 and 13.

32 Case C-367/89, *Aimé Richardt*, ECR [1991] I-4621.

of the national courts. The ECJ however – again referring to *Richardt* – added that it is common ground that the exportation of dual-use goods to a country at war may affect the public security of a Member State.[33]

The Court has adopted a very liberal view on the interpretation of the public security proviso, opening the possibility for Member States to deviate from Community rules without having to comply with rigorous requirements for the justification of this unilateral measure.

3. Evaluation of the Result

The ECJ's jurisprudence in *Werner* and *Leifer* has been regarded as a successful approach as to how to strike the right balance between Community's interest in the uniform implementation of its CCP and Member States' foreign and security policy concerns.[34] Indeed, the recognition of a general Community competence pursuant to Art 133 TEC to set up export controls on dual-use goods enables the Community to safeguard its common interests related to the operation of the Common Market[35] by a uniform trade regime in this area. At the same time, the ECJ managed to mitigate the unqualified restrictions on national prerogatives resulting from the exclusivity of the Community competence in commercial policy matters. By granting the Member State a fairly broad margin of discretion when it feels the necessity to deviate from the common regime because of national security interests, the ECJ has achieved an acceptable reconciliation of these diverging interests.

D. The Validity of the Integrated System in the Light of the Werner/Leifer Jurisprudence

Obviously, the findings in *Werner* and *Leifer* cast doubts on the validity of the cross-pillar nature of the integrated system. The integrated system followed a different road in tackling this potential conflict of interests. Instead of reconciliation, the regime of 1994 sought to establish a rigid separation of political and economic aspects.[36] By shifting the sensitive issues to the CFSP measure, the Council sought to extract the political content from the trade policy

---

[33] See Case C-70/94, *Werner*, ECR [1995] I-3189, paras 12-27 and Case C-83/94, *Leifer*, ECR [1995] I-3231, paras 14-30.

[34] *Emiliou* (1997) 74; *Koutrakos* (1998) 237.

[35] Cf Opinion 1/75, *Local Cost Standard*, ECR [1975] 1355 at 1363ff.

[36] *Koutrakos* (1998) 243.

instrument. Pursuant to Art 1 of joint action 94/942[37], the integrated system involves the Council, the Commission and the Member States "in accordance with their own powers". Recognising the lists of dual-use goods, destinations and guidelines as essential elements of a control system, the fourth recital of the preamble to the former dual-use regulation[38] specifies that the content of these lists is of strategic nature and consequently falls within the competence of the Member States. This argument serves as the explanation for the fact that the issues mentioned are regulated by the CFSP instrument.

The viewpoint on the distribution of competence reflected in these phrases coincides with the general assumption defended by the Member States according to which security issues are a reserve of national sovereignty escaping from the scope of the TEC. In the *Werner* and *Leifer* rulings, the ECJ has clearly dismissed this concept by stating that neither the strategic nature of dual-use goods nor the fact that such measures pursue security policy objectives withdraws export restrictions on dual-use goods from the scope of Community law.[39] Hence the integrated system was based on an erroneous appraisal of the competence distribution.

By withdrawing essential elements of the export regime from the scope of the regulation, the integrated system infringed a central principle governing the relationship between the EC and the intergovernmental pillars of the EU. The requirement to preserve the acquis communautaire enshrined in Arts 2, 3 and 47 TEU rules out any intergovernmental encroachment on exclusive Community competence. According to Art 47 TEU, Community competences are not affected by the TEU. Consequently, the scope of CFSP actions only extends to areas for which Community law does not exclude any action on part of the Member States.[40] In *Werner* and *Leifer*, the ECJ has denied any remaining national competence for export restrictions on dual-use goods. The margin of manoeuvre that Member States still enjoy in this area is only the consequence of the derogation possibility granted by the public security proviso of the export regulation, and not a genuine competence in strict

---

[37] OJ L 367, 31. 12. 1994, 8.

[38] Council Regulation 3381/94 setting up a Community regime for the control of exports of dual-use goods, OJ L 367, 31. 12. 1994, 1.

[39] See C.2.

[40] On the principles governing the demarcation between Community competences and intergovernmental policies see *Weidel* in this volume, 29ff.

legal terms. This differentiation is vital for determining the correct legal base of the export control system and drawing the borderline between CCP and CFSP. In principle, the Community is the sole entity entitled to establish a legal framework in this area. Accordingly, there is no scope for action under the second pillar. Nevertheless, unilateral national actions may be permissible on the basis of an express authorisation laid down in Community law.[41]

V. The Main Features of the Dual-Use Control Regime

A. The Drawing-Up of a New System

As provided for in Art 18 of the former dual-use regulation, the Commission presented a report[42] on the implementation of the integrated system in 1998. Recognising the positive effects for the internal market, the report nevertheless unveiled deficiencies of the current system resulting from the lack of consistent export policies and uniform licensing practices. Due to the coexistence of differing national policies, the system was too complex as to guarantee effective controls and led to delays in customs procedures. According to the Commission's observation, the regime thus failed to establish a real common export system. Based on the results of its report the Commission simultaneously submitted a proposal[43] for a revised version of the Community dual-use control regime to address the weaknesses raised. In June 2000, the Council adopted the new dual-use regulation[44] which entered into force in September 2000. In the light of the ECJ's *Werner* and *Leifer* judgments, it was agreed to base this system exclusively on Art 133 TEC.[45] The lists of items, destinations and guidelines, identified as essential elements for an effective control system[46] have thus been

---

41 Case 41/76, Donckerwolcke, [1976] ECR 1921, para 32.

42 Report to the European Parliament and the Council on the application of Regulation (EC) 3381/94 setting up a Community system of export controls regarding dual-use goods COM 1998 (258) final. See Bulletin EU 5-1998 of 12. 4. 1999.

43 COM 1998 (257) final, OJ C 399, 21. 12. 1998, 1.

44 Council Regulation 1334/2000 setting up a Community regime for the control of exports of dual-use items and technology, OJ L 159, 30. 6. 2000, 1.

45 See the second consideration of Council Decision 2000/402/CFSP repealing Decision 94/942/CFSP on the joint action concerning the control of exports of dual-use goods, OJ L 159, 30. 6. 2000, 218.

46 Cf consideration 5 of Regulation 1334/2000.

incorporated into the new regulation. To guarantee an effective non-proliferation policy, it was intended to extend the controls to services related with dual-use purposes. According to the ECJ's WTO Opinion[47], only a small group of services, namely crossfrontier supplies, is covered by the scope of Art 133 TEC. The integration of services into the regulation would have required recourse to Art 43 TEC. The Council did not use this option. Instead, the regulation was complemented by a joint action providing for a control regime concerning technical assistance related to military end-uses.[48] According to this measure, Member States have to introduce controls for the provision of technical assistance in case it is intended or the provider is aware that it is intended for use in connection with the development, production, handling, detection etc of chemical, biological or nuclear weapons and other explosive devices.[49] Controls shall also extend to assistance in the context with other military end-uses and to assistance provided in countries which are subject to an arms embargo.[50] 'Technical assistance' is defined as technical support related to repairs, development, manufacture, assembly, testing or any other technical service and covers instruction, training, transmission of working knowledge or skills and consulting services.[51]

B. The Control Regime of the New Dual-Use Regulation

1. Scope of the Regulation

In contrast to the former regulation, the new rules do not only cover dual-use products, but also software and technology. In that sense the term "export" also includes transmission of software and technology by electronic media, fax or telephone. In accordance with the limited scope of Art 133 TEC in the service sector, the regulation is not applicable to supply of services or transmissions of technology which involve the cross-border movement of natural

---

[47] Opinion 1/94, *WTO*, [1994] ECR I-5267, para 47.

[48] Council Joint Action 2000/401/CFSP concerning the control of technical assistance related to certain military end-uses. OJ L 159, 30. 6. 2000, 216.

[49] Art 2 of Joint Action 2000/401.

[50] Art 3 of Joint Action 2000/401.

[51] Art 1 of Joint Action 2000/401.

persons[52]. Dual-use items in transit are also excluded from the scope of the regulation.[53]

2. The Requirement of an Export Authorisation

The control system for exports of dual-use items is based on an authorisation scheme administrated by national competent authorities of the Member States. Pursuant to Art 3 para 1 of the dual-use regulation, an authorisation has to be obtained for the export of all items listed in Annex I. As mentioned above, the content of this list reflects the commitments undertaken by the Member States in the framework of the various international non-proliferation regimes. It will be updated by the Member States in accordance with respective modifications agreed upon on the international plane.[54]

Under certain circumstances, the export of dual-use items not contained in Annex I nevertheless requires an authorisation. This is the case when the exporter has been informed by the national authorities that the items are or might be intended for use in connection with the development, production, operation, detection, etc of chemical, biological or nuclear weapons or the development, production, maintenance or storage of missiles capable of delivering such weapons (Art 4 para 1). Such a requirement existed already under the former dual-use regulation. The revised version extended the scope of this "catch-all clause" to two additional cases, in which a licence is necessary for exports of non-Annex I items. First, according to Art 4 para 2, exports have to be authorised when the purchasing country or the country of destination is subject to an arms embargo imposed in the framework of CFSP, the OSCE, or by a resolution of the UN Security Council and the exporter has been informed by the authorities that the items are or may be intended for military end-uses. Second, pursuant to Art 4 para 3, a licence is required when the exporter has been informed by the authorities that the items are or might be intended for use as parts or components of military items which have been exported from that Member State without the necessary authorisation or in violation of its relevant legislation.

In all these cases an export authorisation is compulsory by virtue of the dual-use regulation. Furthermore the regulation establishes an

---

52 Art 3 para 3 of Regulation 1334/2000.

53 Art 3 para 4 of Regulation 1334/2000.

54 Art 11.

obligation for an exporter, who is aware that the dual-use items not listed in Annex I are intended for military end-uses or uses as described above, to notify the national authorities. It is then, however, up to the discretion of these authorities whether the export will be subject to an authorisation.[55] Apart from that, Member States are free to adopt or maintain provisions establishing an authorisation requirement for the export of non-Annex I items, when the exporter has grounds for suspecting that these items are or may be intended for uses mentioned in Art 4 para 1.[56]

3. The Authorisation System

In principle, export authorisations are granted by the national competent authorities of the Member State where the exporter is established. The licences are valid throughout the Community and may be subject to certain requirements and conditions. An important novelty of the new dual-use regulation is the introduction of a Community general export authorisation.[57] It applies to exports of dual-use items listed in Annex I[58] to Australia, Canada, the Czech Republic, Hungary, Japan, New Zealand, Norway, Poland, Switzerland and the US. These exports are exempted from the obligation to acquire an export licence from the national authorities. Since exports to these countries account for approximately 70% of all Community dual-use exports[59], this instrument is expected to entail significant relief in terms of workload for national authorities and a speed up of procedures. Under certain circumstances, however, which mainly correspond to the situations defined by Art 4 para 1, 2 and 4 of the dual-use regulation, the general authorisation may not be used and recourse must be had to the standard procedure.

The dual-use regulation distinguishes between individual, global and general authorisations. A global authorisation can be granted to a specific exporter with respect to a category of dual-use items for one or more countries. Via general (national) authorisations certain categories of dual-use items[60] can be exempted from the requirement to obtain an individual authorisation. If an exporter is

---

[55] Art 4 para 4.
[56] Art 4 para 5.
[57] The details are set out in Annex II of the dual-use regulation.
[58] Except those specified in Annex II part 2 and Annex IV.
[59] *Karpenstein* (2000b) 678.
[60] Except those listed in part 2 of Annex II.

aware or informed by the competent authorities that the items are or might be intended for one of the uses specified in Art 4 para 1–4, the general authorisation may not be used.

In essence, it is up to the discretion of the national authorities whether to grant or to refuse an export licence for dual-use items. When deciding on the export authorisation the competent authorities merely have to "take into account" certain criteria defined by Community law. These considerations set out in Art 8 of the dual-use regulation refer to following aspects:

- obligations that Member States have assumed under international non-proliferation regimes and treaties
- obligations arising from sanctions imposed by a common position or a joint action, by a decision of the OSCE or by a resolution of the UN Security Council
- aspects of national and foreign security policy, including those covered by the EU Code of Conduct on arms exports
- considerations about intended end-use and the risk of diversion.

The regulation does, however, not specify any further requirements to ensure a uniform application of these criteria. Differences in national licensing policies will thus continue to exist.

These possible differences in national licensing policies have been taken into consideration by the dual-use regulation. Art 7 para 1 establishes a system of consultation for situations, in which the goods to be exported are located in a Member State other than the one in which the exporter has applied for the export authorisation. The Member State concerned has to be provided with all relevant information and has the possibility to state objections. In this case, the objections are binding on the Member State in which the application has been made. This procedure prevents exporters from evading stricter or less favourable national licensing policies by filing their applications in other Member States.

A Member State may at any time request another Member State to refuse or suspend an authorisation, if the export might prejudice its essential security interests. Such a request will initiate consultations which are, however, of a non-binding nature.[61] Furthermore a Member State has to consult another Member State which has refused an export license for an essentially identical transaction, before it grants an authorisation for this export. When it

[61] See Art 7 para 2.

nevertheless decides to grant the authorisation, it will inform the other Member States and the Commission and explain the decision.[62]

4. Intra-Community Trade

Whereas one of the objectives of the Community dual-use control regime is the elimination of barriers to the free movement of goods, the former dual-use regulation nevertheless established authorisation requirements for intra-Community transfers of certain dual-use goods, which were intended to apply "for a transitional period"[63]. In its proposal, the Commission had suggested to replace these authorisation requirements by a simple notification requirement.[64] This proposal encountered unified resistance from the Council and was subsequently not taken over in the new regulation. Community transfers of items ranging in Annex IV are still subject to authorisation, for those falling in Part I, Member States may grant a general authorisation. Furthermore, Member States maintain the right to impose authorisations for intra-Community transfers, when the exporter knows that the final destination of these items lies outside the Community, the direct export to this destination is subject to an individual authorisation on the basis of Arts 3, 4 or 5 of the dual-use regulation and the items are not subject to any processing or working in the Member State to which they are transferred.

Nevertheless, some progress in harmonisation has been achieved by the new version: The option to require an authorisation for further specific dual-use goods provided for under the former regulation[65] has now been deleted.

VI. How 'Common' is the Community Export System?

A. The Degree of Harmonisation Achieved by the Dual-Use Regulation

The preamble of the former dual-use regulation set out the prospect of a common system for export controls, which is complete and consistent in all respects. At the same time, the text admitted that the regulation only represented a first step towards

---

62 Art 9 para 3.

63 Art 19 para 1 lit b of regulation 3381/94.

64 See Art 22 para 2 COM (1998) 257 final, OJ C 399, 21. 12. 1998, 1.

65 Art 20 of regulation 3381/94.

this endeavour.[66] In addition, the Community has not met the self-imposed target by the revised regime of 2000. Albeit introducing some further harmonising features, the new version is still far from establishing a common export policy for dual-use items.

In fact, the system introduced is a system of mutual recognition of national policy decisions. The dual-use regulation just defines cases in which an export authorisation has to be obtained from the national authorities.[67] However, the political decision on the permission of the export still rests with the Member States. The regulation neither provides for a uniform procedure nor establishes uniform compulsory criteria, on which a decision to grant or to refuse an authorisation has to be based. The considerations enlisted in Art 8 are formulated in such a vague way that leaves room for very different interpretations and thus grants an ample margin of discretion to the national authorities.[68] Only in a few cases – like the existence of an embargo – the Member States' decision might be predetermined by these aspects. Furthermore, Art 8 only requires Member States to take these aspects into account and does not oblige them to base their decision exclusively on these four considerations. National authorities are not precluded from having recourse to other considerations to justify their decision. In addition to the unrestricted freedom concerning the licensing policy, Member States are entitled to establish further authorisation requirements for reasons of public security or human rights (Art 5 para 1). Under these circumstances there is certainly no harmonisation of export conditions throughout the EC.[69]

The only element actually entailing a harmonising effect is the introduction of the Community general export authorisation for certain goods to a number of "trustworthy" countries.[70] The practical importance of these exports might be quite significant. According to the Commission's estimates, they account for 70% of all dual-use exports effectuated from the Community.[71] This is the one and only piece of a real Community export policy. With regard

66 Consideration 7 of regulation 3381/94.

67 Due to the options laid down in paras 4 and 5 of Art 4, Member States may introduce additional authorisation requirements, which are however predefined by the regulation.

68 See V.B.3.

69 *Karpenstein* (1998) 104; *Koutrakos* (1998) 242.

70 Cf chapter V.B.3.

71 *Karpenstein* (2000b) 678.

to politically much more sensitive exports, a uniform export policy has not yet been established at Community level.

B. Derogation Possibilities

Apart from the ample margin of manoeuvre that Member States enjoy with respect to the authorisation of dual-use goods, national unilateral trade restrictions on dual-use goods may furthermore be justified under certain safeguard clauses. As mentioned above, Member States may introduce further authorisation requirements for reasons of public security or the protection of human rights. According to Art 4 para 8, the dual-use regulation does not prejudice the Member States' rights to take national measures under Art 11 of the export regulation. Furthermore, the regulation does not affect the application of Art 296 TEC (Art 22).

1. The Security Proviso of the Export Regulation

Art 11 of the export regulation[72] enlists a number of reasons under which quantitative export restrictions, generally prohibited by virtue of Art 1 of the regulation, may be justified. Pursuant to this provision, the export regulation does not preclude national quantitative restrictions on exports on grounds of public security. In the *Werner* and *Leifer* cases, the ECJ has already considered the lawfulness of national export restrictions on dual-use goods under this provision. Its findings serve as guidelines, although the ECJ examined the legal situation before the creation of the Community control system on dual-use exports.[73] As has been pointed out above[74], the Court adopted an extremely liberal attitude with respect to the interpretation of the public security proviso. In general, Member States will not have difficulties in justifying the recourse to this provision. However, Art 11 of the export regulation does not constitute a total blanket exception. To comply with the principle of proportionality, the Member State has to prove that the restriction is necessary and adequate and that it constitutes the least restrictive instrument to achieve the aim it pursues.[75]

---

[72] Council Regulation 2603/69 establishing common rules for exports, OJ L 324, 27. 12. 1969, 25.

[73] *Govaere* (1997) 1035 ff.

[74] See chapter IV.C.2.

[75] For more details see *Govaere* (1997) 1029.

2. Article 296 TEC

Under Art 296 para 1(b) TEC, Members States may adopt measures necessary for the protection of essential security interests connected with arms, munitions and war material. It has been established in the foregoing that this provision does not automatically exclude the application of the TEC to arms but merely authorises Member States to deviate from Community law.[76]

Whether dual-use goods do obtain the same status as military goods under this provision has not yet been clarified. The ECJ has avoided pronouncing on this issue in *Richardt, Werner* and *Leifer*. Pursuant to former para 2, the Council established a list enumerating those goods which fall within the scope of Art 296 TEC. This list, which has neither been published nor changed since 1958, has been aligned to CoCom's International Munitions List and comprises hard defence material. Dual-use goods do not appear therein.[77] Whereas the wording of former Art 223 para 2 TEC[78] implies that the list determines the scope of this provision, its exhaustive character has been disputed.[79] So far the ECJ has not pronounced on the question of applicability of Art 296 TEC to dual-use products.[80] The prevailing view in literature suggests that these products are not covered by the security proviso.[81] Precisely because of their dual nature such goods cannot be qualified as weapons, munitions or war material. This argument is supported by the second phrase of para 1(b) requiring the prevention of adverse competitive effects on products "not intended for specifically military purposes".[82]

---

76 See Chapter IV.C.1.

77 See *Eikenberg* (2000) 124 and *Trybus* (2000) 663.

78 The text of former para 2 Art 223 TEC reads as follows: During the first years after the entry into force of this Treaty, the Council shall, acting unanimously, draw up a list of products to which the provisions of paragraph 1(b) shall apply.

79 In the *Leifer* case, the United Kingdom took the view that the list is not exhaustive. See Opinion of AG Jacobs in C-70/94 and C-83/94 *Werner* and *Leifer*, ECR [1995] I-3189 at 3213.

80 Despite being asked to do so in the preliminary ruling C-83/94, *Leifer*, ECR [1995] I-3231.

81 *Govaere/Eeckhout* (1992) 956; *Koutrakos* (1998) 247ff.

82 *Jestaedt/Hohenstatt* (1992) 45; *Karpenstein* (2000) 2340.

In the light of these arguments, it is doubtful whether Art 296 TEC can actually serve as justification for unilateral export restrictions on dual-use items.

VII. Conclusions – Did the Community Reconquer Lost Grounds?

It has been stated that by subjecting goods falling within the Community's commercial policy to an intergovernmental document, the integrated system, "play[ed] into the Commission's worst fears of the pillar arrangement".[83] This observation is by no means exaggerated. The former dual-use regime represented a scenario that critics of the intergovernmental method had warned of in the context of the creation of the second and third pillar. The introduction of the intergovernmental policies risks the shifting of areas from the TEC to CFSP or JHA (Justice and Home Affairs) and undermining the Community method. Due to the ample scope of CFSP, this risk exists in particular in the sphere of external relations. The cross pillar approach employed in the integrated system could have served as precedence for other situations involving a clash of foreign policy and economic interests. Exhaustive recourse to such constructions would have hollowed out the external competences of the Community or degraded them to simple implementation competences[84]. Undoubtedly the Commission's role in the EU's international relations would have been significantly weakened.

The alignment of the regime to the *Werner* and *Leifer* jurisprudence has certainly lead to relief on part of the Commission and other proponents of the Community method. At least from a formal point of view, the Community has actually recovered lost grounds. However, reality does not reflect this division of competence. Due to the wide margin of manoeuvre granted by the Community regulation, Member States de facto retained the main say in export policy on dual-use goods. Nevertheless, the merits of the revised regime should not be underestimated. Respecting Member States' national security concerns, it allows for flexibility without endangering the acquis communautaire.

---

[83] *Ginsberg* (1997) 30.

[84] Cf *Koutrakos* (1998) 243.

Bibliography

Nicholas Emiliou (1996), Strategic Export Controls, National Security and the Common Commercial Policy, EFARev. 1996, 55-78.

Nicholas Emiliou (1997), Restrictions on Strategic Exports, Dual-Use Goods and the Common Commercial Policy, E.L.Rev. 1996, 68-75.

Ulrich Egger (1995), »Dual-use«-Waren: Exportkontrolle und EG-Vertrag, Köln et al. 1996.

Katharina Eikenberg (2000), Article 296 (ex 223) E.C. and external trade in strategic goods, E.L.Rev. 2000, 117-138.

Peter Gilsdorf (1994), Les réserves de sécurité du Traité CEE à la lumière du Traité sur l'Union Européenne, RMCUE 1/1994, 17-25.

Roy H. Ginsberg (1997), The EU's CFSP: the Politics of Procedure, in *Martin Holland* (ed), Common Foreign and Security Policy. The Record and Reforms, London 1997, 12-33.

Inge Govaere/Piet Eeckhout (1992), On Dual Use Goods and Dualist Case Law: The Aimé Richardt Judgement on Export Controls, CMLRev. 1992, 941-965.

Inge Govaere (1997), Case C-70/94 Fritz Werner Industrieausrüstungen GmBH und Case C-83/94 Criminal proceedings against Peter Leifer, CMLRev. 1997 1019-1037.

Thomas Jestaedt/Klaus-Stefan Hohenstatt (1992) Europarecht bricht nationales Exportkontrollrecht. Anmerkung zum Urteil des EuGH im Strafverfahren Aimé Richardt u.a., EuZW 1992, 44-46.

Ulrich Karpenstein (1998), Europäisches Exportkontrollrecht für Dual-use-Güter, Stuttgart et al. 1998.

Ulrich Karpenstein (2000a), Art. 296 (ex-Art. 223) [Nationale Sicherheitsinteressen], in Jürgen *Schwarze* (ed), EU-Kommentar, Baden-Baden 2000, 2336-2342.

Ulrich Karpenstein (2000b), Die neue Dual-use-Verodrnung, EuZW 2000, 677-680.

Panos Koutrakos (1998), Exports of Dual-use Goods Under the Law of the European Union, E.L.Rev. 1998, 235-251.

Olaf Kreuzer (1997), Art. 4 EG-dual-use-Verordnung, AW-Praxis 1997, 308-311.

Pieter Jan Kuijper (1993), Trade Sanctions, Security and Human Rights and Commercial Policy, in *Marc Maresceau* (ed), The European Community's Commercial Policy after 1992: The Legal Dimension, Doordrecht et al. 1993, 387-422.

Paolo Rosa (2001), Non-proliferation and the Europeam Union: An Institutionalist Perspective, The European Union Review 3/2001, 33-61.

Martin Trybus (2000), On the application of the E.C. Treaty to armaments, E.L.Rev. 2000, 663-668.

Barbara Dutzler

EMU and the Representation of the Community in International Organisations

I. Introduction

It is noteworthy that the classical difficulties of the Community in external relations in the field of economic and monetary union (EMU)

> "are increased due to various factors, among them the fact that the euro area [...] does not coincide with the Community legal entity; the lack of precision of the Treaty on what exactly covers the concept of "monetary policy", the presence as an actor in international relations of the ECB; the reluctance of the Member States [...] to give up their role in specialized international fora; and the rigidity of international organizations statutes, specially the IMF."[1]

However, the Community's need to speak with one voice is particularly evident as, with international economic and monetary co-ordination taking place in numerous International Organisations (IOs), issues are discussed and decided that affect the Community's and Member States' EMU policies. In order to develop a clearer picture of the restraints to uniform Community actions or positions at international level, the aim of this paper is to analyse the role which was assigned to the respective bodies in EMU matters, as well as the practical implementation of the relevant Treaty provisions.

II. The Relevant Treaty Provisions

A. The General Scheme

Art 3 TEU sets out the principle of the duty of the Council and of the Commission to ensure the consistency of the external activities of the EU as a whole in the context of its external relations, and imposes on them the responsibility of co-operating to this end and of ensuring implementation. Under Art 111(4) EC, the Council is competent firstly, to decide with qualified majority on the position of the Community on issues of particular relevance to EMU, and secondly, to decide unanimously on its representation "in compliance with the allocation of powers laid down in Articles 99 and 105." Hence, in contrast to Community representation in other fields, for EMU there is an explicit provision (Art 111(4) EC)

---

[1] *Dutheil de la Rochère* (1999) 439.

setting out the principle that the external representation has to mirror the internal competences of the Community entities. As a consequence, the division of responsibilities at Community level between the Council, Commission and ECB becomes an issue. Of similar importance is Para 5, which tackles the division of powers between Community and (EMU) Member States, by reserving for the Member States the right to negotiate in international bodies and to conclude international agreements.

In order to discuss this complex issue in a structured way, it is firstly necessary to determine the scope of Art 111(4). This includes the question to what extent the external representation of the Community is to take account of the competences of the ESCB.

B. *The Scope of Art 111(4) EC*

1. The Setting

Art 111(4) sets out that the Council, acting on a proposal of the Commission and after consulting the ECB, decides with qualified majority on the position of the Community in issues "of particular relevance to economic and monetary union" and, acting unanimously, on the representation of the Community at international level, respecting the allocation of powers as laid down in Art 99 and 105. Para 4 thus expressly confers competence on the Community to act externally in the field of EMU, under the condition that the arrangements of the Community representation adequately ensure the involvement of all competent bodies. In this respect, it should be recalled that due to the non-applicability of Art 111 to derogation states,[2] it is necessary to differentiate strictly between external and internal relation. In other words, there is an obligation of the Community as a whole in international law, whereas at the same time internally, the respective agreements are applicable to the Member States without a derogation only.[3]

As for other definitions or limitations of the scope of Para 4, there is considerable disagreement – concerning the scope of the term "Community", the vertical and the horizontal allocation of powers, and the relationship between Para 3 and 4. These issues will be discussed subsequently.

---

[2] Art 116(3) 2nd Sentence EC.

[3] So *Martenczuk* (1999) 96-97. See also *Louis* (1999) 9 with further references or *Smits* (1997) 403.

2. The Term "Community"

The point is whether "Community" should be read as standing for the international legal person "European Community" and its organs and bodies only. Under this "minimalist approach", as *Smits* referred to it, Para 4 would not give the Council the power to co-ordinate the action of the Member States in the field of external relations concerning EMU, but only to lay down the procedure for deciding who was to represent the EC.[4] *Smits* preferred to see the provision as encompassing both the Community and the Member States, as the minimalist version would deprive Art 111(4) from most of its meaning.[5] This finding is supported by the observation that, if the scope of this paragraph was limited to the Community, the obligation of the Member States to co-ordinate their positions would rest on the general loyalty provision of Art 10 EC alone, and, in the area of economic policy, on the power of the Council to co-ordinate the general economic policies of the Member States under Art 202 EC, first indent.[6] As *Louis* pointed out, this solution would be inconvenient insofar as it does not foresee a precise procedure of arriving at a common position. Subsequently, he therefore understood the term "Community" as not only comprising the legal person "European Community", but the "ensemble communautaire" consisting of Community and Member States.[7] Consequently, the deletion of Art 116 EEC, which provided a procedure to co-ordinate a common approach to be followed by the Member States, was regretted, as it was interpreted as giving the Member States back some of their powers of international operation.[8]

In spite of these considerations, there are arguments supporting the adoption of a different view, for it does not follow from the necessity to co-ordinate action that the scope of Para 4 is to be widened in this manner. This view rests upon the assumption that a reading to the effect that the term Community was exclusive of the Member States and referred only to Community bodies would not deprive Para 4 of most of its meaning. Such an interpretation affects the relation between Para 4 and the external aspect of Art 202 EC, but it does not make it meaningless: As it stands, Art 111(4)

---

4 *Smits* (1997) 410.

5 *Smits* (1997) 411. So also *Dutheil de la Rochére* (1999) 443.

6 So *Louis* (1995) 160.

7 *Louis* (1999) 9.

8 So *Dehousse/Ghemar* (1994) 168.

concerns the power of the Council to decide on the position or representation of the Community at the international level in EMU matters, with respect of the allocation of powers resulting from Arts 99 and 105. Art 99 refers to the powers which the Community commands over economic policies at the internal level, and Art 105 to those of the ECB in the monetary field. Leaving aside the question of remaining Member States competences for a moment, that the ECB is to be seen as Community body, as well as the interpretation of Art 6 ESCB-Statute, deserve a more detailed analysis.

3. The Status of the ECB

Under the view followed hereinafter, the ESCB is to be included in the scope of the term Community, because in spite of its separate legal personality, it is not a third party to the Community, but an instrument of the Community set up to achieve one of its objectives.[9] The contrary view rests mainly on the legal personality of the ESCB and on the distinction between ECB and Community and the ECB's "own field of competence", of which the Council would have to take account.[10] However, if the motivation for such a "conception excessive des conséquences de l'attribution de la personalité juridique"[11] is the ambition to prevent binding effects of possible Council positions in monetary matters, there are built-in safeguards in the Treaty which make such a drastic view unnecessary, as will be shown below.

Whereas in economic union the Community neither internally nor externally commands exclusive powers, this is different for monetary union. Internally, the ESCB conducts monetary policy and performs related central banking tasks, such as management of official reserves, except for some limited areas in which Member States still have residual competences. These relate to the fields of foreign exchange working balances, issue of coins, banking supervision and details of payment systems, agreements predating the

---

[9] See the discussion in *Louis* (1999) 9 (n. 26), 13-15. Cf. *Slot* (1994) 241: "in the field of monetary policy it will be a Community body. The latter may be the ECB." *Seidel* (1992) 427 argues that the law making and instruction giving power is carried out by the System on behalf of the Community. Also *Smits* (1997) 412 sees the ESCB as included in the term "Community".

[10] *Zilioli/Selmayr* (1999) 293 n. 84 or *Weinrichter* (2000) 13-15.

[11] *Louis* (1999) 9 n. 26.

entry into force of the third stage of EMU, and special external monetary regimes expressly mentioned in the Protocols.[12]

The principle of the division of competences is interpreted by the ECB to denote that for the "exclusive" ESCB competences such as monetary policy and related central banking tasks, international representation rested solely with the ESCB.[13] In this view, the ECB has to be represented in all fora where monetary policy is discussed, if statements on the single monetary policy are to be made at the meetings of IOs and fora, such as the International Monetary Fund (IMF) or the G-7.[14] Accordingly, how the representation of the ESCB is to be accomplished would be for the ECB to decide.[15] This would follow from the Arts 6, 23 1st indent and 31.1 ESCB-Statute which determine the ESCB-internal layer or the division of competences of the National Central Banks (NCBs) and ECB respectively.

In order to discuss this assumption appropriately, one must reconcile the ECB's right to decide on the representation of the ESCB (Arts 6.1. and 6.2. ESCB-Statute) with the Council's right to decide on the Community's representation and the Community's position under Art 111(4) EC. Hence, while for monetary union, the problem is not so much to distinguish between Member States and Community competences, it is rather the internal ("horizontal") diffusion of powers between the ESCB, on the one hand, and Council and Commission, on the other hand.

Art 6.1. ESCB-Statute empowers the ECB to decide in the field of international co-operation involving the tasks entrusted to the ESCB. Under Art 6.2. ESCB-Statute, the ECB and, subject to its approval, the NCBs may participate in international monetary institutions. Such a decision can be taken by the Governing Council, which according to Art 12.5. ESCB-Statute may exercise the rights of the ECB in this field. Finally, Art 6.3. provides that Arts 6.1 and 6.2 shall be without prejudice to Art 111(4) EC.

First, it must be noted that the Statute determines *how* and not *if* the ESCB is to be represented. This cannot be read as a derogation from a hypothetical Council decision not to include the ECB in the representation in areas where it would be competent. Rather, Art 6 is simply the reflection of the right of every Community body to

---

12 So *Zilioli/Selmayr* (1999) 298. See also *Smits* (1997) 410.
13 *European Central Bank* (1999) 80.
14 *European Central Bank* (2001) 59.
15 *Padoa-Schioppa* (1999) Chapter 3.

decide in an independent manner on its internal structures. Whereas the Council is not competent to prescribe the ESCB *how* the ECB should be represented, it is the Council, and not the ECB, which is competent to decide on the *if,* as long as this is in accordance with the competences of the ECB as outlined in Art 105.[16]

This is directly related with the second issue, namely the question which institutions are included in the right of the ECB to participate in international *monetary* institutions under Art 6.2. *Zilioli/Selmayr* emphasise that an interpretation which includes IOs dealing at least partly with monetary matters is necessary to allow the participation of the ECB whenever matters are discussed which fall in its competences. A more restrictive interpretation would create the insurmountable difficulty of having to define pure monetary institutions.[17] Likewise, it is proposed that the term "international monetary institutions" should be interpreted in a wide manner, including any bodies which operate in "the field of international co-operation involving the tasks entrusted to the ESCB" under Art 6.1. This would include bodies that control payments systems or co-operate in the field of statistics, agencies supervising financial institutions, or IOs acting to ensure financial markets stability.[18] Art 6.2. would thus even be the legal basis for the ECB to participate in fora which consider international economic co-operation (for instance the OECD). *Smits* submits that this would not collide with a decision of the Council under Art 111(4), since there, the Council decided on the representation of the Community and the Member States (as *Smits* opts for a wide interpretation of the term Community), whereas the ECB was entitled to decide on the representation of the ESCB.[19] Hence, in this view Art 6.3 ESCB-Statute overrides Art 111(4) EC, as a Council decision would not affect the ECB's participation in all international institutions, fora or bodies which in their discussion touched also fields which coincided with tasks that had been entrusted to the ECB.

---

16 As the Council is in the "driver's seat", so *Slot* (1994) 241. See extensively on the question of the external competences of the ECB and the Council's role as principal legislative body *Herrmann* (2002) 5ff. Legal remedies against a decision violating the ECB's prerogatives could be taken under Art 230 EC, so *Louis* (1999) 10.

17 *Zilioli/Selmayr* (1999) 336.

18 *Smits* (1999) Art 6 ESCB-Statute para 20-24.

19 *Smits* (1999) Art 6 ESCB-Statute para 24, n. 5.

It is, however, not necessary to interpret the term "monetary institutions" in such a wide manner, since the same result is achieved by reference to Art 111(4) alone. After all, Art 6.2. ESCB-Statute cannot be understood as giving to the ECB the right to decide, without a contribution of the Council, to participate in organisations in which the Member States, or the Community, are parties.[20] More appropriate seems a more restricted reading of the term "international monetary institutions", referring solely to international gatherings of central banks.[21] In these organisations dealing with rather technical, in contrast to more political, questions, neither country representatives nor the Community as such need to be present. The only examples for such purely monetary institution are the Bank for International Settlements (BIS)[22] and the specialist fora set up under its aegis,[23] whereas IMF, OECD, or G-7 cannot fall within the scope of this term.

Consider, for instance, the G-7, which as an informal forum of states *inter alia*[24] discusses exchange rates. The principle of external representation in accordance with the allocation of powers under Arts 99 and 105, in the absence of formal exchange rate agreements, makes a participation of the ECB necessary. It is, nevertheless, not correct to argue that the ECB is the only participant which is able to ground its participation on Community law, namely on Art 6.1. and 6.2. ESCB-Statute.[25] Quite obviously, the G-7 is not a "monetary institution", and hence, the legal base cannot be Art 6.2.

In this respect, it is telling to compare Art 6.1. with Art 23 ESCB-Statute on the external operations, which gives the ECB and the NCBs the power to "establish relations with central banks and

---

20 Cf. *Louis* (1999) 14.

21 *Dutheil de la Rochère* (1999) 444.

22 Whereas the NCBs remained individual shareholders, on 9 Dec. 1999, also the ECB became a BIS shareholder, following an invitation by the BIS Board of Directors.

23 Such as the meetings of the G10 Central Bank Governors, the Basel Committee on Banking Supervision, or the Committee on Payments and Settlement Systems.

24 The international monetary system is said to have three layers: the BIS for the technical element, the IMF as a regime for balance of payment surveillance, exchange rate stability and capital controls, and the Gx for general macroeconomic co-ordination, including exchange rate co-ordination, *Weinrichter* (2000) 21.

25 *Zilioli/Selmayr* (2000) 639.

financial institutions in other countries and, where appropriate, with *international organisations*". The scope of the term IO is clearly much wider than that of international monetary organisations; the latter are comprised by the former. Hence, for non-monetary organisations, where *prima facie* a permanent representation of the ECB or other central banks does not prove necessary, only working relations may be established. Also, there is nothing in the Treaty which prevents the ECB from developing bilateral relations with central banks or other institutions outside the European Union, or to receive official delegations from non-EU countries, which the ECB did in 1999.[26]

Thus, as the wording of Art 6.1. on the presentation of the ECB in monetary organisations implies, the question is simply which one of the constituent entities of the ESCB – a representative of the Executive Board, of the NCBs, or both – should participate in international monetary institutions. Any decision on this subject has to follow the principle that the internal division of competences must be reflected in external activities. This means, if areas subject to national competence are concerned, the ECB cannot decide how the ESCB is to be represented, but this would remain in the competences of the NCBs representing the respective Member States under national law. The NCBs, in turn, could be authorised by the ESCB, to act in the name and on behalf of the ECB, even if this matter internally was exclusively conducted by the ECB. Under Art 6.2. ESCB-Statute, the ECB could disapprove any NCB participation in international monetary organisations, but given the distribution of votes in the Governing Council (majority of the NCBs vs. Executive Board), in practice, such a decision would not be easily taken.

To conclude, Art 6. ESCB-Statute cannot be used to widen the external powers of the ECB further to the extent as granted in the Treaty. The principles enshrined therein determine that, as soon as Community competences are involved, the Community must be represented by the respective Community body or bodies which is/are competent. Thus, whenever in an international forum issues are discussed which belong to the powers allocated to the ESCB under the Treaty, the Council is bound to reflect this in its formal decision pursuant to Art 111(4) on Community representation.[27]

---

[26] See *European Central Bank* (1999) 84.

[27] On the content of this decision see *infra 455*

This does not mean, however, that the Council is to refrain from deciding "positions" to be taken, "when the matter falls within the exclusive competence of the monetary authority".[28] In this respect, it is necessary to distinguish between decisions on common positions and on representation – only the latter are subject to an automatic "division of labor" between Council and ECB.[29] It is only here that the Council is not totally free to decide which body should negotiate and conclude an agreement on behalf of the Community, but, with a view to the role of the ECB, is bound to respect the internal division of powers and decide only such principles of representations which adequately reflect the powers of the ECB under Art 105 EC. With regard to common positions, however, there are no restraints as to the binding effect, so that it is not possible for the ECB to deviate from a common position voiced at the international level.[30]

This solution prevents that, for instance, the Council could assume by an international agreement competences which, according to the internal division of responsibilities, resided in the ECB.[31] However, this does not "tie" the hands of the Council also in the fields of primarily political "positions" so that it would have to refrain from positions to be taken when the matter fell into the exclusive competence of the ECB.[32] Rather, it could take a common position on the exchange rate policy of the euro area at IOs under Para 4, as this would reflect only the political opinion without imposing an obligation on the ESCB as regards concrete actions to manipulate the exchange rate. Other agreements, fleshing out the political "declaration of intent" would have to be adopted under the procedure of Para 2.[33]

---

28 But so *Smits* (1997) 413.

29 *Stadler* (1996) 174-175. This seems to be overlooked by *Potacs* (1993) 37.

30 *Louis* (1999) 9 makes this subject to the principle of price stability. However, this should be the guiding principle of any Council activity in this field, see Art 4 EC.

31 Cf. *Louis:* "Le Conseil ne peut s'immiscer dans la conduite des affaires monétaires sous le couvert d'une action externe de la Communauté et la BCE doit s'inserer dans le contexte international en tenant compte des aspects de politique globale de la Communauté", *Louis* (1999) 14-15.

32 But so *Smits* (1997) 413.

33 See *Martenczuk* (1999) 98.

Under this view, the ESCB could become subject to the Council and the Commission when the consistency of an external position was at issue. As a result, in case of conflict between an external action of the ESCB and an external political operation, the former would not remain unaffected.[34] Given that the ESCB as the central bank of the Union has to include the external consistency of Union activities in its considerations, it might well be argued that in case of a conflict, the political action by the Council would prevail. In order to understand the full implication of this view, a clarification of the relationship between Art 111(3) and (4) is necessary.

4. The Relationship between Para 3 and Para 4

As to exchange rate management as a part of monetary policy, Art 105(2) 2nd indent determines that the ESCB is to conduct foreign exchange operations consistent with Art 111. Art 111(1) and (2) enable the Council to formulate formal exchange agreements and general orientations. Hence, for both agreements similar to Bretton-Woods or target-zone agreements, there is no residual Member State competence. As to the situation of Member States with a derogation, their internal exemption from EMU matters is also valid externally: they are only subject to the consistency requirement (Art 3 TEU), the general loyalty clause (Art 10 EC) and the duty of treating their exchange-rate policy as a matter of common concern (Art 124 EC).[35]

Art 111(3) regulates the arrangement for the negotiation and conclusion of "agreements concerning monetary or foreign exchange regime matters". On the one hand, the Council is to act "in accordance with the procedure in paragraph 3 for determining the arrangements" for the conclusion of formal agreements. This reference made in Art 111(1) to Para 3 indicates that *foreign exchange regime matters* include *formal agreements.* One extreme view could

---

[34] But so *Smits* (1997) 405 on the consistency requirement of Art 111(3) EC.

[35] The Luxembourg European Council set out that positions to be formulated under Art 111(4) would be limited in their scope in that they reflected only the positions of Eurogroup countries, so that at G-7 meetings, GB's position could be different from the one of the EC, see the Luxembourg Resolution of the European Council of 13 Dec. 1997 on economic policy coordination in stage 3 of EMU and on Arts 109 and 109b of the EC Treaty, para 9, OJC 35, 02/02/1998. For a more detailed discussion see *Vranes* (2000) 366, 377-381.

be that this was the only form which *foreign exchange regime matters* could take, so that the role of Para 3 in this respect would be purely procedural.[36] In this view, Para 3 would be important insofar as it enabled the Council to assign Commission, Council and ECB a specific role during negotiations on the conclusion of *formal agreements,* which would in turn determine the competence, and hence the influence, of the selected body. This arrangement is in contrast to Art 300 EC as *lex generalis*, under which the Commission possesses the sole competence to negotiate. One reason for this could be the lack of political will from Member States to abandon their last possibility to considerably influence, via the Council, the conclusion of such agreements.[37]

Other interpretations envisage a more substantive role for Para 3, authorising the Community to conclude other accords on *monetary and foreign exchange regime matters*.[38] Bearing the constraint in mind that Para 3 cannot be invoked to justify acts of the Ecofin-Council outside the Community competence,[39] *Zilioli/Selmayr*, while submitting that the Community did not need to be substantively externally competent, but that the conclusion of an agreement under Para 3 could be justified by the *need* to enter into such an agreement, argue that this paragraph was not so much a real legal base for an external competence, but more a presumption that such competence existed.[40]

The qualification "where agreements [...] *need* to be negotiated"[41] by the Community deserves some further attention. This could be of importance in cases where it is necessary that the Community expresses a single position, but where the Member States reserved some residual competences, as in the protocols relating to territories inside or outside Europe.[42] In these cases, the Community, although being general exclusively competent for

---

36 See for instance *Martenczuk* (1999) 98, *Smits* (1997) 402.

37 So *Bognar* (1997) 351.

38 See *Louis* (1999) 8, *Zilioli/Selmayr* (1999) 295, *Weinrichter* (2000) 13-15. This would not encompass *all* monetary matters, *Dutheil de la Rocheère* (1999) 441.

39 *Smits* (1997) 402.

40 *Zilioli/Selmayr* (1999) 296, and n. 95.

41 Art 111(3) EC, emphasis added.

42 Protocol (No 8) on Denmark, concerning Greenland and the Faeroes, Protocol (No 9) on Portugal, concerning the Azores and Madeira, Protocol on France (No 13), concerning overseas territories.

monetary and exchange rate matters in the Member States adopting the euro, took account of the historical relations.[43] Para 3 transfers to the Council the competence to decide the *arrangements* for the negotiation and for the conclusion of such an agreement, the agreements themselves being adopted in accordance with those arrangements, whatever they are.

The Council is therefore competent to decide whether – and if so, to which extent – the Member States should have a right to negotiate and conclude such agreements. This has been reflected in practice: As guaranteed by Declaration (No 6) annexed to the Final Act of the Treaty on European Union, the Community facilitated the renegotiations of existing arrangements between Italy and San Marino[44] and the Vatican[45] or between France and Monaco[46] in such fields as banknotes and coins, the access to payment systems, and the legal status of the euro in Vatican City. Para 3 was also used, in the absence of any special exceptional provisions, to allow certain Member States to continue their existing agreements on exchange rate regimes with third countries. The French Franc and the CFA-Franc may serve as an example.[47]

It is only now that it can be tried to clarify the exact scope of Art 111(4). The differentiation between "political" discussions or arrangements and the conclusion of concrete agreements concerns also the unanimous Council decision on the representation of the Community. The formal negotiation and conclusion of an international agreement in order to amend the statutes of an IO to allow for Community participation is considered to be subject to Art 111(3) EC rather than (4), which would be the basis for formal inter-or-

---

[43] Critically on the legitimacy of such an "imperfect" delegation of external Community competence to the Member States *Louis* (1999) 19-20.

[44] Council Decision 1999/97/EC, OJL 30, 04/02/1999, 33.

[45] Council Decision 1999/98/EC, OJL 30, 04/02/1999, 35.

[46] Council Decision 1999/96/EC, OJL 30, 04/02/1999, 31.

[47] Council Decision 98/683/EC concerning exchange rate matters relating to the CFA Franc and the Comorian Franc, OJL 320, 28/11/1998, 58. This does not include the right to conclude a new agreement or to renegotiate the terms of the present agreement, since although it is true that the agreement has no effect on the franc or on the situation of the Banque de France or of the ECB, it is, so the Commission, necessary to avoid any subsequent debate and to ensure legal certainty that any agreement with a third country wanting to maintain the parity of its currency with the euro is to be approved by the Union's institutions.

ganisational relations on the executive level without material substance.[48]

Para 3 is explicitly envisaged for the conclusions of contracts with IOs. It is therefore regarded as the possible legal basis for an agreement concerning the representation of the Community in IOs, as well as agreements with third countries on a general co-operation in currency and exchange rate policies vis-à-vis certain territories.[49] In short, Para 3 should be used for contractual arrangements with an IO, concerning the modalities of Community representation by its various actors (e.g. status of the ECB in the IMF), whereas Para 4 would be only used to regulate the non-contractual aspect of external relations such as discussions or participation in international fora.[50] Agreements on economic issues would similarly need a different legal base, such as Arts 133, 300 and 238 EC.[51]

The key to this understanding is a double meaning of the term "representation", entailing both the *participation* of the Community, and the modalities of its *representation* in the stricter sense, relating to the question which organ or organs would act in which organisation or forum.[52] The former meaning makes Art 111(4) EC the appropriate legal basis for negotiation mandates, the latter requires that any Council decision has to be based upon the competences of the Community as to participation of the Community in IOs. The dividing line to Para 3 is the distinction between the factual secondary law act concluding an agreement at international level, and the more general authorisation of the Community to consider the principles which should gear ordinary work in committees at the international level.

Thereby, the content of Para 4 is restricted, and it has to be asked whether this adds to the internal logic of Art 111. In fact, from the point of view of the ESCB, it does not seem favourable – consider the missing requirement under Para 3 to respect the competences of the various actors, in general, and the ECB's prerogatives, in particular. In addition, according to Para 3 subparagraph 2 such an agreement has binding effect on the ESCB, without that

48 So for instance *Bognar* (1997) 366 and *Martenczuk* (1999) 100.

49 *Bognar* (1997) 362, and n. 103, and *Smits* (1999) para 115, commentary to Art 109. Cf. also *Potacs* (1993) 36.

50 So *Smits* (1997) 410.

51 *Bognar* (1997) 366.

52 *Louis* (1999) 10. See also in this book *Dutzler* at 153.

there is any requirement that the ESCB is to be fully associated with the negotiations, as the Commission. Art 111(3) EC is therefore seen as posing a serious limit to the freedom of the ESCB in monetary policy affairs.[53] However, as *Bognar* elaborates, the justification lies in the presumable weak consequences of corresponding international agreements, as formal exchange rate agreements could not fall under Para 3.[54] In addition, also a further consideration may serve as justification:

Only formal agreements on exchange rate systems are *expressis verbis* exempted from the scope of Para 4: they take precedence over a Council decision under Para 4, but set the frame within which the Council and the other actors might exercise their remaining competences. Were the Council to decide on the representation or a position of the Community in a manner that would infringe a formal agreement under Para 1 (if it existed), its acts of secondary law would not only be invalid in international law, but also according to Community law.[55] Given the lack of an explicit provision that not only agreements under Para 1, but also under Para 3 could derogate from a decision on the representation of the Community, it appears correct to assume that any such agreements concluded under Para 3 would have to be consistent with the principles laid down under Para 4. This rationale would prevent that binding agreements (e.g. on the status of the ECB at the IMF) are concluded pursuant to Para 3 which would run counter to the principles as specified by Para 4.

Lastly, also the wording of Para 3 (agreements concerning monetary or foreign exchange regime matters with IOs) supports the above mentioned interpretation. Informal fora such as the G-7 are not "international organisations",[56] but are included in the wider term "international level" used in Para 4.[57] In informal fora, no agreements on representation under Para 3 will have to be concluded, but representation is discussed and agreed upon informally, in accordance with the principles under Para 4.

---

[53] *Bognar* (1997) 362.

[54] *Ibid.*

[55] *Bognar* (1997) 365.

[56] IOs are defined as forms of co-operation founded on an international agreement creating at least one organ with a will of its own, established under international law, so *Schermers/Blokker* (1999) § 33.

[57] See the proposal of the Commission COM (98) 367 final.

Having addressed the issue of horizontal allocation of powers, equally difficult is the question of the remaining Member States competences.

5. The Vertical Allocation of Powers

According to Art 111(5), the Member States retain, "without prejudice to the competence of the Community and the Community agreements on the Economic and Monetary Union", the right to negotiate in international fora and to conclude international agreements. This cannot be read to imply a concurrent competence of the Member States in EMU matters, since it would be inconsistent with the idea of a monetary union.[58] Moreover, Declaration No 10 of the Final Act to the European Union contains the view of the conference that this paragraph would not affect the principles resulting from the judgement handed down by the ECJ in *AETR*. According to this doctrine, each time the Community adopts provisions laying down common rules, with a view to implementing common policy envisaged by the Treaty, the Member States no longer have the right, acting individually or even collectively, to undertake obligations with third countries which affect those rules.[59]

In the sphere of EMU, there are specific provisions relating to the negotiation and conclusion of international agreements. This is in contrast to the *AETR* case, in which transport policy provisions in the field of relations with third countries were absent, so that a recourse was required to the general system of community law. Art 111(4) commands that the distribution of competences under Arts 99 and 105 are mirrored at the international level. The asymmetry between economic and monetary union results from the different allocation of competences in these areas. As concerns economic union, it is only the field of economic policy co-ordination (guidelines, multilateral surveillance, monitoring of economic convergence) where also at the external level there is no room for any separate Member State actions.[60] This is different for most fields of monetary union including exchange rate agreements, formal or informal, which fall within the exclusive competence of the Com-

---

58 Cf. *Slot* (1994) 241: "Either it [Art 111(5)] states the obvious or it deviates from the *AETR* doctrine."

59 Case C-22/70 *Commission v Council*, European Agreement on Road Transport [1971] ECR I-263, para 17.

60 *Potacs* (1993) 36 n. 94 suggests that this co-ordination competence could not justify an exclusive external representation competence.

munity. Should a Member State participating in the third stage of EMU, by an agreement with third countries or IOs, infringe the exclusive competence of the Community, it could be challenged before the ECJ in the course of an infringement procedure, without recourse to the *AETR* principles being necessary.

It might therefore appear as if the declaration was superfluous. It is evident also from the combined effect of Para 3 and Para 5 alone that the Member State competence can only relate to matters of EMU which are not subject to the explicit competence of the Community as provided for by Art 99 and Art 105 in association with Art 111.[61] Similarly, it follows from Art 4(2) EC that it is the sole competence of the Community to conduct a single monetary and exchange rate policy.

But apart from these areas, and in economic matters in particular, the Member States remain competent, and therefore cannot be prevented from presenting their policies outside the Community framework.[62] In all the fields not covered by Arts 99 and 105 together with Art 111, the *AETR* principles are to be followed, so that it is in this respect that the intention of the Member States not to deviate from the case law on the exclusive external competence of the Community is important.[63]

III. Current Practice

Having tried to establish the principles of external Community representation, the relevance of Art 111 stems from the necessity to articulate the division of responsibilities between Community and Member States, on the one hand, and Council, Commission and ESCB, on the other hand. The outcome should be meaningful and practical solutions, which are also acceptable to third countries, in particular the US. Hence, this chapter is devoted to an overview of the current state of affairs, both as regards a possible Council decision on the representation of the Community as well as the membership at the IMF as an example for the practical difficulties.

---

61 See *Bognar* (1997) 355.

62 So the Luxembourg Conclusions of the European Council of 12/13 December 1997 at para 10, Agence Europe (No 7121) 14/12/1997. This must be evaluated on a case-by-case basis, *Herrmann* (2002) 12.

63 See on this issue also *Dutheil de la Rochère* (1999) 440, 443.

A. Preparations for a Council Decision

1. Commission and Member States' Proposals

The actual modalities of the Community's representation at international level in EMU matters were tackled for the first time at the Luxembourg summit in December 1997.[64] The European Council concluded that the Council and the ECB should carry out their tasks in representing the Community at the international level in an efficient manner and in compliance with the allocation or powers laid down in the Treaty, while the Commission, in addition to its role in the preparation of the decisions (by making proposals) would be involved "to the extent required to enable it to perform the role assigned to it by the Treaty". The Member States, while taking full account of the Community interest, would continue to present their policies outside the Community framework. And lastly, the European Council also emphasised that the representation in IOs should take account of those organisation's rules, calling thus upon the Member States to help the establishment of pragmatic rules, especially as regards the IMF.[65] In the view of *Torrent*, the Council thereby neglected the possibility of a reform of the statutes of the Fund.[66]

Further to these conclusions, the Commission made a proposal for a Council Decision under Art 111(4),[67] in which it proposed a tripartite representation (Council, Commission and ESCB). This would best reflect the allocation of powers as foreseen by the Treaty and would guarantee that the Community spoke with one voice. The representation by the Council should be taken over by the Presidency, if it was a participating Member State. If the Member State currently holding the office of President of the Council did not have the euro as its currency, the participation of the Council would be assumed by the Member State that was next to hold the office of President of the Council and had the euro as its currency. It would therefore always be the Eurogroup President, possibly assisted by a Vice-President.

64 Resolution of the European Council on economic policy coordination in stage 3 of EMU, OJC 35, 02/02/1998 1-4, para 9.

65 Resolution of the European Council of Luxembourg, paragraph 10.

66 *Torrent* (1998) 6.2. (without page numbers).

67 Proposal for a Council Decision on the representation and position taking of the Community at international level in the context of Economic and Monetary Union, COM (98) 637 final.

Commission and ECB would decide the modalities of their participation in accordance with their statutes. In particular, Art 3 of the said proposal imposed the obligation on Member States and institutions of the Community to take the necessary steps to ensure that the principles under Art 1 and 2 – tripartite representation, ensuring that the Community speaks with one voice, and Council participation by the Eurogroup President – were respected. The proposal also specified which procedures had to be implemented in the various fora (G-7, G-20, OECD), in order to ensure adequate Community representation. In cases where institutional constraints impeded the application of the principles (IMF), the proposal provided that the Member States and the institutions of the Community should rapidly adopt and implement transitional arrangements which, as closely as possible, complied with the principles set out above. Under Art 5, the Commission envisaged a central role for the Economic and Financial Committee (EFC) in preparing a position on proposal of the Commission, and tackled the question of coordination between Member States and Community, by making it the duty of the Eurogroup President to ensure that the Community speaks with one voice.[68]

The EP in a resolution welcomed the Commission initiative.[69] However, its rapporteur, *Herman*, criticised the Commission's assumption that Art 3 TEU called for both the Commission and the Council to ensure the consistency of the Union's external activities as a whole. Although this Article was not new in the Treaty, it had not prevented Council and Commission from not ensuring continuity or consistency, in particular as regards the multilateral surveillance procedure of Art 99 and the inability of Commission and Council to co-operate in adopting "detailed rules" as foreseen by Art 99(5).[70] *Herman* therefore asked how the Commission could claim that the role assigned for the Council and the Commission for the preparation and adoption of the Broad Economic Guidelines and surveillance of the budgetary policies of the Member States could make the case for the equal external representation of both institutions.[71] In the end, however, the rapporteur agreed with the "trinity"

---

68 COM (98) 637 final Art 5.

69 Resolution on a proposal from the Commission, OJC 398, 21/12/1998 6.

70 *European Parliament* (1998) 11 of 17.

71 *Ibid.*

representation proposal, for the reason that the Commission could represent also the interests of the Member States with a derogation. Further, the close relation between economic, monetary and exchange rate policies required the participation in the representation of the Community at international level of Council, Commission and ECB in a balanced way.

A separate proposal by the Belgian Finance Minister envisaged to rebalance the representation of the monetary pole and the economic pole, by designating the President of the Eurogroup for a longer period.[72] In this way, also more continuity at the international level could be achieved. The President could be assisted by a Vice-President, who would be national of a "small" Member State if a "large" country held the presidency, and vice versa. The obvious obstacle is that the Eurogroup Presidency has no normative basis in Community law. Acknowledging this, the proposal spoke of the need to find an "adequate co-operation" between the President of the Council, which is the decision-making body in this field, and the informal Eurogroup President.[73]

The final Ecofin-Council report to the European Council of Vienna, however, did not take up this proposal.[74] The Council distinguished between the representation of the *Community* at international level as regards issues of particular relevance to EMU (Art 111(4)), and on matters which do not belong to the *Community competence*, but on which it may be appropriate for *Member States* to express common understandings.[75] For the representation in the first case, the Ecofin-Council applied the same principles as the Commission, namely the tripartite representation, the necessity to ensure that the Community speaks with one voice, and the involvement of the Commission "to the extent required to enable it to perform the role assigned to it by the Treaty". This is, presumably, to say that the Commission must be given the possibility to prepare the decisions of the Council on positions of the Community, and to

---

72 External Representation of the Euro-Zone, proposal by Jean-Jacques Viseur, Minister of Finance of Belgium, in the forefront of an informal Euro-11 meeting in Vienna 1998, published in *Agence Europe Documents* (No 2099) 9/10/1998, Part B para 3.

73 *Ibid*, para 6.

74 Report to the European Council on the state of preparation for stage three of EMU, in particular the external representation of the Community, in *Agence Europe Documents* (No 2116) 23/12/1998.

75 Ecofin Report para 4, emphasis added.

have all the information in order to be able to exert its right of initiative for a formal exchange rate agreement.[76] Nevertheless, this wording certainly means that negotiation by the Commission, although not impossible, should not be considered as the regular case.[77]

In the second case, the matters which do not belong to the Community competence, but where it may be appropriate for Member States to express common understandings, the Council urged that pragmatic solutions must be found for all relevant fora.[78] Here, the Ecofin-Council referred to the area of economic union and the difficulty to find a balance between the expressly reserved right of the Member States to negotiate in international bodies and conclude international agreements,[79] and the Community interest in economic areas which extended also to areas in which the Member States remained competent. As to the composition of Ecofin or Eurogroup delegations for missions to third countries and the inclusion of ECB and Commission representatives, the Ecofin Council did not specify any details, but stated only vaguely that this could vary with the circumstances and the objectives. According to the Ecofin Report, it is in the responsibility of the Council President to make the necessary arrangements.[80] However, in spite of the Vienna European Council's invitation to the (Ecofin)-Council to act, the process was cancelled, and up to now no Council decision has been taken on the subject.

2. Critical Issues

The requirement of unanimity, which has only recently been amended into a qualified majority for a decision on the representation, was certainly a significant obstacle.[81] In addition, the problem

---

76 As argued by the Commission in COM (98) 637 final, explanatory memorandum.

77 *Dutheil de la Rochère* (1999) 441, on the spirit of Art 111(3) EC.

78 Ecofin Report para 5.

79 Art 111(5) EC.

80 Ecofin Report to the Vienna European Council, *Agence Europe Documents* (No 2116) 23/12/1998 para 14.

81 Art 111(4) of the Treaty of Nice: "Subject to paragraph 1, the Council, *acting by a qualified majority* on a proposal from the Commission and after consulting the ECB, shall decide on the position of the Community at international level as regards issues of particular relevance to economic and monetary union and, *[phrase deleted]* on its representa-

lies to some extent in the on-going dispute between those Member States of the euro-area, which are included in informal international fora such as the G-7 or the G-10, and those which are not, over the question which matters should be considered as being of common interest. If the Commission participated, arguably also smaller Member States would be represented by any positions the Community took at this level. In this respect, it is noteworthy that the Conference on the Nice Treaty added a Declaration to be included in the Final Act of the Conference on Art 111 EC, which states that procedures must be such as to enable all the Member States in the euro area to be fully involved in each stage of preparing the position of the Community at international level as regards issues of particular relevance to EMU. It remains to be shown whether this Declaration, after the ratification of the Nice Treaty, will have some practical effects on the formulation of positions of the Community in international fora.

In any event, it is evident that there is a certain mismatch between the limited role assigned to the Commission by Art 111 and its status as an equal partner as envisaged by its proposal. During the Maastricht negotiations, it was even tried to further reduce the Commission's role, by granting also the Member States the right to make an initiative. Reasons identified for this include the lack of political will from Member States to abandon their last opportunity to considerably influence, via the Council, monetary matters in the international sphere.[82] In order to compensate for the loss of sovereignty brought about by EMU, Art 115 was inserted in the Treaty, entailing the right of the Member States to request a Commission recommendation or proposal also in Art 111 matters. The Commission is obliged to examine such a request and to report to the Council on its conclusions, which means that it will need convincing arguments if it does not intend to act.[83] This may be seen as a support for the thesis that the Member States never trusted the Commission's orthodoxy and always sought to restrict its influence in politically sensitive issues,[84] but may also be simply the reflection of the attempt of the Member States to have decision-making

---

tion in compliance with the allocation of powers laid down in Articles 99 and 105" (original emphasis).

82 So *Bognar* (1997) 351.

83 See also *Pipkorn* (1994) 286.

84 So *Westlake* (1995) 84.

procedures in EMU similar to those in the second or third pillar due to the loss of sovereignty involved.

The Commission naturally opposes such intergovernmentalism. Although in EMU, the Council may seem as the appropriate entity for overcoming the difficulty resulting from the division of competences between Community and Member States, in the field of external economic policy,[85] Art 111 is only applicable to Member States without a derogation. In addition, at the international level, primarily the larger states are represented. According to the Commission, this means that wherever the Community is to adopt a common stance on EMU matters at the international level, the Commission should ensure that both the views of the smaller and of the "out" states are represented. This argument is thought to refute the imputation that, although its presence would have the advantage of greater continuity, it lacked legitimate authority.[86]

The other part of the problem lies in the difficulty to find a workable solution at international level, which takes into consideration the distribution of competences between Member States and Community, on the one hand, and which reflects the allocation of powers between the various Community entities, on the other hand, and which at the same time meets the consent of the international partners if these principles meant reform of the statutes of IOs. After all, an overrepresentation of the euro-area in relation to non-European countries could result in the disapproval of such proposals by third countries.

Still another practical problem is that it is in many cases not possible to separate strictly between issues belonging in the sphere of monetary policy, where Art 111(4) EC would call for a representation of the Community by the ESCB, exchange rate matters, where the political power rests upon the Council, and economic policy issues, where the Member States alone or the Member States and the Council together are competent. To give an example, restrictions of foreign-exchange operations are not purely monetary in nature as they affect the supply with capital of the economic subjects.[87] In addition, the various international fora all have a different focus so that for each a different solution has to be found. For the

---

[85] *Torrent* (1998), Chapitre 6.3.3.

[86] *Bénasssy/Italianer/Pisani-Ferry* (1993) 59.

[87] Potacs therefore suggests typological criteria, see *Potacs* (1993) 36 n.93.

sake of brevity, only the case of the IMF as one of the most prominent IO will be presented.

B. Representation in the IMF

1. Community Membership

The IMF, founded in Bretton-Woods in 1944, was in spite of its name not only created to promote international monetary co-operation. By promoting exchange stability, or assisting in the establishment of a multilateral system of payments, it intends to facilitate the expansion and balanced growth of international trade. Furthermore, it makes its general resources temporarily available to its contracting parties experiencing balance of payments difficulties under adequate safeguards, and it shortens the duration and lessens the degree of disequilibrium in the international balances of payments of members.[88]

Such a focus appears to make the membership of the Community necessary.[89] The problem, though, is that the IMF is an IO where external representation of the Community, or also only of the euro area, is difficult, as under Art 2 sec. 2 of the IMF Agreement, only countries are allowed for membership.[90] But as the Fund Agreement is implicitly based on the monetary sovereignty of its members, it could be argued that membership *ipso iure* ended, not only when the respective state seized to be an independent subject of public international law, but also when the respective member changed in such a way that it did no longer comply with the elementary conditions of Fund membership.[91] The Community, and not the Member States, would thus have to be seen as a "country" in the meaning of the IMF Agreement. Though, the practice of the Fund is that of much flexibility with respect to membership, so that countries are regarded as full members, even if they have a common currency with other members.[92]

---

88 Article I of the Agreement of the IMF, at http://www.imf.org/external/pubs/ft/aa/aa02.htm, adopted at the United Nations Monetary and Financial Conference, Bretton-Woods, July 22, 1944, last amendment Nov. 11, 1992.

89 See *Martenczuk* (1999) 102.

90 Art 2 IMF Agreement.

91 Such as independent discharge of the obligations under the Agreement, see *Bognar* (1997) 383, and *Martha* (1993) 754-758.

92 For instance the West African Monetary Union and the Eastern Caribbean Monetary Union, *Martha* (1993) 757.

As regards the relationship between EC law and the IMF Agreement, the latter is binding on the Member States, as long as it is compatible with the EC law.[93] Therefore, the Treaty neither derogates from the rights of third countries stemming from the IMF Agreement, nor from the international duties of the states which are members of the Community.[94] Nevertheless, the Community is bound by such old agreements when duties of the Member States as contracting parties were taken over by the Community, as the ECJ held in its ruling in the *International Fruit Company* case: Where the Community, by means of primary law, had assumed the powers previously exercised by Member States, and the transfer had been put into a concrete form (Member States only act through a Community delegation), and had been recognised by the parties to the agreement, that agreement was binding on the Community.[95]

This principle does not answer the question, whether a *de jure* substitution was the logical consequence of the transition to the third stage of EMU. If the Community became the obligor of the duties of the IMF Agreement, the Member States would be obliged to convince the contracting parties to the Fund of the necessity to amend the Fund Agreement, following from Arts 10 and 307 para 2 EC.[96] The other possibility is that the Community could *de facto* replace the Member States, when the Member States would have been obliged under the Agreement, by acting in common whenever Community competences are involved, without the Community legally taking the place of the Member States as a contracting party.[97] This procedure was, for instance, applied in case of the *ILO Convention*, where the Court reasoned in its Opinion 2/91 that the Community had to conclude the Convention through the medium of the Member States, since international law prevented that the Community itself concluded it.[98] The answer to the question, which of these two possibilities could be pursued, depends *inter alia* on

---

93 Art 307 EC.

94 *Bognar* (1997) 375.

95 Case C-21-24/72 *International Fruit Company*, [1972] ECR 1219, para 15ff.

96 *Martha* (1993) 777.

97 This prominent solution for old agreements is called the "trustee model", since one actor would act as the trustee of the other, not admitted actors, *Zilioli/Selmayr* (1999b) 339. See *Bognar* (1977) 377 for further references.

98 Opinion 2/91 *ILO Convention* No 170 [1993] ECR I-1061 para 37.

whether the Member States lost the ability to perform the essential requirements of membership, so that the Community, in their place, would have to act.[99]

An evaluation of the requirements under the IMF Agreement shows that in the sphere of Art IV on the obligations regarding exchange arrangements,[100] it is the Community which is exclusively competent, as both monetary and exchange rate competence has been vested in the Community.[101] Given that the monetary and exchange rate policy of the Community and the euro area economic policies are under the surveillance of the Fund,[102] the exchange policy of the Community has to be in compliance with the Fund Agreement. Under the present arrangement, it would be upon the President of the Council to act on behalf of the Community in this and similar matters. However, euro area consultations under Art IV IMF Agreement do not preclude the individual membership of the Member States.[103] The IMF, in spite of its euro area analysis in cooperation with the ECB and the Commission or other competent institutions, considers the euro area Art IV consultation to be legally part of the individual Member States consultations, which are continued including the analysis of the monetary conditions.[104]

Also in other spheres of the Fund's tasks and powers, there are still remaining competences of the Member States. As to the obligations under Art VIII, from as early as the beginning of Stage 2, the Community assumed exclusive powers to regulate not only current payments and transfers, but also capital movements.[105] Nevertheless, in the sphere of capital and payment control, Member

---

99 *Martha* (1993) 762.

100 Members are "to collaborate with the Fund and other members to assure orderly exchange arrangements and to promote a stable system of exchange rates", Art IV Section 1 IMF Agreement.

101 So also *Smits* (1997) 431.

102 Under such consultations, not only monetary and exchange rate policies are discussed, but also fiscal and structural policies at the euro-area level, see the 1999 Public Information Notice, http://www.imf.org/external/np/sec/ pn/1999/pn9937.htm.

103 *Bénassy/Italiener/Pisani-Ferry* (1993) 58.

104 See the Decision of the IMF Executive Board No. 11846-(98/125) together with SM/98/257.

105 *Smits* (1997) 433.

States retain some specific concurrent regulatory competences, which makes them also addressees of Fund obligations.[106]

Another obstacle to the replacement of the Member States by the Community is the IMF's practice to subject the economic policies of members to in-depth discussions.[107] The notion that there would be no residual competences, which necessitated the participation of the individual Member States,[108] is rejected by the Member States which doubt whether the co-ordinating role of the Council sufficed to substitute the Member States.[109] In addition, not all Community Members are members of EMU, and there are territories of the Member States to which EMU provisions do not apply. This means that, at least in this respect, these countries would have to remain members of the IMF.

Apart from this special case, however, and since the economic functions of the Fund are subordinate to the monetary ones, it might already be true that

> "over all, the EC is definitely much better equipped with the necessary competences to effectively participate in the IMF than the participating Member States."[110]

Bognar views the problem from a different angle, by arguing that the decisive point was not so much the respective competences after the changeover to the third stage of EMU, but their manifestation, the active or passive behaviour of the Community.[111] Regarding institutional arrangements, the Community certainly followed the passive approach: Although a Community competence would be touched upon if a Member State needed foreign exchange when facing a temporary balance-of-payments problem under Art V IMF Agreement, or when the Community needed to draw on IMF resources,[112] from a technical point of view, financial relations with the IMF are still in the hands of the Member States and their financial agents and depositories, that act as business partner of the IMF.

---

[106] For instance regarding Art 58 EC, so *Bognar* (1997) 385.

[107] See the legal basis of Art IV Section 1 (i) IMF Agreement.

[108] *Martha* (1999) 773, *Herrmann* (2002) 22-23.

[109] *Deutsche Bundesbank* (1999) 21. See also *supra* note 60.

[110] *Herrmann* (2002) 23.

[111] *Bognar* (1997) 376.

[112] Since the "conditionality" of the Fund will involve the economic policies of the Community, the Ecofin-Council and the ECB would be jointly responsible, so *Smits* (1997) 436.

Moreover, the Member States do not have the intention, nor see an economic or technical need, to centralise the fiscal agent and depository functions in view of the introduction of the euro.[113] This means, at present only contracting parties (and not the Community) can request assistance, but at the same time a loan to a Member State would require the consent of the Community.[114]

More generally, the structure of the fund's management poses some problems. The Board of Governors, according to Art XII Para 2 IMF Agreement, is the highest governing body of the IMF, and consists of one Governor per member, usually the Finance Minister.[115] Though, the Board has transferred all powers that can be delegated to the Executive Board, which is thus practically charged with managing the IMF's day-to-day affairs. The Executive Board consists of at the time 24 Directors, 5 of which are permanent ones (USA, Germany, Japan, France and UK). The 19 other Directors are elected by other members with which they form a constituency. A third, important advisory committee is the IMFC, the Interim Monetary and Financial Committee (the successor of the Interim Committee), which advises and reports to the Board of Governors on the supervision of the management and adaptation of the international monetary and financial system, and deals with sudden disturbances that might threaten the system. It reflects the composition of the Executive Board.[116]

For the Board of Governors, the difficulties in taking adequately account of the Community seem surmountable: A common position under Art 111(4) could lead to a uniform vote by all Member States, while either the Eurogroup President or a member of the Commission could take part as an elected member, representing the Community. The difficulty lies in the Executive Board, as the President of the Eurogroup not necessarily will always be one of the three European permanent members, which means that also a member of a country without an Executive Director could be the Council representative.[117] Moreover, due to the peculiarity that the Executive Directors do not only represent the votes of their country,

---

[113] *Deutsche Bundesbank* (1999) 22.

[114] *Weinrichter* (2000) 23.

[115] *Oppermann* (2000) 536.

[116] IMF Press Release No. 99/47, Sept. 30, 1999, available at http://www.imf.org/external/np/sec/pr/1999/PR9947.HTM.

[117] *Martenczuk* (1999) 102. Currently, there are only 4 further EU Member States nationals Executive Directors.

which appointed them, but possibly also of non-EC contracting parties, or that an Executive Director from a non-EC country represents also Member States,[118] it appears possible that Member States would be forced to depart from a common position of the Council, if they could not convince their group.

Due to these difficulties, whereas in the long run an amendment of the Agreement for a *de jure* representation of the Community seems to be the most reasonable solution, at present "pragmatic solutions" which do not require a change in the Articles of Agreement of the IMF[119] predominate. However, even if the Community has not yet become a member, amendments to the Agreement, institutional adaptations and change of informal practices already were necessary. One example is the decision to replace the DM and the FF (but not the Pound Sterling) in the basket of five currencies which used to make up the SDRs[120] by the euro.[121] Moreover, the contribution of the members to the operational budget of the Fund, which to 75% are to be made in the national currency, since January 1, 1999 by EMU participants are made in euro. The IMF also changed the key factor whether a member can be considered a creditor for the operational budget – a sufficiently strong balance of payments and/or reserve position – into IMF quota shares. This was necessitated by the loss of reserve positions' relevance, and the absence of a need for individual balance of payments for different geographical parts of the euro area.[122] A similar solution will have to be found in case an EC Member State wishes to obtain SDRs under Art XIX Section 3 (a) or, more generally, any Fund resources under Art V Section 3 (b) ii.[123]

2. Community Representation

As to Community representation, the Luxembourg resolution of the European Council in 1997 wanted to predicate the representation at the IMF on the provision in that Fund's Articles of Agree-

---

118 See the voting procedure in Art XII Section 3 (b) ii IMF Agreement.

119 Ecofin-Council in its meeting on 1 Dec. 1998, Press Release No. 13462.

120 The IMF created SDRs to lend to countries that need help to finance balance-of-payment deficits, in order to increase international liquidity.

121 Decision of the Executive Board of 17/12/1998, No. 11857 (98/130), http://www.imf.org/external/pubs/ft/seldec/24th/part05.htm.

122 *Deutsche Bundesbank* (1999) 22.

123 *Bognar* (1997) 588-589, and *Martha* (1993) 761.

ment that only countries can be members of that institution. The Member States in their capacities as members of the IMF should help to establish pragmatic arrangements, which would facilitate the conduct of IMF surveillance and the presentation of Community positions, including the views of the ESCB, in IMF fora.[124]

As an expression of this call for pragmatic solutions, the Ecofin report to the Vienna European Council provided that the views of the Community/EMU would be presented by "the relevant member of the Executive Director's office of the Member State holding the euro 11 presidency, assisted by a representative of the Commission."[125] This has been called an "unsatisfactory minimum solution", leaving the euro area without a proper spokesman,[126] as thereby, the Community is not represented by a Director, but by an international officer without voting rights.[127] It is not clear whether the Commission favours a different approach, since it stated only vaguely in its proposal that such "temporary arrangements" would have to be found that allow the Member State which has the Presidency and introduced the euro as its currency to speak for the Community.[128] The EP interpreted this term as denoting that the Member States have to agree amongst themselves and thus include in their delegations representatives from the Commission and the ECB.[129]

The contribution by the Belgium Minister of Finance was more ambitious: For representation at the IMF level, he saw the necessity to distinguish between the short-term requirements and possible medium-term ambitions for the representation. The proposal also dealt with proper organisational questions: at the Executive Board, both the representative of the Presidency of the Eurogroup and an observer from the ECB could represent the euro area, with a clear mandate. The position should be prepared within the EFC on basis of a proposal by the Commission. As regards the Interim Commit-

---

124 Luxembourg Resolution para 10, *Agence Europe* (No 7121) 14/12/1997.

125 Ecofin Report para 13, *Agence Europe Documents* (No 2116) 23/12/1998.

126 *Dutheil de la Rochère* (1999) 445.

127 *Martenczuk* (1999) 102, referring to the possibility of appointing an ad hoc proxy (Art XII Para 3e IMF Agreement), who has the right to vote if the executive director is not present.

128 Com (98) 367 final, Art 4 first indent.

129 *European Parliament* (1998) Explanatory Statement.

tee, a tripartite representation – Presidency of the Eurogroup, ECB president, and Commissioner concerned – was foreseen.[130] This proposal sets already out the lines along which an informal agreement was adopted, which has been severely criticised for the reduction of the Commission's role to a purely technical advisor in contrast to Presidency and ECB, which were awarded the right of external representation.[131]

The participation of the ECB, in contrast to the Commission, never really was an issue. At the IMF Executive Board meeting on 21 Dec. 1998, the ECB was granted observer status, at the level of both the IMFC and the Executive Board.[132] The subjects are explicitly stated in the Observer Decision:[133] Art IV consultations on monetary or exchange rate policy of the euro area countries as a whole and with individual euro area countries; the role of the euro in the international monetary system; the World Economic Outlook; international capital markets report; and world economic and market developments. Moreover, the ECB observer is invited on a case-by-case basis whenever deemed appropriate by the ECB and the Fund. The observer is able to address the Board with the permission of the Chairman on matters within the responsibility of the ECB. The Fund communicates to the ECB the agenda for all Board meetings and, in addition, the documents for those meetings to which the ECB observer has been invited.

In spite of this official recognition of the ECB at the international level, the role of the NCBs is not to be underestimated. The observer status does not mean an active participation of ECB staff in the meetings of the IMF Executive Board, but is conditional on the topics set out above and on permission of the Chairman. Nor has the observer a voting right.[134] Before the transition to the third stage of EMU, the Central Bank Governor of a country as a rule

---

130 Proposals by the Belgian Finance Minister, *Agence Europe Documents* (No 2099) 9/10/1998, IV.

131 *Sack* (2000) 279. Similar informal agreements were also made for G7 and World Bank.

132 IMF Press Release No 98/64. Against this background, the ECB set up a permanent representation in Washington, acting as primary contact between the IMF and the ECB, *Padoa-Schioppa* (1999) Chapter 4.

133 IMF Executive Board Decision 118-75 (99/1), http://www.imf.org/external/pubs/ft/seldec/24th/ part05.htm.

134 This is one of the two characteristics which all observes share, see *Schermers/Blokker* (1999) §177.

was nominated the alternate Executive Board Governor, alongside the Finance minister. In addition, the NCBs, in fulfilment of the members' obligation to ensure the convertibility of the currency,[135] acted as Member States' agencies, by buying balances of their own currency held by other IMF members. This task could also one day be exercised by the ECB on behalf of the Community, regarding transactions resulting from the Member States' membership.[136]

As regards those tasks conferred upon the ESCB, the ESCB-Statute determines that the ECB Governing Council may decide on the distribution of responsibility between the ECB and the NCBs.[137] At the same time, the NCBs are allowed to fulfil their obligations vis-à-vis IOs.[138] This means that the euro area countries can continue their existing financial relations with the IMF as before. As has been noted, the emphasis should lie on the word "existing", Art 31.1. ESCB-Statute being relevant only insofar as the NCBs have to effect transactions which they undertook before the transition to the third stage of EMU. These operations are performed by the NCBs as a part of the ESCB, executing a Community competence.[139]

Existing obligations include a wide range of activities, from additional subscriptions in case of quota agreements to drawing on the Fund's resources. Therefore, the exercise of financial rights and obligations of the euro area countries towards the IMF through national authorities implies a certain overlapping with the ESCB's monetary sovereignty. Provided that payments to the IMF have the size of influencing the European money supply – which is not very likely[140] – the ECB needs to be informed, so that it can take into account large transaction volumes of the national central banks with the IMF in its liquidity management and, as appropriate, offset them. The *German Bundesbank* conceded that, if need be, the ECB would be informed beforehand. The ECB is generally also informed of the situation in the run-up to unusual developments (such as the

---

[135] Art VIII Section 2 (a), Section 3 and 4 IMF Agreement.

[136] So a suggestion of the Committee of the Central Banks Governors of the Member States, *Agence Europe Documents* (No 1669/1670) 8/12/1990, 28.

[137] Art 6.1. and 12.5 ESCB-Statute.

[138] Art 31.1. ESCB-Statute.

[139] Since any use of the single currency concerns exclusive Community monetary functions, *Smits* (1997) 436, n. 283.

[140] *Weinrichter* (2000) 23 and n. 202.

compilation of financial packages for crisis countries), so that the *Bundesbank* does not consider the overlapping as serious.[141]

3. Conclusion

The arrangements presented above show a certain preference for pragmatic solutions. The issue of Community representation at the IMF thus far remains unresolved, the options in a longer-term perspective being common action of the Member States, sole representation by the Community, or double representation as in the WTO case. It is held that for the foreseeable future, the first option, where the Member States are under the obligation to act jointly in the interest of the Community, was the only workable solution: *Zilioli/Selmayr* do not find an amendment of the Fund Agreement to enable Community (or even ECB) participation likely, since this would raise such delicate issues as the redistribution of quotas and of constituencies.[142] The fact that both the Eurogroup President and the ECB observer are responsible for representation at the Executive Board seems to support another possibility advanced by the authors. The ECB could develop from an observer to a representative of the Member States when monetary matters are discussed.[143]

However, given the political component of many decisions of the Fund,[144] it does not seem appropriate to exclude Council and Commission from participation at the work of the IMF, even though internally, monetary policy and foreign exchange interventions belong to the ECB. It is, in this respect, that it can be argued that the Fund, in spite of its focus, which undoubtedly includes monetary functions, does not fall within the scope of the term "monetary institutions" of Art 6.2. ESCB-Statute. After all, "monetary" is usually seen as referring to the means of payment, whereas "financial" refers to the provision or use of monetary resources.[145] It is clear that the Fund's activities, in this terminology, are more financial

---

141 *Deutsche Bundesbank* (1999) 25.

142 *Zilioli/Selmayr* (1999) 339.

143 Also *Smits* mentions the appointment of ESCB representatives as IMF Governors by the Member States as one of the forms, which the common action of the Member States could take, *Smits* (1997) 441. Similar also *Potacs* (1993) 37, *Oppermann* (2000) 538.

144 For instance, regarding Russia, see *Louis* (1999) 23.

145 *Weinrichter* (2000) 19 n. 158, referring to a definition by J. Gold.

than monetary:[146] it is a public international financial institution, with certain objectives in the field of economic policy.[147] This is also very much supported by the traditional perception of the NCBs as *agencies* acting for the member countries in operations with the Fund, only if the respective country so chooses, as demonstrated by Article V (1) IMF.[148]

Hence, membership of the ECB alone would neither be sufficient nor in accordance with the Treaty. The issue is, as a typical problem of joint participation arising under mixed agreements,[149] how Community representation should look like. In agreement with *Bogna*r, the *de facto* substitution of the Member States by the Community (i.e., the delegation formula or trustee model) would appear to be unnecessarily complicated. In addition, even if the "pragmatic solutions" are "quite workable",[150] they do not take account of the loss of monetary sovereignty of the Member States and therefore do not seem to be appropriate.

Therefore, writers favour the more radical solution of an outright, full-fledged Community membership.[151] Of course, this involves the complicated task of analysing and amending the whole institutional system of the Fund, for instance, as regards the election of the Executive Directors.[152] It should be noted that Europe in case of a Community membership would be the "country" with the highest quota, which would induce a transfer of the seat of the IMF from Washington to Brussels.[153] This explains the reluctance of the US to any such proposals.

---

146 Art 23 1st indent ESCB-Statute, however, restricts co-operation to the establishment of relations (e.g. status as observer), thus excluding outright membership.

147 *Torrent* (1999) 1239.

148 *Herrmann* (2002) 9.

149 So *Torrent* (1997) 1240. Cf. also the general discussion of this aspect in the previous contribution by *Dutzler* in this book (152ff, 162ff).

150 So *Deutsche Bundesbank* (1999) 25.

151 *Martha* (1993) 786, *Smits* (1997) 444, *Martenczuk* (1999) 103, *Oppermann* (2000) 538.

152 *Martha* (1993) 780 et seq.

153 The combined voting power in the IMF of the Community would not shrink, as it is the quota of SDRs which determines the voting power of the member, see Art XII Sec 5. There is no reason to assume that Community participation would trigger an adjustment of the quotas of

The nomination of Board members by the Community, continued membership of Member States, which do not participate in the third stage of EMU, and the possibility of a reshuffling of quotas, are politically very sensitive questions, since they touch upon the core of the remaining sovereignty of the Member States. It is thus, in addition, also a Community internal problem, a question of internal unity and political will, and it can only be hoped that there is enough of both.[154] Again, given the amendments of the Nice Treaty, according to which decisions under Art 111(4) can be taken with qualified majority, it remains to be seen whether this will bring about a Community membership. The prospects for actual improvements are ambiguous: On the one hand, the current Presidency (at the time of writing), Spain, is perceived as having little interest in this subject, as first, most of the smaller countries see an advantage of power-sharing and positive effects of a single European representation. Second, as an example for the importance of particular interests, the patronage of Spain as regards Latin America is institutionalised by a common constituency, which it is unlikely to give up. On the other hand, the question of the euro zone's external representation, within the G-7, the IMF and the other international institutions, is on the agenda.[155]

Are solutions analogous to the one at the WTO, when the Community became a member parallel to the Member States, therefore better suited? Although there would be the same legal difficulties of a vertical division of responsibilities between Member States and Community,[156] this parallelism would overcome the difficulty of having to amend the Agreement with every new participant in EMU, as under a *de jure* substitution.[157] In the end, as soon as all participate in the third stage of EMU, the Member States would

---

the Member States, since the quotas are based on the economic position relative to other members.

[154] Louis calls it the question of whether the nostalgia triumphs over the reality, see *Louis* (1999) 29.

[155] Agence Europe (No 8124) 09/01/02.

[156] Louis holds that in this matter, it would not be as easy to produce a list of the respective powers of the Community and the Member States as was done for the FAO, *Louis* (1999) 24.

[157] *Bognar* (1997) 592.

have to give up their Fund membership.[158] Though, it is not clear whether the double representation of the euro area in the transition phase – which could last for a long while, given the enlargement procedure – would be acceptable to non-European Fund members. Whatever solution will finally be found, it is clear that pragmatic solutions alone will not suffice.

IV. Evaluation

To evaluate the external representation of the Community in EMU matters, one has to bear in mind that the goal has to be a Community which is a more consistent and forceful international actor. Pragmatism might in fact be the only available answer to the co-ordination problems at the international level. Yet, it seems justified to conclude that the current practice with the various actors – Member States, Council representative, Commissioner, ECB President and NCBs – taking part in the meetings or leaving them, according to their respective field of competence in order to ensure that those Community entities are present in international fora which are competent to represent the Community, and with the ongoing disputes over vertical and horizontal competences, can hardly be called pragmatic. This "absolutely confused"[159] practice is a result of the special arrangements in the Treaty in the field of EMU.

This finding seems to support the ones who argued that the Community would be the most passive participant in the global policy co-ordination, missing the opportunity of playing an active political role, or leaving it, in the field of exchange rate policy, entirely to the ESCB.[160] It is also in line with the perception of the ESCB as an active participant both at international as well as at Community level, as it is generally regarded as the most appropriate partner and the body which could react fastest. On the other hand, the need for political support also slows the ESCB's effectiveness: the euro had to lose one third of its value vis-à-vis the dollar compared to its introduction, before for the first-time, there was an

---

[158] In spite of the remaining economic competences or their international duties as regards the overseas territories of France, Portugal, Spain and the Netherlands, see *Smits* (1999) para 196-7, n. 100.

[159] So *Sack* (2001) 279 and 284.

[160] So for instance *Torrent* (1998) Chapitre VI 6.2. The fall of the euro exchange rate vis-à-vis the dollar is attributed to the lack of a coherent European economic policy framework, see e.g. *Herrmann* (2002) 6.

overall consensus of ministers and Commission at Community level concerning the low exchange rate of the euro which coincided with the first intervention by the ESCB.[161] This incident underlines, under the present arrangements, that good working relations are an indispensable requirement, in particular in a field such as Art 111 EC. This article presents itself as the typical result of a search for compromise where arguably no compromise is possible, and combines rather than distributes the powers and responsibilities of all players, so that neither body is able to act without the consent of the other.[162]

Relying on informal arrangements alone would be a sub-optimal solution and neglect the political impact of a uniform and effective appearance (or of the lack of it) of the Community at the external level, so that the necessary adjustments with respect to representation – as a matter of time[163] – should not be delayed for too long. It can only be hoped that the lowering of the majority threshold by the Treaty of Nice will open the way for a formal Council decision.

V. References

Bénassy A., Italianer A., Pisani-Ferry J. (1993), Les Implications Extérieures de la Monnaie Unique, L'Ecu oncurrencera le dollar comme monnaie internationale, Économie et Statistique, No 262-263 1993 2/3, 49-62.

Bognar Z. (1997), Europäische Währungsintegration und Außenwirtschaftsbeziehungen: eine Analyse des gemeinschafts- und völkerrechtlichen Rahmens der europäischen Außenwährungsbeziehungen, Baden-Baden 1997.

---

161 Communiqué de l'Eurogroupe (Versailles, 8 September 2000), at http://ue.eu.int/newsroom/. Although the ECB stresses that the actual decision to intervene was taken a day before the intervention by telephone conference of the Governing Council, and that no permission was asked, it should be noted that it had not been taken earlier when there was no political approval.

162 Cf. *Oppermann* (2000) 530.

163 *Martenczuk* (1999) 105-106.

Dehousse F., Ghemar K. (1994), Le traité de Maastricht et les relations extérieures de la Communauté européene, EJIL 5/94, 151-172.

Deutsche Bundesbank (1999), Germany's Relations with the IMF following the introduction of the Euro, Monthly Report September 1999, http://www.bundesbank.de/vo/download/mba/1999/09/ 199909mba_iwf.pdf (accessed July 02).

Dutheil de la Rochère J. (1999), EMU: Constitutional Aspects and External Representation, YEL 1999/2000, 427-446.

European Central Bank (1999), Annual Report 1998, http://www.ecb.int.

European Central Bank (2000), Annual Report 1999, http://www.ecb.int.

European Central Bank (2001), Monthly Bulletin January 2001, http://www.ecb.int.

European Parliament (1998), Report on a proposal from the Commission for a Council Decision on the Representation and Position Taking of the Community at International Level in the context of Economic and Monetary Union (COM(98)0637), by Herman F., A4-0439/1998.

Herrmann C. W. (2002), Monetary Sovereignty over the Euro and External Relations of the Euro Area: Competences, Procedures and Practice, EFARev. 2002, 1-24.

Louis J. V. (1995), L'Union Economique et Monetaire, in: *Louis* et. al. (eds.), Commentaire Mégret, Le Droit de la CEE – Vol 6, Brussels [2]1995, 1-165.

Louis J. V. (1997), Union Monétaire Europeenne et Fonds Monnetaire International, in: *Weber* et al. (eds.), Währung und Wirtschaft, Das Geld im Recht, FS Hahn, Baden-Baden 1997.

Louis J. V. (1999), Les Relations Internationales de L'Union Economique et Monétaire, EUI WP LAW No 99/10.

Martenczuk B. (1999), Die Außenvertretung der Europäischen Gemeinschaft auf dem Gebiet der Währungspolitik, 59 Zeitschrift für Internationales Recht und Völkerrecht 1/1999, 93-107.

Martha R. S. J. (1993), "The Fund Agreement and the Surrender of Monetary Sovereignty to the European Community", CMLRev 1993, 749-786.

Oppermann T. (2000), Die internationale Vertretung von Euroland,. in: *Kirchhof* et al. (ed.), Staaten und Steuern, FS Vogel, Heidelberg 2000, 229-543.

Padoa-Schioppa T. (1999), The external representation of the euro area, Introductory statement at the Sub-Committee on Monetary Affairs at the European Parliament, Brussels 17 March 1999, available at http://www.ecb.int.

Pipkorn J. (1994), Legal Arrangements in the Treaty of Maastricht for the Effectiveness of the Economic and Monetary Union, CMLRev 1994, 263-291.

Potacs M. (1993), Nationale Zentralbanken in der Wirtschafts- und Währungsunion, EuR 1993, 23-40.

Sack J. (2001), Die Europäische Union in den Internationalen Organisationen, Bedeutung der Beteiligung sowie Aktion und Einfluss von Gemeinschaft und Mitgliedstaaten in diesen Gremien, ZEuS 2001, 268-284.

Schermers H. G/Blokker N. M. (1999), International Institutional Law: Unity within Diversity, The Hague et al.[3] 1999.

Seidel M. (1992), Probleme der Verfassung der Europäischen Gemeinschaft als Wirtschafts- und Währungsunion, in *Baur/Müller-Graff/Zuleeg* (eds): Europarecht Energierecht Wirtschaftsrecht, FS Börner, Köln et al., 1992.

Slot P. J. (1994), The Institutional Provisions of the EMU, in: *Curtin* (ed.), Institutional Dynamics of European Integration, Essays in Honour of Schermers, Dordrecht et al. 1994, 229-249.

Smits R. (1997), The European Central Bank: Institutional Aspects, London 1997.

Smits R. (1999), Artikel 105, Artikel 109, in *von der Groeben, H./Thiesing, J./Ehlermann, C. D.* (eds.), Handbuch des Europäischen Rechts: systematische Sammlung mit Erläuterungen, 5th edition, Baden-Baden 1999, 138-164 and 230-272.

Torrent R. (1998), Droit et Pratique des Relations Economiques Exterieures Dans L'Union Europeenne, Bruxelles-Barcelona, 1998, http://www.ub.es/dpecp/ep/livreTorrent.html.

Torrent R. (1999), To Whom is the European Central Bank the Central Bank of: Reaction to Zilioli and Selmayr, CMLRev 1999, 1229-1241.

Vranes E. (2000), The "Internal" External Relations of EMU – on the Legal Framework of the Relationship of "In" and "Out" States, The Columbia Journal of European Law 2000, 361-382.

Westlake M. (1995), The Council of the European Union, London 1995.

Zilioli C/Selmayr M. (1999), The External Relations of the Euro Area: Legal Aspects, CMLRev 1999, 273-349.

Zilioli C., Selmayr M. (2000), The European Central Bank: An Independent Specialized Organization of Community Law, CMLRev 2000, 591-644.

List of Authors

Dr. *Barbara Dutzler*, Research Institute for European Affairs, Vienna University of Economics and Business Administration (Forschungsinstitut für Europafragen der Wirtschaftsuniversität Wien).

Mag. *Katharina Gamharter*, Research Institute for European Affairs, Vienna University of Economics and Business Administration (Forschungsinstitut für Europafragen der Wirtschaftsuniversität Wien).

Univ.-Prof. Dr. *Stefan Griller*, Research Institute for European Affairs, Vienna University of Economics and Business Administration (Forschungsinstitut für Europafragen der Wirtschaftsuniversität Wien).

Ao. Univ.-Prof. Dr. *Peter Hilpold*, Institute for Public and Financial Law and Political Science, University of Innsbruck (Institut für Öffentliches Recht, Finanzrecht und Politikwissenschaft, Universität Innsbruck).

Prof. Dr. *Ulrich Immenga*, Department of International and Foreign Economic Law, University of Göttingen.

Mag. *Anita Lukaschek*, Dorda Brugger & Jordis Rechtsanwälte, Vienna.

MMag. *Lukas von Lutterotti*, Kanzlei Egger & Partner, Bolzano.

Dr. *Bernd Martenczuk*, European Commission, Legal Service, Brussels.

Dr. *Erich Vranes,* Research Institute for European Affairs, Vienna University of Economics and Business Administration (Forschungsinstitut für Europafragen der Wirtschaftsuniversität Wien).

Mag. *Birgit Weidel*, Research Institute for European Affairs, Vienna University of Economics and Business Administration (Forschungsinstitut für Europafragen der Wirtschaftsuniversität Wien).

Abbreviations

AB	Appellate Body of the WTO
ACP	African, Caribbean and Pacific countries
AETR	Agreement on European Road Transport
AFDI	Annuaire Français de droit international
AG	Advocate-General
AIDS	Acquired Immune Deficiency Syndrome
AJIL	American Journal of International Law
ALA	Countries of Latin America and Asia
AöR	Archiv des öffentlichen Rechts
Art	Article
Arts	Articles
BIS	Bank of International Settlements
CAP	Common Agricultural Policy
CARDS	Assistance programme for Balkan Countries
CCP	Common Commercial Policy
CDE	Cahiers de Droit Européen
CEECs	Central and Eastern European countries
CER	Centre for European Reform
Cf.	confer to
CFP	Common Fisheries Policy
CFSP	Common Foreign and Security Policy
CMLRev.	Common Market Law Review
CoCom	Coordination Committee for East West Trade Policy
COREPER	Committee of Permanent Representatives
CS	Common Strategy
CSD	Commission for Social Development
CWC	Chemical Weapons Convention
Dec.	December
DIAC	Draft International Antitrust Code
DISC	Income tax legislation
DM	German Mark
DSB	Dispute Settlement Body
DSU	Dispute Settlement Understanding
e.g.	example given
EAEC	European Atomic Energy Community

EAR	European Agency for Reconstruction
EBRD	European Bank for Reconstruction and Development
EC	European Community
ECB	European Central Bank
ECHR	European Convention on Human Rights
ECJ	European Court of Justice
ECLR	European Competition Law Review
ECOSOC	United Nations Economic and Social Council
ECR	European Court Reports
ed.	editor
EDF	European Development Fund
eds.	editors
EEA	European Economic Area
ECSC	European Community for Steel and Coal
EEC	European Economic Community
EFARev.	European Foreign Affairs Review
EJIL	European Journal of International Law
E.L.Rev.	European Law Review
ELJ	European Law Journal
EMU	Economic and Monetary Union
EP	European Parliament
EPC	European Political Cooperation
EPRD	European Programme for Reconstruction and Development
ERTA	European Road Transport Agreement
ESCB	European System of Central Banks
et al.	et alia
EU	European Union
EuGZR	Europäische Grundrechte-Zeitschrift
EUI	European University Institute
EUMM	European Union Monitoring Mission
EuR	Europarecht
Euratom	European Atomic Energy Community
EuZW	Europäische Zeitschrift für Wirtschaftsrecht
EWS	Europäisches Wirtschafts- und Steuerrecht
f.	and following page
FAO	Food and Agriculture Organisation
Fed. Reg	Federal Regulation
ff.	and following pages

FF	French Francs
fn.	footnote
FRY	Federal Republic of Yugoslavia
FSC	Foreign Sales Cooperations
GATS	General Agreements on Trade in Services
GATT	General Agreement on Tariffs and Trade
GNI	Gross National Income
GPA	Government Procurement Agreement
GSP	General System of Preferences
G.U.	Gazzetta Ufficiale della Repubblica Italiana
GYIL	German Yearbook of International Law
HIV	Human Immunodeficiency Virus
i.e.	id est
IAEA	International Atomic Energy Agency
IAEO	International Atomic Energy Organisation
Ibid.	ibidem
IGC	Intergovernmental Conference
ILO	International Labour Organisation
I.L.M.	International Law Materials
ILSA	Iran and Libya Sanctions Act
IMF	International Monetary Fund
IMFC	Interim Monetary and Financial Committee
IO	International Organisation
ISBA	International
ISPA	Instrument for Structural Policies for Preaccession
JHA	Justice and Home Affairs
JIEL	Journal of International Economic Law
JWT	Journal of World Trade
KEDO	Korean Peninsula Energy Development Organisation
LIBERTAD	Liberty and Democratic Solidarity Act
lit.	litera
LMOs	Living Modified Organisms
MAI	Multilateral Agreement on Investments
MEDA	Countries of North Africa and the Middle East
MEP	Member of the European Parliament
MFN	most favoured nation
NAFO	Northwest Atlantic Fisheries Organisation
NAFTA	North American Free Trade Agreement

NATO	North Atlantic Treaty Organisation
NCB	National Central Bank
NGO	Non-Governmental Organisation
no.	number
NQHR	Netherlands Quarterly of Human Rights
NYIL	Netherlands Yearbook of International Law
OAS	Organisation of African States
OBNOVA	Assistance programme for former Yugoslavia and Albania
OCT	Overseas Countries and Territories
OECD	Organisation for European Cooperation and Development
OJ	Official Journal of the European Union
OSCE	Organisation for Security and Cooperation in Europe
p.	page
para	paragraph
PCA	Partnership and Cooperation Agreement
PHARE	Pre-Accession Assistance Programme for Candidate Countries
PJC	Police and Judicial Cooperation in Criminal Matters
PTIA	British Protection of Trading Interests Act
RdC	Recueil des cours
Riv. Dir. Int.	Rivista di Diritto Internazional
RIW	Recht der Internationalen Wirtschaft
RMC	Revue du Marché Commun
RMU	Revue du Marché Unique
RTDeur	Revue trimestrielle de droit européen
SDRs	Special Drawing Rights
Sec.	Section
Sept.	September
SPS Agreement	Agreement on Sanitary and Phytosanitary Measures
TACIS	Assistance Programme for Eastern European and Asian Countries
TABD	Transatlantic Business Dialogue
TEAEC	Treaty establishing the European Atomic Energy Community
TEC	Treaty establishing the European Community

TECSC	Treaty establishing the European Community for Steel and Coal
TEU	Treaty on European Union
TPPC	Transatlantic Partnership and Political Cooperation
TRIPs	Agreement on Trade related Aspects of Intellectual Property Rights
UK	United Kingdom
UN	United Nations
UN SC	United Nations Security Council
UNCTAD	United Nations Conference on Trade and Development
UNEP	United Nations Environment Programme
UNMIK	United Nations Mission in Kosovo
UNRWA	United Nations Relief and Works Agency for Palestine Refugees
US	United States of America
USC	United States Code
USSR	Union of Socialist Soviet Republics
Vol.	Volume
WA	Wassenaar Arrangement
WP	Working Paper
WTO	World Trade Organisation
YEL	Yearbook of European Law
ZaöRV	Zeitschrift für ausländisches öffentliches Recht und Völkerrecht
ZEuS	Zeitschrift für europarechtliche Studien
ZfV	Zeitschrift für Verwaltung

Index

Springer-Verlag and the Environment